The four books of *The Nature of Order* constitute the ninth, tenth, eleventh and twelfth in a series of books which describe an entirely new attitude to architecture and building. The books are intended to provide a complete working alternative to our present ideas about architecture, building, and planning — an alternative which will, we hope, gradually replace current ideas and practices.

THE LUMINOUS GROUND

Hand painted tile, black glaze, white slip

THE
NATURE
OF
ORDER

*An Essay on the Art of Building and
the Nature of the Universe*

BOOK ONE
THE PHENOMENON OF LIFE

BOOK TWO
THE PROCESS OF CREATING LIFE

BOOK THREE
A VISION OF A LIVING WORLD

BOOK FOUR
THE LUMINOUS GROUND

THE CENTER FOR ENVIRONMENTAL STRUCTURE
BERKELEY CALIFORNIA

in association with

PATTERNLANGUAGE.COM

Published by The Center for Environmental Structure
2701 Shasta Road, Berkeley, California 94708
CES is a trademark of the Center for Environmental Structure.

ISBN 0-9726529-4-9 (Book 4)
ISBN 0-9726529-0-6   (Set)
LIBRARY OF CONGRESS CATALOGING-IN-PUBLICATION DATA
Alexander, Christopher. The Nature of Order: An Essay on the Art of Building and the Nature of the Universe /
Christopher Alexander, p.   cm.   (Center for Environmental Structure Series; v. 12).
Contents: v.1. The Phenomenon of Life — v.2. The Process of Creating Life
v.3. A Vision of a Living World — v.4. The Luminous Ground
1. Architecture—Philosophy.   2. Science—Philosophy.   3. Cosmology
4. Geometry in Architecture.   5. Architecture—Case studies.   6. Community
7. Process philosophy.   8. Color (Philosophy).
I. Center for Environmental Structure.   II. Title.
III. Title: The Luminous Ground.
IV. Series: Center for Environmental Structure series ; v. 12.
NA2500 .A444   2002
720'.1—dc21   2002154265
ISBN 0-9726529-4-9 (cloth: alk. paper: v.4)

Typography by Katalin Bende and Richard Wilson
Manufactured in China by Everbest Printing Co., Ltd.

BOOK ONE

THE PHENOMENON OF LIFE

PROLOGUE TO BOOKS 1-4

BOOK TWO
THE PROCESS OF CREATING LIFE

BOOK THREE

A VISION OF A LIVING WORLD

BOOK FOUR
THE LUMINOUS GROUND

I dedicate these four books to my family:

to my beloved mother, who died many years ago;

to my dear father, who has always helped me and inspired me;

to my darlings Lily and Sophie;

and to my dear wife Pamela who gave them to me,

and who shares them with me.

These books are a summary of what I have understood about

the world in the sixty-third year of my life.

THE

LUMINOUS

GROUND

* * * *

This fourth book presents an aspect of physical reality that is often hidden nowadays — at least in the West — although it was very much part of humankind's conception of the world in past times. There are phenomena in the universe that are explainable only by means of specific models, or approaches, and not by any other means. Nature has many different aspects and is not a single reality; at least the human mind cannot comprehend everything at once using a single model.

I have tried, in the first three books of THE NATURE OF ORDER, to give a complete overview of the phenomenon of life in architecture, together with the issue of value, which is inseparable from life. This has included a description, in Book 1, of the static character of living structure, and a view, in Books 2 and 3, of the living processes which can, successfully, generate living structure. These living phenomena are, I have argued, commonly observable: we see and feel them when they are present in the structure of the world. But they are not easy to explain, and above all, they cannot be explained within the world picture of conventional 19th-century mechanics. Nor, as far as I know, can they be explained in the world view of biology, complex systems theory, and quantum physics as we know them at the end of the 20th century.

These phenomena do not fit within any previous explanatory context. They need their own model.

An analogy may be drawn with quantum mechanics. As a theoretical discipline, when first formulated, it stood apart from other fields of physics, and even today there are still questions and inconsistencies internally. Nevertheless, the theoretical framework of quantum mechanics helps explain certain aspects of physical reality. We can see the interference fringes of electrons, observe the photoelectric effect, calculate the radiative dissipation of a black hole, test Bell's prediction, and measure Josephson tunneling through a barrier, and those phenomena are simply not explainable in the context of classical mechanics. Whether a person has philosophical reservations about the basis of quantum mechanics or not, it remains true that it is useful, and that no other formalism available when it was first formulated, or now, does an equally good job explaining what has to be explained, in a certain range of phenomena.

In the same way, I have attempted to put together a workable explanation of the physical and emotional phenomena which I have observed in buildings and in the living world. The explanation, not surprisingly, clashes with other explanations of physical phenomena which have been studied in physics. Nevertheless, I have very little choice: what I am putting forward in these four books of THE NATURE OF ORDER is — for the present — the only theoretical explanation I can construct (until a better one comes along) to help us understand what I have described. Not only do we want to understand this set of phenomena, but we must also be able to reproduce them: we want to be able to create living structure in the world. Quantum mechanics would not have been of more than academic interest to a few university professors if it were not for its immense field of practical applications, such as in electronics. Here, too, in the sphere of building, we have a practical aim. We wish to create living structure in the built world; we wish to apply this model of the universe in order to reproduce the phenomena that we are interested in.

The explanation that I give is not complete, and it is my hope that it will be improved by others in years to come. Nevertheless, some understanding of these phenomena is necessary at this early stage so that we can use them to better our understanding of the universe.

Is what I propose real? Well, the phenomena are observable, and the results are reproducible (when we create an artifact or building that has the proposed qualities), so this part at least corresponds to reality. The theoretical explanation is simply an attempt to consolidate the observed phenomena. A reader who rejects some aspects of my explanation in Book 4 as too unlikely, should keep in mind that this is but an attempt to explain certain observed phenomena. It helps us to understand a particular aspect of physical reality.

PREFACE

TOWARDS A NEW CONCEPTION OF
THE NATURE OF MATTER

1 / INTRODUCTION

In Book 4 we come to the most personal aspect of THE NATURE OF ORDER: the way in which architecture — indeed, all order in the world — touches the inner human person, our being.

The structure of life I have described in buildings — the structure which I believe to be objective — is deeply and inextricably connected with the human person and with the innermost nature of human feeling. In this fourth book I shall approach this topic of the inner feeling in a building as if there is a kind of personal thickness — a source, or ground, something almost occult — in which we find that the ultimate questions of architecture and art sometimes touch some connection of incalculable depth between the made work (building, painting, ornament, street) and the inner "I" which each of us experiences.

What I call "the I" is that interior element in a work of art, or in a work of nature, which makes one feel related to it. It may occur in a leaf, or in a picture, in a house, in a wave, even in a grain of sand, or in an ornament. It is not ego. It is not me. It is not individual at all, having to do with me, or you. It is humble, and enormous: that thing in common which each one of us has in us. It is the spirit which animates each living center.

2 / BACKGROUND

In Book 1, THE PHENOMENON OF LIFE, I have given an account of the living structure which exists in all those buildings and artifacts which have life, which support life, which are themselves alive. In Book 2, THE PROCESS OF CREATING LIFE, I have given an account of living processes — the class of processes which are needed to create living structure — leading to a new view of the dynamics of architecture. In Book 3, A VISION OF A LIVING WORLD, with hundreds of illustrations, I have given examples of modern towns, buildings, neighborhoods, gardens, columns, and rooms, which have, to some extent, this living structure in them, and which have been generated, in greater or lesser degree, by living process.

But in the pages of Books 1, 2, and 3, I have so far only hinted at what is possibly the most important thing of all. I have not yet described in the most direct terms, the innermost process that lies behind these phenomena.

That is because the real heart of the matter is something which is not so easily talked about, something nearly embarrassing, which we would perhaps not feel entirely comfortable to blurt out too easily, even to mention.

I can introduce it best by talking briefly about my private experience making buildings. When I am part of the making of a building and examine my process, what is happening in me when I do it, myself, in my effort, is that I find that I am nearly always reaching for the same thing. In some form, it is the personal nature of existence, revealed in the building, that I am searching for. It is "I," the I-myself, lying within all things. It is that shining something which draws me on, which I feel in the bones of the world, which comes out of the earth and makes our existence luminous.

This perhaps enigmatic statement about my daily life is not meant to be provocative. Nor is it meant to be profound. It is just a fact for me that when push comes to shove, on a day-to-day basis in my work as an architect, this is how I think about things. I ask myself constantly —

and it is the only question I really ask of myself—What must I do to put this self-like quality into the house, the room, the roof, the path, the tile?

Often, I can feel the possibility of this in a thing before I start to make it or before I start to think, or design, or plan, or build, or before I start to paint. It is the sublime interior, the right thing. I first feel existence shimmering in reality, and I then feel it deep enough in the thing I am looking at and trying to make, to know that it is worth capturing in concrete and wood and tile and paint. I can feel it, nearly always, almost before I *start*. Or, rather, I do not usually let myself start until I can feel this thing.

This thing, this something, is not God, it is not nature, it is not feeling. It is some ultimate, beyond experience. When I reach for it, I try to find—I can partly feel—the illumination of existence, a glimpse of that ultimate. It is always the same thing at root. Yet, of course, it takes an infinite variety of different forms.

Although in Books 1–3 I have only touched upon this ultimate indirectly, I must now dwell on it as all-important. It is unavoidable, this thing, and it is the core of all living structure. If we truly hope to make buildings that have life,

then it is this thing that we must look for, and meet, and face. But in the earlier three books I have not expressed strongly enough, this glimpse of the ultimate as the driving force behind what must be done. In the earlier books, in order to place attention on the questions of living structure, I wanted to speak in a way which was, as far as possible, consistent with our current way of thinking about science and about architecture. I wanted, as far as possible, to present a structure which could be understood in conventional terms. As a result, most of what Books 1–3 contain is consistent, structurally, with what we presently believe about the universe. But underneath that, implied, there is a part which is not consistent with the way we presently think about the universe. Perhaps, in part, I have been *reluctant* to make it clear enough because it rests on academically unmentionable foundations.

But now, in this fourth book, I must finally admit that beyond the formal structure *this* is what I experience. No matter how difficult it is to write down and make it believable, it — this — is what I believe all of us can experience. It is vast and impersonal. Yet it is personal, relating to every person.

3 / THE PERSONAL

When I set out to make the small black and white terrazzo ornaments on the last step of the stairs to my basement office on Shasta Road in Berkeley (illustrated on page 4), in part I reached this state. I knew that I was grazing, just touching, existence itself. I could feel this thing, hovering, shimmering, in the work. I knew that the pearly substance, being created by this pattern of black and white bits of marble dust and cement, does set things in order in such a way as to reveal existence, to make us see it, to see it shining, just beyond our grasp.

Book 4 has to do with this inner meaning, with the task of making and reaching this

shining "something." I want to describe it so that we can talk about it, understand what it means, share it as an aspiration, recognize it as something true, and have some inkling of what it *is*.

My hypothesis is this: that all value depends on a structure in which each center, the life of each center, approaches this simple, forgotten, remembered, unremembered "I" . . . that in the living work each center, in some degree, is a connection to this "I," or self . . . that the living steel and concrete bridge is one in which each part is connected to this self, awakens it in us . . . that the living song is one in which each

Black and white marble-terrazzo inlay in a concrete step, Christopher Alexander, Berkeley, 1974.

phrase, each note, is connected to this self, awakens it in us, reminds us of ourselves . . . that the living picture is one in which every center has this self and, thus, because it was painted there, it reminds us of ourselves . . . and that the living building is one in which each window, each roof, each room, each ceiling, each doorway, the gardens, the flowerbed, the trees, the rambling bramble bushes, the wall by the stream, the seat, and the handle on the door, are all connected to this I, and awaken it in us.

I believe that the ultimate effort of all serious art is to make things which connect with this I of every person. This "I," not normally available, is dredged up, forced to the light, forced into the light of day, by the work of art.

In this, the work of art is similar to nature, because in nature too, this "I" is what we find. The rock, the ripple in the pond, and the fish darting along the stream are connected to this I, reverberate with I, awaken and enliven us, continually refresh the I which sleeps in us. And this I which sleeps in us will not then follow the remembered voice. For this I which comes to life, as we gaze upon the pond, the buttercup, the cloud floating in the purple sky, the rush of water in the thunderstorm — this self is first awakened and then speaks to us, encouraging the I in us to be itself, in a new form taken within us, not similar but awakened in its newness, and speaking, itself, in a voice which will awaken I in other selves.

4 / THAT EXISTS IN ME, AND BEFORE ME, AND AFTER ME

Effectively, what all this amounts to is that in the process of making things through living process, gradually I approach more and more closely knowledge of what is truly in my own heart.

Early in my life as an architect, at first I was confused or deceived by the teaching I received from architectural instructors. I thought that those things which are important — and perhaps the things which I aspired to make — were "other," outside myself, governed by a canon of expertise which lay outside me, but to which I gave due.

Gradually, the older I got, I recognized that little of that had value, and that the thing which did have true value was only that thing which lay in my own heart. Then I learned to value only that which truly activates what is in my heart. I came to value those experiences which activate my heart as it really is. I sought, more and more, only those experiences which have the capacity, the depth, to activate the feeling that is my real feeling, in my true childish heart. And I learned, slowly, to *make* things which are of that nature.

This was a strange process, like coming home. As a young man I started with all my fancy ideas, the ideas and wonderful concepts of late boyhood, early manhood, my student years, the ideas I wondered at, open-mouthed, things which seemed so great to me. Then, from my teachers I learned things even more fantastic — I learned sophisticated taste, cleverness, profundity, seriousness. I tried to make, with my own hands, things of that level of accomplishment. That took me to middle age.

Then, gradually, I began to recognize that in the midst of that cleverness, which I never truly understood anyway, the one thing I could trust was a small voice, a tiny soft-and-hard vulnerable feeling, recognizable, which was something I actually *knew*. Slowly that knowledge grew in me. It was the stuff which I was actually cer-

tain of — not because it aped what others had taught me, but because I knew it to be true of itself, in me.

Usually the things which embodied this knowledge were very small things, things so small that in ordinary discourse they might have seemed insignificant, like the fact that I felt comfortable when my back sank into a pillow arranged in a certain way, and the fact that a cup of tea was more comforting, when I lay thus, with my back in that pillow, staring at the sky.

Then in my later years I gradually began to recognize that this realistic voice, breaking through — and which by now, I had identified in many concrete ways, even to the point of writing this stuff down so others could recognize it also, for themselves, in their way, in their own hearts — was my own voice, the voice that had always been in me, since childhood, but which as a young man I had pushed away and which, now, again, I began to recognize as the only true value.

But this knowing of myself, and what was in my own true heart, was not only childish. Because at the same time that I recognized it in small things — like cups of tea, leaves blowing off an autumn tree, a pebble underfoot — I also began to recognize it in very great things, in works made by artists centuries away from us in time, thousands of miles away in space. In something which one of them had made, suddenly this childish heart, this me, came rushing back. I could feel this, for example, in the mud wall at the back of the sand garden of Ryoan-ji. I could feel it in an ancient fragment of textile. I could feel it in the worn stone of a church, laid fourteen hundred years before. Somehow, I began to realize that the greatest masters of their craft were those who somehow managed to release, in me, that childish heart which is my true voice, and with which I am completely comfortable and completely free.

Ahmedabad, Ahmad Shah's mosque, interior, 1414

An Ottoman tile. Here the geometry of circles within circles has been perfected to the stage where one begins to feel a real connection with some domain beyond the self: the heart beyond the heart.

Knowing this changed my perspective. What at first seemed like a return to childhood or a simple increase of the personal, gradually took on a different character. I begin to realize that what I come in touch with when I go closer and closer to myself is not just "me." It is something vast, existing outside myself and inside myself, as if it were a contact with the eternal, something everlasting existing before me, in me, and around me. I recognized, too, that my most lucid moments occur when I am swept up in this void, and fully conscious of it, as if it were a blinding light.

This is what I have felt on the beach on the north shore of Point Reyes near San Francisco, when the sea comes crashing in with enormous force, when the water and wind are too loud for me to hear my voice, the waves too strong for me to think of swimming, the force of the water and the wind, the white foam of the waves, the blackish green moving water, the huge, loud grinding swells, the beach sand that goes on forever, the seaweeds strewn on the beach that have been hurled by a force greater than they are — as I am, also, when I walk among them.

Yet even though I am next to nothing in the presence of all this force, I am free there. In such a place, at such a moment, I am crushed to understand my own smallness, and then understand the immensity of what exists. But this immensity of what exists — and my connection to it — is not only something in my heart. It is a vastness which is outside me and beyond me and inside of me.

Actions and objects increase or decrease my connection to this vastness, which is in me, and which is also real. A concrete corridor without windows and with an endless line of doors is less likely to awaken it in me than a small apple tree in bloom. The brick on my front doorstep may awaken it, if it is ordinary, soft, like life in its construction.

It is at once enormous in extent and infinitely intimate and personal.

5 / CHANGES IN OUR IDEA OF MATTER

It is the living structure of buildings which awakens a connection with this personal feeling. The more that it appears in a building, the more it awakens this feeling in us. Indeed, we may say, truly, that a building has life in it to the extent that it awakens this connection to the personal. Or, in other language, we may say that a building has life in it, to the extent it awakens the connection to the eternal vastness which existed before me, and around me, and after me.

I believe that this is true, not just a nice way of talking. As I try to explain it quietly, for all its grandeur, and try to make the artist's experience real, I hope that you, with me, will also catch in it a glimpse of a modified picture of the universe. For, in my view, there is a core of fact here — a personal nature in what seems impersonal — that both underpins the nature of architecture in

its ultimate meaning and will also, one day, force a revision in our idea of the universe.

I believe it is in the nature of matter, that it is soaked through with self or "I." The essence of the argument which I am putting before you throughout Book 4 is that the thing we call "the self," which lies at the core of our experience, is a real thing, existing in all matter, beyond ourselves, and that in the end we must understand it, in order to make living structure in buildings. But it is also my argument that this is the nature of *matter*. It is not only necessary to understand it when we wish to make living structure in buildings. It is also necessary if we wish to grasp our place in the universe, our relationship to nature.

That argument — that difficult intellectual path — is the path which lies before us in this book.

It would perhaps be helpful for the reader to consider this book as anchored at three points: chapter 1, OUR PRESENT PICTURE OF THE UNIVERSE, chapter 6, THE BLAZING ONE, and the conclusion, A MODIFIED PICTURE OF THE UNI-VERSE. These three chapters provide the anchors of the argument, and describe the modified picture of reality which I propose. The other chapters provide details from the spheres of architecture and art.

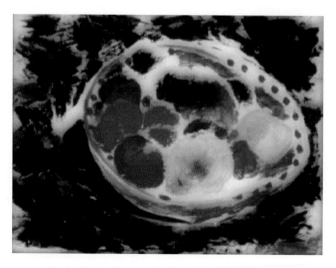

Bowl of fruit, oil on panel, Christopher Alexander, 1991

PART ONE

We stand face to face with art. Can we make the eternal, simple thing, that belongs utterly to the world, and that preserves, sustains, extends, the beauty of the world?

Is this truly possible? Can it be done, in our world of trucks, freeways, computers, and prefabricated furniture and prefabricated drinks?

Throughout Books 1, 2, and 3, I have presented a variety of propositions about living structure. They are results of observation. Many of them rely, explicitly, on unusual methods of observation. Many are based on feeling. They are capable of teaching us a new attitude towards the art of building. They are capable, in principle, of transforming our physical world for the better.

But, powerful and effective as these methods are, they are likely to be ignored or rejected by the reader so long as they are understood within a mechanistic world-view. A person who adheres to classical 19th- or 20th-century beliefs about the nature of matter, will not be able, fully, to accept the revisions in building practice that I have proposed, because the revisions will remain, for that person, too disturbingly inconsistent with the picture of the world. The old world-picture will constantly gnaw at our attempts to find a wholesome architecture, disturb our attempts, interfere with them — to such an extent that they cannot be understood or used successfully.

Unless our world-picture itself is changed and replaced by a new picture, more consistent with the felt reality of life in buildings and in our surroundings, the idea of life in buildings itself (even with all its highly practical revisions in architectural practice) will not be enough to accomplish change.

CHAPTER ONE

OUR PRESENT PICTURE
OF THE UNIVERSE

1 / COSMOLOGY

I have given indications, throughout these four books, that we cannot form a complete picture of the nature of architecture without conceptions that deal with life and self. We need, for our time, a picture which allows us to form a connection, a relatedness with the whole. But the mechanistic scientific world picture we have inherited, as it stands is not capable of this.

It is hardly possible to take the art of building seriously, as a profound task, if what we do when we design a building is merely to aggregate meaningless lumps of matter. Yet that is, within our present world-picture, what we are doing when we design, or build. Within the present scientific picture, if we ask, What it is all for? the only answer that comes back is, *It is for nothing*. Within this picture, if we ask, What is the point? the only scientific answer that comes back is, *There is no point*.

I shall begin, therefore, by examining the great strength and beauty of the scientific world-picture, trying to find a crack where we may inject some new structure that endows the whole with meaning. That cannot be done by wiping away the science and technology we have gained. They are too beautiful, too powerful. We have learned too much from them, and gained too much. But somehow, the abstract mechanism-inspired world-picture must be modified, transformed, in such a way that it becomes something that has meaning for all of us.

2 / THE STRENGTH OF THE PRESENT SCIENTIFIC WORLD-PICTURE

Let us begin by summarizing the strength of our present scientific world-picture. During the last three hundred years we have succeeded in building up an astonishing view of reality. This is a picture in which the parts of the world are to be viewed through mathematical models or mechanisms. That means, mental models have been constructed with precise rules of behavior, and we have managed to make these mental models match the reality in such a powerful degree that we can predict, and manipulate, the behavior of the world, almost throughout the full range of its scales and substances.

We are able to control atomic explosions. Airplanes fly. We can create new materials. We can understand the chemical behavior of matter. We have learned to cure diseases by medicines, and through surgery. We have a level of control of our physical destiny that would have astonished our ancestors in virtually any past period

of human history. We have knowledge of, and control over, the subatomic processes; and have used them to harness energy, to harness communications. We are able to control oscillations throughout the electromagnetic spectrum, using them for every kind of electronic device, for control and communication. We have also begun, in the last decades, to attend to the behavior of highly complex systems, and are now achieving understanding of this subject in biology, in weather, in ecology, in genetics.

And for the most profound material questions, too, we are beginning to have answers. We have models of the origin of the universe and galaxies. We have models of the origins of life. We have models of the human psyche, and of information flow and of cognition.

All in all, we have succeeded in building successful models of the matter in the universe and its behavior, in a way that is wonderful and powerful. It is a collective achievement of an order incomparable with almost any previous human achievement. Our modern world in all its beauty — and fascinating and wonderful as it is to live in it — depends on this achievement.

3 / THE WEAKNESS OF THE PRESENT WORLD-PICTURE

And yet, there is something wrong! Although this modern picture is powerful and remarkable, and must be appreciated for its great intellectual beauty — not merely for its practical effectiveness — still, there is something that does not exactly work. In order to create this effective scientific world-picture we had to use a *device*: the intellectual device of treating entities in nature as if they were inert, as if they were lumps of geometric substance, without feeling, without life — in effect, merely mechanical elements in a larger machine.

This mental trick was invented by Roger Bacon, Descartes, Newton, and others — and has been the foundation of our modern understanding. Even the models of quantum mechanics — they are mathematical mechanisms, to be sure, not actual physical mechanisms — work because they work *like* mechanisms. The elements are defined, and the rules of interaction are defined, and everything then follows when this mechanism is let loose.

Yet we human beings also have, in our daily *experience* of the world, something different, an immediate awareness of self. We are *conscious*. We are aware of our own selves. We have feelings. We experience love. Sometimes we experience unity. As I have shown in Book 1, these experiences of self are profoundly connected with the existence of life in buildings and in our surroundings.

Within the era of the mechanical world-picture, we have been taught to think that the experience of self is somehow an artifact of the interaction of matter, a consequence of the play of machines.[1] Yet thinking so does not contribute any understanding of the self that we experience each day. The self — in each one of us — continues to exist. It is more palpable, more present, in our daily experience than is the world of mental and mathematical mechanisms. Yet our present world-picture has no place in it for this self. The self does not figure in the present world-picture as a real thing. Nor does consciousness. Nor does love. Nor does the experience of unity.

There are thus two worlds in our minds. One is the scientific world which has been pictured through a highly complex system of mechanisms. The other is the world we actually experience. These two worlds, so far, have not been connected in a meaningful fashion. Alfred North Whitehead, writing about 1920, was one of the first philosophers to draw attention to this modern problem, which he called the bifurcation of nature.[2] Whitehead believed that we will not have a proper grasp of the universe and our place in it, until the self which we experience in ourselves, and the machinelike character of matter we see outside ourselves, *can be united in a single picture.* I believe this. And I believe that we shall not have a credible view that shows how human life and architecture are related until Whitehead's bifurcation is dissolved.[3] Indeed, until it is dissolved, we cannot help — at least partially — thinking of ourselves as machines!

4 / THE NEEDS OF ARCHITECTURE

It is little wonder that the mechanistic view of man has been accompanied by a kind of hopelessness and despair. Who wants to live, who can live, when we believe that we are individually indeed nothing but meaningless machines?

Some people seek meaning, and solace for their loneliness, in religion. To try and offset the meaningless and hopeless picture, without meaning, without purpose, spiritualism has re-entered the world with a vengeance. Churches are growing. Fundamentalist movements throughout the world punish their followers for any departure from traditional or conservative canons of behavior. Belief in astrology, visits from outer space, telepathy, are rife. Movements mixing therapy with spiritualism, belief in afterlife, belief in the goodness of man, efforts to exist within some canon of a religious sort, have come back, and grow every day. These religious movements try, somehow, to shield us from the awful import of mechanistic science. They try to make the world bearable, by leavening the machines which we ourselves are, with the incantations of prophesy, of goodness, of liberation, of heaven, perhaps too of hell.

But none of this can really work. I do not believe that religion can improve the situation. Even the most holy, the most serious of these zen monks, new-age priests, new brethren of the new churches in Texas, in the Philippines, in Japan, in Africa — what can they hope to accomplish? The fundamental root of our troubles, of our meaninglessness, lies in our view of the nature of matter. If matter is indeed machinelike, and if then we are indeed ourselves machines — what good is it to call on spirits, to sing hymns of praise, to look for God? The devastating truth is that *if* the world is made of machinelike matter — and we are ourselves therefore machines — we are then doomed to live, for a very short time, in the meaningless and living hell

of Franz Kafka, colored only by the banality of its machinelike pointlessness.

It is the nature of matter itself, which is at stake. Our despair and hopelessness follow from the belief, or certainty, that matter is machinelike in its nature and that we then, being matter also, are machinelike too.

And architecture, too, where is it? Religion cannot inject meaning into architecture, transform what is banal, geometrically, into something that has life and gains life artistically. Again, it is the nature of matter itself which is at stake. The lumps of passive matter, which we arrange, must somehow become meaningful as we try to make them live. But how is that to be done, in a universe which is, in large part, mechanical?

Throughout THE NATURE OF ORDER I have presented a variety of propositions about living structure. All these propositions are, in one sense or another, results of observation. I have presented observations about the degree of life in things — even in buildings, even in concrete and brick and wood — and the surprising way this varies. I have presented comments about the nature of wholeness in the world, and its dependence on centers. I have presented definitions of geometric properties, correlated with degree of life — which seem pervasive in buildings and artifacts and in many parts of nature.

I have tried to show how to make things, in our time, which are truly beautiful. I have presented conclusions about the impact of human process and procedural sequence on the evolution of coherent living structure. I have presented examples — many detailed examples — of harmonious process and its impact on planning of buildings, structure of buildings, on the detailed geometry of buildings and the way a building is constructed from material. I have presented rather surprising facts about the apparent correlation of the mirror of the self test with observed life in thousands of centers. I have presented observations about the way that human feeling seems to correlate with life in material systems.

The ideas I have brought forward — some solid, some more tentative — are in many ways unlike the ideas that are common in our daily experience of science and technology. Many of them rely, explicitly, on unusual methods of observation. Many are based on feeling. They are capable of teaching us a new attitude towards the art of building. They are capable, in principle, of transforming our physical world for the better.

But I believe these arguments will be ignored — or rejected by the reader as a matter of practical necessity — unless the reader also faces, and masters, the changes in *world-view* which these arguments require. A person who adheres to a 19th- or 20th-century belief about the nature of matter, will not be able to accept the revisions in building practice that I propose, because these

revisions would remain too disturbingly inconsistent with that person's picture of the world.

Unless our world-picture *itself* is changed and replaced by another, more consistent with the felt reality of life in buildings and in our surroundings — the idea of life in buildings itself, even with all its ensuing revisions in architectural practice, will not be enough. The old world-picture will constantly gnaw at our attempts to find a wholesome architecture, disturb our attempts, interfere with them — to such an extent that they cannot be understood or used successfully.

That is the reason why I choose, now, in the fourth of these four books, to go — at last — directly to the question of cosmology. What is the universe made of? What might a fully adequate picture of it be like? What is the nature of matter? What is its fundamental character?

5 / SCIENTIFIC EFFORTS TO BUILD AN IMPROVED WORLD-PICTURE

Because our world-picture is inadequate, during the second half of the 20th century many scientists began a serious attempt to repair the world-picture.[4] There was a spate of serious effort, primarily concentrated on the importance of wholeness, and of the whole. This attitude came from a confluence of quantum physics, system theory, chaos theory, the theory of complex adaptive systems, biology, genetics, and other sources. It set out to paint a more holistic picture of the universe — a picture of the universe as an unbroken whole. The picture was widely presented to the public, and widely discussed among scientists. It was a large effort, made jointly by scientists in many different fields, many of them physicsts and biologists. They included, among others, Erwin Schrödinger, David Bohm, Francisco Varela, John Bell, Eugene Wigner, Roger Penrose, Ilya Prigogine, Benoit Mandelbrot,

Brian Goodwin, John Holland, Stuart Kaufmann, Mae-Wan Ho.[5] As a result of their work, especially during the last decade of the 20th century, a new attitude began to emerge.

This new attitude began with results in quantum mechanics which showed that an accurate picture of local particle behavior, cannot be reached merely by looking at the local structure of physical events; rather, that in some compelling way the behavior of each local event must be considered to be influenced by the whole. In a few cases there have even been indications that the local events are influenced by, or been subject to, behavior and structure of the universe as a whole, including influences and interactions which propagate faster than the speed of light.[6] The vital thing, anyway, was that behavior of physical systems is always "behavior of the whole," and cannot be well-understood as a conglomerate of local events acting by themselves.

In parallel with these developments, a similar new attitude was developing in biology. In 19th-century science and in early 20th-century science there had been insufficient attention to the coordinating functions of the organism; to the appearance of complex structure in the course of evolution and in the daily working of ecological systems; to the evolution of whole ecologies and individual organisms. These deficiencies were answered by an attempt to show that complex systems, systems in which many variables interact, have new properties — sometimes called "emergent" properties — that arise merely because of the organized complexity inherent in the network character of the system, its variables, and their interactions. The development of chaos theory, the theory of complex systems, fractals, the idea of autopoesis in complex systems, have led to remarkable new results, which show how unexpected and complex behaviors arise in richly interconnected systems. Theorems have been proved to show how compelling order arises, almost spontaneously, in these systems.[7]

Thus biology, ecology, the emerging fields of complex systems theory, and physics, have all begun to point the way towards a new conception of the world in which the local system is influenced by, and compelled by, the behavior of the whole.

Some science writers have claimed that these developments herald a future new world vision in which humanity, and wonder, and self, are included. Fritjof Capra, in THE TAO OF PHYSICS, was one of the first to express this point of view.[8] More recently, referring to the tradition of late-20th-century science, the ecologist Stuart Cowan wrote me a letter, in which he said: "There is, in both science and theology, a long and important tradition of seeing consciousness, spirit, wholeness, and life immanent in the world of space-time, of matter and energy, of the structure of the universe itself. It is a view of embodiment and incarnation, in which even a hydrogen atom has a profound and mysterious interiority (Teilhard de Chardin's phrase), in which self-organizing structures cohere and communicate, in which interdependence emerges from a fifteen billion year shared story at all levels of scale, in which profound life shimmers forth from the very fabric of the universe . . ."[9]

This is optimistic and positive. And indeed, the newly propagated wisdom seems to suggest that the world-picture has been so profoundly reformulated by these new events in science, that it is a wholly new picture in which even the old aspirations of religion are encompassed.

It is certainly true that within these new scientific writings, one encounters passages of beauty and inspiring thought. For example, Mae-Wan Ho writes of the activity within the organism, "What one must imagine is an incredible hive of activity at every level of magnification — of music being made using more than two thirds of the 73 octaves of the electromagnetic spectrum — locally appearing as though chaotic, and yet perfectly coordinated as a whole. This exquisite music is played in endless variations subject to our changes of mood and physiology, each organism and species with its own repertoire . . ."[10]

The passage is humane and beautiful. Yet even such passages, when examined closely, remain mechanistic in their detail. They deal with the whole and they describe wondrous behavior in the movement of the whole; the writer is deeply holistic in her attitude. But what she describes are still *mechanisms*. No matter how dedicated she is to a new vision, how hard she tries to bring in the new understanding of wholeness in physics, the language of mechanistic science keeps getting in the way. The wholeness itself does not yet appear in the actual calculations *as a structure*.

Some of the scientists referred to imply, and perhaps believe, that the problem of the bifurcation of nature has been solved; that the thoroughgoing emphasis on the whole which has been achieved will now create a vision of the universe in which we may at last be at home; that the enigma of the felt self, coexisting with the machine-like play of fields and atoms, has been resolved by the new emphasis on the coordination of complex systems and the physicist's new way of paying attention to the whole.[11]

I believe their optimism is misplaced. The central dilemma, the split between self and matter — Whitehead's bifurcation — continues today almost as strongly as before. It has been alleviated, perhaps just a little, by the prospect of a new vision and by the prospect of a vision of the whole. But that vision has not yet been *achieved*, scientifically, in a form which allows the human self to find its place. Because these new theories explicitly concern themselves with the whole, they appear to have overcome the mechanistic difficulties. However, the new vision which has emerged from these events in science has still only improved the earlier mechanistic science by focusing better on the whole.

The *personal, the existence of felt "self" in the universe, the presence of consciousness, and the vital relation between self and matter* — none of these have entered the picture yet, in a practical or scientifically workable way. In that sense the world picture, even as modified, *still* deals only with the inert — albeit as a whole. The most fundamental problem with the mechanistic world picture has still not — yet — been solved.

Whitehead's rift remains.

6 / THE CONTINUING LACK OF A UNIFYING COSMOLOGY

Can religion help? Could there be some modification of science by religion, to "combine" (somehow) the material description given by science, with a spiritual description given by religion?

During the last twenty years there has been — worldwide — a surge of renewed interest in religion, among scientists and, of course, among others in the world at large.[12] There has been rekindled interest in various forms of spirituality, schools of religion flourish, seventy percent of scientists readily admit to believing in God in some sense, there is almost a wave to reunite some form of religion, ancient or modern or super-modern, with our understanding of the world. Some forms are invented. Some are combinations of eastern and western, or of primitive with sophisticated. Some of the recent science described above, in section 4, has an almost spiritual tone, or a quasi-spiritual leaning.

But does any of this activity have the capacity to change our world picture, and make it more accurate, more believable, or more able to cement us to the world, more able to unite our knowledge of matter with our feeling of self?

I do not think so. The trouble is that our view of *matter* is flawed: and nothing about religion or spirituality, as practiced or conceived today, has the power to change it.

Briefly stated, the problem is that the many spiritual suggestions and beliefs which resound in the world today are not *coherent* with the underlying mechanistic picture of the substance of the world. They are not on the same playing field. Spiritual overlays on our underlying picture are, in my view, insights — hopes, fears, intuitions, aspirations, a mixture of spiritual truths and wishful thinking — but they are insights which do not add to our understanding of the way the universe actually works. They are undoubtedly sincere. *But they are not made to square with the underlying mechanical picture.* The underlying physical picture has too little room for them, cannot yet accommodate them, has not yet, in my view, been modified to make it possible to include them. The substance which the 20th-century world was made of remained the inert, mechanical space-time of Descartes, Newton and Einstein, of quantum mechanics and the string theorists. This mechanical substance is our cake. So far, our spiritual views and ethical views are only frosting on this cake, which do not penetrate or affect the way the cake works. And make no mistake, quantum mechanics too, though widely heralded as "non-mechanistic," is still a picture in which everything takes place in the space time of inert substance . . . the play of configurations, albeit wonderful configurations, on the canvas of inert space and matter.

Even the Pope and the Dalai Lama today have a mechanical view of the nature of matter. All people alive today are living, for the large part, in a mental world which is dominated by a mechanist picture, *even when they consider themselves to be spiritual, even when they hold spiritual, or religious, or ethical beliefs, and try to live by these beliefs,* because there is no alternative. That, at core, is the rub. A conviction about spirituality is not the same as a coherent picture of things in the world within which spirituality or goodness *make sense.*

It is this ongoing rift between the mechanical-material picture of the world (which we accept as true) and our intuitions about self and spirit (which are intuitively clear but scientifically vague) that has destroyed our architecture. It is destroying us, too. It has destroyed our sense of self-worth. It has destroyed our belief in ourselves. It has destroyed us and our architecture, ultimately, by forcing a collapse of meaning.

In order to have an architecture in which our own lives and the quality of our surroundings, the buildings, too, have meaning, we must find a new form of physics, a modified physics in which self and matter can be reconciled. We have not been sufficiently aware to what extent our own 20th-century cosmology — because of its focus on the inert — has undermined our capacity to produce buildings that have life. Of all the periods of human history, ours is perhaps the period in which architecture has been most barren spiritually, most infected by banality. I myself have become aware only slowly during the last thirty years, of the way that this artistic barrenness follows directly from our contemporary mechanism-inspired cosmology. But I have finally come to believe that it is just the prevailing views we hold about the mechanical nature of the universe which have led directly to a situation in which great buildings — even buildings of true humility — almost cannot be made.[13]

7 / TEN TACIT ASSUMPTIONS WHICH UNDERLIE OUR PRESENT PICTURE OF THE UNIVERSE

To underscore the gravity of the need for modification, I shall now describe ten assumptions — tacit, but widely held in today's world — which must disappear from our world-picture in order to make a vital architecture possible.

Scientists often like to say that the materialist view of present-day science is potentially consistent with nearly *any* view of ethics or religion because it says nothing about these subjects.[14]

Strictly speaking, the logic of this view can be upheld. But what governs people's view of the world is not only logic, but also what is implied by this logic, what is drawn by extension *from* this logic. This is what I meant to say earlier about the meaninglessness of our present conception of the universe. Strictly speaking, the facts of physics and astrophysics do not imply that the universe is meaningless. But the way these facts are presently drawn, the larger conception of the world which we have formed at the same time we have been forming our physics, does suggest — even strongly *imply* — that the world is meaningless. It does this, because along with legitimate assumptions that underlie physics and biology, deeper-lying tacit assumptions are also carried in.

Indeed, tacit assumptions have entered our picture of the world so pervasively that it is from *them* that we have got the picture of the universe that is distressing us. Though they were originally inspired by mechanistic philosophy, they themselves go far beyond the strict discoveries of science. It is these *beyond*-mechanistic or *ultra*-mechanistic assumptions which control much of what we say and think and do today, and did say and think and do throughout the 20th century. In my view these assumptions persist as assumptions about matter, even in the context of the new spiritualized holistic science I have discussed above.

These ultra-mechanistic assumptions about matter — not strictly justified by mechanistic science itself, but inspired by it and encouraged by it — have shaped our attitude to art and architecture and society and environment. They have made good architecture almost impossible.

To keep the text brisk, I have placed discussion of these ten assumptions in the notes at the end of the chapter. That way, a reader to whom these assumptions are already obvious, will not need to struggle through them.

———

The first tacit assumption which has crept in is an exaggerated form of an idea that, in a modest form, is essential as a tool in science:

TACIT ASSUMPTION 1. *What is true, is only the body of those facts which can be represented as lifeless mechanisms.* (Discussion in the note)[15]

A damaging offshoot from assumption # 1 is the widespread and nowadays accepted assumption that value is subjective. This assumption has become nearly the central tenet of modern architecture. Thus:

TACIT ASSUMPTION 2. *Matters of value in architecture are subjective.* (Discussion in the note)[16]

The pressure to view all matters of value as personal and idiosyncratic has been further intensified as a result of a further assumption something like this:

TACIT ASSUMPTION 3. *Modern conceptions of human liberty require that all values be viewed as subjective. The subjective nature of value gives the private striving of each individual person — even when vacuous or image-inspired or greed-inspired — the same weight. Attempts to put value on an objective footing are to be viewed with suspicion.* (Discussion in the note)[17]

A further tacit assumption more directly asserts the meaninglessness of the world:

TACIT ASSUMPTION 4. *The basic matter of the world is neutral with regard to value. Matter is inert. The universe is made of inert material which blindly follows laws of combination and transformation.* (Discussion in the note)[18]

The meaninglessness of the mechanist cosmology we have inherited is further due to the disconnection, within our picture, of what we see as being outside ourselves (the matter which we see as a mechanism) and our experience of what seems to be inside us (which we experience as self). This may be summarized as:

TACIT ASSUMPTION 5. *Matter and mind, the objective outer world and the subjective inner world are taken to be two entirely different realms, different in kind, and utterly disconnected.* (Discussion in the note)[19]

The disconnection between the outer world of physics, and the inner world of self, finds vivid expression in the strange and nearly meaningless view of art which dominated a considerable part of 20th-century life. This view might be characterized as:

TACIT ASSUMPTION 6. *Art is an intense and powerful social phenomenon, but one that has no deep importance in the physical scheme of things, and therefore no basic role in the structure of the universe.* (Discussion in the note)[20]

The "lost" role of art comes nowhere into view as strongly, in my mind, as in our perception of the rift between ornament and function in a building. I believe that, without knowing why, 20th-century people learned to subscribe to:

TACIT ASSUMPTION 7. *Ornament and function in a building are separate and unrelated categories.* (Discussion in the note)[21]

The separated roles given to ornament and function come to a head in a still more "outrageous," though more veiled, tacit assumption:

TACIT ASSUMPTION 8. *At a profound level, architecture is irrelevant. The task of building has no special importance, except in so far as it contributes to practical function through engineering, or to material wealth through image.* (Discussion in the note)[22]

The sequence of assumptions approaches its culmination in what is, perhaps, one of the most damaging assumptions of all:

TACIT ASSUMPTION 9. *The intuition that something profound is happening in a great work of art is, in scientific terms, meaningless.* (Discussion in the note)[23]

And finally one may formulate the following assumption which brings us face to face with the ultimate source of the meaninglessness we experience:

TACIT ASSUMPTION 10. *The instinct that there is some kind of deeper meaning in the world is scientifically useless. It has to be ignored as a subject of serious scientific discussion.* (Discussion in the note)[24]

I believe these ten assumptions do exist *tacitly* throughout our everyday lives today. Although thousands of modern books and poems and paintings have helped people assert and affirm their sense of meaning in the world, the world-picture *itself*, the scientific world-picture, continues to assert the blind meaninglessness of the physical matter in the world, and of the physical matter we ourselves are made of.[25]

8 / INSPIRATION FOR A FUTURE PHYSICS

You may privately consider my formulation of the tacit assumptions to be caricatures which do not correspond to your own convictions about value, or art, or the meaning of things in the world.[25] Nevertheless, even at the very moment of trying to preserve some thread of a connection to the value of existence — some way of doing it the homage which the intensity of feeling it evokes demands — in almost every attempt, the modern person is prevented from embracing his own feelings in any full sense, because today's cosmology and the undercurrents I have tried to articulate in the ten tacit assumptions simply don't allow it.

Sad as it is to insist on it, I believe we must admit to ourselves that, broadly speaking, some version of these ten tacit assumptions *does* represent the general *ultra*-mechanistic tradition of 20th-century science and technology, especially as this tradition has impact on questions of value and art, and on the art of building. These tacit assumptions form the mental prison which we currently inhabit; they are the origin of the meaningless world-picture which quietly makes people depressed and alienated. Even though we may kick, and rail, and protest that we are after all connected to some deeper substance, this system of assumptions *is* the current view of the universe in which we live.

Yet nearly every sensitive person who examines his own feelings carefully will recognize that he experiences great discomfort in the framework of these tacit assumptions. Who has not had the feeling, listening to a Mozart's 40th symphony, or to Bach's B-minor Mass, that something magnificent is happening, that in some inner sense, the heavens are opening, and that this structure of sound somehow reaches in and hits the heart? But no matter how deep this feeling, the mechanistic cosmology contained in the ten assumptions of the last few pages is not consistent with it. According to this mechanistic cosmology, the Mozart is a soothing pattern of sound which happens (for physiological or cognitive reasons) to be soothing. Perhaps it activates some pleasure center in the brain. But certainly this cosmology cannot admit, or formulate, the idea that the Mozart somehow strikes to the core of the cosmos ... and that our pleasure in it happens because we recognize this fact, and take part in it. Thus the Mozart is, in the mechanistic framework, ultimately considered trivial. Whether it gives pleasure or not, it certainly does not in any physicist's sense strike to the core of existence.

Until now, this kind of problem has not been thought of as a serious problem by physicists. The lack of a serious answer to the question: What is happening when you hear a piece of Mozart? has not been seen as a problem in *physics*. If it has been seen at all, it has been seen as a minor problem in applied psychology, certainly not as a clue to a possible mismatch between the current physical picture of the world, and the way the world really is. *But that is the whole problem.* In physics there are repeated enunciations of the idea that the laws of physics constitute, or might constitute, a theory of *everything*. For example, Stephen Hawking, Professor of Astronomy at Cambridge, speaking of physics: "Our goal is nothing less than a complete description of the universe we live in. In the next chapter I will try to . . . explain how people are trying to fit together the partial theories I have described to form a complete unified theory that would cover *everything* in the universe." and "A complete consistent unified theory is only the first step; our goal is a *complete* understanding of the events around us, and of our own existence."[26]

This is the underlying belief shared widely, sometimes perhaps unconsciously, by many educated people in society. Physics has constructed a picture of reality, which purports to be a picture of *everything* and the way that everything really *is* — yet it fails to incorporate fundamental experience, and fundamental intuitions. We *experience* the fact, intuitively, that the Mozart seems to have something essential in it. But the present theory of physics cannot make sense of it.

So far, within the framework of physics, this mismatch between feeling and theory has been ignored. But look what happens as a result. What it means is that we have a certain experience, momentary perhaps, something we consider a haze of emotion . . . a feeling we recognize as

deep, as vitally important . . . it lasts for a few seconds, perhaps even for a few minutes . . . and then our rude cosmology dismisses it.

The same thing happens a thousand times a day. When we enter a great building, see the deep blue of the light in the nave of Chartres fill the church, or walk down a lane in a forgotten village in England, and the same feelings pass across our consciousness . . . again we rule it out. The same happens even with a fleeting moment at a children's birthday, when the cake is brought in, candles flickering, glowing in the half dark, and for a moment a small voice in us gasps . . . but quickly, once again, we are brought back (more truly, we bring ourselves back) to our ordinary reality.

It happens even with the beauty of a flower at the roadside. Looking at this flower, again the feeling strikes: the knowledge that in this miracle, somehow, lies the whole beauty of the world. But again, because there is no room for this thought in our cosmology, we brush away the thought, dismiss it as too soft, too romantic . . . and come back once again to our harsh reality in which space is neutral, the flower is neutral, we are neutral, all well-behaved machines, following the rules of our creation and behavior.

The ultra-mechanist cosmology we have taken in with our 20th-century mother's milk therefore cuts across our experience constantly. It forces us to dismiss, treat lightly, all those precious feelings we have, of meaning in the world, of something wonderful . . . and replaces it by a dull, gray, matter-of-factness which is not matter-of-fact at all, but was invented by Descartes and others of his time, and is now merely mouthed by us because we do not know of an alternative.[27]

9 / THE CONFRONTATION OF ART AND SCIENCE

Let us go back to the essential question that must lie at the root of any believable cosmology: What is the life that we discern in things?[28]

In Book 1, I described the inner life of buildings as a real phenomenon. What kind of phenomenon is that inner life? In chapter 6 of Book

4, I shall go further to describe how in a great building or great painting where the most profound color phenomena occur, something sometimes happens that I call inner light, a state where colors are both subdued and shining brilliantly. I suggest you look at the examples on pages 158–239. The inner light is an extension of the life in things, a deeper version of the phenomenon of life. What is this inner light which can occur in paintings?

Contemporary science — if it tried to deal with the phenomenon of life in works of art — would probably have to say something along the following lines: Perhaps when the colors are combined in a very subtle and harmonious way, somehow a special resulting structure or condition arises, and this structure or condition then causes an effect, or a reverberation, or response, in the body, or in the central nervous system. Perhaps it is an archetypal connection to inner cognitive structures. Crudely put, the arrangement of colors zaps the central system. And there you are.[29]

Yet I am quite certain, intuitively, that what is happening when colors form inner light in a great painting, is something more significant, something which has real meaning. Somehow, I believe that it touches to the core of things. Somehow, something deep and essential in the universe — not just in us — is being awakened by the inner light of a great painting. In short, I believe in the seriousness and significance of the phenomenon.

The present-day scientific mode of thinking is forced to bypass this intuition. It has no good way of letting it be true. But we still face the question, What *is* the inner light which occurs in a great painting by Fra Angelico or in the nave of Chartres? Is this merely a subjective phenomenon where a certain arrangement of colors zaps the central nervous system? Or is it a phenomenon in which something penetrates to the heart of *existence*, to the heart of what the universe *is*?

Today's scientists, especially the more technologically oriented, may tend to believe the former. Whether or not they are privately artistic or religious, as professional *scientists* they will tend — today — to assume that some "zapping" model of the first kind must explain the phenomenon, even though we do not yet know how such a zapping model works! They will tend to want to say that all that is happening is that the nervous system, its cognitive structure, is somehow being zapped.

Painters, musicians, and architects, on the other hand — especially the better ones — will say that in some form it is the *second* of these two which must be true. The zapping idea is too trivial and ridiculous to be taken seriously.

Here lies a confrontation. It is not true that scientists don't appreciate art. Many appreciate art very deeply. But they have not, usually, thought about art as a *phenomenon* in the deep and serious scientific way they think about other phenomena. They enjoy art, they appreciate it. But in their present mode of thought, if forced to consider some particular event in art — like the shining of the inner light in a great painting — then they will feel virtually forced to assume some kind of model of the cognitive system being zapped, because that is the only kind of model they know at the moment. It is the only way they can imagine, of making sense.

This, precisely, is my point. The only reason scientists might have a naive picture of the phenomenon is that, *as scientists*, they haven't thought about this kind of thing very carefully. What I have presented in THE NATURE OF ORDER is an extension of science, written by someone who has thought about these kinds of phenomena carefully, and has begun — just begun — to see what the structure of these phenomena must be. According to what I have described in these four books, it seems that matter-space must somehow be a potentially living kind of stuff, perhaps even a potentially conscious stuff — anyway, at the very least, center-making stuff, or whole-making stuff.

Somehow, and for some reason, the more intensely that centers are created in any given region in space, the more intensely this region of space becomes connected with the human person or the human self. That is the origin of life and inner light. But there is simply nothing in our present scientific picture of the physical universe which hints at anything like that.

The apparent confrontation between art and science is not really between "art" and "science" as two disciplines. Rather, it is between two different views of what kind of stuff the universe is made of. It is a confrontation between the idea that the world is made of purely mechanical stuff, similar in essence to the kind of inert and abstract Cartesian matter-space scientists have taken for granted for the last three hundred years . . . and the idea that it must be some other kind of stuff, more personal, and far more mysterious in its nature.

10 / A FUSION OF SELF AND MATTER

Physicists, certainly, must face this confrontation. Architects, too, *must* face it.

What I have to say in the next chapters, rests on the search for such a new cosmology: one in which the idea of great art is possible — even necessary — as something which connects us to the universe, something which can provide a proper underpinning for the art of building.

The cosmology which I describe, as I work my way through the task of reaching a deeper view of building, rests on the recognition of the I — the source of our own self — as something real, existing together with space and matter in the universe, something which must be given its status, together with space and time, as part of a new view of living structure in a more comprehensive material view of things.

In these chapters, and finally in the conclusion of the book on pages 317–38, I put forward a sketch of a modified cosmology that extends physics — a way of extending our view of matter that leaves our present physics nearly intact, yet adds to it and injects into it new features, not presently part of our picture of matter, but capable, in principle, of making better sense of everything, and making better sense of architecture.

NOTES

1. A sophisticated example of this attempt to see the self which we experience as a by-product of the play of matter (neurological process, etc), is to be found in Daniel Dennett, CONSCIOUSNESS EXPLAINED (Boston: Little, Brown and Co, 1991). This is a sophisticated book, with an attempt to build a workable and believable theory. But it does not, in the least, explain the interior awareness of self. The argument simply sidesteps the real question, as any mechanistic explanation is bound to have to do.

2. As Whitehead says, "How unfortunate that we should be forced to conclude that in its own sad reality nature is a dull affair, soundless, scentless, colorless; merely the hurrying of material, endlessly, meaninglessly . . ." from Alfred North Whitehead, SCIENCE AND THE MODERN WORLD (Cambridge: Cambridge University Press, 1925, reissued 1932), 69. And again: "For us the red glow of the sunset should be as much part of nature as are the molecules and electric waves by which men of science would explain the phenomenon. It is for natural philosophy to analyze how these various elements of nature are connected . . . What I am essentially protesting against is the bifurcation of nature into two systems of reality, which, insofar as they are real, are real in different senses. One reality would be the entities such as electrons which are the study of speculative physics. This would be the reality which is there for knowledge; although on this theory it is never known. For what is known is the other sort of reality, which is the byplay of the mind. Thus there would be two natures, one is the conjecture, and the other is the dream." From Alfred North Whitehead, THE CONCEPT OF NATURE (Cambridge: Cambridge University Press, 1920). See, also, Laurence Bright, O. P., WHITEHEAD'S PHILOSOPHY OF PHYSICS (London and New York: Sheed and Ward, 1958), 19–24. Whitehead's problem remains unsolved today.

3. For a fuller explanation of my views, please see Book 1, chapters 7–10, especially chapter 8.

4. The text of this section was inspired by a series of very stimulating discussions with Stuart Cowan. Stu-

art felt, at first, that my emphasis on cosmological shift, as presented in this book, gave too little credit to the emerging theories of the many writers mentioned in this chapter. I, on my side, felt that the enormous contribution made by these scientists did not yet solve the core problem. In the course of several months of 1998 and 1999, in a series of conversations Stuart and I succeeded in reconciling our views, and the text of this chapter, and of chapter 6, THE BLAZING ONE, both benefited greatly from our discussions. I am deeply grateful to him.

5. The work of these scientists may be found in a long list of publications including the following key titles: H. R. Maturana and Francisco Varela, THE TREE OF KNOWLEDGE (Boston: Shambala, 1987); Stuart Kaufmann, THE ORIGINS OF ORDER, SELF-ORGANIZATION AND SELECTION IN EVOLUTION (New York: Oxford University Press, 1993); David Bohm WHOLENESS AND THE IMPLICATE ORDER (London: Routledge & Kegan Paul, 1980); J. S. Bell, SPEAKABLE AND UNSPEAKABLE IN QUANTUM MECHANICS (Cambridge: Cambridge University Press, 1987); Mae-Wan Ho, THE RAINBOW AND THE WORM: THE PHYSICS OF ORGANISMS (Singapore: World Scientific Publishing Co, 1998); Brian Goodwin, HOW THE LEOPARD CHANGED HIS SPOTS (New York: Simon and Schuster, 1994).

6. Results mainly stemming from Bell's theorem, and since then widely discussed. For Bell's original paper, see J. S. Bell, SPEAKABLE AND UNSPEAKABLE IN QUANTUM MECHANICS, 1987.

7. For example, in Stuart Kaufmann, THE ORIGINS OF ORDER, SELF-ORGANIZATION AND SELECTION IN EVOLUTION, 1993.

8. Fritjof Capra, THE TAO OF PHYSICS (Berkeley: Shambala, 1975).

9. Quoted from a letter Stuart wrote to me in 1998. In this letter, Stuart also referred to the works of Teilhard de Chardin, Thomas Berry, Brian Swimme, Erich Jantsch, Lee Smolin, and Matthew Fox as major contributors to the new emerging vision.

10. Mae-Wan Ho, THE RAINBOW AND THE WORM : THE PHYSICS OF ORGANISMS, 1998, pp. 10–11 and 115.

11. Such confidence is implied, for instance, in the last pages of Stuart Kaufmann's AT HOME IN THE UNIVERSE (New York: Oxford University Press, 1993).

12. See, for example, Henry Margenau and Roy Abraham Varghese, COSMOS, BIOS, THEOS (Illinois: La Salle, 1992). In another book, Ken Wilbur assembled quotations from Heisenberg, Schroedinger, Einstein, De Broglie, Jeans, Planck, Pauli and Eddington, showing that every one of these men was a mystic, and "the very compelling reasons that they all became mystics," QUANTUM QUESTIONS (Boston: New Science Library, 1984).

13. I say that even humble buildings cannot be made, because the infection which comes from our mechanistic cosmology, is mainly one of arbitrariness — and the arbitrariness breeds pretension. In the presence of pretentiousness, true humility is almost impossible. A truly humble cottage even, seems beyond the reach of most builders today.

14. This is a very commonly expressed point of view. John Polkinghorne — both professor of mathematical physics at the University of Cambridge and an Anglican priest — has, among many others, emphasized it, and written about it. See, for instance, John Polkinghorne, THE PARTICLE PLAY (Oxford: W. H. Freeman and Co., 1981), especially 124–26.

15. Articles in thousands of scientific journals presently control our growing picture of the world. Each year they contain hundreds of thousands of pages of argument. These pages of scientific argument have one common thread: they are all built on the assumption that what is discussable in science is the totality of models that can be represented, in one form or another, as inanimate mechanisms. Even biological life itself is represented in such a fashion, as a phenomenon in a system of non-living parts.

This was the central invention of Bacon and Descartes, and has been the prototype for virtually all scientific explanations since the time of Descartes. Of course, the word mechanism is crude, and a more accurate modern version of the same idea would use the word "model" instead, where a model is understood to be any abstract mathematical system or mechanism, susceptible to exact thought, operating according to exactly formulated rules such as those formulated by modern philosophers of science such as Percy Bridgeman and Karl Popper.

As scientists, we propagate this assumption among ourselves, in order to understand how things work. We focus on models, to make the models help us understand what is going on. But the careful use of models does not require us, also, to inject gratuitous assumptions about the inertness of the models into our thought, or into the aura of thought with which we surround the models. Most scientists will tell you that you are entitled to hold whatever additional extra beliefs you wish. But the "extras" will be characterized as *beliefs* thus excluding them once again from the world-picture, while the material in the scientific journals will be characterized as *hypothesis about fact*.

As a result, although the use of Cartesian models in science is beautiful, and useful, and powerful, it does not yet provide us with a wholly accurate picture of the way things are. Its use means that vital aspects of reality, especially those which we can only see accurately through feeling — such as the degree of life in buildings — can be represented only in a crude and distorted fashion.

Our society is corrupted by this approach. The tacit assumption that what is true is only that which can be represented as a mechanical model, almost prohibits us from seeing life around us, or life in buildings, as it really is. Love, feeling, faith, art — the human dignities — have been subtly undermined because, regardless what their real status is, they have become second-class citizens in the world of ideas. That has happened because they cannot be fitted nicely into the world of mechanisms.

16. Before the age of enlightenment there was, in most cultures, some group of values to which one could appeal, and to which people did appeal while building the parts of their world. The source of these values was

different in different cultures. In some it was thought to be "God," in others "ancestors," in others "tradition" or "law." Whatever the source, there was no doubt, at that time, that there was indeed a (partially) uniform source of value widely understood throughout the culture, and of such a kind that nearly any act might be judged against it, inspired by it.

Today the situation is different indeed. Who among us has not had the uneasy feeling that it is best not to assert one's own feelings of value too strongly in public, except as personal expressions of individual taste or opinion? It is socially acceptable to state values publicly—but only so long as they are clearly presented as matters of opinion, hence as matters of *private* value? Few people today will dare to assert that some value they perceive is in any sense actually true.

Among architects sober, public discussion of value in buildings is rare. (One exception was the symposium held in Austin, Texas, March 1998, under the chairmanship of Michael Benedikt, which explicitly invited and encouraged architects to discuss value in buildings, and to do so in a way which took value as a real phenomenon, not as a subjective one.) Newspaper critics only rarely try to discuss value of buildings as if it were something real, not merely an idiosyncrasy. Even then, there is little public debate about buildings. That is because the lack of a basis for judging the life of buildings is a profound embarrassment within the architecture profession. The great secret that contemporary architecture has no sound ethical basis, would be let out of the bag the moment serious debate about right and wrong, or good and bad in buildings, were to begin. So public discussion of the merits of buildings is kept to a minimum, in order to avoid revealing the arbitrary and private character of the discussion.

17. During the 18th and 19th centuries, European and American imperialism created a view of the world in which many people on earth were considered ignorant, and in which it was taken for granted that the views of white Victorian gentlemen were correct. At the end of the 19th century the new discipline of anthropology was gradually able to attack this Victorian point of view, by establishing the idea that each culture is coherent in its own terms. This crucial idea helped to dissolve racist and imperialist mentality, and helped to forge a mental platform on which one could assert that each culture had its own dignity, its own rightness in its own terms.

In the last decades of the 20th century this movement was extended to protect the rights of many groups in society. Many distinguishable groups are now able to assert the dignity of their values—whether it be handicapped people, people with various sexual preferences, subcultures of ethnic or religious particularity, groups of particular age, and so on. But the importance of these movements, and the increase in human dignity they have created, make it almost more difficult to assert general truths in the realm of value. So, by the end of the 20th century, the liberality and freedom of the century's early years had helped to create an atmosphere of

pluralism in which nearly "anything goes," and in which it had become intellectually almost impossible to assert the rightness of any value — since to do so, would challenge, and possibly undermine again, the political freedoms which had been so hard won.

Thus the idiosyncratic and private view of value, which began with the scientific revolution of the 17th century, has led to the assumption that value, valuation, and judgment and taste, are so deeply embedded in the realm of individual rights that they almost *cannot* be seen as based on an objective reality.

Perhaps because of this tacit assumption # 3, efforts to identify the living character of buildings are too often met with skepticism, even anger.

18. Even the enormous changes in physics which have taken place during the 20th century, have not fundamentally changed this view. In the 19th century physicists thought that the world was made of little atoms, like billiard balls, moving and rearranging themselves on the billiard table of space. Today, we have a conception of ultimate matter which is vastly more interesting, where particles are more like whirlpools of energy, wavelike in character, and where the process of combination and destruction, more resembles some beautiful dance.

However, the physicist's idea that this matter or energy is essentially lifeless, and moves blindly according to the laws of its process, has *not* changed. The particles and fields are more interesting now — they even go so far as to include the possibility of instantaneous connection of particles on opposite sides of the universe in a great undivided wholeness (demonstrated by Bell's theorem, J. S. Bell, op cit., by the experiments of Freedman and Clauser, and by the experiments of Alain Aspect and his coworkers, J. Clauser, M. Horn, A. Shimony and R. Holt, PHYS. REV. LETT, volume 28, 1972, 934–41, and A. Aspect, P. Grangier, and G. Roger, PHYS. REV. LETT, volume 47, 1981, 460–66). Even the provocative and startling conceptions introduced by these physicists, retain a view of inert matter, following certain rules, as the basis of their revisions in physics). But in spite of this advance, the underlying philosophical idea has changed very little. The matter, or energy, is still conceived as essentially machine-like, following certain rules, blindly buffeting, pushing, changing, fascinating, capable of amazing surprises and great combinations, but still, nevertheless, at bottom a machine made of inert parts dancing neutrally according to the rules. Sir James Jeans's words "The universe begins to look more like a great thought than like a great machine," written in 1930, have, so far, remained a beautiful and inspiring, but still empty, promise. (See THE MYSTERIOUS UNIVERSE [Cambridge: Cambridge University Press, 1930], 148.) And it should be said, too, that recent developments in complexity theory, for all their ability to simulate complex life-like systems, also remain machine-like in their ultimate character. They illustrate the advances made in our understanding of complexity, and our ability to define machines (models) which create life-like structures. But our cosmology itself, the machine-like picture of space, substance, and process, remains unaltered by these developments.

19. This is the core of Whitehead's bifurcation. But historically it goes back much further in time. The idea that the outer world can be thought of as having a structure which is distinct from ourselves, the division of world into mind and matter, goes back at least to the scholastics of the 14th century. (See, for example, the discussion throughout Pierre Duhem, MEDIEVAL COSMOLOGY: THEORIES OF IN-FINITY, PLACE, TIME, VOID, AND THE PLURALITY OF WORLDS [Chicago: University of Chicago Press, 1985]). And the assumption that the structure of the outer world is separate from our own self combined with the assumption that we can only reach truth by distinguishing objective (agreed-upon) outer reality from individual (and not agreed-upon) inner reality, is the very foundation of modern science. It is the idea that observations and experiments must be made independent of the observer.

The first 20th-century cracks in the iceberg of this assumption arrived within physics itself. They came with Bohr's and Heisenberg's demonstrations that completely observer-free observations cannot exist at the level of photons and electrons (Niels Bohr, "The Quantum Postulate and the Recent Development of Atomic Theory," NATURE [1928], volume 121, 580–90 and Werner Heisenberg, "The Physical Content of Quantum Kinematics and Mechanics" [1927], reprinted in J. A. Wheeler and W. H. Zurek, QUANTUM THEORY AND MEASUREMENT [Princeton: Princeton University Press, 1983], 62–86). But today, seventy years after Heisenberg, mind and self still do not have a status in the world-picture that is comparable to the status of the underlying entities of 20th-century physics. Even among the scientists who accept the existence of cognitive structures, it is still generally accepted that a cognitive structure is an artefact or product of some particular neurological activity. Even among those who agree that many cognitive structures are similar from one person to another, there are few who believe that the inner experience of self has any fundamental connection to the outer structures we observe in physics.

The mental conditions imposed on us by assumption # 5 make it hard to be at peace with oneself. Within such a dualistic world-picture the self cannot itself be successfully included into the larger view of the universe (Again, Whitehead, THE CONCEPT OF NATURE.). Yet self is what we experience of ourselves. How, then, could the universe seem comfortable to us?

20. I can imagine a reader reacting to this formulation with angry denial. "I would never hold such a crass view," one can imagine the reader thinking . . . "on the *contrary*, many would *insist* that art *is* important, vital."

Yet how can the view that art is truly important be taken seriously, or even make sense, if it has to be consistent with a mechanist view of the universe? Since the mechanical view of the world makes no room for value, except as an outpouring of personal idiosyncrasy, it creates no serious basis for art except as an outpouring of private value, or as a cynical construction of artificial images. And that is exactly what the 20th century — in architecture anyway — created time and again.

A mechanistic cosmology makes it difficult to formulate the idea that a building, or a painting, or a piece of music could have any *inherent* value. At best, for explanations of art to be coherent with the present mechanistic framework, they might be based on social realism (ascribing functional importance to works which help society), or psychological realism (describing the value of works of art in terms which appeal to human emotion).

These ideas are deeply conflicted. Is it not undeniably true that certain works of art — works that we describe as great works of the spirit — go much further than mere social or psychological impact? For a person who is inspired by the last paintings of van Gogh, by Bach's Goldberg Variations, by Mahler's 9th symphony, by the sculptures of Jean Arp or Constantin Brancusi, or by the Baptistry in Florence, it is hard to escape the certainty that these works are *somehow* genuinely profound and do, somehow, interact with the fundamental scheme of things in the universe. Yet so far, in our scientific picture of the world, such an intuition has no coherent place at all. Within the material universe of our current cosmology, the intuition cannot even be formulated.

21. Why is this a cosmological matter? It had its origin in the 19th century, when ornament became something to be applied, not something arising organically from its context. Adolf Loos, trying to overcome a spurious and disconnected attitude to ornament, began the early 20th-century revolt against irrelevant and decadent ornament. In pursuit of a less decadent form of art, he argued, in a famous catchword, that "ornament is a crime." See Adolf Loos, ORNAMENT AND CRIME: SELECTED ESSAYS, 1897–1900 (Riverside, California: Ariadne Press, 1998). By mid-20th century, later versions of this assumption then said, essentially, that all ornament should be removed from buildings and that their geometry should be derived from function. This hinged on the tacit message that what is practical is only mechanical; and that any ornament or form which is not mechanical, is removable, unecessary. A profound way of seeing form in which both ornament and function arose from a single evolving morphology, did not yet exist.

Mid-century purity lasted until about 1970, when architects started again, like builders of old, bringing in ornament and shape out of sheer enjoyment. But even then, in the post-1970's postmodern works of the 20th century (which often have a frivolous attitude to shape and ornament) the conceptual split caused by our mechanistic world-picture still exist. There is a functioning part (the practical part), and an image part (the art part). In some of the latest buildings, built during the last three decades of the 20th century, this image part, because of the conceptual context, became truly arbitrary and absurd.

The separation of ornament from function is a cosmological matter because it fits, and supports, and stems from, the mechanistic view. In a machine, the geometry of a thing exists in order to perform in a certain way. The alternative — that both geometry and function are part of one greater whole — implies that order, geometry, ornament, might have meaning and significance together with function, as one body. This is indeed what I would argue. The goal of architecture is to intensify the degree of life in space. Function cannot then be a practical matter separate from beauty. All functional forms will also be ornamental, as they are in nature. The artist, working from this spirit, will naturally and spontaneously bring color, detail, and ornament into his work, because it is necessary to bring that space to greater life. And if that is true, it will imply, right away, that this thing is *not* a machine. So, it is no surprise at all, that at the outset of the 20th century Adolf Loos established the doctrine that ornament is a crime. And it is no surprise at all that in the late 20th century, when beauty of shape could no longer be entirely ignored, a new and drastic form of separation between form and function was introduced in architecture, whereby shapes often became trivial — sometimes even funny or ridiculous. To see such buildings which border on the absurd because of drastic separation of form and function, one has only to look through the pages of any avant-garde magazine on architecture. Outlandish examples, made for reasons having to do with image, not truth, are presented every month for the pleasure of their readers.

22. Few people would willingly admit that they make *this* assumption. And yet I do believe that in our tacit mechanistic world this assumption, too, exists without acknowledgement. It is visible daily throughout contemporary behavior and practice. Is it not commonplace, for instance, that the design of a building starts with a program that defines different numbers of square feet to different functions, and that these square footage estimates are then used by client, architect, banker, planning committee, and so on, as a basis for deciding the adequacy of the design? This is true in most of the houses and office-buildings built in technological society.

Yet I have proved in Books 2 and 3 that a living building cannot be conceived this way, because the inner laws of centers, the wholeness of the conception, the relation to the surroundings, are pushed into a subsidiary position by too great an emphasis on the program. (In Book 2, I have given some idea of the negative impact that can be made on a building design by this kind of mechanistic adherence to program.) Here is a tiny but clear example of the way the building process in our society is routinely mechanized. Few contemporary architects would reject the use of a building program; few lay people would question it either. It is the norm. Yet their acceptance of this norm (and this is only one tiny example) means that real beauty, real life, are pushed into a subsidiary position while the building program, more concerned with efficiency of administration than with life, stays in a higher position.

It is reasonable to conclude that architecture is viewed as irrelevant. A society in which people routinely do something different from that which creates life or beauty, cannot be said to care much about life or beauty. Our daily behavior proves again and again, in thousands of examples like this, that a tacit assumption about the irrelevance of architecture is indeed part of the mechanistic world picture that we live by. However much one might *want* to say that buildings *ought to be* important in some deep sense, still, so long as we live in a mental world governed by our present cosmological assumptions, we shall continually accept (and create) a world in which the shaping of buildings has only the most banal kind of practical importance.

23. Millions of people have experienced, in the presence of some ancient work of art, the conviction that something of massive importance is going on there. Yet our prevailing cosmology provides no way in which this conviction may be understood coherently together with the rest of our scientific knowledge. By default, our cosmology relegates art to the status of an interesting psychological phenomenon. Certainly it does not allow art equal status with the awe-inspiring realities of the atom, or of the galactic universe.

This is not to say that scientists, like others, do not have instincts which make them feel the deep importance that a work of art can have. But, scientifically speaking, that is only a vague instinct at best. So far, it has no place in the body of thoughts and concepts which make up our fundamental picture of the world.

24. That is what our scientific civilization has been telling us for three to four hundred years. Yet it is hard to deny the fact that many of us have instincts about deeper meaning in the world. The experience may come, perhaps, as a result of love, as a result of gazing at the ocean, at a small flower.

The official position of 20th-century scientific philosophy said, explicitly, that science is neutral: it neither confirms nor denies the instinct that this experience is important (A nice discussion of "the official position" is to be found several writings of James Wilk, for example, "Metamorphology: Mind, Nature and the Emerging Science of Change," in Diederik Aerts, ed., EINSTEIN MEETS MAGRITTE, VOLUME 6, THE BLUE BOOK [New York: Kluwer Academic Publishers, 1995]). However, the *actual* state of mind encouraged by our current scientific cosmology is not neutral but negative. Since there is no official place for an instinct of deeper meaning to be realized as part of the consequences of present day science, adherents of the current world-picture (our teenagers for example) are given little intellectual support for dwelling on such thoughts. The assumption therefore exists — nearly always tacit, of course, rarely explicit — that experiences, ideas, which might lead to a feeling of profound meaning in the world are scientifically empty, and best kept at arm's length, away from the body of precise thought about the world.

25. You the reader, yourself, may or may not make these ten assumptions. But I suspect, even if you believe that you are free of them, or rise above them — that, in fact, to an extent which may surprise you, it is these assumptions which inform your underlying picture of yourself and your place in the world.

There are two ways in which such hidden assumptions may be revealed within a person's picture of the world. Suppose a person tells you that he believes the earth is round, not flat. However, you notice that this person has a surprising reluctance to go far to the east, or far to the west. No matter what he says, you may wonder if after all, this person does not believe the earth is flat. With each of the mechanistic assumptions, I have given examples of the kind of behavior which we may each find in ourselves — and which, in my view, show that the more subtle view is just frosting, and that the mechanistic assumption does exist in us — even if concealed.

It is my view that the mechanistic view does exist in most of us as a mild form of practical certainty, while the more life-centered or spiritual beliefs do not — they are more like empty decoration on the surface, which are not capable of having any coherent impact, because they do not all make practical sense together with everything else. In this sense, once again, I take the view that people are still caught in the mechanistic paradigm. No matter what people say, they often continue to *behave* as if these assumptions are true. There is no practical certainty attached to the other more spiritual views, which lead directly to different behavior; so once again the residue of behavior suggests that the ten assumptions are what is, in fact, controlling our mental picture of ourselves and of the universe.

26. The quotations are taken from Stephen Hawking, A BRIEF HISTORY OF TIME (New York: Bantam Books, 1988), 13, 153, 169. Stephen Weinberg and other important cosmologists and contemporary physicists commonly make similar claims and assertions. Incidentally, although Hawking became famous for his reference to the mind of God (BRIEF HISTORY, 175), nevertheless the substance of his cosmology remains steadfastly mechanist, and addresses none of the problems I have raised in this chapter. He may be commended for having the instinct that the subject needed to be mentioned by a physicist, but not for dealing with it, which he did not do.

27. For an artist the situation is perhaps even worse. It is only possible to make things well, and deeply, out of the feelings that a deeper consciousness ignites. But here again, the old cosmology refuses to allow it in. Once again, if we want to retain our picture of the world, as it has been presented to us by physics and biology, we must constantly attack, invade, undermine, refuse, these feelings. And on the other hand, if someone does choose to live perpetually in the knowledge of these *feelings*, then the old cosmology itself must be forced out, and this person then lives without a forceful or coherent scientific picture of the world. Is it any wonder that some of those we call artists, during the period of this cosmology, become insane, are forced to turn their backs upon the world?

28. I am very grateful to Ingrid Fiksdahl-King, with whom I had an extensive discussion about these matters in 1980. The text of the following section is based on our conversation.

29. I have no doubt some readers will say to themselves, "Here Alexander is going too far, surely no one could be silly enough to propose such a thing seriously." No? As I write, a book by a prominent professor of psychology has appeared, in which he describes the human mind as a mechanical system, and where he explicitly states that within the mind, music works merely as "auditory cheesecake." Steven Pinker, HOW THE MIND WORKS, (London: Allen Lane, 1998). See also the humorous review of Pinker's book by James Langton, "The man who thinks he is a computer," THE SUNDAY TELEGRAPH, December 7, 1997, Sunday Review, 3.

CHAPTER TWO

CLUES FROM THE HISTORY OF ART

The fan-vaulted ceiling of the Chapel of Henry VII in Westminster Abbey, early 16th century

1 / INTRODUCTION

I begin the search for a world-picture in which self and matter might be fused, with a short discussion of art history.

There is, in the historical facts about traditional builders, an aspect which paves a possible direction. A view in which matter and spirit, or matter and self are somehow connected, pervades the buildings of history. This view was most often rooted in religion, and was in some fashion or another God-centered. However, I believe the facts about this building effort, without needing a whole-hearted embracing of traditional religion, show us possible connections, and point the way to a foundation in which we may get a new view that allows us to see the world in its wholeness, and allows us to see our own relatedness, as a core issue in the character of matter.

Throughout THE NATURE OF ORDER, I have drawn inspiration from great works of history, works where men and women have created buildings and artifacts that possess the greatest life. Especially in Book 1, I have shown historical examples of buildings, gardens, paintings, tiles, stones, brickwork, woodwork, and artifacts. We have looked at examples from North Africa, China, Japan, Norway, Russia, England, France, Mexico, Korea, Persia, Turkey, Italy, India, Ireland, the culture of the Shoshone, Thailand, Armenia, Greece, Egypt, the Philippines, the Inuit . . . in short, from many, many cultures of the world. I have repeatedly used such examples as instances of living structure. Among those that I know, I have tried to illustrate the artifacts that possess the greatest life. Throughout Book 1, I have described the *structure* which these works have in common.

In Book 2, especially in chapter 3, I have discussed the *process* which these works have in common. I have described the fact that all truly living works are created by unfolding — a continuous structure-preserving process. This led to the further analysis, in Books 2 and 3, of the kinds of process which are capable of creating life in buildings and in towns.

Now, in Book 4, I shall come back to these great living works once again. There is a further aspect of these works, created so often in history, which I have not yet touched. It concerns the *cosmology* within which these works were created, and the concepts of our relatedness to matter. In the vast majority of cases, the works which have life and which stand, for us, as supreme examples of living structure — were created in a mystical-religious context.

2 / AN OBSERVATION

As a matter of observation, it is simply true to say that many of the most beautiful works of art in the world's history, and many of the most profoundly living structures, large and small, that human beings have created, *have been created within the cultural context of some religion.* One might also say that living structure, when it has been created successfully in villages, in churches, in glassware, in paintings, rooftiles, hedgerows, forests, necklaces, masks, columns, and statues, also has most often been made in a mystical-religious context.

The great works of the European Dark Ages were made by Christian mystics. The great buildings of Japan were made by adepts of Zen. The great Turkish carpets and illuminated miniatures were made and inspired by Sufis. The Tantric paintings of India were made by the

Islamic mysticism: green Sufi tiles in the Mosque at Kairouan, North Africa

Minoan art: a ceremonial vase, 18th century B.C.

mystics of an obscure Hindu sect.[1] The beautiful pieces of Shaker furniture were made as acts of devotion, in the closed religious communities of the Shakers.[2] The tiles and carvings of the Alhambra were made, as far as we know, as acts of devotion in the Muslim canon. The North African tiles with beautiful green paintings were

made for the mosque at Kairouan.[3] The tea bowl of Kizaemon was made by humble Korean craftsmen, within the Buddhist canon.[4] The cathedral at Pisa and the stone floors of the baptistery in Florence were made by early Christian craftsmen. The marble panels, the black and green and white floors of San Miniato, the great

Christian mysticism: illuminated manuscript from the Durham Gospel fragment, 7th century A.D.

Taoism: the Tower of the Wild Goose

*Tibetan Buddhism: Thyangboche Lamasery,
Mount Everest*

*Buddhist mysticism: Zen: the Korean
tea bowl of Kizaemon*

paintings of the early 15th century in Florence and Siena, were inspired by passionate religious devotion, by a daily awareness, throughout these cities, of the presence of God.

I would go further. The profound wholeness which I have described with care in Book 1, the "mirror of the self" in these things which ties them somehow to a person's deep experience of life, has historically been created millions of times. After spending my life looking for these profound examples, I have reached the conclusion that the specific living quality I have identified and shown in these four books, almost every time that it has been done most profoundly, *has been done in a mystical-religious context*.

This observation is not intended suddenly to pave the way to a religious interpretation of what I have said in Books 1 and 2. It is a simple statement of fact which needs some reflection. It suggests that there is some aspect of the process of creation which has not yet been covered; that there is some specific quality, introduced into the act of creation by work done in a traditional mystical religious context, which contributes to the formation of living structure.

What, then, about the modern works I have also shown repeatedly, the paintings of van Gogh and Bonnard and Nolde and Matisse, most of which are not inspired — at least explicitly — by a belief in God? What of the traditional-modern buildings I have cited, such as the communist walk along the Danube at Estergom, the railroad tracks in Chicago, Jefferson's University of Virginia, the works of Gunnar Asplund?[5] I do argue that these works touch a modern wellspring, which is almost the same wellspring that arose in history to inspire the works which came from mystical traditions. In other words, it is not my claim that the works which are the greatest, or deepest, are necessarily *religious* in origin. Nor that they are necessarily old. I am, rather, seeking to identify a quality in these works, which can be explained. If these great works from all periods of history, including even our own, shared a certain cosmological or spiritual background, then that background may have information for us, may give us some hint about the conditions which are *necessary* for the creation of living structure.

3 / RELATEDNESS

All these works, I think, stand out because we experience in them a special quality of relatedness, relatedness of ourselves to the universe. We feel that there must have existed, in their makers, a special relatedness with all things, which shows through and is reflected in their works. And we, privileged to see these works or visit them, also ourselves feel a special relatedness within ourselves, and to the world, while we are in the presence of these works.

It is this relatedness which holds a clue to the process of creation. It is the relatedness to Self. It is that relatedness between our individual self, and the matter of the universe, which is touched, and illuminated.

I am seeking to probe the existence of the Self in these works, because it appears there, sometimes, as a palpable fact — and is illuminated, to some extent, by the historical religious context of Christian mysticism, Tantric buddhism, zen, tribal mysteries, and so on — all of which tapped, and connected with, the same ground of self to which I am referring.

It is not the *religious* nature of these works, as such, which draws me to them. It is not their formal locus within organized religion, that is at issue. Works inspired by religion (the mass-produced effigies sold in cathedral tourist shops, for instance) can easily be banal, very often *are* banal, and certainly do not automatically have life or living structure.

The works which I have chosen to illustrate — and I chose them for their artistic weight, not for their religious origin — apparently achieve their weight because they were conceived and made within the framework of a spiritual tradition.

It is not their age per se. The importance of these great old mystical works has little to do with their *age*. There are many other historical works of art which are old, but less mystical-religious in origin, and less inspiring.[6] The baths

of Caracalla, the great Roman mosaics, the paintings of Rembrandt and Rubens, of Corot in France, the Elizabethan portrait miniatures, the decoration of traditional country furniture in Austria, even the statues of Michelangelo are nice, interesting — but all are more trivial. Though also historical, though also belonging to what many might think of as the great historical tradition of art, these do not have the same spiritual core as the works which I have mainly used as examples in THE NATURE OF ORDER — and through which I have mainly been inspired. It is precisely my point that these secular historical works embody the values which I have sought to describe *to a lesser degree*.

Why might all this be true? What is it about the works made in a mystical tradition, that marks them, and sets them apart?

If we had the opportunity to ask a craftsman from the early Christian period what he was doing and what he was aiming at in the things he made, he might have told us that he was making the church, the stone, the window, or the column "for the glory of God."

In a similar fashion, if we had been able to ask a 15th-century Sufi woman weaving a carpet or painting tiles what she was doing and what the aim of her work was, she would have replied in something like the following terms: that in their work she and her colleagues were seeking to become "drunk" in God, that they were trying to lose themselves, to become one with God.

Mother Ann, the spiritual leader of the Shakers, gave carpenters and cabinet makers this advice: "Make it as though you were going to live a thousand years, and as though you were going to die tomorrow."

If we had asked a master carpenter of a zen temple like Tofuku ji in Kyoto or Myohon-ji ("Subtle-reality temple") in Kamakura what his purpose was, he might simply have answered that the work itself was what mattered: "When I eat, I eat; when I drink, I drink; when I plane the board, I only plane the board." But there too, after more careful inquiry, and if we managed to break through his desire to avoid talking nonsense, we would have found out that his main purpose was to lose himself and become one with the "principle of things."

Each one of these views was, in some form, based on an assumption that there exists a ground material of the universe, and that this ground material can somehow be "reached." But what they meant by this "ground-material" was something simpler, that which I choose to call relatedness. In reaching the ground people felt related to themselves. In reaching the ground they felt related to their fellow human beings. In reaching the ground they felt related, somehow, to all that is.

Most of the artists in these traditions believed that human beings are somehow alienated from this ground material, and that the hard work of becoming an artist, like any other spiritual journey, consists of somehow removing the barriers between one's self and the ground. That is not greatly different from the view of modern doctors and teachers who believe that we, as a

people, are too often alienated from our own true self.

The details of the artistic or spiritual path proposed by different mystical teachings as a method for reaching the ground varied from one religion to another. Muslims emphasized prayer and communication with God; Christians emphasized love; St. Francis emphasized the love of every living creature; some Buddhists emphasized meditation; others, especially those of the Zen sects, approach life with the greatest matter-of-factness possible, and emphasized the ordinariness of the process, declaring that it is only hard work and the absence of irrelevant thought which leads us in the right direction.

However, though they varied, all these teachings had certain essentials in common. They all emphasized the need to abandon concern with one's own ego. They all emphasized the importance of hard work and repeated simple, even menial tasks. Above all, they all emphasized the desire to reach God, or the ground of all things, directly, face to face. In all these cases, the task of making, the task of building itself, was to be understood as a spiritual exercise, a direct attempt to come face to face with the ground of the universe.

4 / A POSSIBLE EXPLANATION

The success of mystical tradition in helping traditional builders to create life in buildings and parts of buildings has a practical explanation.

According to my analysis in Book 2, success in making living structure in a building comes from the ability of the maker, at each step in the unfolding process, to do the thing which is *required* — at each instant to do that thing which is most consistent with wholeness. I have described at length, in Book 2, how the life of a building comes about to the degree that all the steps in its making are structure-preserving steps — and that, of course, depends on the ex-

tent to which the makers could *see* the structure of the wholeness that was there while they were making it.[7] Yet while one works as an artist or a builder it is *hard* to see what is required, it is *hard* to see wholeness.[8] To see wholeness as it is requires purity of mind, because the thoughts, mental constructs, theories, ideas, and images one has all interfere with perception of wholeness, and make it difficult to see.

Historically, for an artist, belief in God worked — I think — by focusing attention on wholeness. By asking the believer to concentrate on God — that means, in some operationally understandable fashion, on the ground of all things, in pure humility, not on some other thing — it helped the artist dissolve his images, constructs, and concepts — and focus on reality as it is — in other words on the structure of the wholeness *as it is*.

This connection is straightforward and practical. Mystical tradition, in one form or another, helped a person focus on wholeness, and therefore helped the artist or the builder, at each step in a building process, take a step which was structure-preserving, not something else. Works made in this mental atmosphere then took on life, because the artists were empowered by their humility to see wholeness and to act accordingly.

There was too, the matter of pace. The essence of these works, made in a devotional atmosphere, was that the maker had time, the mind was concentrated. The step-by-step nature of slow unfolding, which I have characterized in Book 2 as a necessary part of making life, was made possible.

This explanation creates, perhaps, a partial understanding of why it may be that the greatest built works of humankind were those which were inspired within a framework of traditional mysticism.

But I must admit that I also feel something more, and that the profound life which was created in some of these traditional cases cannot be grasped *fully* by saying that the builders were able to work in a structure-preserving manner, or that they were enabled to find living process in what they did. In the spring of 1997, I was lucky to be immersed once again, as I had been long ago, in the buildings and paintings of Florence, immersed in those buildings which, even now, still shine and reverberate with the content that was created 600 or 800 years ago. I was again shaken. And I was convinced that what had happened in these buildings was something more than just the outgrowth of the *practical* mental atmosphere and pace of great religion. It felt as if something more specific had been intended, reached for, and then achieved.

The Hotel Palumbo, an 11th-century palace in Ravello, Italy, even after being rebuilt and repaired a hundred times, after 900 years still shows us a depth of which we, ourselves, are hardly capable.

Thinking of those buildings, wondering what it is that we must do to reach these heights, I became convinced, again, that for us to do something similar, to make works of the same depth, we must ourselves somehow share the path which the builders from Florence — or the great builders from Tibet, or those of Nubia (now gone), or Russia, or China, or India — all shared.

In some form I cannot articulate perfectly, I believe that the connection between the creation of living structure and ancient and mystical religion goes further. I doubt if we shall plumb the full extent to which a living structure is created until we have thoroughly explored and understood just what these ancient builders did, in what frame of mind they did it, and with what attitude.

Illustrated here, for example, is a building referred to in Book 1, the Hotel Palumbo in Ravello. It was built, originally, in the 11th century, at a time when that early Italian civilization was immersed in the Catholic view of God, saturated with a holy feeling. The building, originally a small palace, was secular, not religious. It has been changed, rebuilt, and modified, continuously, for 900 years. Yet still today, in its transformed state, it contains a quality that is deep, pure, and profound.

That is the quality which, I believe, is typical of all living structure, at its best. In pursuing living structure, in hoping to reach it for ourselves, it is this we must search for, and ultimately in some form reach, before we can claim that we know how to make living structure in our world.

5 / A CONNECTION TO THE SELF

The core of what I want to say, is that I believe many traditional religions did, in their search for God, create the conditions for the perception and creation of buildings which were profoundly connected to the human self. They did this out of a search for ultimate truths in the universe. Indeed, I am suggesting that it is even possible they may have come much closer to discovering, or gaining access to, the actual nature of the universe, than we have allowed ourselves to think. That is precisely the relatedness between self and cosmos that I have hinted at in chapter 1.

But because of our classification of religion, the possibility that such a nearly religious path may be necessary as a road to living structure, or may be a structural prerequisite for the attainment of living structure — all that is still nearly invisible in our time, simply because of certain prejudices against religion. And fundamentalist religion has taken on a peculiar mask in modern times, so fanatic that it hides this vital practical content. Moreover, present-day religion does not compare, in intensity of content, with the pro-

found belief of those other eras. What they were doing and thinking in that era, was simply something else from what we, in our time, typically conceive.

For all these reasons, in the next chapters I have deliberately framed my remarks outside the context of religion and have tried to formulate the self as a more neutrally defined entity which may be grasped, understood, and used, as a necessary part of our practical effort to make living structure.

Yet the existence of this self — let us call it "a something" which lies in me and beyond me — is the basis of almost all human religion: certainly of all mystical religion. Time and again, in one discipline and another, it has been reaffirmed that a pure life can be led only under conditions where one recognizes, and lives, in connection to this eternal something — what some mystics also called "the ground" or "the void." The fact that this something is nameless, without substance, without form — and yet is also intensely personal — is one of the great

Madonna, detail from Gentile de Fabriano, The Coronation of the Virgin, c. 1450. In the attitude, the demeanor, the drawing of every scale and every thread of the cloth, our relatedness with I, with our own self, and with the self of the universe, is made manifest.

Giovanni di Paolo, Paradise, detail, c. 1470

mysteries at the source of art. It appears in the writings and teachings of the early Christian mystics — for example in THE CLOUD OF UN-KNOWING, and in the writings of William of Wykeham.[9] Essentially similar teachings appear in Zen,[10] in Mahayana Buddhism,[11] in Tibetan Buddhism,[12] in Tantric scriptures, in the spoken word of the Hopi, in the Jewish mystical writings of the Cabala, in the practice of Islam, in the Tao, in the poems and teaching of sufis like Jala-l'a'din Rumi or Shams,[13] and in the thought of St. Francis of Assisi.[14] The similarity of these different teachings has been emphasized many times:[15] *"Before heaven and earth, there was something nebulous, silent, isolated, unchanging and alone, eternal, the Mother of All Things, I do not know its name, I call it Tao."*[16]

In every case, the essential point concerns the existence of some realm, or some entity, variously referred to as the Void, the great Self, maha-Atman, God, the Friend, and the fact that human life approaches its clear meaning, when and only when, a person makes contact with this Void. The belief, widely expressed, is that as this connection occurs, the person becomes connected to all things, and at one and the same time more personal, more human, more transparent, and more peaceful.

So human beings have felt the existence of the Void, have contemplated it, have tried to define it, have sought union with it. And it has, for the reasons sketched above, also been the source of practical results in making living structure.

What I call the eternal self is yet another name for it. The use of the word "self" focuses concentration on the fact that this void does contain all that is in *us*: it gives primacy to the fact that this void is *already* in us: that it is a part of the human being which exists already, and is available to us. In this sense, no matter what its ultimate character may be in the universe, or as a substrate of the universe, it is something which appears in you and me, every day, and is there for the asking.

It is that which makes it powerful, which makes it useful. And this self — or "I" — is the core of every living center.

6 / WHAT OF OUR MODERN WORKS?

Let us leave traditional art and look at 20th-century works. It is not true to say that *all* great spiritual works have been religious in origin. In the 20th century (and in the late 19th) there have been great paintings and buildings which came — in my view — from the same rootstock, yet are not founded in religious origins. Some of the works of Nolde, for example. Some of the works of Matisse. Some of the works of Bonnard. Some of the works of van Gogh.

I choose these names carefully. I do not say that all famous modern painters reached this level. On the contrary, I select a few, and contrast them with the far greater number of modern painters whose works do not have this quality. Still, it is undeniable that this quality *has* been reached outside a religious context, and has been reached quite often. 20th-century examples of buildings which have reached this quality exist, too. But they are more rare.[17] Indeed, in recent architecture, truly profound works hardly exist. We must regretfully admit that the more "shiny" modern works and postmodern works almost never reach this substance. They cannot, because they have not been trying to. Rather they are defined by a search for commercial images, and are governed by style, image, form without substance, effect without content, appearance instead of satisfying emotional reality. Yet there are occasional works which express something that might be seen as similarly religious in achieved quality (though not in origin). One example of such a work might be the Golden Gate Bridge in San Francisco. On a minor level, the works of Mackintosh, Maybeck, Lutyens, and Vesey might be seen like this. Or the works of Frank Lloyd Wright or Geoffrey Bawa. Perhaps some of the buildings of Gunnar Asplund or Peter Behrens. Occasional folk-works, a café made by a proprietor on an unnamed street; the tiny nearly unknown pioneer cemetery of Yoncalla in Oregon.

These last — as do the paintings — contain a similar rough quality, a blinding light of some kind, a quiet humility, which has its origins in personal thought, private inspiration, a trace of an even deeper source perhaps, finding its origin in every person, yet not necessarily stoked or inspired or animated by social religious yearning for God. Yet, the very profound connection with God which we find in the works of the 14th century is almost unattainable for us — just because of our scientific sophistication.

What can we do, then? If this quality is *necessary* in order for us to gain living structure in the world, what is it, and how might we attain it? Our form of this search will not succeed if it is merely colored with historical religiosity. Yet is there any way we can reach it, the real article? And can it be the same thing, the same true thing, which we might make to shine in our new works? Is there a new way in which we can reach it?

Charles Rennie Mackintosh, Drawing room of the Hill house, c. 1916

Emil Nolde, Stilles Meer (Calm Sea), 1936

Henri Matisse, Park in the Rain, Nice, 1918

To make living structure — *really* to make living structure — it seems almost as though somehow, we are charged, for our time, with finding a new form of God, a new way of understanding the deepest origins of our experience, of the matter in the universe so that we, too, when lucky, with devotion, might find it possible to reveal this "something" and its blinding light. Yet any new approach to the creation of living structure which is to succeed, cannot be sentimental, cannot be rooted in some old kind of religion. The old kind of religion will not work for most of us and, I think, in its old form, *cannot* work successfully for us.

The builders of Florence, especially those building from about the year 1000 A.D. to 1500 A.D., lived and worked with an unshakable belief in God. As one looks at the works that came from their hands, God is everywhere: in the paintings now hanging in the Uffizi, in

the Baptistery, in San Miniato, in the life and death of Beato Angelico living in his cell in the monastery of San Marco. For them, every stone was a gift to that unshakable belief in God they shared. It is the belief, the unshakable nature of the belief, its authenticity, and above all *its solidity*, which made it work effectively for them. We, in our time, need an authentic belief, a certainty, connected with the ultimate reaches of space and time — which does the same for us.

The living character of their *stones* came directly from their *belief*. We see in the churches and paintings and ramparts and inlays of medieval Florence, the shaking experience of what can be made by people living day after day in such a God-centered world, under the inspiration of a God-centered vision of the universe. But it is not realistic to imagine that the belief which *they* had, and which inspired them and led them on

North wall, The West Dean Visitor's Centre, West Sussex, England. Christopher Alexander, 1996

*Child's bed alcove which I made from one-inch boards, cut and ornamented
with small flowers with a fretsaw, Berkeley, California, 1985*

and then released them to make these marvelous works, could, in the same form, be ours again. That era has passed.

Somehow, our own version of this relatedness between man and the universe, our own way of making a connection to the "I," must be more direct, must be more rooted in truths consistent with the 21st century. If there is to be such a thing in the future, it must — if we ever reach it — be a transformed version, perhaps a vision of something *like* God, a future vision of the universe that arises from our time, consistent with our biology and physics, that makes sense for us of our world, that can inspire us in a way that is connected with our own state of 21st-century evolution.

7 / MORE ON THE PROBLEM OF OUR ERA

An understanding of a new relatedness will arrive, I believe, the more we come to recognize that entity which I call the self or I, lying within matter, lying within ourselves, lying, above all, in the special relatedness between ourselves and living structure. It will arrive, because the existence of this entity I call the "I" can be confirmed by experience, and it will — I believe — one day become part of physics, part of our understanding of the material universe, which reunites self and matter, ourselves with the world.

The dilemma of belief in *relatedness* as a wellspring of art and living structure — the difficulty of the search for this new form of vision, and yet the near necessity of our finding something like it for our time simply in order to create living structure at all — is visible in a discussion recorded by the conductor Bruno Walter. In 1956, in Los Angeles, toward the end of his life, maestro Walter was interviewed about the music of Mahler (the interview is preserved on CD).[18] In the course of the interview, he also spoke about Mozart. Walter speaks of the way that Mozart had a clear and unshakable faith in God, as a real and definite thing. In one letter to his father Mozart writes with joy, of the prospect of dying, because as he says, he will then be able to see God and be with God. The beautiful music of Mozart is written in the context of this concrete and sublime faith. By contrast, Walter describes Mahler as religious, too, but engaged in a more brooding search, not a person who *did* believe in God, but a person who *wanted* to believe, someone who struggled to find, define, manifest a faith of some new kind. In many ways Mahler did not succeed. The magnificent brooding quality of his symphonies is a testament, rather, to a faith not fully realized and to the struggle to find it, rather than to one that *has* been found.

In rather similar fashion, if we are to reach living structure of comparable depth in our built works, something that would virtually have to be a new faith for our time *must* be found: some modern way in which we can make — for our time — a realistic and satisfying connection with the I.

But it also seems certain that we, the first builders of a new era, cannot hope to anchor our work in the religious traditions of the old faith. For example in the late 20th century a few architects began building neoclassicist and buildings. These buildings — built by neoclassicists who were yearning perhaps for the religious certainty of the 18th century — have a lukewarm quality, an absence of feeling, something nearly puerile, too "sticky." They do not touch the unbearable reality of our 20th-century experience, which is needed to create true life. Some religious devotion might possibly exist in some of them. But the inspired release of great life, contemporary

to our own spirit, and the connection to *our* ground of existence, is far less present in these postmodern and neoclassical works, than in the searing works of Nolde or Derain.

Yet, I believe some form of concrete connection to the "I" such as that which existed in the great early works of building, which their builders found through mystical religion, is necessary as an underpinning for a successful art of building. I believe this, because I find it to be a necessary precondition for the creation of living structure by human beings.

If I am right, that means that living structure, to an extent beyond the reach of my analysis so far, must — and will always — rely on its connection to the same ground which underlay traditional forms of mysticism. If so, that means that we must find in our way, through something else, something additional, supplementing the fundamental process I have described in Books 2 and 3, something of some kind which we, too, must have in our buildings if we are to give them life. In short, to create living structure, we need a vision of the universe in which meaning exists, in which a vision of relatedness and self have a primary place. But it must be a vision whose feelings, whose depth of understanding, is as real for us — true and vibrant and real as part of daily life in the third millennium — as much as God was at home in Mozart's heart.

That, I believe, is the challenge of our era.

When I look at the Madonnas of Gentile de Fabriano or Duccio, when I listen to Mozart's *Requiem*, or to the ecstasy of Bach's Hosannas, it seems almost unreachable for us to accomplish such things in our time. To do it in our buildings, to create a comparable heavenly light, as of a living thing, in a column, or a ceiling, or a roof as builders once did, seems like a near-impossibility for us to achieve in 20th- or 21st-century terms. It is not the beauty which is unreachable; it is the spiritual depth of what is achieved in the works. Yet I am sure that is what we must set out to do. And I do want to warn the reader that, in my view, the things which Nolde did, which Mahler did, were only a begin-

Detail of The Adoration of the Magi by Gentile de Fabriano, Florence, 1450.
One of the three kings. Again, in every button of his tunic, our relatedness with I,
with our own self, and with the self of the universe, is made manifest.

ning, not ultimately what we should be aiming at. It does not go far enough. In architecture of 20th-century examples, it is even more difficult to see.

According to this argument, if we wish to create a living world, finding our own contemporary version of the I, and learning how we may connect ourselves to it, is a challenge we must meet. I have become quite certain that the deepest living structure in buildings is not attainable without some new understanding like this, without a new faith based on a new *physical* and *intellectual* grasp

of the nature of the *material* universe. For us, I believe it is quite certain that the old forms of mysticism that we know as religious cannot provide us with this "something." It is too late. By the end of the 19th century, unshakable faith in God — as human beings had known it in the world's religions for some two thousand years — no longer worked. For us of the 20th and 21st centuries, our faith, if there is to be faith, our deep understanding, must come from some new vision — a new vision able to do for us and for the future what the vision of God did for the builders of the 14th century.

8 / THE BLACK PLASTER

I should like to tell a story of Mr. Ishiguro, the eighty-year-old master plasterer who did the black shikkui for us in the Eishin project. Mr Ishiguro was known as one of the last great plasterers of Japan. The art of making shikkui, a lime plaster mixed with organic gum and polished to a fine finish with a series of blades of greater and greater suppleness, is one of the great old arts of Japan.

Mr. Ishiguro offered to come to our construction yard, when we were considering the idea of working with him, to make samples. He and his son made a rough framework, and on it the elder Mr. Ishiguro plastered an area of about one-square meter in black plaster. His son, sixty years old, and the head of their two-man company, made a similar area of light green plaster.

His son finished first. The light green plaster was very nice by any ordinary standards. But the elder Mr. Ishiguro worked at his black plaster for a long, long time, lovingly stroking the small square of plaster, for hours it seemed, with his softest trowel, as gently as one might stroke a beloved woman's skin. He went on with it. And he went on with it. His plaster, the black panel, shone in an almost unbelievable way. It had a surface of satin gloss and sheen, yet so deep as if the world itself were in that plaster.

Whatever quality it was, it did not exist in the green plaster his son had made. I asked the elder Mr. Ishiguro, as we were all three standing there, what it was, and what the difference was. He said, quite openly, that his son, though he had been plastering for forty years, had never understood this "something." He is interested in the business, he takes care of the money, he is a good plasterer. But I was never able to teach him this. And he shook his head.

That is a whisper of the something, a direct relatedness between person and matter, which has escaped our modern consciousness.

9 / FOOTNOTE

I remain continuously *and exclusively* occupied with the problem of creating living structure. There is no additional agenda, no psychic, religious, or spiritual agenda. There is only the desire to create living structure and to create it well. But this means, as we shall find out, *creating* relatedness. And it is my desire that we may actually *succeed* in this, do it successfully — and, therefore, do everything that must be done to achieve it.

From the study of history, I have become convinced that we cannot successfully create living structure in full degree without paying attention to the ground of all things — whatever that may be. We cannot do it, therefore, without allowing the formation of centers to be guided by the principle that (as far as possible) all living centers do make a connection with the ground. In the next chapter I shall examine this more closely.

NOTES

1. See tantric painting illustrated in Book 1, chapter 1, page 49.

2. See, for example, the photograph illustrated in Book 1, chapter 5, page 226.

3. For large color illustration of these tiles see Book 1, chapter 1, page 43.

4. For a color illustration of the Kizaemon bowl see Book 1, chapter 1, page 47.

5. A number of these living modern works are illustrated in Book 2, chapter 6.

6. Here I mean to use the word "inspiring" literally, as in "it breathes life into us."

7. Book 2, throughout.

8. One experiment which demonstrates the difficulty of seeing wholeness accurately is described in appendix 3 of Book 1. The experiment describes, too, the extraordinary difficulty of teaching a person to see wholeness. It is a process which essentially requires that person to give up all categories, give up focused forms of perception, and give way instead to a wide-open, all embracing form of perception in which he/she "drinks in" the wholeness. The experiment was published in Christopher Alexander and Bill Huggins, "On Changing the Way People See," PERCEPTUAL AND MOTOR SKILLS 19 (1964): 235–53. This training, which I discovered in a series of laboratory experiments at Harvard, is very similar indeed, to the many religious techniques used by Zen, by Sufism, and by other mystical branches of religion.

9. THE CLOUD OF UNKNOWING, anonymous, written in the second half of the 14th century by an unknown English monk, translated into modern English by Clifton Wolpers (London: Penguin, 1961).

10. One of the clearest expositions of zen in a western language is by Hubert Benoit, THE SUPREME DOCTRINE (New York: Viking Press, 1959), translated from the French, LA DOCTRINE SUPREME SELON LA PENSEE ZEN, Paris, Le Courrier du Livre, 1951.

11. Peter Matthiessen, THE SNOW LEOPARD (New York, 1978).

12. W. Y. Evans-Wentz, TIBETAN YOGA AND SECRET DOCTRINES (New York: Oxford University Press, 1967), and THE TIBETAN BOOK OF THE DEAD (New York, 1927).

13. Hafiz, Shams-al-Din Muhammad Hafiz, POEMS FROM THE DIVAN OF HAFIZ, trans. Gertrude Lowthian Bell (London: Heinemann, 1928); Rumi, Jalal al-Din, MYSTICAL POEMS OF RUMI. trans. by A.J. Arberry. 1968.

14. Julien Green, GOD'S FOOL: THE LIFE AND TIMES OF FRANCIS OF ASSISI (San Francisco: Harper and Row,); Nikos Kazantzakis, GOD'S PAUPER: ST. FRANCIS OF ASSISI (London, Boston: Faber and Faber, 1962).

15. First perhaps by Aldous Huxley, THE PERENNIAL PHILOSOPHY, New York, 1945, paperback Meridian 1962, especially chapter 1, That Art Thou, and chapter 2, the Ground.

16. From the TAO TE CHING.

17. Of course, other architects in the 20th century — not all — sought spiritual depth in some degree. Wright in the Imperial hotel, and in some of his Prairie houses, perhaps in the Johnson Wax building. Not, I think, in the Guggenheim Museum, nor in the Marin County Civic center. Mackintosh, Julai Morgan, Geoffrey Bawa, Asplund, Berlage. In some degree they all succeeded. Rudolf Steiner tried to get it, but I think he failed. Honestly, I believe his work is too syrupy to be the real thing; perhaps Steiner himself was after all, not practiced in making buildings. Although his spiritual aspirations were undoubtedly most serious, I do not think it can be said that the Goetheaneum itself actually does penetrate the I enough — or make us feel its existence.

The Golden Gate Bridge also does not reach it. It is a wonderful structure, one which embodies much of what I have said in this book. But I do not know that it goes deep enough to make much of a connection to the "I." I feel in awe of it, and find it beautiful. But it does not connect me to myself, in any very profound way. Now, on the other hand, do the rounded shapes of "spiritual" architects who have now started to make an intentional effort to arrive at the spiritual — these, too, are (so far) usually too soft, too gooey, not hard enough or cold enough for the genuinely spiritual.

18. "A Talking Portrait: Bruno Walter in Conversation with Arnold Michaelis," track #1 on MAHLER'S NINTH SYMPHONY (New York: Sony Classical Records, CD£ SM2K 64452, 1994).

CHAPTER THREE

THE EXISTENCE

OF AN "I"

I BELIEVE THAT ALL ARCHITECTURE DEPENDS ON RELATEDNESS. THOSE BUILDINGS
WHICH WORK ARE THE ONES WHICH CREATE RELATEDNESS
BETWEEN A PERSON AND THE UNIVERSE.

1 / A DEWDROP

Please consider for a moment that you are gazing at some dewdrops, hanging, glistening, on a few blades of grass. The morning frost is there.

I believe that you, looking at one of these dewdrops in the cold weather, feel some relatedness between yourself and the dewdrop. It is beautiful, yes. But what you feel goes beyond that, I think. You feel related to it.

You may tell me, for example, that you "respond" to the dewdrops, enjoy them, find them beautiful. But I want to insist that it goes further, that you experience an actual relatedness, between you and the dewdrops, as if your eternal soul, your existence, and the drops, are entangled, related to each other.

I do not mean to say that it is your daily self, exactly, that is related to the drops. It is more, I suggest, as if your eternal self, the eternal part of you, is related to the drops. Almost as if it exists as a presence in the drops. You feel something like that.

But of course, since there is no basis for asserting something so fantastic in a scientific discussion, when I try to pursue it, or establish it, you may pull back hastily, and say, "No, I am not sure I really experience anything like that." A

Dewdrops in winter

cautious reader might even, at this moment, pull back, and say to me, "If you are trying to drag me into that kind of thing, I will go back over the discussion, and deny that I feel any real relatedness."

And yet, I believe you do feel it. I believe if you allow yourself an impetuous reaction, if you are not too careful, you may find in yourself some version of the experience I describe, that you do feel — whether it is true or not — some thread connecting you to the dewdrop, a feeling, no matter how uncertain, that you and the dewdrop are related, that the drop and your relationship with the drop, shed light on your existence.

2 / RELATEDNESS

If I look at a traditional old bench in the garden, I feel related to it. If I look at an old naturally broken tree stump, I feel related to it. If I look at a steel window or at a computer casing I feel less related to them.

The buildings and objects of the ancient world, too, were usually made so that if people looked at them they felt related to them. Today, if I look at an apartment building of recent times, or at the parking lot of a big supermarket, I feel less related to these things. They *seem* vacant. The onset of the modern era has created a world full of configurations to which we do *not* feel related.

I have written about this extensively in Books 1 to 3, and have shown what we may do to create and generate a world to which we do feel related. I have done this by using the concept of life, and by proving, I hope, that living structure is a real kind of structure, something which can

The stump of our 300-year-old oak, which finally blew over in the winter of 1996,
after being weakened ten years earlier by the great hurricane of 1987

*Something of the modern world, to which I barely feel related:
only with the greatest difficulty can I find my self in this building.*

occur in greater and lesser degree in any part of space. I have done it, too, by showing that human beings are nourished by this living structure when it occurs.

I believe one could make a good theory of architecture, and remake the world successfully, on the basis of the theories and practice which I have sketched in Books 1 to 3. There is enough concrete scientific substance there, and there are enough practical demonstrations, so that the importance of this subject and its practical feasibility can hardly be ignored.

However, the quality of relatedness remains undeveloped. The fact that we of the 20th century have created huge parts of the modern world in ways which are alien, not related to us, brings the question of the relatedness between ourselves and the world more sharply into focus. I shall now try to show that intensive focus on this relatedness itself can lead to a level of understanding about ourselves and about matter that

could altogether change the distinction between matter and self we make today. Consideration of an apparently minor aspect of our world — typified by the pleasant relationship between me and a tree-stump — can, as I hope to show, give us a new picture of the way self and matter interact. It will show us that, inextricably, we belong in the world.

The core of what I intend to prove is this: *Each of us, as we are, is connected to the world.* We are connected to it in a concrete way. The character of this relatedness is not invented or concocted in our minds, but actual. I seek to demonstrate that the tree which stands is entangled with my self, and I am entangled with it. This entanglement exists in a fashion which — when I understand it thoroughly — will forever change my conception of my place in the world. Once we understand it, it will change our conception of the universe and our conception of the matter of which we are made.

In this place I feel myself related to every part of it.

3 / THE MIRROR-OF-THE-SELF EXPERIMENTS

In Book 1, I have shown that we are able to distinguish, with rather consistent results, configurations that are more and less like our own selves (my experiments were general, but focused especially on the perception of various artifacts and works of art).[1] When comparing different configurations, we can see, tell, and decide which of them is more like a picture of our own self, and which is less.

Most important is the fact that when we compare two things and concentrate on the question "Which of the two is more or less like my eternal self?" we find that different human beings agree, to a significant extent. This result is experimentally verifiable. There are further aspects of the experiments which are significant:

1. To a very large degree, people agree about the results. That is, people from the same culture tend to choose the same things as embodying the eternal self. More remarkably still, even people from different cultures agree, on the whole, and choose the same things as pictures of their eternal self.

2. People are sometimes uneasy about participating in this experiment, because they wonder if the questions they are being asked "make sense." In order to get the best results, I usually found it necessary to tell the subject of the experiment, "Of course, it does not mean anything. Don't worry, this is just a game; of course it doesn't make sense, just forget all that and try to answer the question. Please just do it to humor me, just tell me, if you *had* to choose one or the other as a picture of your eternal self, then which one would you choose?" Once people do the experiment, just for the hell of it, we get consistent

results. But, it has always seemed to me that people are uneasy because the "official version" of current cosmology does not allow the question to make sense. As a result, people do not know how to regard it or think about it, even if their feelings tell them that it does make sense, once they try to answer it.

3. The judgments people make about works of art, when using this criterion, tend to coincide in considerable degree with informed judgments about art. Thus by using this criterion, people find in themselves some wellspring or source of information which allows them to supercede the "beauty is in the eye of the beholder" view of art, and instead allows them to make informed judgments similar to the judgments made by experts in different fields of the visual arts.

This third result raises the importance of the experiment, strikingly, and makes it clear that it has a profound content. I invented the experiment, originally, at some time in the 1970s, as a way of helping students get beyond the idea that "liking" and artistic judgement are subjective, and to give them a way of reaching consistent and reliable judgment about the quality of things, objects, artifacts, buildings, and so on.

Now, I shall go further. I did not, when I first described the experiment in Book 1, ask the reader to pay attention to the *meaning* the experiment might have. I simply introduced it as a way

of getting an experimental grip on questions of life and value. Now, instead of treating it as a merely convenient and objective way of measuring the life in things, I shall look at the result *itself* — the observation that people experience living structure as like, or similar to their own *self* — and ask: What does this mean?

Since people consistently say that living things resemble their own eternal self, and since they show consistent results from person to person in judging things which have this quality, I shall move forward on the assumption that what is reflected in this similarity must be about something real.

Of course the question is, *What* is it that is real? What real phenomenon is reflected in these experiments? *Why* do I feel that my own self, my personal self, me, is more connected to the tree, and less connected to the parking lot? Why do I feel that my self is more connected to a cloud or a river, or to an ancient tea bowl, less connected to a pressed steel computer casing?

My description of living structure in the first three books has an obvious role here. The tree and the cloud and the tea bowl have more living structure than the steel computer casing. That means that the structure of living centers is more developed in them; and the process which generated these structures was an unfolding process, more biological in character,

The Kizaemon tea bowl, Korea, 16th century

*This traditional Norwegian storehouse is a building so replete with boundaries and
living centers, that it is almost entirely made of them.
Here I feel the relatedness between my self and this thing
almost as strongly as I do in nature.*

more natural. They have more life. The computer casing has less life.

It would seem obvious, then, to say that I,
who am alive, feel a greater affinity for the things
around me which have living structure, and less
affinity for those which lack living structure. For
this reason (one would expect to say) of course I
feel more related to the tea bowl or to the carved
traditional Norwegian hut shown on this page,
than to the more alien structure of the freeway
bridge and supermarket parking lot.

I have, in Book 1, also put the connection we
feel between these living structures and our own
self on an empirical basis. In the experiments reported in Book 1, I have established experimentally that this connection of our own self to
things, exists.[2] I have established that different
trees, or different vases, to the extent that they
have living structure in different degree, do appear to us in comparable degree, as pictures of
our own self. That is our impression. The existence of this impression is empirically verifiable.

It would therefore seem that there is such a
thing as *the* deep or eternal self. If we take the
experiments literally, focusing on the wide
agreement on the content, one way to express the
results is to conclude that it is possible to find
configurations which resemble *the* deep self of

humanity. It seems astonishing that there really is such a thing as *the* eternal self.

Perhaps more fundamental and more immediate as content is the *relationship* which people experience with the world. Here I am referring to the actual relationship you, or I, or someone else, experiences between themselves and the world they look at, when it appears to have this mirror-of-the-self quality.

In all the years I did these experiments, I do not remember anyone ever saying, "I cannot do this, it is nonsense, I refuse to do it because I cannot make sense of the question." Once prompted to play the game, people took part willingly, and gave largely consistent answers. We must conclude, I think, that the *relationship* between people and the world which makes it appear that some parts of the world have more relationship to our own self and others less *should be understood as something real*.

Yet one might conclude, too, from the fact that I felt obliged in many of the experiments to say to the participants, "Don't worry, this is just a game; of course it doesn't make sense, just forget all that and answer the question," that the relationship is *deep*, that it is hidden, and that people almost want to *keep* it hidden. For us, steeped in our present cosmology, it is not, perhaps, an entirely comfortable subject. Perhaps people feel most able to be honest about it, when they pretend that it is not really being talked about.

4 / THE REAL RELATEDNESS EXISTING UNDERNEATH THE SKIN

Let me focus more intently, now, on the relatedness itself, the relatedness I feel with the bowl, or with the dewdrop or the tree. *Why* do I feel so related to them? Why do I feel that my self, particularly my deepest self — my own *self* that I experience in me — is related to the tree? Remember that I do not feel this equally for all things. I experience it in lesser degree for some things, very little in other things (the supermarket), and very much indeed in a few special and remarkable places (Ryoan-ji, for example, or the Parthenon).

I believe — and will try to demonstrate in the chapters which follow — that we are, each of us, literally connected to the tree stump and to these other things. People in a primitive society, where both the world which they themselves built and nature too had living structure, felt this connection with almost everything around them.[3] We, in our world, where less of the built world has living structure, feel it more rarely. We feel such relatedness weakly with nature and for things which occur in nature. But I dare to say that it is, indeed, only *experienced weakly*. It is not an encompassing feeling of relationship, such as was felt by a farmer in a primitive traditional society.

John North, a Sussex man who looks after our sheep, summarized this for me one day. We were talking about the miserable, wet, windy weather of the day before. "How did you like that?" I asked him half-jokingly. He answered quietly but seriously, "I like the weather every day." In that simple phrase he expresses his contentment and his happiness in his world. The relatedness between him and the world is profound, and does not need to be mentioned. To him the relatedness I write about is obvious. For us it seems almost like a mystery.

It is easy to imagine a positivistic explanation saying that the tree (bowl, cloud, doorway, etc.) has a structure which is similar to certain cognitive structures, and that this creates the feeling of relatedness. However, I believe such a positivistic explanation is not very interesting, and is probably wrong.[4]

I wish to assert something altogether different. I wish to say that *the relatedness through which I feel that my own self and the tree in the field are directly connected is the most fundamental relation that there is*. I wish to say that it is *in* this relatedness — *in* realizing my connection between my own self and the tree, or the pond, or the road or the grass — that I learn, feel, understand, that I am of the world, that I partake of the world, and it is in this relation that my real connection with the universe may be understood and experienced by me. Far from being a minor cognitive resemblance between me and the tree, this relatedness which exists between us and the living things in the world occurs, I think, because of a fundamental connection between our own self and *something* which is in those things.

What is that "something?" I say that this relatedness occurs, because there is, in the very matter we are made of, a connection to self, a rootedness in self.

Thus it is only in connection with these living things that I am fully real. Only then is my relatedness to the world fully expressed, fully developed, fully manifest. In a place surrounded by alien non-living structure where I do not feel such a feeling of relatedness, my *actual* relatedness to the world is interrupted or destroyed. Then I myself am not *as* real. My reality is damaged and inhibited.

I claim that the relatedness between myself and a thing in the world which encourages my relatedness *is the most fundamental, most vivid way in which I exist as a human being*. When it occurs, my own self — the degree to which I am connected to the world, the degree in which I partake of the interior "something" that underlies all matter — is then glorified, is at its zenith, and I then experience myself, as I truly am, a child of the universe, a creature which is undivided and a part of everything: a small extension of a greater and infinite self.

I claim, therefore, that this simple relation between myself and the treestump by the pond, which moves me, is a connection so profound that my full existence in the universe is made solid, is manifested, is captured by it in its entirety. It is not a small moment. It is the glory of my existence as a person — no matter how humble I am — which I can feel so long as I am in the presence of nature or in the presence of other human-made structures which, too, have the same living structure and hence the capacity to form this bond with me.[5]

Thus the fullness of my existence, my capacity to be a person, my capacity to drink in, enjoy, and commune with the full depth of living matter in the universe is sanctified, and allowed, and enlarged, by my relatedness with the treestump. It is prevented, atrophied, cut off, by my not-relatedness with the plate-glass window, the fashionable facade, and the deadness of the supermarket parking lot.

Further, I want to draw attention to the role of buildings in maintaining the existence of this relatedness between us and the world. The relatedness between the self and the world, the relationship which begins to exist wherever there is living structure, is as important in the sphere of building, as it is in the sphere of nature. Indeed, it is my view that our ability to experience the relatedness with nature or with buildings is damaged when we live in a world of objects and structures that are non-living structures. Thus, the modern person who "loves" nature and goes to visit nature is not able to enter this relatedness with nature as easily, because the daily proximity with so many non-living structures — freeways, motels, traffic lights, office buildings — dominates our awareness, cauterizes the person and the person's capacity to enter into this relatedness, to see it and feel it. This is true even in the case of nature.

So whether our buildings have this quality or not — whether they themselves have this interior relation with the I — is of the greatest importance. If I am right, it is the presence of living structure in our built world that decides the extent of our relatedness with earth. Buildings which lack living structure not only destroy our ability to feel relatedness through them. They also inhibit, somehow, and reduce the ability we have to feel relatedness at all, even in nature — places where we would otherwise feel it naturally.

5 / THE ANCIENT AND ETERNAL TRUTH
OF THE RELATEDNESS

Among anthropologists, it is widely accepted, and has been written about often, that the people in primitive societies had a more all-encompassing relationship with nature; felt themselves to be part of nature in a way that we do not; and understood that there was, or is, an intermingling of their own selves, with nature.

This has been written about, but nearly always from a distance. Although it has been described for the Hopi, for the Aborigines, for traditional farmers in India, or Iran, or Italy, or Africa, I do not know whether any anthropologist has ever suggested that there might be something *necessary* about the views these traditional people held. It may have seemed too quaint to suggest that *we ourselves* might have, or must have, such a relationship.[6] Yet I believe this is so.

When the Hopi chief says that he looks out and sees the desert and the stars, and that he and his people are related to them, we take this, we listen to it, we love it; but it is no longer entirely real for us. We listen to it as poetry. We think to ourselves, How marvelous! But it is as literature that we consider it marvelous. We think how wonderful it was that people saw the world like that, and regret its passing — what a shame the world is no longer like that. But, of course, we consider it as fiction, the thinking of primitives. It has not occurred to us, that what the Indian chief says *might actually be true*. Literally true. That the relation he and his people spoke about, and felt, between themselves and all things, was a relationship that is actually there, but one that we no longer see, or acknowledge, or are willing to experience, because in our cosmology it is not understandable that such a thing could be true.

However, I am proposing that this is literally true. That the relation between a person, and the living structure in the world, is an *actual* and *tangible* relationship of a kind that we have not yet grasped. The essence common to all these cases, is that people really saw all of nature as a single embracing whole, *of which they were a part*. Their sacred relationship to this whole was the foundation of their lives. It hinged, I think, on the awareness that they and it — we and it — are not separate, cannot be separate, are two halves of a single whole.

In a non-traditional form, in a new cosmological form consistent with modern physics, I too wish to make such a claim. I wish to claim that there is such a thing as an "I," lying behind matter, and that all *living* structure (though certainly not *all* structure) is connected, necessarily, with this I. I shall claim, too, that, on examination, this relatedness will turn out to be part of *physics*.

In order to sustain this claim, we must begin by grasping it as something rooted in experience. That is, we must learn to acknowledge the experience of relatedness with living things, and the depth of this relationship. Once we have it, and it is rooted in our experience, we may then go on to ask what kind of physical explanation might make sense of it. But we must start with verifiable experience.

6 / THE NUMINOUS EXPERIENCE

A way to verify the experience behind these statements is by doing experiments. As I walk about the world, I can look at each thing, each car fender, each table with its cups and saucers, each bush, each knot of people on Fifth Avenue, each configuration, and ask myself to what extent it has "it" — by that I mean, to what extent I feel related to it, and to what extent it forms this relatedness with me, to what *degree* it touches me, and appears to embody a relatedness between me and the eternal, in it. Above all, the question, again and again, is this: *To what extent do I feel a personal relationship with it? To what extent does it serve as a pool in which I can see my dreams, sorrows, the beauty of the world?*

It is an unusual frame of mind. We look at one stone set against the hedge and it has this element to a greater extent than another. One patch of wall with peeling paint and broken plaster has this quality. Another wall, freshly stuccoed, and of uniform color, has it far less. Another wall, peeling and broken, merely looks crummy: it does not have this quality.

The base assumption is that there are places in the world which have more of this relation with our own selves, and there are places that have less. The primitive spoke of certain spots in the forest, or on the hills, which were sacred. We have dismissed this as something fanciful. But, from the perspective I am taking, it is not fanciful at all. It is just fact, consistent with what I have described in Books 1 to 3, and empirically verifiable. Some places in the world carry the relationship with our own selves more deeply than others.[7]

Human beings have, in the past, recognized such places as numinous. They are places which carry the spirit. They are places which carry the soul. That language may or may not be useful. But what I want to insist on, is only the one thing: some places, some things, are of such a nature that we feel more intensely related to

them, we feel a relationship with them, a direct relationship between our own self and that thing, that place. We feel it most strongly, and when we feel it we feel that we are connected with all things, with the universe.

That is the core experience which underlies everything that I am describing here.

In the language of Book 1, the wholeness of the world may be seen as a vast system of centers, each one induced by the existence of others. Some of these centers are transitory (ripples in a pond or forces in a beam); some are hard to see (the centers induced in the sheet of paper with a dot); some are normal to the functions in a building but only visible in the hidden structure (the centers that make up a living room); others are clear, tangible, and distinct (tables, chairs, houses, people, cars, benches and trees).

In this view of living structure, each center which exists has its own degree of life. Otherwise stated, it has more or less existence "as a center." Within those centers which have intense life the component centers themselves also have intense life.

The more deeply a particular center has its centeredness or intensity of life, the more it resembles *me* or *you*. In a building which has great intensity of life, not only the building itself seen as a center has this quality, but all the centers which exist within it and all the centers it induces in the world, *all of them* have this property of being pictures of self.

The vision created by this idea not only covers the nature of a single building, but of the whole world. Flowerbeds, rivers, mudflats — the same rules apply. The continuity and life of the fabric is what counts. Each of these things will be alive, to the extent that it, and each one of the others, has its field of centers as intense as possible. Such a world will have an almost perfect relation to ourselves. Since everything with an intense field of centers is also a picture of the human self, it is a world in which every single part we encounter is somehow a picture of the soul. The self-like character which is pervasive, produces unity. It is a comforting world. It is also, in a fundamental sense, a normal world.[8]

This is the kind of world which existed in many cultures for much of human history. In traditional society nearly every place, nearly every part of the world, contained an intense field of centers. Nearly every doorknob, handrail, window, chair, step, room, street, building, roof, bush, tree bole, walkway, doorpost, and doorway could be experienced as a picture of the human self. Wherever you went in such a world, wherever you looked, at every scale, you recognized yourself, you saw things as familiar and felt related to them. This world was friendly. Though often frightening in its physical dangers, every part of it was animated, like a human face. I can identify with each part of it. Even though many of them were made by people remote from me in time and place and civilization, still, the remarkable thing is that I see my face in each of them. Each of them deeply resembles me.

Now compare another kind of world, the world that has become common in the last few decades. In this world living centers exist far more rarely in objects or in places. The structure of most buildings and artifacts is such that the field of centers they contain is weak. Only very rarely can they be felt as pictures of the human self. The placemat at a McDonald's is a good example. Like that placemat, altogether, everywhere, there are impersonal artifacts. They may have images behind them, but no real humanity. Plastic sheets, shiny sheets of dark glass, brickwork laid in artificial patterns, concrete which only reflects the steel pans of the forms, columns in unusual shapes, arches which are not quite right. As you meet the things in this second world — doorknobs, handrails, doors, windows, buildings, roofs, streets — the great majority *fail* to have the structure of the mirror of the self.

Things seem chilling, alien, distant, unrelated. You feel frightened, disconnected, without heart. This world is an unfriendly world. Little is related to you, little seems human. You have no place. You do not belong.

The difference between these two worlds — though we have accepted it — is *staggering*. The recently constructed world is often abstract — and for those who have eyes to see, deeply frightening — by comparison with the traditional world. Terrible. Empty. Deserted. Is it too much to expect that men and women may become insane in this second kind of world? Yet this is the reality of the conditions under which a great majority of human beings live today.

The two worlds are not only physically different. They also communicate images of two different kinds of universe ... images of two different cosmologies, two different conceptions of the universe. One is a world in which the universe is friendly — human-related — and in which we are related to the universe. The other is a world in which the universe is unfriendly, alien, and we are unrelated to it.

When there is living structure, it is related to me, to you, to every person. You look out, around you, and you see things in which you see yourself; it is astonishing, absorbing. It is the most fundamental experience. No other experience is as comforting. It is beyond what the phrase "living structure" suggests. Path, tree, sunset, are related to me. They contain a presence, the presence of some I-like thing. All of it, when it has the right structure, is undeniably related to you. It is related to YOU: A matter of degree, but the degree is not the main issue. The main issue is the *fact* of the relationship. We love one thing more than another.

In a world which has deep life, the world belongs to me, and feels like mine, when it has a structure of wholeness, deeply within it.[9] It becomes alien, or dead, when it is made of impersonal structures, abstract structures, and when self-like qualities are no longer present.

7 / TRUE MEANING OF RELATEDNESS

Let us now probe more deeply into the nature of the relatedness we feel with living matter: our feeling that we, in our own selves, are connected to all living material. When I see the wild duck fly off the pond and hear the beating of its wings, I am filled with a sensation that it touches me. It has to do with me. It is related to me. This is entirely different from the feeling I experience when I see the modern apartment building with gaping windows, which strikes me as vacuous. In the supermodern apartment building, as one of my friends put it, "it seems that there is no one home."

What, then, is the distinction between the vacuous feeling we get from one not-living artefact and the feeling of relatedness we experience with a living artefact or with nature?

I have slowly become certain that the relatedness we experience in things with living structure is not a psychological trick or an illusion. What we experience as a link is, I am certain, real. The apparently self-like presence which I seem to see in the world—in the column bracket, in the tree stump, in the water of the pond, in the scudding clouds—is an actual thing *in* the thing. It is not a mental construct. It is not an idea we have formed in our minds. It is an actual presence in the material thing itself. When I experience the relationship of my self to that pond, when I see this thing and recognize myself in it, I am related to that thing. I recognize it, and feel related to it, because—somehow—I am of the same substance. The self-like quality I experience in it is what I also experience as self-like in me.

Above all, the relatedness I feel between me and it—I with the tree, I with the pond, I with the upturned boat on the sea shore, I with the window sill as the sun gleams on it, or as the rain falls—is a real relationship. It is a connection between me and it which exists, which is important, which is not an idea but an actual material connection. It is something like the fact that we are made of the same atoms, they and I, but it is a far greater thing. It is that we are both made of the same Self, we share the same inner character, the I which I experience in me as myself, and the I which I experience in them, as a feeling of love or relatedness.

Go back to the dewdrops on page 50. If there is such a thing, such a feeling of relatedness between you and the dewdrops, what might it be caused by? I do not know of any part of contemporary physics or biology which sheds light on this. Yet if this relatedness is there—literally there, not as an illusion, but as a fact—it needs to be explained.

Of course, as I have suggested, we may turn to modern psychology for an explanation. One might, for instance, interpret it as a matter of a structural or cognitive similarity, claiming—for instance—that the cognitive structure of the human mind has structural features in common with the structure of the dewdrop.

But if I turn back to you and ask you, "Does your feeling of relatedness with the dewdrop shining and glistening on the branch, truly *feel* to you as if it is explained as a structural similarity between your cognition and the dewdrop?" then I believe you may well reject this explanation. It is a *possible* explanation, of course. But I believe you will recognize what I mean when I say that it leaves me unsatisfied, that it does not somehow go to the pith of the experience we have in front of the dewdrop. The feeling of relatedness we have with that dewdrop feels like something more, something more basic, something more essential. If you examine your feeling carefully, you will find, I think, that your instinct is that the nature of the relatedness means more, and *is* more.

Throughout this experiment, I am hoping, of course, that you are being as honest as possible, admitting to what you truly experience, and

A small blue hill is visible in the distance of this miniature
in a Book of Hours, Rouen, 15th century.

not shielding your experienced feeling with a careful or more artificial point of view that you believe might be acceptable to science.

Let me expand the example a little bit. Look at the medieval illumination shown here. There is a painting of hills, green in front, yellow blossoms, in the distance a shining haze and a brilliant light blue, azure hill. Now, let me describe, in a little more detail, how you might experience this phenomenon. I imagine, for example, that you are looking at this painting. Again (let us say) you feel a direct relationship with this small piercing blue hill in the picture.

This relatedness that occurs is something *between* you and the bit of blue in the painting. You do not, I think, experience the bit of blue as if it *were* your self. I believe rather, that you expe-

rience something stretching between yourself and the blue hill, something that seems to mobilize your self, stretch it out towards the bit of blue, connect with it. The thing which comes into play, is the *something* stretching between you as you stand there, and the bit of blue. That is the relationship I am referring to.

What happens? You look at the blue hill and something, stretching between you and the blue hill, then comes into existence. But it is a very important thing that comes into existence. It is not the mundane, everyday self, which is being mobilized. It is as if the eternal you, the eternal part of you, your eternal self, is somehow being mobilized — and has been mobilized — simply because you are looking at that bit of blue.

8 / A JUMP TO SPEAKING ABOUT THE EXISTENCE OF AN "I"

Within this feeling of relatedness with the tree (or the dewdrop or the patch of blue), and because each one of us feels it more or less the same way, there must be *something* — an actual something — in the tree. This "something" needs a name. Although the relatedness is something ancient — something experienced, I believe, by many generations of human beings — in our time it is so unusual even to talk about it, it runs against the grain so strongly, that it can hardly even be referred to in modern parlance, because we no longer have the words for it, we no longer even have a single word for it: neither for the relationship itself, nor for the "thing" to which I feel related.

We could call it simply living structure since we know, from what has gone before, that living structure is there. But this fails to communicate the numinous sense that accompanies my experience of it, and my experience of the relationship. Above all, I feel the experience of relatedness with the tree as *personal*. It has to do with ME. I feel related to the tree, I feel that my own existence grows, extends, and becomes wholly good, as I experience my connection with the tree. So a phrase like "living structure" is far too abstract. Though there is indeed living structure that lies in the tree, that phrase alone does not express — nor does it suffice to contain — the personal feeling of relatedness.

Inside the experience, there is something much more personal, almost the most personal thing there is to me. So the "thing," if thing there is, must have unusual features.

I might describe what I experience as a "presence" in the tree or in the dewdrop. In this way of talking I would say there is a presence, and I feel related to that presence. Looking for a name for this presence, we might call it "the eternal self," felt in the tree, felt in me, stretching between the tree and me.

Once again, however, it does not communicate, fully, the very *personal* nature of the experience, nor the feeling of *relatedness* which occurs. The fact that the dewdrop has to do with ME. The fact that the tree has to do with YOU. And the fact that, in this relationship, we are mobilized utterly, and that it is our person, all that is personal in us, which is mobilized.

Further, that it is above all a *relationship*. It is never only in the thing itself, nor is it only within me. It lies between us. It is almost like a single all-embracing thing, which I have tripped up against, stumbled into. It is an object which lies outside the boundaries of space and time. Whatever it is, it is not limited in its position. And it does not fluctuate with time.

Because it is so personal, and because it is also one thing, and because, yet, it is so related to all that is, so vital — I must coin a phrase for it. I call it "I."[10]

I am not using the word "I" to mean the many selves, all of us, which each of us refers to severally, as I. There is, in this view I am putting forward, only *one* I, altogether. But I use the word "I" to mean the deep and individual aspect of our universal experience, it is something we experience as personally, as intimately, as we experience our own small I every day.

For this reason I have adopted the word "I" for it, and have coined the phrase "the I" to stand for it. I fully recognize that this language of "the I" could strike the reader as stilted and unusual. But I hope the reader will forgive what might seem like a pretension, and recognize that I do this of necessity, as I believe, because I must speak of this thing for which our language does not have a word; and therefore I must find — and use — a phrase which summons it up.

Above all, I must be able to refer to it in such a way as to make clear that "it" has three qualities: (1) first, that it is *personal* — of you, and of me; (2) second, that there is only *one* of it — the relationship we feel is with a single I-like thing, lying in all the universe; (3) third, that it is so personal that it is suffused with *relatedness*, and expresses, when I refer to it, the intimate relatedness I feel for a tree or for my favorite bowl. The use of "I" — rather than self, or ground, or universe, or eternal self — does convey just these three things.

I hope that the reader will be willing to accept my discussion of the eternal self in the next chapters, using this language of an I-like presence. It was — in every era except our own — of the essence for human beings, the most important thing there was, the form in which people kept and cherished their connection to the world, and thus the form in which they experienced themselves as part of the world, and in which they experienced the world as "theirs."

The existence of this relatedness, our right to exist, our love for the world, acknowledged as a real thing, and our relationship to all of it as something permitted, endorsed, supported: there can hardly be anything greater than that. Our lives will be changed, utterly, if we can establish as factual, this personal relatedness between each person and the living world; establish it as part of the nature of the world, and as part of the nature of our selves.

9 / AN EXPERIMENT TO DETERMINE THE EXTENSION OF THE I

An experiment: this shows a little of the way our relatedness to the world appears in us, and something of its quality.

One day I was visiting my editor, Bill McClung, talking to him about relatedness, and about the I. We were in his study. In front of us were two old armchairs, each chair had a cushion on it. The left hand chair had a brownish grey, somewhat battered cushion. The right hand chair had a cushion which was red, with yellow lines forming a kind of tracery. The red cushion was old, too, so it was worn, and the colors a little faded by age. Overall, it had a faintly glowing quality. It was attractive to the heart.

I asked Bill, then, if he could feel his own I in either of these cushions. Not surprisingly, he chose the right hand, red cushion, and told me that with the red cushion, he felt something of his own self in it. He felt more related to it. I, too, felt the same, so we discussed this briefly.

Then I asked him, "Where does your own I stop?" Pressing him about the physical extension of the I he experienced, I asked, "When you look at the grey-brown cushion, *where* exactly is your I, where is your experience of I?" He indicated his own body, his head, his body, and said, "It is in here." I nodded.

And then, I asked him, "Look at the red cushion now, the one on the right." He looked at it. Now, while you are looking at the red cushion, tell me again where your own I starts and stops. We had by then already established that the red cushion had somewhat greater substance in it, to which one could relate (both for him and for me).

So, I asked again, "Where is your I, exactly, in this case, when you are looking at the *red* cushion?" Remarkably, then, he said to me, "It seems to go out *toward* the cushion. Somehow, for some reason, I feel my I exists beyond my body, it includes the cushion . . . or (he corrected himself), at least it goes out toward the cushion; when I look at the red cushion my I seems larger than before, and it tends to expand toward the cushion, includes it."

I too felt the same. So here we had a very primitive experience, which indicates the I as being larger than our own bodies, experienced in this instance as being outside our bodies occupying the space between our bodies and the thing we were looking at — apparently because of the more I-like nature of the second cushion. It appeared that a substance like the red cushion, because more deeply connected to the I, will actually expand the experience of I in us, make our connection to a larger "something" more plainly visible.

Apparently, we do experience the world like that. Here, for the first time, we have modest empirical confirmation that those things which have more I in them really do enlarge, and open, our connection to the I, and that this I which we partake of is larger; its existence beyond ourselves is, for the first time, seen experimentally.

10 / THE I OF OUR EXPERIENCE ORIGINATING WITH THE I IN THINGS

The I-like substance is visible in things which have life, according to the degree of living structure which exists. I do not make it happen by being there. It is not subjective. It is there. Thus the I is not something imagined, but an actual thing, in matter itself.

Illustrated below is a seedling nursery, run by Charli Danielsen, in the Berkeley hills, with seedlings of native California plants set out on tables under the pine trees of Tilden Park.

It is a wonderful, free, Zen-like place. The place is orderly, ramshackle. What is done is done, entirely, by common sense and, I believe,

feeling. The seedling tables are placed, the pots stacked, the chairs, the tools, all placed to make a profound feeling.

It seems almost like nature, almost abandoned. Yet it is a place where one feels oneself just right, all the time. Immense energy and concentration have gone into the making of this ordinary of ordinary places. It is lovely there. It works. Speaking personally, it fills my heart to be there.

It is important to see that a subtle structure has been firmly made, molded, to create this much feeling. It is not like a typical nursery. In

Charli Danielsen's Zen nursery in Tilden Park, Berkeley

deciding how to place the tables, she could have made them in rigid lines. She chose to place them, perhaps unconsciously, where the deeper feeling was. In deciding how to place the pots of plants she could have decided to place them for ease of access to the watering hose. She placed them where the deeper feeling was. She could have placed the tables in a position for maximum sun, or shade, whatever the plants required. She chose a dappled sun and shade, undoubtedly good for the plants — but inspired, I think, by the deeper feeling it creates.

The place is not strange. It is a different level of human experience that has been drawn on there; and it gives out a different level of experience. Speaking to Charli, it is obvious that these decisions, the feeling of the place, an attitude to life have informed each decision that she and her helpers have made while building it: they have consciously made the place a celebration of life. You have undoubtedly had a similar feeling about some other place. What was it that was wonderful about that place? Why did I remark on this one? Why did yours create such freedom in your heart?

First, I experienced that place as something in itself truly wonderful, itself so harmonious, so ordinary, I could see that a great thing had happened there. But while I was standing there, something like that also happened in *me*. *Because* of being there, the best there is in me came to the surface, inside *me*. The ultimate worthwhile occurred in me, drawn out by the presence of that place, almost as if it rose up in me to meet the same thing from that place.

The feeling that arose in me . . . you will not object, I think, if I call it a feeling of I. It was a precious feeling of my own self that I experienced while standing there. The same life that was mobilized in the place, was then mobilized in me.

But I want, now, to say something much more strange. I believe this existence of the life in me, the feeling of I that arose in me when I was in that place in Berkeley *is not, was not, secondary in the phenomenon, but primary*. I do not think that the "life" first occurred in the place and then repeated as an I-like feeling in me. It is rather as if the life which occurred in that place was already, *of its very own nature I-like* — in the thing, and independently of me. What seemed like life, the life which then caused an I-like reaction in me, was rather — I now believe — the submerged I-like presence in the place itself, which was arising, as if from the sea, touched, revealed, and then — because it was arising there — it also communicated with the I-like thing in me.

In other words, the very I-phenomenon which occurred in me, also existed first, I think, in the place, before I had anything to do with it or came on the scene. That is what I experienced as its life.

And I believe the same thing happens every time we experience living structure in a thing. It also arises in the dewdrop or in the little patch of azure blue paint. It occurs, in lesser degree perhaps, in each brick that is correctly placed, in the wall of a building, in each window that is correctly, beautifully made.

11 / A HYPOTHESIS

At root, these assertions lead, in my mind, to one conclusion: that the "I-like presence in the universe" is real, is somehow a real thing, and plays a real role in the scheme of things, and in the structure of matter, in the way the universe behaves. In slightly more detail, I have myself concluded this: *There must be some relation between the ultimate nature of a living center, and the nature of this "I."*

I began the preface to Book 4 with the statement that all great art hinges on the formation of the I in things. The relation of ourselves with

Did a tiny fraction of the I become visible here? Perhaps. The interior of the kitchen of the concrete Sala House, 1983.
There are wooden columns, brackets, beams, and this hand-painted alcove.

some presence in things that animates them also makes them feel related to us. But the subject of the I, and our perception of it, is deeper than that. For, as part of our experience, the I appears in nature, too. It touches our relation with all the things in the world.

Let us go back to the glistening dewdrop and its evident relation to the I, a leaf on a tree glistening in the dew, a waterfall. In various forms we experience the I as being *in* these things, *in* the leaf, *in* the raindrops, *in* the waterfall.

Some experience of I, within the things of the world, and especially within the things of nature, is shared, I think, by every human being, in some degree. In the notes below, I show by example how the I in these things may be experienced with various degrees of intensity. Many people reading this book will themselves have experienced a few of these possible forms of relationship between themselves and the I in the world — at least the more modest versions. And regardless of what the reader has experienced personally, I suspect every reader will accept that similar things have been experienced by others. And I would guess that almost everyone has experienced, as fleeting sensations, even some of the more extreme stages I describe. In the mildest version of this experience, I look at the waterfall and say I find it pleasing. I may be aware of a relation between me and the waterfall. But I stop short of saying that I identify with the waterfall, or that there is any possible identification between me and the waterfall. It is simply pleasing.

In a second, also mild, version of this experience, I enjoy the waterfall, and I feel a stirring of some relationship to it. I feel related to it. Virtually all of us, at one time or another, experience this feeling of a mild relationship between ourselves and the waterfall, or between ourselves and the tree.

A further stage of this experience occurs, if I find the relationship strong. Then I may go from saying that I experience some relatedness to the waterfall to saying that I experience this relationship as somehow interior to me. The rela-

tionship is touching to me. It matters. Here I experience a strong emotional linkage between myself and the tree or waterfall.

In a fourth version, I may even feel that the waterfall, the tree, or the bush touches the core of me. This happens, for instance, when as a lover, I feel profoundly stirred by the drop of water glistening in the grass, or by the steady pounding of the waterfall. Being there, being filled with the experience, I know that an essential core of me, the best part of me, is stirred, touched by the "I" which I perceive within the thing.

In a stronger version yet, I begin to feel some actual identification with the waterfall, or with the tree. I identify with the waterfall. I experience that it is profoundly related to my being. In this kind of experience, the relationship is strong enough so that I *identify* with the waterfall in some fashion. What I experience is not only my feeling, but that my own *self* and the waterfall are somehow related. This does not mean that I actually feel my self to be present in the waterfall. But I am aware that in some refreshing way, the waterfall — more than a hamburger bun, say, or today's morning newspaper — nourishes me, releases me, refreshes me. In this sense, I become aware of a relation to my self, which exists in the waterfall, or in the tree. In our society today, this kind of experience may not be as common as versions 1–4. Still, many contemporary people do have experiences of this kind.

There is a stronger version yet of the experience which, according to the reports of anthropologists, was common in preindustrial cultures. In these primitive experiences the person experienced the waterfall or the tree as a spirit, that is, as an animate being of some kind. Reports from (so-called) primitive societies describe the way that people not only identified with trees or with the forest, but endowed the entities of the forest, the rocks of the ocean, with spirit. I believe this was an expression of a situation where people felt, or experienced a presence, as being *in* the tree or in the waterfall. As such it is a direct, and even stronger version of the last.

A tunnel on the island of Tínos, Cyclades, although nearly rudimentary, shows profoundly what it means for people to make something ordinary, with their own hands, in which the I is present, visible, felt.

A still stronger form of such identification also existed in primitive cultures when it had currency in ritual. This occurred, for instance, when people of the culture reified the identification by giving it explicit substance, as for instance when a California Yurok Indian made an explicit identity between himself and a seal or an eagle at the time of adulthood, and from then on wore that animal's skin, took the name of the animal. Although anthropological texts categorize this kind of experience perhaps too patronizingly as animism, I believe it was simply another way (at a further level of intensity) in which people have asserted the identity they sometimes feel with natural things.

There is even a stronger version of this experienced identity that occasionally occurs in us when we recognize explicitly, and feel that our own self exists *in* the beach, or *in* a wave, or *in* a bush. And a stronger version still — different again in kind — is reached when we experience the relationship with the waterfall so that it is not merely that I identify with the waterfall, but that in some fashion I am the waterfall: not merely identification, but actual *identity*. In this case, when I see the waterfall and feel related to it, I experience the relationship as more fundamental, not merely "I *feel* identified with this waterfall," but something more like "There *is* some kind of an identity between my self, and the waterfall. My I is really in the waterfall. My self and the waterfall are not merely similar, but it feels as if they are the *same*, as if both are parts of one thing."[11]

Here we begin to enter metaphysics. This experience is no longer merely a statement about psychology. It is now asserting that the I which I experience as my own self, is in some fashion the same thing as the I which I feel and see in the waterfall. It appears to the person experiencing this, that both are expressions or manifestations of a single thing. I experience nature as if everything in me and without me is made of the same stuff.

12 / MOBILIZING THE STORM

Is it perhaps clear, now, why I do not believe that one can make sense of the facts surrounding life in buildings, or of the process of making this life, without explicit recognition of this relationship between the living centers in the world, and what I call the presence of the I. I am certain that some fairly strong version of the connection between centeredness in the world and this "I" must exist. I am not sure just how far this connection goes, but it seems to me that to make sense of the life of buildings, degrees of relatedness, as I have analyzed them in the previous section, need to be comparable to the higher levels of intensity I have described. They do not need to be expressed in transcendental terms. But, at the very least, they must be acknowledged as a core of human experience.

When we succeed in making a living thing from this point of view, we achieve a building (ornament, painting, garden, street) in which strong centers are connected to our own (individual and collective) eternal self. That is, the center becomes something so close to us emotionally that we experience a yearning for it and belonging from it and from being in its presence. It is tied to us, as if by blood. It is ours. We shine in its presence. Such a building endows us with knowledge of ourselves, makes us feel awake, conscious, more human, more ourselves, and in the end makes us experience ourselves as if dissolved in a flood of tears.

The success of every truly great work — town, street, building, painting, windowsill —

lies simply in the extent to which the living I appears in it. For every artist, every builder, this must be true: as I work I must try to create a structure which appears like I to me. I must try to arrange the colors in a painting in such a way that living breathing I appears in it. This effort makes the centers live; it makes me communicate with the ultimate beyond all things; and at the very same time it mobilizes myself, animates me, makes my person, my being, awaken, because I am then more present. It is this mobilizing of my self in the great work which chills me, devastates me, wakes me to the bone. And this, which is so personal because it reaches the personal in me, also connects me to the great ultimate beyond all things: to the ocean and the wind and the fire.

So, the work which means something is at one and the same time something religious, spiritual, something which connects me to God. And, at the very same time, it is also personal and childish. It connects me to me.

In human terms it is down to earth. It is the core of the earth and child in me. This "something" is black as night. It may be yellow or red. There may be touches of white around the greenish-white incandescent light. And perhaps at the core are black, purple, and dark tones of red.

What it touches is beyond reason, and before reason. It may be a connection to some realm, where I no longer am, and where I shall always be.

That is our task, as makers of things: to mobilize — to open — this eye to the storm.

NOTES

It is the core of the earth and child in me.

1. Book 1, chapters 10 and 11.

2. I use the word *established* advisedly, after showing that the items which have more living structure are, reliably, considered by most people to be more like their own deep self. It is true that the experiments reported in Book 1, like all psychological experiments, have statistical, not absolute results. However, the level of agreement is considerably stronger than that typical for many experiments in psychology. From the point of view of social science, the experiments described in chapters 10 and 11 may therefore be said to show this result conclusively.

3. The existence of such a close, intimate, interwoven character in the relation between early people and their surroundings, has been documented repeatedly in the anthropological literature.

4. I have presented a more extended discussion of this point, and of the relationship between a positivistic "psychological" explanation, and the metaphysical or mystical explanation, in chapter 10.

5. Although this conception of a self, intertwined and not distinguishable, may seem strange in our highly rational period of history, there is some fascinating evidence that this attitude may be a consequence of sharply drawn ego-boundaries, more associated with the masculine temperament, less with the feminine. David Gutmann, "Female Ego Styles and Generational Conflict," chapter 4 in Judith M. Bardwick, FEMININE PERSONALITY AND CONFLICT (Belmont, Calif.: Brooks-Cole, 1970), 77–96. Gutman describes women as tending towards what he calls autocentric, and men as tending towards what he calls allocentric. There is some suspicion that this allocentric, the sharply defined self, divided from the world, is a product of the highly sequential and rational mode of perception that was on the rise in the second half of the 20th century, and may now once again be declining.

6. However, other books written in the last decades have suggested this quite strongly. Helena Norberg-Hodge, LEARNING FROM LADAKH (San Francisco: Sierra Club, 1991) is one example among many.

7. I use the word "place" very loosely. Some of the places I mean are very, very large, hundreds of yards or miles across. Others are tiny, no bigger than a brick or two.

8. A full description of this kind of situation is given in chapter 4.

9. See chapter 10 of Book 1. If we go back to the blue bench and the grey stool of chapter 10, we see it clearly. The blue bench feels as if it is "mine" and it makes me feel, in my heart, that it is mine. The grey stool feels not-mine, and makes me feel alien from it. This does not have to do with literal ownership, or with social rules or conditions. It has to do with the fact that

one of them is made in such a way that *it* is related to me. The other is made so that *it* is not related to me. In each case this depends on the pattern of centers it contains. The same thing is true of roads, parks, gardens, passages, entrances and rooms.

10. It is significant, I think, that the use of the word "I," in this chapter, to mean something as large as it is, is similar, both in spirit and in meaning to the Hebrew name of God, Yahweh. which, literally means "I am." The idea that "I am" as a name of God expresses just what God is, has intellectual origins and a concrete meaning very similar indeed to the meaning I am trying to give the word "I" in this text.

An interesting discussion of a similar point occurs in one of David Bohm's dialogues (David Bohm, UN-FOLDING MEANING, ed. by Donald Factor [Mickleton, Gloucestershire: Foundation House Publications, 1985], 151–56).

11. Father Tom McGelligot has kindly shown me that an almost identical formulation appears in St. Ignatius, MEDITATIONS ON LOVE, 1548, in the "Contemplation to Gain Love," section 235. This may be found reprinted and translated in THE SPIRITUAL EXCERCISE OF ST. IGNATIUS: A LITERAL TRANSLATION AND A CONTEMPORARY READING, trans., David L. Fleming (St. Louis: Institute of Jesuit Sources, 1978), 140–41.

CHAPTER FOUR

THE TEN THOUSAND BEINGS

1 / INTRODUCTION

Let us now consider a model that builds on the conception of I. In this model, I consider living structure as I have before, as a system of centers, each center having some different degree of life.[1] The model is similar to the one presented in Book 1, especially as it is presented in chapters 3 and 4. But I now introduce one very important change. Let us also include the fact that every center in the system of centers is, to some degree, a picture of the self.

Of course, in a real building the many centers will not all have this quality to an equal degree. Some will contain the self-like, I-like character more intensely, others less intensely. But, in *some* degree, all the centers are related to self. In Book 1, we spoke of the degree of life which different centers have. That is a structural matter. We now add the idea that each center has a degree of quality, an intensity of life according to the degree in which it is a picture of the self.

This model is consistent with two propositions which were introduced in Book 1: (1) *that every living structure contains thousands of living centers*, and (2) *that every living center may be distinguished as living, to the degree that it is a picture of the eternal self.* But, in Book 1, I did not go on to draw the conclusion that comes from these two propositions.

When we put these two propositions together, we can hardly avoid reaching the conclusion that *every living structure is composed of thousands of pictures of the eternal self.* In this model, a living structure, is not merely composed of thousands, or millions, of interacting centers. It is, equally, composed of millions of interacting pictures of the "I."

2 / CONSIDER THE POSSIBILITY OF VIEWING ALL LIVING CENTERS AS BEINGS

Essentially, then, we are now viewing a living center from a new point of view. It is related to the self.

I ask you to contemplate further, and without prejudice, the idea that a living center is something almost being-like. What do I mean by a "being"? What is the difference between the "I" and a "being"? And what, then, is the I?

The I, as discussed already, is a huge thing, of enormous significance. It is everywhere. Whenever a thing takes on life, this thing is connected, in some measure, with the I. It is the connection with the I which endows things with life, which constitutes their life. But the I is a vastness, a something in the universe, as large as the universe itself, from which living structure draws its life.

A being is a small thing. It is a name for a center which is connected to the I. It is not a new kind of entity at all, merely another way of talking about living things and living centers, because they are connected to the I. It is just another word for a living center. But, unlike the phrase "living center," or "living structure," the word "being" draws attention to the nearly animate quality that appears when something is connected to the I.

In Book 1, we saw that strong centers are built up recursively from other centers.[2] We saw the effect of the recursion. We saw that as centers are built up, toughened, strengthened, then gradually the centers which appear as geometrical configurations *of* other centers become deeper, tougher in the artistic sense, and more

Brass rubbing of a horse from Thailand, 12th century. The remarkable thing about this brass is that it is made of many, many parts, each one of which is beautifully shaped in its own right, each one essentially being-like. Each of the parts invites me to have a relation with it. I can enter into, love each of these parts, have a feeling in relation to each of the beings, one by one, whether these beings are small, or large, or in between other beings.

profound; they reach deeper, somehow they penetrate a realm in which "something" happens. We saw how this recursion applies to many kinds of structures: buildings, paintings, living systems, even to living groups of human beings. And we saw it even more clearly in the simple geometric examples from the realm of ancient carpets and ornaments — interesting because they are so abstract that there are no distractions.

If we reexamine these examples from the point of view I have proposed, we begin to see that the recursion may be said, then, to create a being-like connection to the I. Each living center is, to some extent, an I-like picture of the self. The more life a given living center has, the more I-like it is: the *more* it is a picture of the self. As centers are built, strengthened, and toughened, the larger structures which contain them then, too, become more I-like. In short, the recursion, which allows us to build living structure in the world, not only makes living centers more and

more strong. *It also causes the appearance, somehow, of pictures of the self, throughout every nook and cranny of a region of space.*

How is a modern person to interpret, within normal and reasonable cognitive categories, the idea — in nature or in architecture — that as the build-up of centers proceeds recursively, space becomes filled, gradually, with I-like stuff, with living structure made of thousands of pictures of the living self? Within our present picture of the world, it is hard — one might say, nearly impossible — even to consider such a phenomenon. How then, are we to react to it?

Should we regard it as nonsense? I do not think so. I believe this model will help us to cement the rift in our world-picture, come to a graspable and sensible account of how architecture works, yet retain the physical world-picture we presently have without too much damage. If so, we may reasonably say then that it is a step toward an understanding of how things actually are.

3 / THE JEWEL NET OF INDRA

The model is not entirely new. In traditional Buddhism, there is a vision of the world considered as a ten thousand pictures of the self. It occurs in a fascinating but relatively unknown branch of Buddhism known as *Hua-Yen*. According to this vision, the world is seen as ten thousand raindrops, each an eye, each reflecting all ten thousand others.

A beautifully written overview of this branch of Buddhist thought is given by Francis H. Cook in HUA-YEN BUDDHISM: THE JEWEL NET OF INDRA.[3] In Cook's summary of Hua-Yen, "Far away in the heavenly abode of the great god Indra, there is a wonderful net which has been hung by some cunning artificer in such a manner that it stretches out infinitely in all directions. In accordance with the extravagant tastes of deities, the artificer has hung a single glittering jewel in each "eye" of the net, and since the net itself is infinite in dimension, the jewels are infinite in number. There hang the jewels, glittering like stars of the first magnitude, a wonderful sight to behold. If we now arbitrarily select one of these jewels for inspection and look closely at it, we will discover that in its polished surface there are reflected all the other jewels in the net, infinite in number. Not only that, but each of the jewels reflected in this one jewel is also reflecting all the other jewels, so that there is an infinite reflecting process occurring."

The jewels in the net of Indra, the living centers in the world, are what I call "beings."

4 / WHAT IT MEANS FOR A CENTER TO BE BEING-LIKE

Look at the African head on the next page. If I speak only of my experience, I can say that the I really is in there. I am related to it, and to every part of it. Each part of it is made to be like the I, reveals the I. If you are in doubt, for contrast look at the diskette cover shown on page 78: a graphic design from about 1985. There I cannot so easily enter into its parts, I am not related to the parts, my self finds no home in them. I am not as strongly related to it, or to every part of it.

What exactly do these statements mean? To answer the question, of course, I can start by asking the reader to repeat the mirror-of-the-self experiments described in Book 1, chapters 8 and 9, laboriously, piece by piece, going through five centers in the diskette cover, comparing them with five centers from the African head.

Look at just the eyelids of the African head, their slightly bulbous swelling. Ask of this thing, "Do I feel related to it?" I answer "Yes, I do." Is that eyelid a being? Yes. Is the eyelid a picture of my self? Certainly a better picture than the inside of the diskette's capital "C."

Look at the space inside the "C" of the word "certified" (top of page 78). It is a rounded rectangle, with a keyhole shape where it passes out into the space beyond. If I ask whether I find myself in this black bit of space, I may hesitate, be unsure. Is it a being? Is it a good picture of my self? Obviously it is not very strong. Certainly not as strong as the eyelid of the mask, or as a strand of its hair, or the slit between the eyelid and the eye.

Let us try again. Consider the space inside the bars of the capital "E" on the diskette cover. Is *this* a picture of myself? Do I love it, feel related to it? Again I have to answer "No." How about the bar of the E: Is this a picture of my self? No, it is nothing. Subtly, it makes me feel nothing.

Or, look at something larger on the diskette cover: the wedge-shaped triangle of space above

Look at the way the massive, elongated, 17th-century African head—and its beauty as a center—helps to make the eyes more self-like. In this statue, the character and life arise because every part, even the individual tresses of the hair, the eyes, the lips, the space below the lips, is developed to a great height as a being in its own right.

and below the writing. Is this a picture of self? It is not. Is it a living center? No! But look, for comparison at the great elongated form of the top of the head of the African statue. The head alone, the beautiful filled, shape of the hair and head, with its three ornaments along the front. Is my self related to this shape? It is. Do I find myself in this head? I do.

If I look slowly at every part and every crevice of the diskette cover, again and again, I shall get the answer "No!" And if I look at every part and every particle of the African head, again and again I shall answer "Yes."

Do you think that this is happening because the statue is a *head?* Look instead then, at this type from a book (page 78): a few letters on a page, entirely abstract, formed of nothing but black and white and space, just like the diskette cover. But what a difference! Here, again and again throughout the piece of paper, I find myself related to the serifs, to the space between the bars of the E, to the triangular space between the

A paper diskette cover from 1985 is mainly made from entities which do not reflect the human self.

great letters G and A, to the inner triangle of the large A, to the space between the G and the smaller T which it contains, to every letter, to every particle of space between the letters and around the letters.

Look carefully at the space inside the small "o" of the text. At a distance you think it is a circle. When you look closely, you see a beautiful, subtle, egg-shaped form sloped to the left, inside the black of the type. This shape, the egg itself, gently sloping, makes me related to it; I feel my self in it, just as with the crude shape inside the C of the diskette I feel unrelated. The feeling of relatedness — the being-character — lies in the *geometry*. It is in the space.

In case you think the computer diskette is too negative, too close to being a strawman, let us consider another artifact from our time: a pair of scissors used for haircutting. The scissors are rather beautiful and have abundant life — but not because they are symmetrical. Leave prejudice aside, and do the mirror test. You will, I

THE PLAN OF
GSt GtALL

A STUDY OF THE ARCHITECTURE & ECONOMY OF, &
LIFE IN A PARADIGMATIC CAROLINGIAN MONASTERY

Here the letters and spaces between the letters are all beings, all pictures of the self.
The letters are from the title page of THE PLAN OF ST GALL, *typography by Ernest Born, 1979.*

think, feel some connection to the pair of scissors, an inner connection between this pair of scissors and yourself. It is somewhat I-like. It is a being. And its interior centers are, each of them, also being-like. When we take them one by one, each is I-like, each is being-like, each is a being in its own right. It speaks to us, it evokes our cognizance of its being nature as we encounter it, use it, and look at it. And that is, indeed, exactly what we find. When we examine the internal entities within the scissors, the thumb-hole of the handle, the bolt that makes the pivot, the chamfer on the blade, the point, the fleshy shaped piece of metal between bolt and handle, the cross section of the steel that forms the handle — in every case, the smaller center is again being-like, is a mirror of the self.

To be an I-like center, a center must also be composed of centers which are themselves I-like. To be a being-like center, a center must also be composed of centers which are themselves being-like. Beings can only be made of beings. If it is not made of beings, it cannot be a being.

So the fact that the pair of scissors is made of many centers which are themselves life-filled and being-like is empirically connected to the strong I-like character — and to the life — of the pair of scissors as a whole: the overall life of the scissors hinges on the fact that it is made of beings.

There is no apriori reason to expect this to be true. It is an empirical result, and one which we must remember again and again, as a fundamental aspect of the nature of centers which come to life.

Most of the argument that follows depends on your willingness to understand this, assimilate it, make it yours. If you are to grasp the argument, it is imperative that you concentrate on this idea of beings and thoroughly understand what it means. In that way you will have access to your own intuitive knowledge, and you will develop an uncomplicated ability to tell when centers are beings and in what degree each center is a being, by knowing when they are related to your self — when they are truly I-like — and when they are not.

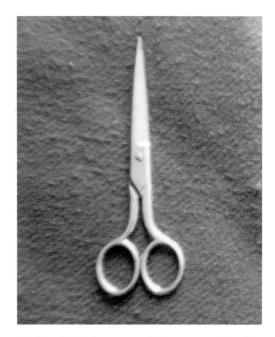

In this pair of scissors most of the centers are being-like. This is where the life of the scissors comes from.

The I-like character of living centers is crucial; it is at the core of everything. And yet, although it could be easy for the reader to nod agreement, and could also be easy to dismiss it out of hand as absurd, actually to understand it, to grasp it, to experience it, is hard. It takes perception, care, and a willingness to be connected with your own feelings. And it takes concentration and effort to make such a structure appear in space. It requires, too, an operational willingness. It is easy enough to say to oneself that it is clear: but immensely hard to transform that intellectual understanding, into a daily operational willingness to make this I-like structure appear, in every center, throughout the vast fabric of a building or something else which you are making.

For this reason, I beg your indulgence if the examples of this chapter are in any way repetitive. I go on and on with the argument and with examples, because after years of teaching I know, only too well, how long it takes for a person to reach a point where this understanding is thoroughly assimilated, familiar, and understood so that it is really understood, and almost second nature.

Clematis, growing on the stable wall

Even in this meadow, and its saplings, we feel each stem, each leaf, each rib, and each vein, as pictures of our self.
We are related, fundamentally, to each one of them.

5 / A CORNER OF A FARMER'S FIELD

The life formed from the many-being structure does not occur in the way things *look*. It occurs in the way things *are*. And it occurs in the way they *work*.

Let us consider the organic nature of a living system, part nature, part man-made; for instance a stand of trees and an old fence, in the corner of a field. The living nature of the trees, first of all, is visible in the leaves, in the shady places under the trees, the branches, limbs, sap-veins, in the rings and layers of wood of the trunk, in the root system. Each of these elements is I-like. A biologist has no immediate reason for linking these naturally formed elements to the wholesome human self. Still, it is so. The leaf, branch, root, and crown are all beautiful things with which I can identify. They are thus I-like centers in the whole.[4]

The less visible parts of the wholeness — the space between the lowest branches and the ground, the space between individual leaves, the sap-filled spaces between rings of wood, the spaces between the veins and ribs of a single leaf — are also I-like in the same sense. The parts of the bush themselves, are I-like. Whatever their biological origin, there is hardly any doubt that they are I-like in every particle.

We may check this by experiment. If I compare any one of these things, anything in the meadow, anything in the bush, with the computer diskette cover illustrated before, each of them is more I-like than this computer cover. Consider the leaves, twigs, spaces between the branches of this bush. Each space is being-like and self-like. Though it is made by nature, not by people, I feel myself related to each one of them.

Compare the space between the leaves, shown above. Is it more like the African carved woman's eyes? Or is it more like the space inside the C of the diskette cover? I think you will agree it is the former.

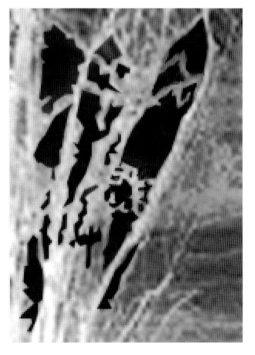

A blow-up of a bush in the photograph opposite, emphasizing the space between the branches. Again, it is more like the African carved woman's eyes than like the space inside the C of the diskette cover.

6 / A SHIPYARD

The multiplicity of I-like centers which occurs in nature is also visible to some extent in certain early industrial landscapes. If, for instance, we look at this pictures of early 20th-century ocean-liners on Merseyside in Liverpool, we may be struck by that character, in every stanchion, handrail, even in some of the dirtiest bits of machinery, in the steelwork it is visible in almost in every bolt and nut and rod and plate.

The fact that the early great industrial places had enormous life was recognized by many, including Le Corbusier.[5] Since we can be nearly certain that these places were not created by conscious religious intent, and only by practical business-like intensity, we need to ask what process created these things, successfully making I-like centers in them, that nevertheless fails so often today when building modern warehouses, airports and so on, and fails when architects self-consciously try to use an "industrial aesthetic." This is the core of the intellectual problem I have addressed in Book 2. The industrial process of the *early* 20th century *was* an unfolding process in its straightforward directness. But the post-industrial processes of the late 20th century have been contaminated by images, and no longer have the directness of real-world creation and unfolding needed to make life.

Circa 1920. A thousand pictures of the human self in every ship, crane, stanchion, handrail, funnel, bucket along the Merseyside in Liverpool

HMS Aquitania on the dock, 1914, another picture of ten-thousand beings among the industrial dockyards of Merseyside

Although nostalgia may be partly responsible for this retrospective appreciation of the early industrial period, I believe that our appreciation of these 19th- and early 20th-century engineering structures mainly comes from the fact that they are actually *visible* as having the multiplicity of I-like living centers — hence real life — in them. Even the simplest stanchion, railing, barrel of oil, smokestack, steel plate, bolt or rivet — as shown in these photographs from the early 20th century — makes us feel related to it.

A computer casing, a freeway bridge, or a packaged machine of our own era rarely has the same depth of feeling, and is less related to the I because what few centers it does have are not I-like to the same degree.

What is certain is that these machines, made by builders and engineers, were made for practical ends. It is their practicality we see made flesh in the structure of living centers. The manifold living centers we see in them arise *because of* their practical nature. That is what caused and sustained their practical effectiveness.

7 / LOOKING AT CHARTRES

Let us now look at a building which is composed nearly completely of I-like centers. I have 200 slides of Chartres, a few of them shown here. To go through them all, one after the other, all 200, is a stunning experience. They show that place, that building, is a multitude — truly a fantastic multitude — of millions upon millions of living centers, all worked through, established, shaped, as pictures of the "I." Living centers, existing everywhere, are virtually the only things that happen there.

In this building you see the level of exceptional life that can be created in space. It is not overlaid by too much abstract thought. It is a

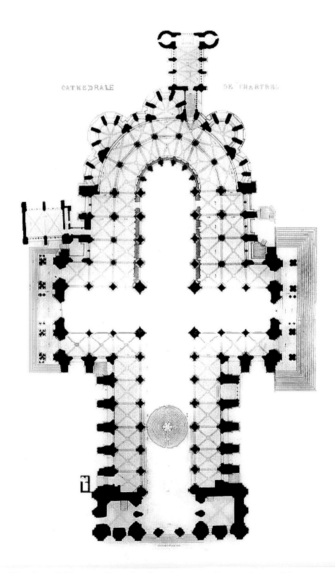

The plan of Chartres. Even the plan alone contains ten thousand beings:
columns, bays, vaults, transepts, choir, even the buttresses themselves,
are visible as Selves.

Chartres: the being on the rock, in which each tower and spire is a being, too.

beautiful, undying construction — ultimately all ornament in nature — in which the properties create life innocently, in centers and in which the centers themselves are multiplied, each one made deeper by the next.

The blue glass in the windows, the colored light: Is this not a question of material, technique? I have heard it said that we no longer know how to make such a blue glass. Yes, but even in this very important case, it is the life in the centers which makes the blue. These glass makers knew how to put just such a blue that the blue itself is so intense, it captures my soul when I look at it, I am deeply engaged, only by the blue itself — so the makers of that glass worked for

years and years just to learn how to make a tiny piece of glass which has this power to capture the human heart, to make me feel. *That* is a living center. Each living center has *that* power, above all.

There is little doubt, I think, that the makers of Chartres consciously created a structure filled with beings. When we examine the church, and try to count the living centers, there are hundreds of beings even in a few inches or feet of glass and stone, millions of living centers in a single bay, and perhaps as many as a hundred million in the building as a whole. Each one is so intense that it captures me, touches me. The life of the building, and its life as a center, *is* this fact.

The beings are in the glass; in the fragments of color in the wonderful blue glass that make the light shine (left). Each buttress is a being; each section of the buttress with its own stone cap is a being; the small arched openings are beings; the space between the buttresses is calculated and proportioned, in plan, section, and volume, to be a being, too (right).

The main doors as beings too: and each of these doors is also made of beings, literally, dozens upon dozens of human beings, forming the doorway, bringing it to life in an almost literal, though symbolic and geometric, sense.

Here we see the columns as beings, the majesty of the shafts, the tapering thinner shafts grouped as if in conversation, the vaults as beings, the springing of the vaults and bosses and ribs as beings, too.

8 / EACH LIVING CENTER IS A BEING

In a successful work, in a living thing, though there may be ten thousand living centers, each one of these centers is a picture of the "I," or that part of our selves that is most deeply grounded.

The carved stone ornaments in Chartres (shown below) are from the apse. From the point of view of abstract structure, the most remarkable feature of these carvings is their extraordinary compactness of design, in which every single particle of space is well formed and functions as a center. This frieze is a supreme example of positive space and multiple centers. We have a perfect distribution of beings — at the scale of the column, at the scale of the field, at the scale of half the field, at the scale of the column shafts, at the scale of the carvings between the columns, at the scale of the cartouches in the border at the scale of the column capitals, at the scale of the smaller octagons between the medallions, at the scale of the triangles between the cartouches, at the scale of the triangles which make up the guls themselves, at the scale of the flower motifs within the cartouches, the whirling stars within the octagons, at the small rhombuses forming the stars in the octagons, and down to the very smallest triangles of all in the flowers between the cartouches and between the points of the stars in the octagons.

This dazzling display of levels — although simple and severe — is scarcely equalled. The discipline, simplicity, and enormous complexity of space that is achieved in this small panel

Here, in the carved stone ornaments, even the squares and diamonds are centers shaped to be pictures of the "I."
Shapes that would elsewhere be ordinary are brought to life. Each one, each geometric shape,
is animated by its proportion and detail until it, too, in itself, becomes a being.
In this one photograph we see, perhaps, two thousand to five thousand beings.

*Every stone is a picture of the ''I''—every shaft, every column, every base, is
a being which reflects and embodies the ''I.''*

of stone is absolutely fascinating. And it is all
the more fascinating because at first sight the
stone is so simple. The key thing about these
many different wholes we see, is that each of
them has a relation with us, me, you. Each shape
is made in such a way that you can establish a
relationship with it; indeed, you want to establish
a relation with it.

If we look carefully at the stained glass window, the remarkable thing about it is that it is
made of many, many parts, each one of which
is beautifully shaped in its own right. Each one
invites me to have a relation with it. Whether
these parts are small, or large, or in between
things, I like them, and have a relation with each
of them.

Every piece of stone and every piece of glass is a picture of the "I." Of all the parts of Chartres, it is perhaps here where the beings are most explicit: in the jewelled lights of the south window.

Here every shadow is a picture of the "I," every void, every hollow—even these are I-like centers in this carving.

The same is true in this statue from the apse. Each of its many, many parts, the hair, the braids, the nose, the breast, the cloth, the folds of the cloth is hewn, so that I have a relation with it. Each one—no matter how apparently insignificant—is a center that is a picture of the self. I have a beautiful relationship with the eyes, I experience this relationship with the braids of hair, with the individual locks in the braids of hair, with the mouth, the lips, the curve at the

The glorious glass, here mainly red, helps the I-like quality of the blue by intensifying it.

Stone tracery made entirely of I-like centers

The folds of cloth are pictures of the "I." Even the hinges and the bolt-heads on the door
are yet again shaped to be pictures of the "I."

The eyes and beard are I-like beings, too.

Even the individual strands of hair, the knots and whorls, and the jewels in the crown
are chosen, individually, to be beings that are pictures of the "I."

top of the lips. Each part, as in the ornament and in the glass, is drawn and shaped in such a way that I feel my relationship with it.

The same is true in the ceiling vault. Every rib is a being. The divisions are beings. The dividing lines are beings. The small bosses are beings. The triangular bay, made of hundreds of smaller ones, is a being itself. And the whole thing is a being.

Even in the roof, where ordinary tiles simply repeat, there is this extraordinary quality. Every tile is a being to which I feel related. Every fold in every tile is a being to which I feel related. The space between the tiles is a being. The assembly of the tiles together, like a dragon's back, is a being, too.

In each case I experience each of these centers as something nearly sentient. I experience the feeling in the thing, not only in me, as I look at this being, contemplate it, meet it, confront it. Thus, literally, as I look at the cathedral, which is made of a hundred million beings, I see and feel life in everything. That is the measure of its unity and greatness as a whole.

9 / PURE UNITY

Let me try to summarize the situation. In a profoundly living thing, the life which is there is not only present as a multiplicity of centers, in recursion. With the example of Chartres, we begin to see that there may be a special quality of such a thing, that the qualitative fact that may come into being, as the recursion becomes more and more intense, is that this thing gradually and more and more deeply, makes contact with the I. And, at the same time, it becomes more unified. As the structure approaches I in every center, then as a whole, it begins to reach a single unity.

Later, in chapter 7, we shall see this unity very explicitly in the realm of color, where we sometimes feel space melt, nearly swimming together, as if it became a single substance, not a multitude, but a many-faceted thing which glows with a single quality. But what we experience in color is simply a version of something more general, which is the ultimate experience of living structure. *Living structure is unified.* It is that *unity* which is the aim of life. It is the *unity* which is created by living structure.

Perhaps above all, we must always remember that a living center is living, is a being, only according to its position in a larger whole. It must help some larger whole. And if it is a being, it is helped by smaller wholes inside it, to the side of it, and far away from it.

So the being-like living center is a phenomenon, a nearly electric entity in space which gains its life by action at a distance, from the cooperation of the others all around it, from its contribution to the larger wholes with which it appears. This truly living quality is the being nature.

Thus as we begin to see living centers as beings, not as component parts, we begin to approach the idea of pure sheet-like unity, which is achieved in the space made of beings, to recognize that beings partake in a living structure, to the extent that this structure approaches becoming an undivided whole, and the extent to which the beings — centers — help it to become an undivided whole.

The beings create unity, and by definition are part of unity. Each being — that is, each center — gets its life from the existence of the other centers around it within the unity they form together. But the interwoven life of these beings, all essentially stemming from the same I-like character, is then like a proliferation, an elaboration of the I. It is all I. It is all manifestation, elaboration, intensification of the same. The structure which contains ten thousand beings is not ten thousand separate entities. It is one entity, only shouting the same name, one sound, one voice, one I, one unity.

10 / THE FUNDAMENTAL PROCESS

In cathedrals, how was such extraordinary unity made?

During the last thirty years I have often asked myself how people in traditional societies were able to make things which had such life and embodied living centers to such a high degree. It is unlikely, I think, that they used such detailed structural formulations as I have given in Books 1 to 3. However, it also seems unlikely that they had no formulations at all to guide them. One needs something clear to hang onto while one is working. It is therefore almost certain, in my mind, that the people of ancient cultures had at least some kind of intellectual formulation to guide them — even if it was very different from what I have given.

What did a 14th-century mason say to himself while carving the stone of a cathedral vault? What did a Turkish weaver say to herself while knotting a carpet? What did a Japanese temple carpenter think about while laying out his roof or planing the beams? These craftspeople made living structures — I believe — at a level of intensity and sophistication often far beyond our own capacities. How then, did they talk about it? What did they have in their minds while they were doing it?

In 1981, I made an exhibit for a fair in Austria, showing pictures of the fifteen properties, and explaining how they work to create living centers.[6] It happened that an Austrian cabinetmaker from the mountains, who was working for me at the time, and who came from a long line of traditional cabinetmakers, saw my exhibition. He was not a literate man, but a deeply skilled craftsman. After visiting the fifteen properties in the exhibit, he astonished me by saying: "Anybody who doesn't understand these things can never be a cabinetmaker." I was surprised that these intellectual formulations were not too abstract for him — on the contrary he found them natural.

Nevertheless, I do not believe that traditional craftspeople — in 14th-century Europe, for example — usually carried such explicit theories in their minds. They worked; they acted; they knew what they were doing.

How did they know what they were doing? I believe that, in some form, they used the fundamental process in virtually everything they did. The fundamental process, discussed extensively in Books 2 and 3, is a process in which centers are made progressively more and more profound, more and more living, by an iterated, repeated, sequence of transformations.

How did they carry this process in their minds, and keep it before them? What was their view of it, their formulation? Whatever it was, it must have been brief, simple, to the point. To be passed on from person to person, to have been present in every act, even when a mason was chipping a stone, it must have been easy to remember, and highly compressed.

I believe the following sentence expresses the kind of thing they might have carried, mentally, with them:

Whatever you make must be a being.

Stated at slightly greater length, it could be stated thus:

While you are making something you must always arrange things, or work things out, in such a way that all the elements you make are self-like beings, and the elements from which the elements are made are beings, and the spaces between these elements are beings, and the largest structures are beings, too. Thus your effort is directed toward the goal that everything, every portion of space, must be made a being.

Such a short rule could easily have been carried about consciously by a 14th-century craftsman as the secret of his art. If you follow this rule at all scales, in the large and in the small, whatever you are doing, you get the centers, you then get the density of centers, and you get life. The

Look at the eyes, the eyelids, the beard, the shin, the arms in this 9th-century Irish carving.
What was the instruction which the carver carried in his mind? "While you are making something
you must always arrange things, or work things out, in such a way that all the elements you make
are beings, and the elements from which the elements are made are beings, and the spaces
between these elements are beings, and the largest structures are beings, too.
Thus everything, every portion of space, must be made a being."

word "being," used instead of the word "center," catches the fact that every center which has life is a self-like thing, and conveys its animated, self-like character. And, because it is very easy to see how the life of each being depends on the life of the other beings, it also contains, in capsule form, the whole of the theoretical idea of the field of centers. It is this formulation of the fundamental process that first led me to consider that "being" is a rather good summary or synonym for "living center."

The idea of a spirit which might reside in every stone or every speck of matter is a concept that would have been natural in the 14th century, almost anywhere in the world. It is less natural now, but with the idea of beings in mind it is easy to see how, in the mental context of the 14th cen-

tury, this one sentence would have been capable of standing for very much of what I have said in these four books. I believe that a builder who makes *everything* a hierarchy of beings in that primitive religious sense, will, with no further instruction, succeed in making life in buildings.

Of course, what this sentence means is simply another way of saying what I have said throughout these four books. *Only a deliberate process of creating being-like (and self-like) centers in buildings throughout the world will encourage the world to become more alive.* By this I mean that the successful maker consciously moves towards those things which most deeply reflect or touch his own self, his inner feeling, and consciously moves away from those which do not. This does not merely create places which are pleasant, or liked, but this process creates places which are profoundly practical, harmonious, adequate for conduct of life, respectful of ecology and all living forms — even sometimes profound as works of art.

In Book 3 I have shown hundreds of examples where my colleagues and I used such a process. Although I argued from the point of view of the fundamental process, and tried to show the results of using the fundamental process repeatedly, it is also true that a process of consciously creating beings, something I was fully aware of throughout, also informed many of the projects.[7] So the fundamental process *does* work, *does* create life. The effort to create beings, when pursued honestly and carefully, does create living structure in the world.

Careful construction of the world, according to the principle that every center is made as profoundly as possible as a being — hence to be related to the true I of the maker — will result in a world which is practical, harmonious, functional. If this is true, astonishingly then it appears that the safest road to the creation of living structure is one in which people do what is most nearly in their hearts: that they make each part

in such a way that it reflects their true feeling, that it makes them feel wholesome in themselves, and is, in this sense, related in the deepest way to their own true I.

This is enigmatic. It means that a world constructed in the most personal and individual fashion, made by people who are searching deeply to follow the nature of their own true selves, will be — in the most public, objective, and universal sense — a world which is functional, adequate, and harmonious.

The enigma which arises, then, is that the process by which human beings create the world, in their own image, gradually creates a living world, and this is — I have come to believe — the best and most efficient way a living world can be created.

But, of course, the phrase "in their own image" requires that it be the *true* self, and the personal search for the true self cannot be separated from this process which each person strives for. This means, then, that the making of a living world cannot be separated from each person's search for the true self.

This is the most basic formulation of the fundamental process that I know how to give.

11 / THE DIFFICULTY OF THE TASK

The beauty of a living structure made of beings can, in my experience, only be fully understood once a person has struggled to *create* this structure, found out how hard it is, failed, failed, failed again, and then succeeded.

Creation does not happen easily. But I have found out that readers of this book often believe, from the text and from the examples, that it is actually not too hard to do. They assume they understand what is involved. "A center, after all — what is so hard about making *that*!" But the "something" they create, while assuming they understand it, is then shockingly unlike the real

thing, because it lacks *beings* — often almost entirely.

Look at the examples in the top row on the next page. They are typical of drawings made by students who have read this book, enjoy discussion of it, and who then try, as best they can, to make drawings of buildings which embody the fifteen properties. The drawings are far from the real thing. They are not beings, they do not contain beings, they are not densely packed with beings in space. You may see it by comparing them with the drawings in the bottom row of the next page, which *are* made of beings. In the student

NO BEINGS IN THESE TWO EXAMPLES

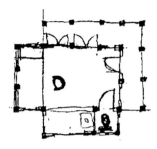

This student-drawn plan is intended to be practical, but there are no beings here. The student is laboring. He tries to do what is wanted of him, but has too little joy. There is a half-hearted functional sense in the design, but the building has little existence as a center or an ornament, hence there are no felt centers that live and breathe.

Here the student's ability is hampered by the sense that this must be a section of a building. He feels that it must be professional, and is thereby hamstrung by a lack of freedom to create real beings. There is no ability, nor even any real effort, to create living centers, because he has not yet grasped what "center" means.

THESE TWO EXAMPLES ARE REPLETE WITH BEINGS

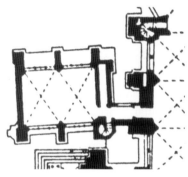 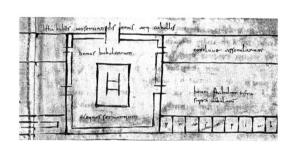

This—a tiny part of the plan of Chartres, (left) blown up—is quite different from the student drawings above. It is a powerful center, made of beings. Here too in a fragment from the 9th-century monk's drawing of the St. Gall plan (right), we have a plan which is genuinely made of beings, throughout. Each entity which appears in the drawing has feeling and character which make a connection to the I. It allows us to experience relatedness.
In this, it is quite different from the student plans above.

drawing at the top left, the individual columns are not beings. The alcove is not a being. The wall between the columns is not a being. The space behind the door is not a being. The windows are not beings. But in the two fragments shown at the bottom of the page, *every* single part is a being — each column is fat and shaped, the space between the columns is positive and definite and being-like. Column, space, window, door, gap, repeated small rooms — *all* are beings. And in the St. Gall fragment, the entities are even more subtle, quiet, but contemplative, once again being-like. Each rectangle is distinct, different from its neighbors, has its own character. That is what makes them being-like.

I present these positive and negative examples for comparison, as a warning, because I believe many readers may too easily assume that they understand the argument, and that they know how to do it. Yet, when they try they, too, might make something like the student drawings. It is the slap in the face, the difficulty between the spoken word and the idea, the actual geometric substance and its difficulty, which one must experience to find out how awesome this structure is.

We must study the drawings at the top, though they seem negative, in order to heighten our appreciation and awe for the living structure itself, as it appears below, and as men and women have managed to create it through the centuries.

We must be certain that our appreciation of this structures on the bottom row is real, substantial, factual, not merely a wishy-washy positive feeling, but appreciation of the hard-edged power and discipline of the structure which can contain such joy.

Consider this. If I look at your face, or at your hand, or at a tree, I see positive space, definite shapes, selves, beings, which I can love. I see the gaps between your fingers are positive. The leaf of the tree is a being. The shape between your wrist and your shirt is a being and has positive shape. The space between the tree and the ground, is positive and is a being. Nature does this almost everywhere. But to *draw* it is immensely hard. Even knowing how to create a two-dimensional arrangement in which these gaps between the fingers, and the finger nails, and the space below your hand, and the gap be-

tween the wrist and the shirtsleeve are all beings is immensely difficult to do. So difficult that only a few artists — Matisse, Leonardo, Dürer, Vermeer, Bonnard, and a few unknown great ones who made brass and stone etchings — have been able to do it consistently. Of the millions of people on earth who have known how to draw, just a handful could create this multi-being structure, even when copying from nature, from a structure which already has the being structure in it. That is how hard it is to do.

To do it in a building is perhaps even harder, since here we are not copying, but we have to arrange, create, and shape the building so that every stone, every brick, every window, every gap between two rooms, every space outside every door, is a thing to love, an actual being.

To see just how hard it is, it is useful to look again at the student drawings, where students were explicitly asked to create positive structure in a building. Sadly they fail. Well-meaning as they are, excellent as they are as students, the first drawings are dreary, they do not have this life in them, because the multi-being structure is not there and because the student does not *truly* realize that putting that structure of beautiful being-like shapes into the thing is what it takes to make it live.

12 / INNOCENCE

It may help for me to describe a class I once conducted, in an effort to improve the students' ability to form buildings from beings. I first asked each student to give an example of an innocent process of drawing or making ornament which they had most enjoyed. I was looking for something which had been truly joyful for them, not part of their student training. They gave various answers. As I listened, I noticed that the smaller the examples were the more true — that is, the more innocent they were, the less contaminated. Then one student said, in a very soft voice, that

he had enjoyed painting Easter eggs in his childhood. That was something that was pure joy, unaffected by guilt, or by a feeling that he must "do well." At first I could not hear him. He was shy about it, didn't want to repeat what he said. I persuaded him to speak a little more loudly, and finally we all heard him say, embarrassed, that he had loved painting Easter eggs.

I felt at once that this love, of all those which had been mentioned, was one of the most pure. It was simple. In that work, there is nothing except the egg and the pattern on its surface,

In the gaily painted Easter eggs the students made, they, perhaps for the first time, experienced
the real meaning of the creation of living centers and found themselves able to do it.

no mental constraints of what one "ought" to do — only the thing itself. No one really judges or censors the outcome — so it is easy and alright, not festering with complicated concepts about architecture when you do it.

So I asked each student to make holes in the ends of a raw egg, blow out the yolk and white, and then paint the egg, decorate it like an Easter egg. I made it clear that they did *not* have to use the fifteen properties. All I wanted them to do was to make the egg beautiful, to enjoy what they were doing.[8] Here are some of the eggs they painted. The shapes and spaces in the ornaments took their shape, and became what they are, just to be beautiful and to have the maker's depth of feeling visible and shining in them. That was the only principle which governed them. And this, I believe, is what one *has* to do to make a serious work. Naive as it sounds, it is this, too — I believe — that the great traditional builders did.

The students' other architectural work improved greatly once they understood that making a good building is more like the joyous work of painting an Easter egg than like the practical task of being an "architect."

13 / THE VISION OF MATISSE AND BONNARD

Matisse was one of the first 20th-century artists to bring this vision into a modern form. In his work, we see love in every shape. Each shape is lovingly made, lovingly filled out — the page, the canvas, is entirely made of beings which are loved.

Here, even the pudgy fingers, the spaces between the fingers, the rings, the woman's breast,
the necklace, the sleeve, even the space inside the sleeve, even these are beings.
Henri Matisse, Odalisque voilee, 1940.

I have told my students on occasion, when they are struggling with an architectural plan, failing to put into it this multitude of beings because they are too much obsessed with practicalities, and therefore blinded to the beings that must be made in every part: "Make it like Matisse. Show me a plan that looks like this cut-out of Matisse, in which each part of space is made with love and each part of space is positively shaped." In a building design it takes hours, sometimes weeks, for them to do it. But this instruction almost never fails.

The importance of emphasizing the beings, treating each entity as a separate building block

Here every cut of the scissors, every white piece of space, is lovingly shaped, each piece of the blue paper is a shape with which we have a relationship. This space in and around the woman's body, is fully loved, and fully made of beings. Paper cut-out, Henri Matisse, 1945.

In Pierre Bonnard's Nude in a Bathtub (1946), a profusion of living centers exists in the details and in the whole.

of unity, has been echoed in recent times by Bonnard, who, speaking of his most realistic paintings, said: "A painting is a succession of blobs that connect up and finally compose the subject, the piece over which the eye can stray without a hitch."[9]

14 / IN OUR OWN ERA

What does all this have to do with our world? Chartres was built in the 13th century. Bonnard and Matisse are possibly an avant-garde, holding visions of our future. But they do not yet represent the reality of freeways, motels, apartment buildings, or the world of mass construction. Our present world is more rough and ready: the majority of our environments do not contain the same multitude of living centers. And they do not, therefore, so easily contain centers which are beings — beings which remind me of myself. In many cases, rather, the world is more alien from us, more separated from us, its centers not developed as I-like beings.

Of course, even in our rough and ready world, there is some aspect of the being nature which appears. Here, for instance, is a place in Oakland, California, an ordinary street on Lake Merritt, which has some life. Somewhere between the trashbasket, the view of the lake, the styrofoam coffee cups, the people sitting at a busstop, the trees, and the markings on the road, there is some life. The joggers along the lake enjoy the glistening buildings in the dawn light.

Where does this life come from? It comes from the fact that many of these places are, though very weakly, self-like centers. The busstop bench is not much to look at. But here, across from the lake, people sit, talk, joke, shout. I sit drawing. A little girl watches me, and talks to me about the figures I am drawing. The bus comes — massive, but still a necessity, again a being at a low level which animates the street — and takes people home.

The buildings across the lake — at this distance I do feel related to them as beings even though, as buildings, they are really not so good. At five in the morning, the time when I took this photograph, they shine in the dawn light, each has its own distinctive character. Close up, they are ugly and impractical in many respects. But at this distance, seeing them across the lake, I feel them being-like, too. I feel related to them. And in part the people jogging also feel themselves related to the distant, gleaming buildings. So there is something of the being-world in the most ordinary scene. And I see it because I cannot help loving the beauty of the world, even the imperfect fragmented world.

Could these beings, visible or half visible in the banal reality, be transformed to become beings in a truer sense, as they are in this painting I made on that same day?

Sometimes I am mesmerized by the beauty of our joyous, ugly world. The Bay Bridge, for instance, I love it on that bridge, I love driving over to San Francisco in all its modern exuberance, and ugliness. There I seem to see a thousand beings in the world, when I am driving, and I feel the world is wonderful, nowhere is it so wonderful, it is only good, and glorious to be alive. The sheer beauty of that experience is shaking. I see the grey shining towers of the bridge, arcing above, the great X-braces of the steel; the cars, in their hundreds, crossing the bridge in front of me; tail lights, light of the city, light of the fog, sometimes the green light over the Bay, and the shining yellow light coming off the Bay water like phosphorescence. Then, every bolt-head on the bridge seems wonderful, the cars and lights seem like beings; the light in the sky, the edges of the clouds are beings, the rainwater on the asphalt is a being, the small lights of a plane in the distance, the dark edges of the roadway — all beings, all wonderful.

Is there, then, something as profound as Chartres in this modern world of ours?

Again, what I experience when I drive over the bridge, when I gulp in like beer the beauty of my existence — the lights on the road, the cars, the trees, the sky. The inner thing, the beauty of that freeway, the beautiful world which surrounds the freeway, which makes us realize how marvelous it is to be alive, for one second only, one day, to experience all this.

15 / A NEW VISION OF BUILDING: MAKING LIVING STRUCTURE IN OUR BRUTAL WORLD

So what does it mean to make beings in our world? We live in a world of freeways, bridges, Coca-Cola machines, advertisements, cars, office buildings; there are homeless people sleeping on the streets; a drug addict may be lying in a dark alley. High-priced, ugly condominiums line the beach. Trash cans. Hamburger stands. Used cars. Ugly as it is, it is also wonderful because it speaks,

The shore of Lake Merritt, Oakland, California. Here there are fewer beings, the centers are barely living.

Lake Merritt at Dawn, 5.30 a.m., Oil and digital painting, Christopher Alexander, 1995

The work of finding beings always starts at the very simplest level, as we see in our efforts to make rosettes in concrete, during a construction experiment from one of our building sites.

in some degree, of freedom, our freedom — driving a truck across the bridge, making something in the back yard, the struggling homeless person selling old shirts to eke out a living, the styrofoam cup which, ugly as it may be, allows me to have my cup of coffee as I drive along, singing, in the truck.

We cannot make the world over. We must accept our world, and within it, make our beings, in a fashion consistent with this world, and its demands, and its harsh realities.

So, I see the beings throughout the fabric of the world, I experience them. I can be aware of them in the beauty of the world — even the harsh, broken world. And I can paint the beings I see behind the scenes, bring them into existence, create a vision of reality, which shows the beings in the lake, or in the freeway.

But this is not the same as Chartres. In Chartres, the beings were not only seen and felt — they were made actual in the stones of the church, in the interval of silence in the footfalls within the church, in the glass, in the rooftiles, and in the hinges of the doors. That we do not have in our time. And, I believe it is not appropriate, it is nearly impossible for us, in our time, to have this perfection in light of the harsh cruelty of the world, the overpopulation of our planet, the inhumanity we are aware of, the unfairness inherent in money and education.

Strangely, I believe the beauty of the world is almost more touching, more profound, if this harsh, ugly world of ours, is married, mixed, with the more perfect world in which the beings are fully living. I believe that it is possible for us to create a world, less perfect than the world of Chartres, but perhaps even more true, in which both ugliness and beauty are reconciled. A world in which the banal street signs of Oakland are combined with the beauty of stones and cherry blossoms; a world in which the ugliness of poverty is accepted in a downtown city neighborhood, is laid side by side with the beauty of

Freeway At Night, Oil painting, Christopher Alexander, 1991

beings in a sidewalk, in a window; a world in which the dirty machineshop of a gas station and its Coca-Cola machine sits comfortable, and happy, side by side, with something inner. A world in which even the banality of the developer's cheap apartment can be illuminated with the beings in the window, or in the furniture, or in the car outside the door, and in the lights around the garden.

But it is necessary for us to *cross* that bridge. The beings we can sense in the freeway, and which can be painted, are not enough to sustain our lives, even in a modern form. I believe they must be welded into a newer structure, which we can so far only glimpse, in which both worlds are visible.

It must not be forgotten just how *hard* this is. At Chartres, the stones, the hair on the statue, the beautifully shaped triangles on the buttress, the foot of the column, the ornament on the belt of the statue, the glass, the individual pieces of glass, the roundels, the carvings in the ornament — each one is worked and worked until it is full of feeling and until, then, the self-like character is very deep. This is hard won. It does not come easy. But when it happens a living thing is made. And this comes, above all, from the impulse we call ornament: to fill living space. *Above all, then, a building is an ornament.*

This statement is difficult to grasp since, in the last two centuries, we have become used to thinking of an ornament as something trivial. I

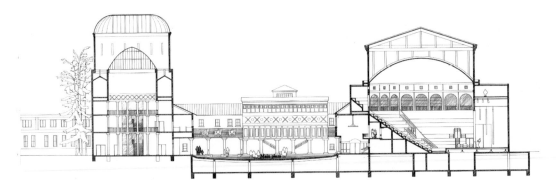

Each entity is distinct, and works as "something" in this cross-section of a design for the Mountain View Civic Center, Christopher Alexander and Artemis Anninou, 1989

was brought up during the middle years of the 20th century, in a family with (as they were then called) good middle-class values, and with an appreciation of art as defined by Beethoven, Raphael, Cezanne — the romantic meaning of art: art with significance.

I was astonished when, as a university student, I first read Josef Strzygowski, and realized that ornament *itself* is a profound thing.[10] The idea that the ornament on a carpet or the edge of an illuminated manuscript could be something of significance as a work of art — a concept not widely accepted or understood in 1950 — was a revelation to me, and something I never forgot in later life. It meant that Bach and Biber were as significant as Schubert and Beethoven — something that was not at all clear even as recently as 1950.[11] It meant that a Persian miniature might be as significant as a statue by Michelangelo, or even more significant.

My meaning, when I say that a building, to be living, must be an ornament, goes even deeper. What I mean is that this sense of ornament — a profound, organized object reaching to heaven — applies equally to a functional object: to a freeway, or to a car, or to a flower which is a living thing. There the word "ornament" is a profound comment on the contribution which something makes to the world, through its order and its relation to the world. When I take all that, and summarize it in the statement, "A building is an ornament," we get close to the meaning I have in mind. In this sense, the living centers, the structure of living self-like centers, created by the fifteen properties, is the utmost that a building can provide.

Preparing to finish this chapter, I want to hint, too, what the many-being character may look like in the buildings of our time. It will not look like Chartres. It will not look, I think, like the Bay Bridge with its glowing elements and lights. It will not look, directly, like a painting by Bonnard.

Shown here is a cross-section of modern urban civic space, at high density, a design for the civic center of Mountain View, in California. Unlike normal conceptions of urban space in which the car dominates and regular lots divide the space, in this conception every part is positive and being-like: the gardens are regular, shaped in themselves; the pedestrian paths have their own weight and integrity and are protected from the cars; the auditorium has a shape and existence as a thing in its own right; domes, and columns, and arcades exist as beings; even the car streets and parking places have weight as pleasant living space, forcing the car to move more awkwardly than is usual, to reduce its speed and pace, leaving each part with its life.[12]

In the preface of Book 3, I show a painting and other details of this project, to bring out its living character.

16 / THE LIFE OF THE ENVIRONMENT

I finish, then, with this conclusion: *The environment is good, or bad, according to the degree that its thousands and thousands of centers are pictures of the self, what we might call "beings."*

On the face of it this proposition appears scientifically outrageous, because the relation of the great environment in the world to our own person would seem irrelevant to its quality. Is it not absurdly presumptuous to declare that whether or not a certain street in the city of San Francisco works is in any sense dependent upon its relation with the personal self of you, the reader, who may be sitting in a chair in London or Baghdad? And is it not absurd to declare that the life of apartment buildings in East Oakland is independent of fire codes, cultural heritage, climate, cost, window area — but that it is dependent on the way these buildings are composed, or not, of beings?[13]

Yet that is just what I have come to believe. The practical matters of fire, cost, family structure, wall construction, structural efficiency, ecology, solar energy, wind, water, pedestrian traffic — all these have their place. Function must be at the core of everything.[14] But what governs the life of the buildings is not to be found in these matters, alone, but in a single question, always built on the foundation of these matters, but elevating them to a different level of understanding: *To what extent is every building, and the whole building, and every garden, and the whole street, all made of beings?* Asking this question is the right criterion to apply, because your self, and my self, and each person's self, are all somehow linked — either by similarity, caused by genetic and biological homology, or by some deeper connection — to one another.

The thought expressed by my conclusion, though it seems at first frivolous, is precisely the watershed between the alienated world of mechanism and the non-alienated world of life. I well know that it may take time for you to appreciate the fact behind the thought. You need to test it, experimentally, as I have done, for years. You need to examine each piece of the environment you come across from this point of view. And you need time to weigh its unlikely character against the fact that, nevertheless, it seems to be true.

To do this, you need to become clear in your own mind about the distinction between centers which are more like beings — more genuinely related to your self — and those which are less so. That in itself takes practice, and discussion, and honesty about your inner feeling. If you try to develop that ability, slowly, by observation and experiment, you will then be in a position to conduct the larger experiment of trying to judge the difference between places which have more life and places which have less life. You will then gradually become persuaded, I believe, as I have been persuaded in the last fifteen years, that this one criterion, absurdly simple though it seems to be, does correlate accurately with the presence of life in the environment. It is that empirical fact, once you encounter it for yourself, which may then persuade you of the truth of what I am recording here.

It should perhaps be said that the word "being," though I believe it is a true and helpful description, has such a heavy character that it cannot be used every day. In discussion with my colleagues, I find that we rarely speak about this "being" nature of the centers in a building that is being made: it is just too much to keep on talking about it. In ordinary discourse one says, perhaps, that a given bit of garden, or a given bit of ceiling, should be "something," more of a "thing," more solid, more of an entity. That kind of language conveys the same essential meaning, and is easier for everyday professional discussion. But those of us who speak like that, and think like that, know that it is the *being* we are referring to; and in our hearts, as we work, it is this I-like nature which we try to reach, in every particle.

In thirty years of work, struggling to understand what makes the difference between buildings which have life and those which do not have life, I have found no other formula of this simplicity, nor of this accuracy.

NOTES

1. I do, of course, use the word "life" here, as I have used it throughout the four books, to mean that life in buildings, towns, and artifacts, where we experience life to be present, thus going well beyond the usual biological meaning of the word.

2. Book 1, chapter 4.

3. Francis H. Cook, HUA-YEN BUDDHISM: THE JEWEL NET OF INDRA (University Park, PA: The Pennsylvania State University Press, 1977). The original treatise HUA-YEN I-CH'ENG CHIAO I FEN-CH'I CHANG, was written by Fa-tsang in the 7th century.

4. That nature does this is amazing. It is discussed, in part, in Book 2, chapters 1 and 2. The possibility that biological matter may indeed be considered as made of thousands of living centers, and that this is not a metaphor, but a crucial insight into the nature of matter within living and non-living material systems, is discussed in the conclusion to Book 4.

5. Le Corbusier, TOWARDS A NEW ARCHITECTURE (London: Architectural Press, 1927) trans. by Frederick Etchells from VERS UNE ARCHITECTURE (Paris: Editions Crès, 1923). See illustrations of grain elevators, ships, planes, automobiles, and other industrial artifacts and machines, pp. 81–138.

6. "Individuelle Designkonzepte: Christopher Alexander," in FORUM DESIGN, LINZ, 1980 (Vienna: Löcker Verlag, 1981).

7. The fundamental process is described, at great length, both in Book 2 and in Book 3. In Book 2 it is defined in chapter 6. In Book 3 it is discussed throughout, with hundreds of examples. The process is once again, defined, and summarized, in the preface to Book 3.

8. I was virtually certain that the difficulty they had putting the fifteen properties into a building, would go away when they painted the Easter egg, and that they would probably use the fifteen properties anyway, without even thinking of them or worrying about them.

9. Pierre Bonnard, in "Conversation with Teriade," VERVE (Paris: Teriade, 1947), Volume V, Nos. 17 and 18, quoted in Sargy Mann and Belinda Thomson, BONNARD AT LE BOSQUET (London: Publications Office, South Bank Centre, Royal Festival Hall, 1994), 78.

10. Josef Strzygowski, ORIGIN OF CHRISTIAN CHURCH ART (Oxford: Clarendon Press, 1923).

11. Now, thirty years later, this will seem obvious to the reader. However, in the musical climate of 1955, when these thoughts were first becoming clear to me they were far from obvious — and seemed like mysterious and forbidden revelations.

12. It is made in the very same way, and in the same spirit, that the students made their ornamented Easter eggs.

13. Even the language of "beings" is difficult, even uncomfortable for us modern people. Consider a parking lot. In discussion with my editor Bill McClung, I asked him, "Do you now have the opinion that a good parking lot, a sensible one, and a good one, is made of beings?" "No," he said, "that is pushing me too far." "But," I said, "you have accepted that a good parking lot is one that is made of strong centers. You have told me that you almost completely accept the truth of chapters 4 and 7 in Book 1." "Yes," he said, "that seems true to me." "What then is the difference? I have defined 'being' as a shorthand expression for a living center that is made of other living centers. Why do you accept one, and reject the other?" "I do not feel comfortable using this language," he replied. "Yes, I too, do not usually use the language," I told him. "But the fact remains. A good parking lot is one which is made of beings. This is true for you. And it is true for me. It is this *fact* with which I am most concerned."

14. I have described how this works in Book 1, chapter 11, and throughout Book 3. But what we now call function only plays a partial role in the formation of a being.

CHAPTER FIVE

THE PRACTICAL MATTER
OF FORGING A LIVING CENTER

1 / INTENSIFYING SHAPE

Let us go back to buildings, and building design. What is it like actually to do it? What is it like to make a building, or part of a building, which has the being nature, in an ordinary action?

For ordinary work, Chartres is too much. Such things are, for the most part, almost inaccessible, at least as daily work. But whatever we do, in simpler tasks, we may always aspire to make a thing which lives as a center, and which has the being nature. Even then, it is hard work, intense work. It is something we must concentrate on, to get it done right. To approach the subject of the I-like character as the substrate of living centers, let us go back to elementary examples, and discuss the way they have been made, and how we must behave, mentally and physically, in order to achieve the being nature in our ordinary work.

2 / UNITY ACHIEVED IN A GREAT BLOSSOM

In my experience, few human-made objects more powerfully demonstrate the nature of living structure and the role strong centers play as the building blocks of wholeness, than certain ancient carpets.[1] Because of the devotional nature of these carpets, and the likely cosmology of their makers, we may reasonably assume that they were made by a slow process in which spiritually inspired weavers, probably women, sought to reach the eternal, to make "a picture of the face of God." Here, then, is a pure, premodern context. Here is pure abstract art, only two-dimensional patterns of color on the plane, and we see the creation of intense living centers and structure.[2] How did they do this?

An unknown weaver sought to fuse her heartfelt self, her own experience of self, with what I am calling the I — No mind, or the One, or God. She made a God-like carpet possessed of a unity of being — its I — and that carpet is suffused throughout with living centers. She succeeded, I believe, in creating a living connection to the I, linking the structure of life in herself with the structure of life in the thing she made, and in so doing I believe she was also probably making connection with the structure of life in the world.

This is the nature of order. It is life constructed of living centers. It is life, I believe, constructed by the same means we have available to us today, although we must learn anew how to make such inspired living things.

What is crucial about the best centers we observe in the carpets, in the illustrations that follow, is that individually the component centers are I-like. Each one in its way reflects and reminds us of the I. That is where its detailed shape comes from. *The intention that each part should be I-like is what governs its shape, and is what makes the weaver weave this shape, and not some other.*

It may help if I ask you to try using the powerful instrument of your own ability to feel the I, to reach the I in the blossom fragment shown here from a Caucasian carpet. It was possibly made in the 13th century. Please try to concentrate on the fact that your own I is connected with the I that appears in this carpet blossom. I want to create some sense, in your mind, of how *hard* this is, to have "found" or made this shape, how much effort it takes and must have taken for the weaver to reach something I-like in the blossom.

Yet the blossom illustrated here *is* like this.[3] We see the deeply etched shape of the two diago-

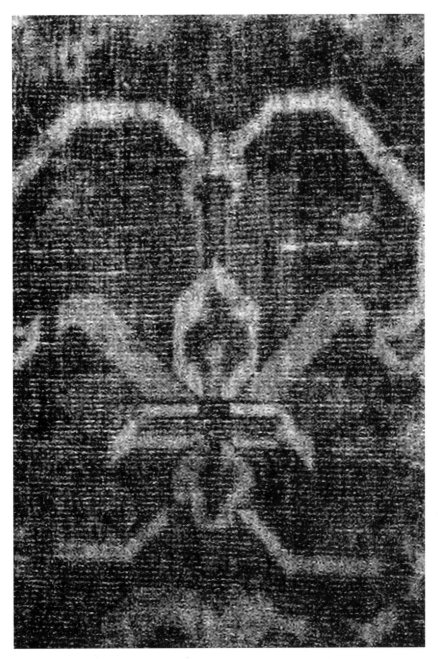

Pure and forceful, this very worn 13th-century blossom carpet fragment in my possession is shown with computer enhancement of the image.

nals going away from the base of the flower, and the shape of the tips, drooping over. It is in the precisely drawn hexagon at the core of the whole thing, filled with a mysterious dark cloud. This is the recursion which I have discussed at length in Book 1. Living structure has appeared more and more deeply as this recursion progressed.

The recursion of living centers we see in this almost incredible blossom figure is more than a fascinating intellectual idea. It shows, I think, how plain hard work by the maker, when correctly oriented, made the recursion happen, and simultaneously connected the structure to the I, rooted it deeply in the I. Here, in this

Two other versions of the blossom.

The lower one is beautiful, but mainly decorative. The upper one does have some force, but its connection to the eternal self is not as developed as it is in the great blossom on the previous page.

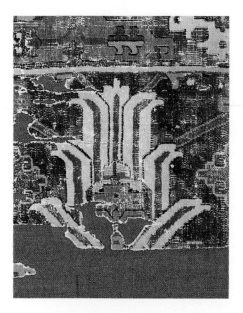

15th-century version of the blossom design in a carpet from Herat.

16th-century version of the blossom in a carpet from Tabriz.

It is extraordinary to compare the different examples from the 16th, 15th and 13th centuries, to see how powerful the great blossom of the 13th century really is.

design, as a matter of practical work, we may see how the recursion, applied to the formation of these centers in the design, makes them nearly *shine* with their geometric forcefulness.

This can be seen vividly, by comparing this particular blossom with two other similar-looking blossoms from other carpets in the same tradition.[4] In these blossoms, the weavers — though following a similar drawing — achieved a living connection to the I less strongly. The blossoms are more schematic. Though elegant, even beautiful, they just do not have the force of the main example.

I have no doubt — indeed, I am quite certain — that the weaver who made the 13th-century blossom that I am showing experienced exactly the same feeling regarding the forcefulness of the blossom as a being, and its effect on her as she made it. This giant blossom, so much more powerful than the other blossoms I have shown, was reached by a person who consciously, knowingly, yearning for it, reached to touch the I, and did in this case reach it, and in doing so opened a door which we, centuries later, can go through again.

I do not mean this as a metaphor, but as a literal description of what I believe this weaver must have been doing, to create this thing. In my own experience of this process, it cannot be done merely by working at details, or by working at individual centers, trying to make them good. To achieve this last bit of power, it is necessary to focus directly on the I, to yearn for it, to seek it out, to strive towards it, to try and try to reach it. Under these conditions, one actually tries to embrace the I, reach for it, try to recreate the feeling of the I, in the stubborn material — but one feels it, is aware of it, feels it drawing you, as a poetic muse, or as a limitless horizon.

I am afraid these words *sound* too poetic, too romantic, too flimsy to capture the hard intention of my thought. My difficulty as a writer, here, is that I mean them literally.

I know of only one way to do this thing, and that it is to conjure up the I, in one's mind, in the unseeing eye, strive for it, reach out for

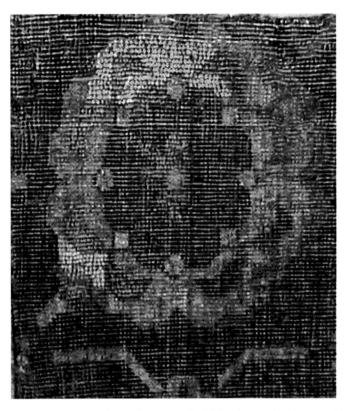

A far more powerful blossom. Compared with the blossoms on the left hand page, this blossom, which is another part of the 13th-century carpet fragment of page 113, is a far more powerful and subtle center.

it. Although this may sound almost like nonsense, my experience is that it is literally true, and that when one does reach for this state, then something happens, and the actual material that one creates can, on occasion, be moved, modified, and that the structural part of the hard work then comes into play, and sometimes helps to create a thing which really and truly does connect us with this I — at least to some extent.[5]

What we see happening in the solidification of the main blossom on page 113, and in the blossom on this page, is a process in which the individual component centers, their relative sizes, their individual existence as living centers, one by one, always including, of course, the centers which form the spaces between centers, and above all the unity of the whole, are all being progressively refined until a unique and powerful figure of great impact arrives upon the scene. From humble beginnings, it achieves a connection to the I so strong that one must call it being-like.

My sketch of the blossom center shown above. Even though this sketch shows the detailed forms and centers that make the blossom I-like and gives a hint as to why it is profound, still, I have not captured the intensity of the real thing at all.

The shapes visible in the upper photograph are more mysterious, the subtle relationships of tone and color create a more magnificent being — altogether more wonderful, more I-like, than I could capture. Each detail has more life, each subsidiary center is just a little more a picture of the I than I could manage to catch in this sketch. That shows how much the real I-character depends on the detailed attention, the detailed hard work, which makes every center as much as possible an I.

3 / EMERGENCE OF A "BEING" FROM THE FIELD OF CENTERS

What we see happening in the two-dimensional case of the carpet, is, I believe, happening all the time, throughout the three-dimensional world, whenever true unfolding happens. All kinds of structures — bricks, mortar, arches, roofs and streets — were all shaped, at certain times, by certain cultures in ways that had similar profound effect. Tough-minded creation of deep centers, worked together with other centers to create, sometimes, remarkable depth of structure all around us. And then we see living structure appearing, in a plethora of forms, all over our planet, in profusion.

In nature this seems to happen by itself, merely through unfolding. In things made by human beings, it happens when the maker concentrates deeply — intently — on the I itself, as far as it exists in him, in her, as far as he or she can perceive it, focus on it, draw on it, draw it out, and make a thing which comes from it, is of it, is of its form, is of its origin. This is not different from doing what has to be done to be practical. The farmer who mends his fence and makes it I-like is far more intently tuned to the

harmony of nature than he will let on to a city person who does not understand.

That original I-like matter has then been composed to embody unity, and shows us what we are ourselves. It is this focus on each living center as an I-like being, elaborated, intensified, which brings the emergence of life to a building. That is the main task: to connect to the I, the creation of a being.

I show, here, an extremely simple example of such a being arising in a building. The carpentry shop my apprentices and I built for the CES office in Martinez was a simple, ordinary structure, with massive wooden columns and beams. After we finished building it, I looked at it. It was straightforward, but somehow it lacked its life.

I spent several days trying to imagine what the building would it be like if it existed, more or less as it was, but was more filled with life? After a few days, I began to get a clear vision of the building with a large white star on the central bay. At first it was just a vision, caused by the fact that the three bays of the building formed an invisible center in the central bay, which needed to be completed. So in practice the star came from my ability to feel the field of centers in the building as a whole.[6]

I went to the office a few days later, and tried to explain this to one of my apprentices. It didn't make sense to him completely. At a certain point, I picked up an old piece of styrofoam and a penknife, and very quickly, without making any measurements, cut a big star from the styrofoam sheet. I hacked it out, as fast as I could. The star was crude and jagged. Not all the points were pointed. The arms had different lengths and different angles. I went outside, and put a single nail through it, to hang it up. The whole thing took literally no more than forty seconds. But it did bring the building to life.

Somehow, within the particular field of this

The giant star as cut by hand

The star in its position on the barn. How strong this irregular star, with its spontaneity, compared with the perfectly drawn star below.

building, with its massive columns and calm, equal structural bays, this animated and irregular star created life and had being. If the same star had been in another context, it probably would not have made sense at all. But here, it had a being quality. Here, it connected to the I.

Now a surprising thing happened. I assumed that the crude star I had cut out was just a mock-up, and that we would use it to cut a "perfect" star. We began trying various exactly regular nine pointed stars in the same place. I got the average diameter of the star I had made. We tried to get the average distance of the inner points, and one of my apprentices then cut star after star, trying to find a regular and "properly made" star, which would catch the life in the same way, have the same feeling. He and I kept on trying for three months. None of the regular stars we made had the same life in them.

Finally, I gave up. I acknowledged that the irregular, jagged star had some kind of life in it which was perfectly in tune with the building, and that I was just lucky to have found it. It was

best to leave it alone. We cut a permanent star exactly on the template of the jagged styrofoam which I had originally made.

It is not the method which is hard to understand here; the *structure* is hard to understand. Even after looking at it, it is not easy to say analytically why the irregular star creates a more profound being than the regular star. But it does. Somehow, it brings the thing to life. This is the spirit. This is the contact with the I.[7]

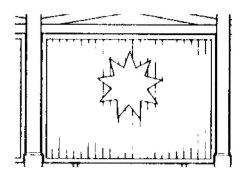

A drawing from my office which shows the lack of living substance in the exactly drawn star

4 / BEINGS IN ARCHES, SPACES, AND COLUMNS:
THE EXAMPLE OF WEST DEAN

The site in the distance, and the river Lavant

The site, two flint cottages, and, on the right, my earliest mockups of brick and flint where I first tried to find
combinations of material that felt right on that land

West Dean Visitor's Centre: my first detailed sketch of the brickwork on the north face of the building, 1994

I now describe the West Dean Visitor's Centre, a public building I built in England, where some of these concepts are visible. The upper photograph on the left-hand page shows the character of the site before I started work. All that arose later originated from the feeling and wholeness of this site as it was then.

After I had only the roughest idea of where to place the building (see lower sketch) I then began, within no more than two or three days, to build assemblies of bricks, flints, block, concrete, and stone, to find out what kind of structure, and what kind of colors, would best preserve and extend the quality of light that dominated the

Shown here are some of the early samples we made, while I was trying to grasp the true being nature of materials, on the site, and to find what balance of materials would best create the whole.

feeling and wholeness of the site. Some of these early tests are visible in the lower photograph on the left page opposite (right-hand side of picture), others in the photograph shown here.

What began with a few very light sketches drawn on the site, was followed by a period of experiment in which we built very ordinary mockups on the site itself to find out what assemblies of brick, mortar, and flint had the capacity to feel harmonious in that place. That was followed by

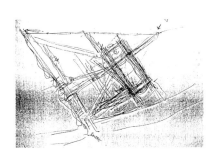

An early site sketch, working out building position

Standing on the open slab, one could already feel the character of a bay window, looking towards the view. On page 127, one sees the later development of this window as it slowly took shape.

Getting a first fix on the position, size, width, and splay of the large southern windows. By placing chairs, and sitting down as if one were in the finished building, it was possible to give the window opening the being-character that emerges most naturally from this situation (middle left). Testing the size, width, position, and extent of the tiny stairs that come from the gallery into the main dining room—looking, once again, for the exact proportion and size which would make these stairs connect us with the I (lower left). Sitting in a mockup of the upper gallery, and testing the splay and depth of the window reveals, to get their shape and character just right (bottom right).

Our only remaining photo of this model. This first wood and cardboard study model of the Centre was made brick by brick — each brick a separate piece of balsawood — allowing us to visualize and work out a coherent structure pattern which would also be harmonious and beautiful.

Here we see the handling of brick, headers, flint, and stone, that we worked out, course by course, to give the cornice at the top of the north wall a true I-like character. It took many experiments, and every course had to be placed by eye, in mock-ups, to make the whole thing come out right.

an intense period in which students made models for me to find out the physical possibilities of making a structure which captured the feeling I had shown in the sketches.

Then the real work began. We built that building and — step by step, board by board, stone by stone — we learned what it meant to make that building solid, and to make the structure congruent with the space.

I can hear someone saying to himself as he lays out the structure of a building, "Here I am doing just what it says in Alexander's book. Every column is a center. Every bay is a center. The structure is working just fine. But the result I am getting from this process is just the same dead stuff! What should I do?"

The key, of course, is whether you work hard enough to make each element have its life. Does each column have life? Does each beam have life? Is the shape of the bay just that one which makes it have life? Does the volume of the bay have life? Is it true, when you stand in the room and look at the result, that you are met and overwhelmed, and left in peace, by an overarching subtle life which exists in the volume, in the space, and in the members?

The issue that this will — if done faithfully — produce the goods is not in doubt. What might be in doubt is whether you have the stamina, the sheer will, and stick-to-itiveness, to make sure this happens, *because you keep rejecting every version where it doesn't happen*, until it *does* happen. Do you keep throwing away versions because they do not have enough life? Do you wait, at each step, until you get the best life in the member that you *can* get?

Ultimately, the internal coherence of the building as a structure is what counts above all else. The space and structure, dark and light, form interlocking systems of centers. Often, towards the end of the fiddling around, the spaces are adjusted so that the pattern as a whole becomes beautiful. Deep coherence within the whole, and the feeling of the whole pattern, ultimately gives life to the building. That is far more important than any too-detailed consideration about any one part.

At each moment in the West Dean project we were dealing with the solid mass of the concrete, brick, flint, and raw poured concrete. These materials were, in our hands, day to day on the site, like clay which we molded to form the next small piece.

During some parts of the work I was in California six thousand miles away. John Hewitt, my partner and the engineer in charge, was on the site with two apprentices. Nearly every day we exchanged fax messages, phone calls, and

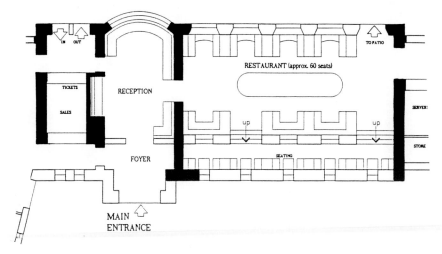

The plan of the building, with the four cross-walls shown in black. These four cross-walls, when pierced with arches, would begin to get a being-nature in themselves.

sketches, going through the possibilities of the next step in painstaking detail. Often we sent faxed pictures and photos of our next step — samples of how the brick would look if it were two and a half inches high, or two inches high; what the corner would look like if the brick arrangement went three then one then three then one, and all the other possible combinations. There was not one piece of stonework on the building we did not discuss like this as the project evolved, and where we did not use the fundamental process to choose the thing which made the greatest — and best — impact on the whole.

To give the reader some idea how extreme this plastic treatment of the building was, this nearly sculptor's attitude towards every bit of brick, I will describe the emergence of the arches in the interior.

5 / EMERGENCE OF THE ARCHES

When we made the initial drawings of the building for a building permit, I found myself unable to visualize just how the cross-structure of the building worked. I could visualize the space rather clearly, and the structure, I knew, was a big thick wall, with a ring beam, surmounted by a wooden truss and rafter roof.

But I also knew that there was some missing thing, something I had not visualized. I found out what it was only at a relatively late stage, when the walls were already going up, after we had the exterior walls up to about three meters and could experience the rooms, interior space, windows, gallery, and the smaller rooms. Walking about inside, I saw a tremendous lack of coherence in the cross-walls. They did not make sense. Structurally they were OK, but as space, the rooms did not end properly. In fact, all the cross-walls of the main building, four of them, were missing something. I had sensed that this problem might be coming. During the design phase I had wondered how the cross-walls were going to work, but at that early stage there wasn't enough information to make a realistic judgment about what to do. Intentionally, I left it as an open question to be solved when we could experience enough to make a realistic judgment.

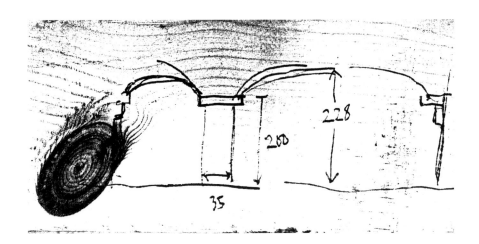

Early sketch of a cross-wall, made on a piece of scrap wood, after it first became possible to judge the presence, scale, and effect of the arches in these walls.

I began to see that what was needed in the cross-walls was an arched structure.

So far, we had beautiful openings in the long walls — doors and windows, these beautifully, gently, arched openings. But there was nothing yet of a similar character in the cross-walls. To make the space feel three-dimensional, whole, solid, and at one, a similar series of arched openings was needed — I felt — in all the cross-walls, something that would tie the walls together structurally, that would make openings in the cross-walls correctly.

It was only a small step from that thought to the thought that the very same arches, if introduced into a system of four walls, would provide a kind of cross-structural stability which would reinforce the action of the massive walls and ring beam.

We then began to examine each of these cross-walls, one by one. They told us rather simply what to do. All we needed was a kind of language which would allow any combination of arched openings to be created, and we could lay out all four cross-walls without difficulty.

This final touch (at a fairly massive scale), not foreseen or contemplated at the time of the initial drawings or even construction, is what now holds the building together most firmly, gives it a solid and definite unity as a thing.

As this unity came into being, so did the being nature of the centers themselves, individually, together, all at once. The thickness of the members feels profound. Windows are the right size, in the right positions. Alcoves are the right size. Ceilings are the right height. The coherence of the whole has no need to be wrong on these points. It is careful consideration of the feeling of these kinds of things which informs the whole and makes it sensible.

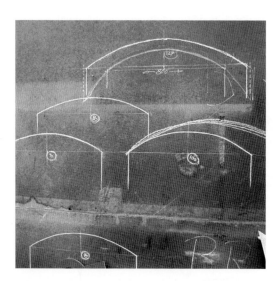

These sketches of the arch curves, made on the wall of our construction shack and very exactly drawn, gave us the ability to see the difference in being-character between curves of only slightly different radius and span. From them, we finally got the templates of the curve we used to build the forms. The top sketch gave us the best line for the bigger arches; the central, inner sketch gave us the line for the smaller openings.

Something approaching true living structure: a sequence of arches in the building.

One of the openings, as it developed in rough block and concrete

6 / DETAILED DESIGN OF THE STRUCTURAL COLUMNS

In order to understand the character of this one act — that of being guided by the emergence of a being nature in the elements that are physically created — it is useful, perhaps, to follow it through a step or two further. Having decided that these arches and columns were to be in the building, we began to try and visualize the columns which might support the arches. We did this using cardboard columns, made at full size, and placed in the building.

My greatest surprise came when I began to notice that the heavy, friendly character of the building led to — and seemed to need — very low, squat columns. As we made our experiments, I noticed that the columns that were actually best in feeling were so low that the capital of the column was literally grazing your face, at head height, no higher. It seemed insane at first.

How could a column capital be so low that a person would bang their head on it? But in fact, it was a correct intuition. Even though the arches are low, there was just enough lift in them to carry each arch well above head height, from the capital at some 1.70 meters to about 2.10 meters in the middle. And it is this low column capital that makes the arches seem so intimate, that make the whole building intimate, because it is literally in a position where you can touch it, smell it, see it right in front of your nose. All this is reinforced by the squat, thick character of the columns themselves and by the rather heavy capitals, all cast in concrete.

Here the feeling of intimacy in the building, the correct carrying-through of the building's emerging feeling, created the size, weight, and position of the columns — and their almost ani-

While trying to work out the column capital with the most being-quality, we made a series of full-size cardboard mock-ups, and looked at them in the space where they were going to be built. In the end, all of these shown here were rejected, and the much simpler shape shown on page 128 was chosen as the one which had deep life most profoundly.

The bay window and its many subsidiary centers beginning to develop

A being-quality finally appears in the windows themselves.

*Early cardboard and wooden mock-ups of the furniture we were designing for the building.
After reconciling the feeling of the furniture with the actual place while it was still in construction,
we then built the tables and chairs according to these mock-ups.*

Arched entrance to the main dining room. The column capitals as finally decided, and built.
West Dean Visitor's Centre, Christopher Alexander and John Hewitt, 1996.

mal character. There is a stubborn smallness, just right for the building, seeming big and grand, yet intimate.

The emergence, then, visible in the photographs, is of a being-like unity, both in each part of the building — to an extent — and in the whole. Just as I have written in chapter 4, there are now ten thousand beings in the buildings. And because of the patient effort in each individual entity, the centers became, in some cases, not only living centers that carry some emotional weight and character.

The arches have a little of this quality. I show one of them on pages 124–5. The columns have something of it. The squat, rugged capitals have a little of it. The steps and the windows, splayed, did manage to reach something of this character.

What we reached falls far short of the great beings in the history of art: the stones of St. Mark's, the window glass of Chartres, the brass rubbings of Thailand, the domes of Isphahan. Nevertheless in some small measure, by reaching for the I, we did manage to pluck, from that ground, some small portion of a thing which is like self, which speaks back, which makes one feel one's ordinary association with the brick, and tile, and concrete, and with the gravel on the ground.

If you look at the arches, the capitals, the rooms, the terraces, the ornaments, the windows, and the ceiling of the main dining room, I believe you will feel some measure of the I was reached in some of them. And because of this, standing in the building, you do feel relatedness with much of it.

*The finished West Dean Visitor's Centre, West Sussex, England,
seen from the park, 1996*

7 / A WALL

To show the universal character of the process of seeking a connection to the I, let me go to the simple example of an ordinary wall in California. Compared with many walls we may experience today, this wall is fatter, and lower, and heavier. You may say that it is so simple, it could hardly have opportunities in it for centers, or for the being nature. But this is not true.

Even in the most ordinary judgments about height, volume, mass, and overhang of a utilitarian wall, the same factors come into play, the same questions arise: whether it is connected to the self, or not, whether its individual centers are connected to the self, or not.

Let us begin with the height of the wall. The first idea was that it would be a wall for separating the property from surrounding land, yet of a height to sit on. Usually such a wall would be, say, about 16 inches high. But in this instance, I got some concrete blocks and placed a few of them to indicate a wall 16 inches high, and 16 inches wide. It was not enough. If I asked myself, then, did this fill me with the I of that place, did it create and strengthen a permanent relation between me and that land, the 16-inch wall was not substantial enough. I added some boards to find out what *would* be substantial enough. It became both higher, and a little fatter. At a certain stage, as increments of dimension were added, one could see the being of the wall existing like a bull in a field. I had made it in such a way that the wall would feel, as far as possible, related to me.

When I had the height fixed, then I went on to the width. I tried to imagine the wall of that height, having a width across the top that would be related to me as deeply as possible. Again I made experiments with my hands, with sticks, now also with cardboard — until the thickness of the wall took on substance and became, as far as I could make it so, related to me.

When it came to the actual making of the wall, once again I used the same process: I tried to find a way of making the substance of the wall so that I could feel a glimmering of I in it. I felt it had to be solid. So I chose to make the wall from a pallet or two of old cement sacks which had hardened and were going to waste. The dimension of the solid, useless sacks of cement was just about right for the thickness, and would make the wall beautifully solid, too. I physically stacked the cement sacks, to make the volume and profile I had decided on, following the contour of the land gently up and down. Then I shot the sides (covered the surface of the old concrete sacks with Gunite), so that the wall surface took on a rough and straightforward feeling. I used a Reed gun, with a small nozzle to get fairly fine control over the surface of the concrete — but not too fine.[8]

Once the body of the wall was shot, I went on to make the top. Most important, I had to fix the dimensions of the top — its thickness. I tried to settle on a thickness for this top, which would make the wall as deeply related to me as possible. I used scraps of wooden boards, propped or nailed in position, and stood back to judge them, and the volume of the top they made. I tried variations in the thickness of the top and the total width across the top (one-and-a-half to four inches for the thickness, and from seventeen to about twenty-two inches for the width.)

You may ask just how those judgments were to be made. The experiment is simple. As I have written in Book 1, there is a classic experiment, where we compare two things, A and B, and ask which of the two seems more a picture of my own eternal self.[9] With a bit of concentration, and paying attention specifically to the *thickness* of the top (only), you can answer that question. If you *only* pay attention to the thickness of the top, nothing else, you will find it easier to make the judgment successfully. If it seems hard, you can also ask in

A wall that is simple and massive and contains, in each part, the self.

which of them the wall makes you feel more whole, in which the world seems more whole, which makes you more connected to the world, which of the two walls would make a better gift for God. All of these questions allow you to form a judgment and to decide whether A or B is more like the eternal I. You choose from *that* pair — say you choose A. Then you try another pair, A and C. Again you ask these questions. This time, C seems a little better. Next you compare C and D. C remains better. Now compare C against E. Still C seems better of the two. The reality of these questions is easily visible in the accompanying sketches. Among these three, and focusing on the thickness of the top in relation to the height, the bottom one of the three sketches has the greatest depth of feeling, and the most "I."

But one has to go on, finer and finer, refining and refining. You compare C with F, something you had not thought of before, a minor variation of height or thickness. And again you ask of F and C, Which is the one which is better picture of your own eternal self? Again, C remains the stronger of the two. By now you have perhaps concluded that you cannot find a G, or an H which does better than the C. So the decision to make C is settled.

Then once that is done, you go to another question. For example, once having the thickness and height of the top, there is a remaining variable — the dimension of the overhang. Does the top hang over by one inch, or one-and-a-half inches, or two inches from the wall?

A

B

C

Three sketches of the wall cross-section, with different degrees of emotional weight.

Since the top is already set, this is a judgment about the position of the surface of the wall. Using the same question as before, you can now make *this* judgment. In this instance, yet another center is involved, the center that lies in the angle between the wall surface and the overhanging top. As nearly as possible, you make that space positive, so make even *this* center which sits in the air next to the overhang as much a being as possible.

By the time you have done your best on each of these decisions, the wall begin to have the being nature — at least to some degree. It makes us all feel related to the I. Even though it is an ordinary wall, made of old hardened cement sacks, it has a touch of the eternal I in it.

And to this day, people like that wall. They sit on it, drink beer on it, children run along the top of the wall. All of them love the wall, because the wall is related to them, and they feel related to it. It increases the relatedness which people feel in the world.

8 / CATCHING A BEING IN COLOR

In color, just as in form, the same process dominates. To make something which is really whole, we play and play, and try and try, until we catch a being shining through.

A painting of Fra Angelico's shows the being-nature very strongly. I will try to reconstruct a process that I believe he must have experienced in making it. The painting is Fra Angelico's *The Dream of Innocent*, a small panel at the bottom of The Coronation of the Virgin, now hanging in the Louvre. It is a beautiful example of inner light — the clear sequence of colors, from the white to the grey to the pale blue to the black to the deep blue to the shimmering pale golden white, centering around the deep blue. Here we can see the being-nature very directly, and can, I think, even glimpse the way this being-nature appeared in the painting as it was created.

You remember the strange being-like "creature" I have been advising you, in chapter 4, to seek as you search for the I. Can you not see this

Fra Angelico: The Dream of Innocent

strangeness — this I-like "creature" — in this painting? It is not the strangeness of the subject matter that I am talking about. It is a quality in the color itself, in the feeling of the color, caused especially by the interaction of the black with the other colors.[10]

Suppose, for instance, that you decided to paint something with this beautiful blue. Can you see how you would probably place other bright, nice colors around it, try to make it interact with reds, or yellows? Can you feel the intensity of the strange way in which grey and white and black, and pale blue, are all used to make and support this luminous blue?

I can try to make my point more operational. Let us imagine the picture when Fra Angelico himself was painting it. Imagine some moment before the black of the door and priest's robe had been painted, but when everything else is more or less already there. (I have no idea whether there was such a moment, but it doesn't matter.) You can see what I mean by putting your hand over the picture, so as not to see the black parts. Do you see that the picture loses much of its haunting character. The blue is still beautiful and intense, but far more subdued. Above all, the feeling of spiritual depth in the painting is almost completely gone.

Now, try to imagine yourself in the position of the painter at that moment. Try to imagine that some color is needed, somewhere, to complete the picture. You search your mind for what this color might be. Do this, just as if you were actually painting the painting, and looking for the inner light, in the way that is described in

chapter 7. Try to imagine the possibilities — red perhaps, or purple, green, deep yellow. All these are conventional, and they do little to produce the inner light.

And now imagine that you suddenly have the idea of putting black there. To get the feeling of such a moment, cover the black up with your hand, look at the rest of the painting and its colors — and now try to imagine, in your inner eye, your mind's eye, some areas of black on the left.

Can you feel the strange intensity which this suddenly creates? And can you see how immensely surprising it is? It is strange, almost haunting, and somehow it seems odd that just this color would produce so magical an effect. And do you see how especially strange it is, that the black could affect the blue at such a distance? Often the colors that affect a given color are near it, but here, this black produces dazzling light, almost on the other side of the picture, where the blue is. It is this inner light, which the black creates — which makes the blue shine, from so far away, and in such a strange, intensity — this is the inner light, in a form where you especially see its being nature.

In this example we begin to see how the process of looking for inner light, and the process of looking for the slightly mysterious being — like a haunting melody, half heard, suddenly grasped — really works. It is very hard to do. But it seems to be a real, and attainable process, which each of us, if we only concentrated enough, might be able to do ourselves.

9 / THE HAUNTING MELODY

Many years ago I lived in India. In the village where I lived, at night especially, some sounds travel a long way. (The country, when I was living there, was less industrial, so in general it was more quiet.) I remember walking around in the

fields at night, and once hearing in the very far distance, very, very far off, a flute playing in the night. You could barely pick out the strains of that flute music. Twilight time; and there I was just listening, and trying to, trying to get that haunting melody; I could just hear it, and then I could just partially hear it. It was way, way off in the distance.

Searching for the being in a thing is rather like that, whether you're searching for it in a building, or in a window, even in a windowsill. I get a glimpse of something that is starting to happen. I hear something like this haunting strange distant flute. My feeling is like the quality of hearing such a sound. Then I look at the thing that I am doing — the building, or the window — and I ask myself: Is it in fact carrying that haunting sound, or not?

———

Learning to see wholeness, or self, in a thing is not unlike the process of straining one's ears to catch that haunting tune. I look at the thing which I am making, I keep on looking at it, and slowly I begin to see a spirit in the thing. I become aware of an emerging wholeness, only dimly heard at first. It is hard work to see the wholeness. But if I do work hard, don't take the thing for granted, don't assume that I am doing the right thing, but if I do search for the wholeness, and keep assuming that there may be more to see, if I can only strain my ears a little harder, then I can move towards it, and gradually produce it more and more.

This is the process which really produces life. I become aware of the self beyond the thing as a very faintly heard tune that I can hardly hear. I strain for it, try to listen for it, try to catch it, and then as I make the thing, as I develop the field of centers in the thing, I do my best to bring this half-heard whisper of a being out in the material.

NOTES

1. Some of the carpets I am speaking about here are described and discussed in detail in Christopher Alexander, A FORESHADOWING OF TWENTY-FIRST CENTURY ART: THE COLOR AND GEOMETRY OF VERY EARLY TURKISH CARPETS (New York: Oxford University Press, 1993). The argument of the next few paragraphs is taken from the carpet book, pages 31–42.

2. Ibid.

3. Ibid.

4. Both these blossoms are also from A FORESHADOWING OF TWENTY-FIRST CENTURY ART. The Herat carpet is illustrated, in full, on page 239, and the Tabriz carpet on page 258.

5. For a detailed discussion of the being-nature as it appears in carpets, ibid., pages 79–88.

6. The mental state which allows me to grasp this field, is that which I described long ago, in appendix 3 of Book 1, where I described the laid back, passive, receptive state of mind needed to feel wholeness. It takes time to learn to open one's self, remove one's active mind, and allow awareness of the wholeness *as it is*, to generate the being.

7. The teachings attributed to Hermes Trimegistus, and practiced by the medieval masons, included some knowledge similar to what I am describing here. For instance, in Nigel Pennick, MYSTERIES OF KING'S COLLEGE CHAPEL, Thorson's publishers, Wellingborough, Northamptonshire, 1978, pages 87, 92, 93, we find a number of figures which clearly show systems of centers as the underlying structure to be followed by a mason.

8. For discussion of the Reed gun, and the process of shooting gunite, something I used to do a great deal at one time in my life, see Book 3, chapters 15–16.

9. Book 1, chapters 8 and 9.

10. See this book, chapter 7.

MID-BOOK APPENDIX

RECAPITULATION OF THE ARGUMENT

1 / INTRODUCTION

In the course of this book, I shall arrive at some remarkable conclusions about the nature of things and the nature of the world we live in.

Before launching into them, I should like to provide the reader with a kind of road map. In the four books, there are many kinds of facts that have been introduced, and there are a few more still to come in the remaining chapters. By themselves these many kinds of facts are multifarious. They touch different subjects, and different practical issues, different theoretical issues.

My purpose, of course, in all this, is to help people make a better architecture: a more living architecture, that is good for the surface of the Earth, good for people. My assumption is that many of the ideas, facts, and observations I have put before the reader, are potentially helpful in this regard. They have the power to help people do a better job, and to approach more closely the goal of reaching harmony, in the large and in the small, on the surface of the Earth.

But I know very well, from my own experience, that it is hard to use the multitude of facts, ideas and concepts, so long as they remain disconnected, fragmentary things that can be understood only one at a time. In my experience, one does not fully reach the stage of being able to use this material effectively, until one also understands the details as part of a coherent, larger picture. Only then, does one have sufficient grasp of the whole, the motivation, the mental ability to work with these complex ideas most effectively — when one understands them as part of one, coherent, sensible picture, in which each thing makes sense in relation to every other. Without such a unified coherence in one's understanding, one cannot put the material to sufficiently good use.

I therefore aim, in this last book of the four, to establish a single and coherent view, in which all these ideas make sense together, and are visible, perceivable, as part of a single whole.

To help the reader arrive at such a state, where all the details make sense together, I shall, in the next few pages, begin to arrange the assorted facts that have appeared along the way, and show how one may infer from them, the existence of a larger picture, one which is capable, of providing a vehicle that allows the artist to act with understanding, and in which acts of building, acts of planning, are coherent within a larger framework, so that it all makes sense.

2 / THE POSSIBILITY OF A COHERENT VERIFIABLE THEORY

Let us begin by asking: Is the theory which I have begun putting forward in the early chapters of Book 4 true, or is it merely a fantasy, a dream for children? Might it actually be a true description of things around us — so true, that it might ultimately change our picture of the space and matter in the universe?

Some readers, kind enough to be enthusiastic, do see it as a possible picture, a helpful and poetic picture. Their enthusiasm is, of course, positive. But it is still a far cry from thinking or acknowledging that it *might* be true, to seeing that this picture actually *is* true. If it is poetically satisfying, one can be inspired by it. It can help people to think about architecture in a more constructive way. But, if the theory were actually *true*, if our picture of the nature of space and time *requires* modification to include the I, and if such a modification of our physical picture ultimately turned out to be a real feature of the universe, then that would be a discovery, an intellectual

waking up of a very different order — something vast in its implications.

When thinking as a scientist, it must of course be this question of truth which occupies one's mind. It is for this reason that I have kept records, and written down my observations, for the last thirty years, as carefully as possible. As a result of my observations, and as a result of my experiences in the field — as an architect building buildings, as a craftsman making things, as a planner laying out buildings and precincts and seeing them come to life — I have gradually become convinced that this theory, or at least something very much like it, is indeed *likely* to be true. In short, as a scientist, I have gradually come to the belief that the I must be real. And as a architect, I have also become convinced that the I is certainly real in buildings, and must necessarily play a fundamental role in architecture.

I shall now try to summarize the combination of observation and scientific argument that has led me to these beliefs.

3 / THE ARGUMENT FROM VERIFIABLE DETAILS

The argument hinges, first of all, on the fact that the theory of centers *works* in practice. By that I mean (1) that it works empirically in getting good results in architecture; and further, (2) that it works as a coherent theory in which the various pieces fit together nicely and make sense of the whole. These two criteria, verifiable results

in many details, and the fit and coherence of the details with many pieces as a whole, are, in the end, the two most important scientific criteria for deciding the truth of any theory.

It helps, I think, to start by taking the solid bits of fact which have been established, without too much fanfare — treating them as isolated and useful bits of information about the way the world works. In this modest sense, I believe the reader will agree that many of the concrete ideas put forward in various places in these four volumes do work empirically. Their results are verified or potentially verifiable. Like any other evolving science, many individual details of the theory have predictive force.

For example, in Book 1 there is an idea of life in things as an objectively existing quality that exists in the world, and which can be measured by experiment. I put forward fifteen structural properties which are associated with this kind of life. They *work* scientifically. By this I mean that they have predictive force. They enable us to predict the distinctions people make between buildings with more life and buildings with less life. They also do this successfully for works of art, and for other living systems, too. This leads to the idea of living structure as a *general* kind of structure which exists in nature and in artifacts to the extent these properties are present.

Book 1 sets out to describe wholeness *as a structure*, thus replacing vague ideas of the whole with the idea that what we refer to as "wholeness" in a configuration is a defined global structure which can be established for any configuration. The system of nested and interdependent centers is an operationally defined approach to capturing the wholeness. Life occurs to the degree that centers help each other and cement their wholeness: the helping between centers is caused by the fifteen properties, and on the recursive appearance of these properties among the centers from which wholeness is made. Although the precise nature of a center remains partly mysterious, nevertheless it is clear that the idea of these fifteen properties defining and linking centers, *works* in the sense that it predicts, with some accuracy, which structures will be living and which will not.

These ideas also provide insight into the *functional* nature of buildings. With the same tools we gain scientific insight into the nature of function in buildings in many specific cases, and into the close connection between function and ornament — previously unexplained and often denied in contemporary thought about architecture. This again has predictive force because it adds to our ability to predict which kinds of buildings will work well.

Further, the degree of life that a system has is in some fashion connected to *ourselves* and correlates with the degree to which the system is seen as a picture of our own selves. This, too, is confirmed experimentally. So this idea, too, works empirically and gives answers to questions about value in architecture and art, questions which, until now, have been left largely unanswered in the last hundred years.

In summary, then, the concept of living structure provides us with a precise, reasonable, and sharable way of understanding many phenomena. Book 1 gives us a powerful set of tools with which to understand architecture, and with which to understand thorny problems of value that, up until now, have remained almost abandoned scientifically and have been treated, instead, as matters of individual taste and personal judgement.

In Book 2, the structural ideas of Book 1 are extended to a dynamic analysis of *process*. The argument of Book 2 leads to verifiable accounts of the ways in which people succeed in *making* environments possessing life. It also leads to verifiable techniques for judging processes according to their ability to help generate living structure in towns and buildings. The life-filled buildings and works of art which were examined from a static point of view in Book 1, when looked at dynamically, are seen to be the products of some very definite kind of step-by-step operations: the operations of unfolding. Reasons for the good quality of traditional buildings and towns come into view simply and directly as a result of this dynamic analysis. This theory, too, *works* — at least approximately — since it leads to verifiable distinctions among processes from the point of view of their efficacy in creating living structure.

As part of the analysis of unfolding, the idea of a structure-preserving transformation is introduced as an essential concept arising from wholeness. From what appears in Book 2, one may conclude that living structure can only be created by structure-preserving transformations. This surprising and much deeper conclusion is also verifiable in principle. A number of experiments demonstrating it for buildings have been done so far.

In the latter half of Book 2, particular types of structure-preserving transformation are specified as the necessary underpinning of any successful social process capable of creating living structure in neighborhoods and buildings and rural land. Living processes are defined as linked chains of applications of structure-preserving transformations, and one sees verification of the fact that these living processes are uniquely able to create living structure in the environment. In many instances, the effect of living processes on buildings and environments is described in detail, and their capacity to create living structure has been documented. All this is testable and has been tested in many cases. Once again, the ideas have predictive force.

In Book 3, the idea of structure-preserving transformations is married with practical information about the care of land, layout of buildings, creation of public space, the placing of buildings on a site, the development of building volume, creation of building plans, the interior design of rooms, the development of building structure in its engineering aspects, the creation and construction of myriad building details.

Useful and verifiable insights are generated about the ways in which practical and effective town plans, buildings, gardens, and rooms can be built to be in harmony with their surroundings. Even the making and construction of buildings, the way in which the microstructure of buildings supports or does not support the macrostructure is seen in a new way, with verifiable criteria for success and failure. All this has beneficial practical results, and has practical results even in the realms of materials, engineering, and construction. It creates practical tools which make it possible to design and build buildings which have real, verifiable, degrees of life. This is, once again, what I mean by saying that the theory has predictive force and that it works.

In Book 4, I have introduced the concept of the I in the early chapters. It is more adventurous and perhaps less well-founded empirically than my other results (at least so far). But it provides a practical underpinning of considerable power, by showing us how the strength of centers is associated with personal conditions which significantly change what one is able to do when building living structure. Empirically, it seems certain that it enables artists and builders to make their work more profound. As far as I can judge, the ancients who used similar methods also reached deeper, *and were able to go still deeper* in their search for living structure by using some version of this conception. Although the empirical aspects of Book 4 may so far be the least well-tested, still, it can hardly be denied that the idea of the I as present in material configurations does have empirical content, and that this content is effective in creating good results. It therefore sets forth an astounding, if controversial way of understanding the foregoing theory, and does it in a way that cements it to rather deep aspects of human nature.

4 / THE ARGUMENT FROM COHERENCE

Let us now go to the *coherence* of the theory. What had to be done to make this theory of architecture work? What was the origin of its empirical success? To answer this question I ask that the reader come with me while I briefly retrace the path I have followed for thirty years while reaching these results.

I started out trying, simply, to make a practical theory of architecture: one which makes sense of things we know and feel, and which helps us to make better buildings. That apparently straightforward task led to the construction of the theory put forward in Books 1 and 2 and 3: A theory which allows us (as previous theories of architecture perhaps did not) to recognize the essential life in things, to recognize the objective nature of this quality, and to ask again and again: What *is* the puzzling and recurrent structure of this life? What process can create this living structure?

But as part of my practical effort to get a sensible, consistent, and truthful theory, I had to make several key decisions about the underpinnings of the theory. In any science, getting a workable theory is usually a roundabout process where one tries again and again, muddles along, accumulates facts, tries to formulate apparently disparate facts in language which makes them fit each other. In effect we are always searching for the most *coherent* picture, and along the way we try various different formulations of the underpinnings of the new theory, worrying, from day to day, which of them makes the theory work most simply and most elegantly (and, if possible, does so in a way that sheds the most light on many of the currently unanswered questions and annoying puzzles in the field).

In the course of this work, the underpinnings shift and change as the theory gets refined. For example, at the very beginning of my work on this theory (around 1975) the fifteen properties described in Book 1 played a fundamental role. These fifteen properties were, at the beginning, the underpinnings of the whole theory. Later, I realized that these properties were not the most fundamental aspect of the theory, and that they occur as consequences of an even more fundamental structure — the system of living centers, and are simply the ways that centers support each other to create more life. So the fifteen properties shifted within the theory, and turned out to be consequences of the existence of centers and their interdependence. The idea of centers then came into the limelight.

Later the *dynamic* aspects of wholeness and the idea of structure-preserving transformations

became even more important. It turned out that centers have to be understood dynamically in order to be understood at all, hence as results of unfolding and structure-preserving transformations. And it turned out that living structure, which I had first identified statically, is more profoundly understood when it is understood as a product of dynamics.

In many ways like these, during the last thirty years, the theory shifted again and again as I continually tried to make it more and more practical, more and more effective, and — as far as possible — more and more true to real experience.

Today the idea of a center remains at the heart of the theory. Centers are fundamental as the building blocks of wholeness. They are fundamental to the unfolding process and to the idea of structure-preserving transformations.

Yet throughout the last thirty years, even while it has become clear that centers and their structure play a fundamental role in all living structure, the actual *nature* of centers still remains partially elusive. From early on, the mathematical nature of a center was partially clear, and could (in principle) be made entirely clear. But the *content* of the idea, what a center *is*, that remains uncertain. To pin this down, to provide underpinnings for the nature of centers, I therefore had to introduce other theoretical foundations. These may be summarized in four propositions, all expressing some further explication of the nature of wholeness:

Proposition 1: Each center is a focused zone of space which may be characterized by saying that, to some degree, space in that zone itself comes to life.

To make sense of the idea that life is an observable phenomenon which appears in greater and lesser degree in *every* part of space, I suggested that the degree of life which occurs in things must be understood, not only as a construct of the organization of space, but also as a quality which happens to the space *itself*. According to this idea, the pure geometric space *itself* has the capacity to come to life. In Book 1, chapters 4 and 7, I invited the reader to accept this idea as the basis for a new kind of calculus, a calculus in which the life of each center was defined recursively, as a function of the life of all the other centers it contains. And I think I managed to establish, in a very preliminary fashion, that *if* we accept this, then it gives us a tool with which we can essentially calculate the greater and greater life that occurs in things. Like a recursive arithmetic, by assuming it is true for limited cases, we can then use it in bootstrap fashion to explain more and more complex examples, deeper examples. It gives us a new kind of practical handle on things. It gives insight into structure of buildings, natural systems, and works of art.

But what *is* all this? Remember, I am arguing (and necessarily so, to make the calculus work) not that life exists in some *mechanical* fashion, as a complex mechanism built out of simpler parts. What I am suggesting, instead, is that pure life *itself*, as an attribute of space *itself*, increases in some measure according to the organization of the space. The degree of life of any given portion of space, thus appears like a color, or like an overall attribute — a *quality* which appears in the space itself, along with the structural organization that also signals its appearance.

If true, this idea would be as startling, I think, as Maxwell's idea, introduced in the 19th century, that light is created by electromagnetic waves in space itself. The idea that space *itself*, vibrating, should create light, was startling to people who thought of light as something that occurred *in* space. Maxwell's idea must have been almost impossible to accept in 1865. Even now, when I myself really stop and think about Maxwell's idea, I find it very hard to grasp — truly to grasp — the fact that it is true. Yet we now know that it is true.[5]

The idea that life, too, might be an inherent attribute of space itself, as I have suggested, is no less hard to grasp. Yet I believe it is a necessary consequence of the theory I have put forward.

It is needed, conceptually, to make the recursion in the mathematics work consistently. And this implies that it is likely not merely to be an artificial device, but that it is actually true.

Proposition 2: To the degree a center is a living center, it is also a picture of the true self, and — very startling — has this character for all people, not just for any individual.

According to the discussion in Book 1, chapters 8–9, the degree of life of each center is correlated with the degree to which that center is a picture of the self. To the degree it is alive, it reminds us of our own self. In this suggestion I laid the groundwork for the concept of "I" which appears throughout Book 4.

I first proposed this in Book 1, as a form of *measurement*, simply because it works experimentally and practically. It gives us one way of getting agreement among different observers about the degree of life in a given wholeness. It is a useful and effective way to find out what degree of life there is in any given center. I am not sure that, at root, it is not the *only* way we have of getting a reliable measure of life in things. As far as I have been able to determine, nearly all — and perhaps all — of the effective ways of measuring degree of life experimentally are related in one way or another to this experimental method that depends on our awareness of self.

It is remarkable that such a simple experimental method provides agreement on such a subtle subject. As I explained in the discussion of oriental carpets (Book 1, page 228), the criterion allows complex judgments of quality (which could normally be made reliably only by a museum curator or connoisseur with many years of experience) to be made successfully by a person almost without training, after a few hours. The criterion seems to short-cut a process of learning which would normally take years.

But the mystery is hardly yet plumbed. After all, degree of life, though measured by the degree of self-ness, and discussed in other empirical ways throughout Book 1, is not only reflective of aesthetic or emotional life in a building. It is indicative of *actual* life, of *practical, functional* life. It includes the way a parking lot works. It includes the life of ecological systems. It includes the practical way an auditorium works from an acoustic point of view. It even includes the practical efficiency of the entrance to a house and the structural efficiency of the Golden Gate Bridge. What is there in the way things are hooked up in the universe, that can explain such a deeply surprising correlation?*Why should the practical beauty and efficiency of a girder in a bridge have anything to do with I?*

Why should centers, in a structure which has *practical* life, in any sense at all resemble the human I, the self which each of us experiences at the core of our being? Why indeed, should what appears as my self, and what appears as your self, be in any sense similar? And why should it be that the things of the world, rank-ordered by the degree of life they have, have approximately the same rank order for you, and for me, and for almost everyone else?

Remember, too, that these phenomena are not limited to human artifacts. If it were true only for human artifacts, we could perhaps explain it by claiming that the artists who made them, consciously or unconsciously made them in such a way as to make them resemble the human self. If we assume that there is enough uniformity among different persons — a species-wide psychological core having to do with similarity of structure in our cognitive make-up — we might then reasonably expect that artists could "see" this psychological core, and could then put it into the centers of the buildings and artifacts they make.

But, as I have pointed out in both Book 1 and Book 2, the structure of living centers appears in *nature*, too, not just in buildings and works of art. It appears in snowdrops, in waves, in the billowing clouds, in mountains, glaciers, and rushing streams. It appears in a fox, in a snake, in a butterfly. It appears in grains of sand. What reason might there be, that the centers which appear in these things, and which are

created by the apparently mechanical process of nature itself unfolding, would *also* resemble your self, and my self? Why should they resemble the self at all? Why should the self resemble *them*? There must be a connection, under the surface, which accounts for the correlation. Without proposition #2, the theory does not cohere.

Proposition 3: The structure-preserving transformations which continually modify one wholeness in space and replace it by another that preserves the structure of the first, slowly cause space to be filled with unfolded I-like centers.

This view of the unfolding process presents us with yet another mystery. The unfolding of wholeness is modest and conservative. It governs the emergence of all structure in nature (I have conjectured). It governs the emergence of structure in building and in art. It is related to the gradual intensification of that structural wholeness which exists naturally in space. Nevertheless that structure is essentially mathematical in nature. As a result of this unfolding action, in nature as well as in art, space slowly generates centers which are more and more deeply alive, and which more and more deeply reflect the human self. Thus the I-like character of space — if it exists at all — seems to arise physically, in both nature and in buildings, as a result of the unfolding process.

Why might *this* be true? On the face of it, as a mathematical process, the process of unfolding itself has nothing whatever to do with self or I — as far as one initially understands it. It is merely structure-preserving. The process of a wave forming in the ocean is not apparently connected with I. Yet it creates a structure which does profoundly connect with the I in me. The process of the unfolding of a buttercup is not apparently connected with my I. Yet again, what it leads to does then profoundly connect with my I almost as if it knew beforehand that my I existed.

The cumbersome explanation that we appreciate these natural forms, and recognize their naturalness, and *therefore* feel linked to them, does not really explain the sense one has from the phenomena, that the I-ness which develops in them is really *there* — not merely an after-the-fact invention of our perception. Once again, proposition #3 is more simple, and is inevitable. Though startling, with this proposition, the theory becomes more coherent, and more graspable.

A fourth proposition, also needed to understand the theory deeply, may be culled from the material I have put forward so far in Book 4.

Proposition 4: Only a deliberate process of creating being-like (or self-like) centers in built structure throughout the world, encourages the world to become more alive.

Here we come to the last of these four propositions to crystallize in my mind: the one I myself understood last. As I have said, it has become my conviction, through observation and experiment, that the successful maker of life consciously moves towards those structures which most deeply reflect or touch his own experience of I, his own contact with the eternal and universal I, his inner feeling, and consciously moves away from those which do not. My experience is that this does not merely create places which are pleasant, or liked, but that this process then creates places which are profoundly practical, harmonious, adequate for conduct of life, and respectful of ecology and all living forms.

If you look at the pages of Book 3 you see examples of living processes in action. Although many of the works illustrated are my own or the work of those whom I admire, nevertheless I believe it is still true to say that many of these things do have as much life as most that have been built near the end of the 20th century (possibly even a little more than most). So to some extent the process defined in this way *does* work, *does* create life. The effort of creating I-like centers, when pursued honestly and carefully, does create living structure in the world.

My conclusion is that careful construction of the world, according to the principle that every center is made to be related to the true I of the maker, will result in a world which is practical, harmonious, functional. If this is true, astonishingly then, it would appear that the safest road to the creation of living structure is one in which people do what is most nearly in their hearts: that they make each part in such a way that it reflects their true feeling, in such a way that it makes them feel wholesome in themselves and is, in this sense, related in the deepest way to their own true I.

For someone educated in the 20th-century way of looking at the world, this is enigmatic, if not ridiculous. It means that a world constructed in the most personal and individual fashion, made by people who are searching deeply to follow the nature of their own true I, their own true selves, will be — in the most public, objective, and universal sense — a world which is functional, adequate, and harmonious.

The enigma which arises, then, is that the process by which human beings create the world in their own image, gradually creates a living world, and this is — apparently — the best, and most efficient way in which a living world *can* be created. Of course, the phrase "in their own image" requires that it be the *true* self they are looking for; and implies that this larger process of building the world cannot be separated from each person's personal search for the true self.

From the appearance of I-like phenomena throughout the occurrence of natural systems, it would appear, too, that the ordinary process of physical nature, efficient as it often is, also works for some reason when it makes connections with the same I. This is true, apparently, whether it occurs easily — as it does in nature by itself — or with great difficulty as it does when created as a result of an egoless effort by human beings. And those centers which unfold most smoothly remind us *most* of our own I.

In the next chapters I shall try to give a glimpse of the I itself, as nearly as I believe that we can actually see it. Then in the remaining chapters, I try to show, in further ways, what it means to behave, live, and work, within the knowledge that this I is real.

PART TWO

What I have presented in these four books is intended to become a part of a new science — a first sketch of a new kind of scientific theory.

Since the creation of a work of building must always be, at root, creation of living structure, I have built to the best of my ability a picture of living structure and of the processes that can generate living structure. The picture is sufficient, I believe, for working architects to carry in our minds, a vision of our task.

But this picture necessarily touches physics. The existence of living structure, as I have defined it, requires modifications in our physical picture of the world, not only in the picture which we have of architecture. And, in the most subtle phases of this work, we are forced — I believe — by the arguments presented in Book 4, to go still further. It is not enough merely to have a picture of living structure, but necessary, also, to recognize that there is something ineffable, a mystical core in things, that is deeply related to our own individual self, and that THIS — *not something else — is the true core both of matter and of architecture. That, too, must find expression.*

CHAPTER SIX

THE BLAZING ONE

THE UNITY THAT SPEAKS OF I

I now embark on the most ambitious, and possibly the most thought-provoking chapter in the four books.

To make the reader share with me my sense of what is really happening in the architectural examples where life appears, I shall now try to describe something — a feeling so remote from our ordinary sense of things, that it may have to be called *meta*-physical — truly beyond physics.

However, even here, in this metaphysical discussion, I try to keep to the straight and narrow of experience. Although what I shall describe would be far-fetched if viewed first as a physicist's picture of the matter in the universe, I shall first describe it, simply, as my experience. I hope the reader will accept that it is indeed my true experience. This — what I describe in this chapter — is how I experience the reaching for the ultimate unity when a building or an ornament is being made. It is also how I experience its effect when it *has* been made. Far-fetched or not, this is what appears to me to be going on, this is how I *do* experience the presence of the mysterious and ultimate quality that can occur in a made thing.

The experience concerns the universal I — how it is felt, how it appears when it comes into a work, what it appears *as*, how it functions in establishing a relatedness between the work and the person and the universe.

Somehow — whether it be in color, or in a harmonious garden, or in a room whose light and mood are just right, or in the awesome wall of a great building which allows us to walk near it — some placid, piercing unity occurs, sharp and soft, embracing, tying all things together, wrapping us up in it, allowing us to feel our own unity.

What, physically, is this unity which seems to speak to us of I?

1 / THE FAINTLY GLOWING QUALITY WHICH CAN BE SEEN IN A THING WHICH HAS LIFE

When I look at a thing which has a living quality, sometimes I am aware of it, almost as if it is faintly glowing. I am aware of something like light — not actual light itself, but something softer, something very like it — in the thing. The more it is alive, the more it seems faintly to shine.

In my later years, as I have encountered this sensation more and more concretely, and with more and more certainty, it seems to me, that I am seeing God, the glowing of all things, shining out from that old brick wall, or from that bush, or from that face, or from the flowers in a vase.

It is the same life, already described so many times. But in the end, this is what I am left with, the sensation that somehow, in this living thing, there is somethig faintly luminous, there is something streaming from it, something visible, and something real.

It has been said that God is immanent, that all matter is imbued with God, that God is the ultimate material of the Universe. And that may be so. But if so, why is it that this shining forth of God is visible more in some things than others; why is God visible more in some events, and less in others. What causes the life in things; what causes God to be more visible in one thing, more visible in one moment, less visible in another.

The moss garden of Ryo-an-ji, Kyoto

Gold and mosaic ceiling, Baptistery, Florence

This small, humble panel, made of marble strips, is inlaid into the west wall of the Baptistery, Florence, 11th century. Though small and rough, it impresses us as reaching the depth of mystery, merely by its quiet shape.

2 / A PSYCHOLOGICAL EXPLANATION

One rational explanation for the existence of this I — one which would have been consistent with 20th-century modes of thought — is a psychological explanation. Let us suppose that all living structure happens to be a structure which is related to certain (presently unknown) deep structures in human cognition. These cognitive structures, when they occur in the outer world, might easily somehow convey the sense of "self." In this interpretation, the structure of all living matter would be related to a fundamental part of human cognition. Living structure therefore *seems* "self-like" when it appears in things.[1]

According to such a psychological explanation everything with life would *appear* to be made of ten thousand beings simply because of the coincidence between the structure of every living system (in nature or in architecture), and the structure of self as experienced cognitively. What I have been calling "I" would then be no more than a name for the structural universal, common to the cognitive self, and common to all living centers. We would see it, potentially, in bridges, walls, columns, roofs, buttresses, and streets whenever they have living structure. The fact that living centers appear self-like or being-like would then merely be a coincidence — but a very useful one which gives us a natural way to judge the depth of living structures in the world around us.

It is quite possible that this is true. But, even if it is true, this explanation does not correspond to *all* that we feel when experiencing the I, when experiencing the relationship between the old wall at Ryoan-ji and ourselves, when visiting the Baptistery in Florence and looking at the black and white marble floor and on the wall under the golden ceiling-dome of the mosaics.

More vital than that, it does not explain how, or why, we have the sense that this I is beckoning us, leading us on, pulling us towards it, trying to help us reach it, trying to help us infuse the lesser works of our own hands, with this same living substance.

3 / POSSIBLE EXISTENCE OF A SINGLE UNDERLYING SUBSTANCE

To make these experiences understandable, and our picture of the I more complete, I am going to add an element to the physical picture I have given so far of how things in the universe may be.

The detailed content of this picture contains features which are quite surprising, because these features require a different conception of physical nature from the one that we are used to.

I am going to start with the idea that the I exists physically, that there is some plenum, not part of the physical space and matter, as we have modeled them in Cartesian science, but nevertheless there in fact, at every point of what we think of as space and matter. This is another possible way of expressing the I-hypothesis. In this version, we postulate that there is, in the universe, and underlying all matter, a single plenum or Ground. Above all, it is single, and it is personal. This plenum is the "something" which shall simply be called "I."

However, I now add the idea that it really exists everywhere, it is single, underlying all things. It may exist in another dimension curled up in space, or it may exist in some other linkage we cannot yet imagine. I am viewing this plenum as being perfectly connected to all the physical reality that we know about, like a deeper reality which shadows and underlies the first. For the time being I shall say that this plenum is either "I" or "Self," a huge, single Self, underlying all the matter in the universe.

According to this second version of the I-hypothesis, this plenum of I, or ground, really exists. It is not a metaphor. It lies behind, and inside matter and space. It is enveloped by them, and communicates with them, stands behind them and beneath them. It is everywhere. Wherever matter is, this I is also there.[2]

Now I am going to say that some kind of tunneling can occur, to connect physical structures in our familiar physical domain with the single I-stuff of the plenum. I use the word "tunneling" in the sense that modern physics uses it,

to mean a direct connection between two regions which are in different dimensions.[3] I am asserting that some connection can occur between the physical structure of the everyday world of matter and the underlying I.

The most common example of this tunneling would be the one which occurs in the experience of I and self which each person has. In a human body, which is at least in part a structure of matter alone, the experience of I or "self" arises. In spite of various sociological attempts at explanation, this everyday experience of our own selves is not yet understood in a satisfactory way by physics. But it would be relatively easy to understand if we postulate the plenum of I, universal and general, linked to matter, and if it were a fact that the matter in a body, once organized, is able to make direct connection with this I. We would then experience the bridge or tunnel to the I *as our own self*, not realizing that it is in fact merely one bridge, of a million similar bridges, between the matter in different beings and the I. That is to say, in such a conception the I which one of us experiences as his own self is not a private and individual thing, as most of us imagine it to be, but a partial connection of our *own* physical matter (my body) to this very great, and single, plenum of I-stuff.

Now I am going to say, much more generally, that *every* living center in the matter of the universe — even the smallest center which is induced in space — starts this kind of tunneling towards the I-stuff. And, the stronger the center is, the bigger the tunnel, the stronger the connection of the matter to the I. That means, that every beautiful object, to the extent it has the structure which I have described, also begins to open the door towards the I-stuff or the self.

4 / THE BLAZING ONE

Let me say more about the plenum of I, from the point of view of our experience. When a thing

has life, our experience is that, somehow, in being with this thing, or in looking at it, we catch a glimpse of something luminous in it, of a deeper more significant domain or realm beyond. Some reality, more pure and more fundamental than the one we are used to in our everyday world. I can say the same thing in another way by saying that in a very beautiful tile, or in the fragmentary Parthenon, as I gaze at it, I feel clearly as though I am looking through at heaven. Of course, this expression may seem far-fetched or romantic. However, in the conception I am describing, this should be understood as a literal and structural feature of material reality, not as a metaphor.

Let me try to describe it in another way, to bring out this realistic quality. If there is indeed an all-embracing single plenum of which we are catching glimpses, whether we call it "I" or "self" or heaven, it is reasonable to ask, What is the structure of this domain? Could it, for example, ever be given a coherent mathematical description? The answer is that it could not, in principle, for a very simple and fundamental reason. Of necessity, those things which we describe as mathematical structures — insofar as we can describe them as structures — are not truly *one*. They are — in our description — *multiples*. They are, necessarily, made up of various elements with relationship between them. We have to use these elements in our descriptions, because it is only through using elements and relationships that we can describe the structure. But what is achieved in an *actual* thing when wholeness occurs? It is not some multiple phenomenon of interacting structures but actual unity. That means "meltedness," "one-ness." This actual unity cannot be described as a structure. Yet it is this actual unity which is the source of life in the things we admire, and the goal of all our efforts when we make a building or a work of art.

Let me now go back to the plenum of I. Instead of calling it "I" or "self," I may also assert that what is in this deeper domain is pure unity. I assert that this domain exists as a real thing; that it is parallel to the material world, but that it is inherently incapable of having structure, because it is pure "one." But it is occasionally visible. At least it is potentially visible, some of the time, under some special circumstances. It becomes visible when the structure of a strong field of centers gently raises the lid, lifts the veil, and through the partial oepning, we see, or sense, the glow of the Blazing One beyond.

What I am saying, then, is that this pure "one," which may be like a blazing furnace or intense light, is partially available to our inspection.

When I see the beautiful tile, or walk into the beautiful building, it is as if I just lift up the corner of the flap and temporarily see into that blazing "one." It looks like heaven. The idea, then, is that every part of our physical world is shadowed by this parallel domain of I-stuff, and that each part of our ordinary world, if it is given the right structure, will lift the flap or open the door, and give us a glimpse into that domain.

That is what happens when we are in the presence of a work of art, to the extent it has true living structure.

5 / WHAT, THEN, IS A CENTER?

To a scientifically minded person this description cannot help but seem fanciful. To some it will seem absurd. Nevertheless, I have come to believe that it — or something like it — is a necessary feature of physical nature, and that without it we cannot hope to understand the real na-ture of art, or to understand what we are doing when we make a building. Although the picture is undoubtedly far-fetched, and may be wrong in its detail, I believe the general outlines of this picture are necessary to explain the facts coherently.

I also believe that this proposal helps us to make sense of nature — not only art — in a way which overcomes, once and for all, the dichotomy in our understanding of the nature of things, which we have experienced ever since the era of Descartes. That is because it asserts, essentially, that underlying all matter is this plenum or substance which is entirely "I." The self is connected to all matter; all matter is connected to the self.

In the light of the picture which I have just painted, let us return once more to the key question: What is a center?

If you go with me in assuming that underlying all matter there really is a ground of I, as in my model, you can see the answer. Behind matter, or within matter, there is the ground, or the domain of I. Each center, then, would be a window on the eternal blinding light of this domain. The nature of space and matter is linked to this eternal I in the following way. Any center which appears in space, to some extent opens a window to the I. If the center is a weak center, the window is tiny, the glimpse is tiny. If the center becomes more powerful, the curtain is pulled back a little more. If the center is very powerful, and has life, the window is bigger, and the center allows us to experience the I or self, permanently. A great work of art makes a permanent connection with the I. To the extent that it comes to life, it works as a window to the I, and reveals this I.

According to my thought — or, if you wish, according to my model — it is the nature of space and matter that they are linked to the I in this fashion. They reveal the I to the extent that any center which forms in space, does come to life.

In the matter which hovers over the ground, and is anchored in it, in the fabric of matter/ space, each center which is formed is in essence a window to the ground. If you prefer, you may imagine it as a camshaft, a structure of centers which has the ability to lift the veil, to lift, as it were, a small trap door like the cover on a flute is lifted off the hole, by the action of the levers. The recursive structure of centers, inherent in the field effect, lifts the trap door, and reveals the ground. When we are in contact with a living center, in some degree the center itself enables us to see through to the domain of I, to blazing unity itself.

Within this picture, space is a material whose most important feature is its capacity to form centers. As I have explained in Book 1, centers are formed by a geometric bootstrap structure in which each center makes other centers more alive.[4] Now, I would go on to say further that the life of a center is a phenomenon in which the center, like a window, makes contact with the plenum of absolute unity. At the same time, because this plenum of absolute unity has a personal and self-like character, the center itself — when it is living — seems personal and full of feeling according to the degree of life it has.

This description of the centers would hold for all centers, in all their different degrees of life. At one extreme, at the most modest level, it would hold even for the smallest and weakest center — a dot upon a page. To an immeasurably greater degree, it would hold for a living organism, and would explain the nature of its life. And it would hold too, for the centers formed by a great building like Chartres, and would explain the way this building seems to connect us directly to all that is.

I suggest that, so long as space/matter remains undifferentiated, the I which stands behind it remains incommunicado, not reachable, not connected with the matter. It becomes connected with matter — and visible to us — only as centers form. The stronger a center forms, the more it becomes window-like, and the more it allows us to see the I. Every center, to some degree, is a window which communicates with this inner plenum of I, reveals it, opens it to view. In this hypothesis, a center *is*, in the last analysis, any zone of matter which to some extent opens a window towards this I, and so allows us — however partially — to see the I *directly*. In this view, the extent to which a center is a living center is dependent on the degree to which this window on the I is opened.

6 / THOUGH A STRANGE MODEL, IT PROVIDES A VIABLE EXPLANATION

Suppose that my conception of the Blazing One, a ground of Self as the ultimate substance of the material universe, were not merely a model. This conception of a ground, if taken seriously as part of science, would be very surprising. That is because, in the last three hundred years, the fundamental assumption of all science has been precisely the opposite: namely, that there is just one kind of matter, and that the mechanical view of what this matter is, what we call space-time, is sufficient — viewed as a mechanism — to allow us to build a complete and comprehensive view of the universe. Spirit has been exorcised from science.

The proposal I am making here — that the I which lies behind or inside all matter is an underlying substance, or "original substance" underlying all matter — partially reunites us, part of the way, not all the way, towards a world of spirit. It does not make a separation between spirit and matter. Rather it asserts and insists that matter is not a purely mechanical material, but rather a spirit-like, Self-like substance, a material grounded in I, hence a different kind of substance from the space-time of Descartes and Einstein which were both postulated in the mechanistic tradition. That is surprising. Of course, too, it is open to question.

But no matter how surprising and unfamiliar, it does, for the first time, make sense of everything that has gone before. When you think about it carefully, the structural explanations that I have given in these four books have perhaps remained puzzling, incomplete.

The concept of a living center, and the degree of life which different centers have in them, have been defined and explained recursively and structurally. But the *quality* that appears in a living center — the quality of life *itself* that appears in centers — has not been explained. Throughout it all, the nagging question keeps on raising its head: Just what *is* a center? What does it really mean for a center to come to life? What is the intrinsic meaning of the character of its "life"? And further nagging questions have arisen, too: Even if a beautiful building can be understood in terms of centers, why does the structure of centers make it *beautiful*? Why then does it have *life*?

The description I have given in this chapter — if you could accept it — would for the first time finally make sense of all of that, because it finally answers these questions fully. In that sense, although my theory of the plenum of I might seem fantastic, it does finally take all the complex structural facts of these four books, and does tie them together in a single whole.

For this reason, although you may very reasonably be skeptical of the model I have put forward in this chapter, I suggest that you should suspend some part of your disbelief. It is no small thing to be able to make sense of all that has been set down in these four books and to understand the phenomenon of centers in a way which finally leaves important questions about their ultimate nature answered, instead of half-answered or unanswered.

7 / WHICH I-HYPOTHESIS IS TRUE?

Should we take the description literally? Or should we take it as a truth of psychology? Of course, I fully realize that if this physical/meta-

physical hypothesis of the I-plenum turned out to be true, it would force a radical reappraisal of the nature of matter and would, in effect, provide a starting point for thinking about an altogether new view of the physical universe. That is a very tall order. A reasonable person may reject the wisdom of even thinking about such a thing.

Even if this picture is too much for you, and you consider it to be just a model — at best partially correct — still, the I in one form or another, does remain as a necessary part of the world-picture.

The humane view of the ground as a psychological and structural phenomenon is undoubtedly more easy to accept. *In this view we keep a view of the I as something in our experience, as a psychological ground, which exists in every human being: and we recognize that we cannot make a living building unless each one of its centers is connected to the structure of this self or psychological ground.* Then the blazing one, the blazing furnace, which is seeable, reachable, reached by the artist trying to find union with the I, or reached by the observer who, through the existence of a living work, sees and makes contact with the I, makes sense as psychology. Even in that case, the blazing one remains as an experienced reality.

The plenum model of the Ground — the idea that the I is actually real in the universe, not only in the mind — is harder to accept. But in the rare moments when I dare to consider it, it helps me, because it enlarges my understanding. It also nourishes my mind and stimulates my inspiration. *In this view we see the same ground — but we now think of it as a great thing in the universe, far beyond ourselves, haunting, otherworldly, ultimate in its beauty and light.* It is reached only when a great work breaks through to it.

Whether the humane, psychological and positivistic view, or the more dream-like plenum view is more accurate, I do not know. But the overall picture I am trying to present in either case remains. One way or the other, the ground of I is real. Either the ground is a psychological description of the way we *experience* living structure. Or it is a factually supportable, previously unknown aspect of matter. There can be no doubt, I think, that at least *one* of these two versions is true. The I, in some form, exists.

Although you and I probably cannot help being skeptical about the more difficult metaphysical view, because it is so far beyond what we currently allow ourselves to think, there is one cogent reason for believing it that I have not mentioned. It is very, very hard to make a beautiful building. Even the methods and processes I have described in Books 2 and 3, with all their structure, are *still* very hard. As a practical matter, the metaphysical view of the Ground put forward in this chapter makes this hard task more attainable. As we shall see in chapter 12, the artist or builder is then making the building as a gift for "God" — an instrument through which one seeks union with God, reality beyond reality. The buildings themselves, and all the centers of the buildings, are made as windows through which one can reach contact with that blazing One, through which I touch eternity.

When I do my work in this conscious spirit, then all that living structure which is so hard to reach does become slightly more attainable, slightly easier. It then *seems* to be within reach, and as a practical matter, it *can* then sometimes be reached.

8 / A NON-MATERIAL VIEW OF MATTER

The transcendental I, in the model I have put forward, exists as the core of all living matter and becomes visible in every center to the degree that the center comes to life. Even though it must seem extraordinary by present standards, this does help to make the building process work better in practical terms. It adds something new which allows a person to make sense of all, in such a way that he can work more profoundly, more effectively.

It may work because the model I have described is *true*. Or it may work because the psychology is true, and this psychological reality, what *seems* like the blazing one, releases our ability and makes us, as artists, more profound. I cannot say, for sure, which of these is more accurate. But my instinct goes towards the former, the metaphysical and physical model, not merely the psychological. When I make a building as deeply as possible, in my own experience the work seems more like an objective process in which my yearning to reach that thing — that Blazing One, out there in the universe — activates in me some opening of the window to the I. It does, sometimes, help me to make a marvelous, simple thing in which I then feel my heart and the existence of my soul.

If we are to understand thoroughly what I have said about architecture, we can only with great difficulty accept a purely mechanical interpretation of the nature of matter. I have become convinced, indeed, that so long as we try to stay within a mechanical interpretation, we shall very likely get our understanding wrong.

It comes down to this: the facts, when carefully analyzed, may lead to and make neces-sary a new view of the universe, one in which the ultimate ground of all things is seen as a kind of I-substance, lying behind matter, or wrapped up within matter. This will be true whether we use the first, psychological view of this substance, or the second, nearly physical view of it. In either case, we must see that it is not possible to understand either the life of artifacts, or the process which creates this life, without realizing that in the end all living processes are processes which lead towards this I, and that the artifacts which have life are just those which are most deeply connected to this I.

If I am right, a non-mechanical interpretation of space and matter is indicated, necessarily, by careful reflection on the facts of architecture I have presented. Indeed, I believe that any attempt to keep the discussion, or our understanding, on a strictly mechanical plane will fail to encompass the real meaning, or the real basis of the facts themselves.

In the end perhaps the most stunning conclusion of all, is that a vision of the universe and its luminous ground, follows as a necessary result of the empirical truths about architecture which, throughout these four books, I have been trying to explain.[5]

NOTES

1. This would be consistent, too, with the dynamic view. Indeed, the unfolded character of living structure, and the way it always appears as a product of smooth unfolding, could also be a reason it appears in cognition.

2. The idea is not new. Thousands of writers throughout many centuries have posited the existence of such a Ground. For example, see the words of several mystical writers quoted under footnote 5, on the next two pages.

3. Tunneling of this kind, first described at the quantum level by Brian Josephson, has played an important part in modern physics. In a looser and more general sense, the word has been used widely by a variety of writers to describe such phenomena.

4. Book 1, chapters 4 and 7.

5. The connection of the individual person to the great Self, or Void, and its appearance in works of art, has long been a theme of mystical religious texts. In the works of nature, and in serious work of art, this connection of a person with the Self is brought forward, in-creased, intensified. It is that work in which the work itself, conceals, reveals, hints at, and approaches God. Thus, the Koran, quoted in Titus Burkhardt, SACRED ART IN EAST AND WEST (London: 1967), 111:

"According to a saying of the prophet, God hides himself behind seventy thousand curtains of light and of darkness; if they were taken away, all that His sight reaches would be consumed by the lightnings of His Countenance. The curtains are made of light in that they hide the Divine 'obscurity,' and of darkness in that they veil the Divine Light."

But the Void spoken of, the Divine light spoken of, is not abstract. It is always, ultimately, personal. In one form or another, all these teachings say that what has to be reached, above all, in a person, and in a considered life, is the human heart itself. For example, from Martin Lings, WHAT IS SUFISM? (Berkeley: University of California Press, 1975), 58:

"Since everyone has always a center of consciousness, everyone may be said to have a 'heart.' But the sufis use the

Capital of an ancient building in Lhasa, Tibet

term on principle in a transcendent sense to denote a centre of consciousness which corresponds at least to the inward Moon."

In Zen, too, it is understood that a person reaches contact with the eternal just to that extent that he makes contact with his own heart. Thus Soen Roshi, quoted in Matthiessen, NINE-HEADED DRAGON RIVER (Boston: Shambala, 1986), 62:

"In the midst of winter, I find in myself at last, invincible summer."

And again, in Sufism, the message that in the unfolding of the heart, the soul of the person, which is carried in each of us, and which may be reached, naked, at the moment of being comfortable and true to one's own heart, this Void or I is reached. It is most beautifully and simply expressed in the 10th-century poem written by the Sufi saint and poet Hallaj, quoted in Martin Lings, op. cit., p 49:

"I saw my Lord with the Eye of the Heart. I said 'WHO ART THOU?' He answered 'Thou.' "

Throughout these teachings there is a subtle ambiguity. This event — the process of reaching the heart or reaching the void — may be thought of as purely psychological. Or it may be thought of as objective, something about the universe which is being reached.

To understand it and grasp it as something practical to be attained, it must be understood as "both." It is a process in which a person casts off all mental affiliations, all concepts, all trains of thought, all opinions, leaving only the simple truth of their own naked heart. This process, in which action, object, and person come only from the heart, is psychological. It is a core "heart" which exists in each of us. It is revealed, universal, shared, more or less the same in each of us. Seven hundred years ago Meister Eckhardt described it like this (MEISTER ECKHARDT: WORKS, trans. C. B. Evans, London, 1924):

"There is a spirit in the soul, untouched by time and flesh, flowing from the Spirit, remaining in the Spirit, wholly spiritual. In this principle is God, ever verdant, ever flowering in all the joy and glory of His actual Self. Sometimes I have called this principle the tabernacle of the soul, sometimes a spiritual Light, anon I say it is a Spark. But now I say that it is more exalted over this and that than the heavens are exalted above the earth. So now I name it in nobler fashion . . . It is free of all names and void of all forms. It is one and simple, as God is one and simple, and no man can in any wise behold it."

At the same time, at the moment this true heart in us is reached, there is contact with some "thing," something beyond us, an actual entity of some kind in the universe, something before us, after us, an eternal substance which exists not only inside us, but underneath the substance of the world, before the substance of the world: it may be called the ultimate material from which the world is made. This entity — or the claim to its existence, and to the possibility of meeting "it," is "not" psychological. From THE TIBETAN BOOK OF THE DEAD.

"O nobly born, the time has now come for thee to seek the Path. Thy breathing is about to cease. In the past thy teacher hath set thee face to face with the Clear Light; and no thou art about to experience it in its Reality in the 'Bardo' state (the intermediate state immediately following death, in which the soul is judged — or rather judges itself by choosing, in accord with the character formed during its life on earth, what sort of an after life it shall have). In this 'Bardo' state all things are like the cloudless sky, and the naked immaculate Intellect is like unto a translucent void without circumference or center. At this moment know thou thyself and abide in that state. I too, at this time, am setting thee face to face."

The claim that this self, what the Tibetan Book calls the "clear light," exists is asserting something in the realm of physics. It used to be called metaphysics, simply because it appeared to be a part of the nature of matter which could not be treated by the contemporary methods of physics. Still, it is in fact a part of physics, since it asserts something — admittedly hard to pin down and hard to understand — about the nature of matter and the nature of the universe.

The key fact which makes all this so important is that the two entities, or two interpretations — the "heart" and the "void" — are linked. In approaching our own heart, we make contact with this ultimate self from which the universe is made. In approaching this ultimate self-substance, we also make contact with our own heart. That is the core of all the religious teaching in the great tradition. Thus Aldous Huxley, in THE PERENNIAL PHILOSOPHY (1962), 35:

"So far then, as a fully adequate expression of the perennial philosophy is concerned, there exists a problem in semantics that is finally insoluble. The fact is one which must be steadily borne in mind by all who read its formulations. Only in this way shall we be able to understand even remotely what is being talked about. Consider, for example, those negative definitions of the transcendent and immanent Ground of being. In statements such as Eckhardt's, God is equated with nothing. And in a certain sense the equation is exact; for God is certainly no thing. In the phrase used by Scotus Erigena God is not a what; He is a That. In other words, the Ground can be denoted as being "there"; but not defined as having qualities. This means that discursive knowledge about the Ground is not merely, like all inferential knowledge, a thing at one remove, or even at several removes, from the reality of immediate acquaintance; it is and, because of the very nature of our language and our standard patterns of thought, it must be, paradoxical knowledge. Direct knowledge 'of' the Ground cannot be had except by union, and union can be achieved only by the annihilation of the self-regarding ego, which is the barrier separating the 'thou' from the 'That.' "

The Ground is, I believe, unavoidable as the core of architecture. If I look at the golden capital of the Tibetan building on page 155, it has an extraordinary shape and color, which penetrates the Ground, and penetrates the Self, and penetrates the individual human heart, that which we are made of. Architecture cannot be undertaken, in a sensible way, without intended and deliberate contact with this Self. Conversely, the thought and practice of architecture — the facts about structure — which I have defined in the preceding chapters, shed, I think, a great deal of practical light on this ultimate mystery, and so show us, concretely, something essential about the way the universe is made.

Although these arguments have chiefly been brought forward in the mystical traditions of the world's religions, I must emphasize that I bring them forth here in a scientific spirit. I believe that some concept along these lines is necessary as a part of *physics*. I do not believe we can accurately describe the way the world works — at least that aspect of the world which I have been describing in these books — without some concept like this. Without it we simply cannot account for the essential facts about the personal quality of works of art, the apparent emergence of *being*, as a quality, when the field of centers becomes intensified, and the role of simplicity and ultimate purity in great works of art.

CHAPTER SEVEN

COLOR AND INNER LIGHT

1 / INTRODUCTION: A DIRECT GLIMPSE OF THE I

It is my impression — even more accurately, my considered judgement — that the I or ground is a real thing, something which exists in the world, perhaps attached to matter or a part of matter, which is connected to the world in which we exist, in which matter exists, and that this I forms a necessary substratum to all that exists. It is, in effect, a kind of blinding unity, underlying all matter.

In this chapter, I shall try to show directly, visibly, as nearly as I can, the I *itself*. I shall do this by showing you color, and, in particular, a certain kind of color which I believe allows the I to be seen. Of all the phenomena I know, this is the one which comes closest to letting us see the I directly, as if we were actually looking at it. It is what I call the phenomenon of inner light.[1]

2 / COLOR AS AN ESSENTIAL FEATURE OF REALITY

In the first half of the 20th century, color in architecture was weakened as a way of understanding the world. Buildings, especially those built in the early part of the century, often had little or no color, just grey, white, brown, and black. Even now, in a time when color is permissible again, we live in an era when profound *color* (in the sense of unified deep color, in the singular) plays a rather minor role in things, even though there are lurid *colors* (in the plural) everywhere. Even our prevailing mental picture of the world leaves color out: for example, the color of a thing is rarely part of its scientific description.

Yet the black and white Cartesian scientific picture fails to describe things as they are, and certainly fails to describe pure unity as we experience it. Can you imagine daffodils which are blue, not yellow? Or consider the beauty of a forest. The green light breaks through the leaves, and fills the space below the trees. Can you imagine it without imagining that it is green? Would it be possible to see its unity if it were not green? Isn't the beauty, the harmony we feel there, to an enormous degree, a result of the thousands of soft greens, dark greens, light green, yellowish green, bluish green, blackish green, light white green at the tips of the leaves, and of the glimpses of blue sky, or grey cloud, shining through?

We see here a weakness in our mental picture of the field of centers. So long as we are trying to understand the wholeness of the forest structurally, we can understand it through its field of centers. And yet, when we contemplate the *pure* wholeness of the forest, one of the overwhelming things about it is its greenness. The unity is green. This unity is not directly captured by the field of centers.

The unity is colored

Little Hawk Lake, Ontario: colors of sky and tree and water

This is why it is so important to see unity itself beyond the field of centers. As scientists, we are used to thinking geometrically. To understand the unity of the forest, we naturally start with the kind of analysis which I have made in Book 1. This can give us the structure of the forest, the biology, the ecology, its life. And it is certainly true that the unity of the forest is explained in large part by its structure, by its centers.

But its color is also an essential part of its beauty — and this color goes beyond the "structure" we can analyze. If we leave this colored aspect of the forest out of our picture, we still have only a half-dead, impersonal picture of the world, which fails to capture its wholeness fully.

The same is true of buildings. We look at a cathedral or a temple, and we think of lines on paper, planes, volumes, columns, beams, arches, doorways. Obsessed by geometry we may imagine that the beauty, the harmony of the thing is a result of its geometrical organization, and the

Greens of an inland valley

way these elements form wholeness through their geometry alone. Once again, the real thing is beautiful, harmonious, because of the soft grey stone, the darker grey of roof tiles against the sky, the green moss growing out of the ground and onto the stones, the deep blackish brown wood of window frames, the soft pinkish grey of tiles on pathways, because of the light yellow or yellowish grey and startling white where the sunlight hits the stone.

To modern ears, all this might sound romantic. But it sounds romantic only because the Cartesian world-view we have inherited has excluded these subtle features of pure unity from consideration. So, we have been brainwashed into

assuming that the "essence" of a building lies in its so-called primary characteristics — its shape, volume, line, and spatial organization. But this coldly geometric point of view is not a thoughtful and intentional result of observation. It certainly does not describe reality as we experience it.

Reality as we *experience* it is full of color, saturated by color, dominated by color at every turn, in every point, in every line, in every shadow. And life is especially influenced by color. Indeed, color is one of the few aspects of wholeness where we experience wholeness directly, because the sensations of color are not analyzable into parts. We are simply aware of the overall color quality of something as a whole.

3 / INNER LIGHT

Inner light is the color quality which arises as something comes to life, and as it approaches and reveals the I.[2]

Inner light occurs almost everywhere in nature, as in the examples shown on pages 161–72. The color in nature almost always has inner light. In things made by human beings it is rather more rare and happens, chiefly, when it is made in some almost visionary mode. It occurs, for instance, in the painted wall of certain Tibetan monasteries, like that shown opposite, made by the monks. It occurs in some of the Turkish and Persian miniatures of the 15th century; in medieval illuminations; in the pale milky blue interior of the Cabalistic synagogue of Josef Caro at Safad in northern Israel; in some ancient carpets; in the clothes of certain Himalayan monks; in the paintings of Gauguin and occasionally van Gogh; in some of the buildings of Mexico; in a few Japanese silks; in the buildings and sea and sky in the Greek islands. Here and there it may be found, scattered throughout human experience.

In order to understand the inner light which these things and most parts of nature all

have, let us begin experimentally. Suppose we look at pairs of colored scenes or objects from the point of view of their color and make comparisons among them. We may do this by paying special attention to their color and looking, within the color, for the same "life" we have discussed in earlier chapters of Books 1 and 2. To do so, we may use the same experimental tests already defined in chapters 8 and 9 of Book 1. In essence, these tests require that you compare the two colored things and ask which one comes closer to being a picture of your own self. Or you may ask which one makes you feel more wholesome in yourself while you are looking at it.

On pages 162 and 163, the double-spread after this, four things are illustrated: an interior, a painting, and two examples of Turkish tilework. All four seem nicely colored. But when you compare them for the degree in which their color makes you feel a profound wholeness within yourself, two are positive, and two are weak. On page 162, the interior is weak in its effect; the Derain painting strong in its effect. On page 163, the ancient 13th-century tilework is

Dazzling inner light in painted walls: Drepung Monastery, Tibet

THIS HAS INNER LIGHT: Hyde Park, by Andre Derain, 1906. Though unrealistic, even harsh, this color is connected to the "I." I feel more whole because of contact with it. Even if I do not recognize at first, that this is so, ultimately it becomes so, undeniably, and in spite of any prejudice I have.

WHILE THIS DOES NOT: This interior seems nicely colored, pleasant, perhaps "well-designed" or beautiful. But it has no inner light. It does not make you feel more whole deep in yourself. There is, from it, no contact with the I. Bedroom corridor at Monkton, Sussex, by Kit Nicholson and Hugh Casson, with the help of Salvador Dali, c. 1930.

profound in its effect, the 16th-century tilework rather weaker.

This judgment does not lie in the realm of opinion. Two of them have a more profound effect on our spirits than the other two. Although it is possible that you may not agree, my experience in asking people to make similar judgments is that most people will agree. The difference exists.

If we examine the origin of this difference, we find something even more profound than the geometric wholeness or living structure we have learnt to identify. There is now a visible difference in the actual *quality* of color itself. Especially in the good cases (the Derain and the 13th-century tiles), the quality lies in the overall color as a whole. In the second group of colored things — the ones with more life — the color is a single thing, field-like, it is more pungent, more touching as a *whole*, it goes to the heart more strongly.

Whereas the wholeness of geometric things can be understood as a living structure (caused by the field of centers and by the fifteen proper-

THIS HAS INNER LIGHT: This tilework does connect me to the I. This becomes clear if I compare it with the other, later tile panel shown to the right. Here, though the design seems foreign, barbaric, my contact with my self is made more profound by contact with it. This does have inner light. 13th-century Turkish tile, Sircali Medrese, Konya.

ties) in the case of color, the life or wholeness comes in a single package. You cannot take it apart. When color is whole we experience the color as a single field, as pure, unbroken unity.

This is the quality which I call "inner light."

Possibly the greatest examples of inner light occur in nature. You may see it in a field of yellow anemones. It is in a single white apple blossom. It is in the pink and blue morning sky. It is in the water of a blackish pond. It is in the waters of the ocean. It is in earth and rocks. It is in snow. It is in dust. It is in thunderclouds. It is on a horse's coat or a cat's fur. It is in almost everything colored we see in the natural world.

In things which we have made, this quality of inner light is much more rare. But in certain cultures, at certain periods, it has also been understood and created intentionally and systematically by artists, who were intentionally seeking to do it. Some of the greatest examples occurred

in ancient Persian and Turkish miniatures of the 15th century. Others may be seen in early medieval painting and decoration. Others come in early Anatolian carpets. Others come in Japanese silks and pottery. Others in prehistoric Chinese bronzes, simply in the surface of the metal. Occasionally it occurs in gardens. The phenomenon also occurs in certain European paintings — conspicuously in the works of Piero della Francesca, Fra Angelico, Vermeer — and in the works of a few modern painters, sometimes to an almost astonishing degree: van Gogh, Gauguin,

WHILE THIS DOES NOT: It seems pretty, at first; and was prized at the time it was made. But it does not deepen my sense of myself. It has no inner light. 16th-century Turkish tile panel from the Mehmet Pasha Mosque, Istanbul.

Pale gold and blue which embodies inner light: Henri Matisse, Corner of the Artist's Studio, 1912

Matisse, and Bonnard especially. It also occurred as a more everyday matter in the textiles and hand-painted artifacts and buildings of many traditional cultures: Africa, India, Tibet, medieval Russia, the Caribbean, and the Mayan cultures of Central America, all come to mind.

In every case where it occurs, color which has inner light has a special kind of subdued brilliance. It is quiet, very quiet, yet bright at the same time. It is an overall single sensation,

not a composition of colors, but a single overall color field — almost like a musical chord — which strikes simultaneously from all parts of the picture at once. It comes from the picture as a whole.

Even *seeing* inner light may need a little help. In our period (late 20th century, early 21st) it is not so easy to see this subdued brilliance, because we are not used to it. To learn to see it, we must recognize that it is entirely different

Inner light in a medieval manuscript illumination: Gospels of St. Willibrord

from the harsher, brighter color we have become used to. We have learned to enjoy bright *colors*. But we know too little about unitary *color*, an integrated field-like harmony in which a thing becomes truly one because the colors are perfectly in tune.

Wherever there is inner light we always see two phenomena simultaneously. On the one hand, the overall feeling of the color field is muted. It is not gaudy, or garish. It is calm, soft-toned, subdued. At the same time, the colors are usually quite intense and brilliant; they are not, themselves subdued, or muted, tones of gray with tints of colors.

The combination of these two methods is very surprising: 1) the use of brilliant colors to produce a muted whole or an overall unity so profound that nothing stands out, everything melts together, and yet the actual colors that are used are brilliant; or 2) the actual colors that are

Here inner light is apparent even in the yellow orange of the traditional robe, and the deep blue of the sky: Tibetan lama in traditional clothes.

used are subdued, but everything together seems extremely brilliant.

To understand the idea of subdued brilliance better, it is very helpful to think about nature. Very often, when we look at nature, we experience a feeling of intense and lovely color. Even on a dull day, the colors we see are soft, varied, and full of life. On a bright spring day the world seems literally filled with color. Yet objectively, even on a bright spring day, the colors are extremely pale and muted if we compare them with the paint colors we consider bright — primary red, primary yellow, primary blue. These primary colors which come out of tubes of paint are extremely crude, shouting and harsh compared with the colors we see in nature. In nature, even the color of the sky, which we think of as bright blue, is *objectively* an immensely pale watery blue, compared with the ultramarine, cerulean blue, and cobalt blue of the paint box. The rich green of a meadow is often — objectively — a grayish, brownish green, far yellower, browner, greyer, lighter, and more subtle than the chromium or brilliant green in the tube. So nature uses colors that are subdued, muted. Yet

Inner light in a rather ordinary setting: paint, stone, and color reminiscent of the sea on a Greek island

Inner light in a Turkish prayer carpet, 17th century

Bright intense inner light in a Persian miniature: from the Shah-Nama of Muhammad Juki, Herat, 1440

the brilliance of a field of flowers, on a spring day, is legendary — and a thousand times more brilliant than an advertisement which uses red and yellow and blue.

This is the essence of inner light. It is like the brilliance which we experience in nature.

The brilliance, and the intensity of color, is not caused by the saturation of hue, by the crude massive use of primaries. It is caused by the *interaction* of the colors, by the way that many subtle colors interact to *become* brilliant and to give off light.

4 / THE UNFOLDING WHICH PRODUCES INNER LIGHT

This subdued light which follows in the softest cases seems, when it occurs, to come from the underbelly of our experience. It shocks, grasps us directly in our emotion, takes on the character I have discussed at length in Book 1 as the mirror of the self. For this reason too, I believe it provides us with a direct vision of the I. Somehow, this quality reminds us of ourselves, makes us

feel our own existence. It shocks us into awareness of our innermost feeling.

Like every other kind of life, inner light is created — always I think — by the unfolding process. The artist works at the whole which exists and then asks himself, at each step, what has to be done next, to intensify the light. The extraordinary thing is that while working, if we

Inner light in the intense darkness of a Bonnard painting: The Terrace at Vernon, 1928

Fragment of a carpet from Turkestan with the subtle light of green and yellow and red

*Inner light in a somber and beautiful painted room: interior of a 17th-century house
from Nieblum on the Island of Föhr, now in the museum in Flensburg.*

Toulouse-Lautrec, Officer on Horseback, c. 1890

The Castle of Auvers, 1890: one of van Gogh's last paintings

half close our eyes and look at the half-completed work in a passive and receptive state, we can *answer* that question. That is, the color which will produce light comes to my eye by itself, presents itself to me autonomously, arrives in me without my effort. The only effort I need to make is to make myself passive enough to *receive* the color which will then come into my eye. I have to get rid of other mental influences and keep paying attention only to the question: what dot of color — where, how much, how intense — will create that flash of deeper, more inner light in the thing before me? Usually, I can sense, intuitively, autonomously, what kind of color it is. We have the ability to see this color, partially formed, in our mind's eye. Then we have to try and *make* the color. And then, with actual paint I have to try and see if an amount of that color, in the place where I imagined it, really will *create* a more brilliant light in the thing.

This is an empirical matter. I place the color, then check to see if it does have this kind of effect. And I must remember, while I am doing it, that I am not looking for some superficial brightness. I am truly looking to see if the process I have just done, increases the *inner* light. That means, does it increase the extent to which this thing I have made now seems to go deeper into the realm of I, makes me more vulnerable, reaches further into the light behind all things.

By asking *this* question, again and again for each new speck of color, for each brushstroke — and by working — I gradually make progress towards the kind of thing which has some value, and which has the seamless unity which reflects the I.[3]

5 / THE ELEVEN COLOR PROPERTIES

While showing examples of nearly perfect color in these eighty pages I shall suggest that even the extreme and seamless unity that I call inner light still has a structural origin. It is not *just* a feeling. It is a feeling which arises as life occurs and which is still linked to structure. Thus, the feeling we experience is not an isolated feeling, or a subjective feeling of color. It is the feeling experience of the I, direct experience of that objective structural reality.

The inner light is directly linked to the field of centers. Each color exists as a center and becomes more intense as a result of its intensification by the other centers. At the same time, the whole also becomes more intense, more alive, more unified, through the action of the field. So, like the centers we have examined in other contexts, the centers of color come to life by a bootstrap process in which they work on each other and bring life to one another.

Stated more precisely, subdued brilliance and inner light only occur when certain definite things are happening in the color field. These "things"—and I have identified eleven of them—are very similar to the fifteen geometric properties described in Book 1. To make the similarity with the fifteen geometric properties clear, I have put the name of the most similar geometric property in parentheses.[4]

1. HIERARCHY OF COLORS
   (LEVELS OF SCALE)
2. COLORS CREATE LIGHT TOGETHER
   (POSITIVE SPACE)
   (ALTERNATING REPETITION)
3. CONTRAST OF DARK AND LIGHT
   (CONTRAST)
4. MUTUAL EMBEDDING
   (DEEP INTERLOCK AND AMBIGUITY)
5. BOUNDARIES AND HAIRLINES
   (BOUNDARIES)

6. SEQUENCE OF LINKED COLOR PAIRS
   (GRADIENTS)
   (THE VOID)
7. FAMILIES OF COLOR
   (ECHOES)
8. COLOR VARIATION
   (ROUGHNESS)
9. INTENSITY AND CLARITY OF INDIVIDUAL COLOR
   (STRONG CENTERS)
   (GOOD SHAPE)
10. SUBDUED BRILLIANCE
    (SIMPLICITY AND INNER CALM)
    (NOT-SEPARATENESS)
11. COLOR DEPENDS ON GEOMETRY
    (LOCAL SYMMETRIES)

As stated, these eleven color properties are similar—though not identical—to the fifteen ways that centers give each other life. In my work with color, I classify them a little differently, and list only the eleven properties that I have identified and found most useful. It is odd that there are eleven, not fifteen, and that the correspondence is not exact. I do not know the reason for it. But I have examined these properties, carefully, for many years, and no matter how hard I try to fit them to the mold of the fifteen, still, obstinately, at least as I have observed them, they remain eleven. They are, I think, *the* ways that centers of color create and intensify life in one another. And, insofar as the phenomenon of inner light is a direct vision of the I, perhaps they are as close as we may ever come to seeing the ground directly. These properties may even be considered qualities of the ground itself, qualities of the I which is behind all things and all appearance.

What we find out, as we try to create light, and as we work step by step to create inner light in a painting or a building, is that there are no alternatives: we have to use *these* ways of helping color centers to bring life to each other. In these ways, whatever we do intuitively to make light happen, we find these eleven color properties coming, of necessity, into our work where we are trying to induce the inner light. In the great works of color, by the greatest painters, as in nature, we find these eleven properties again and again. In my experience, these eleven provide the structural backbone of all color unity, of all inner light.

Because I believe that the inner light is a direct experience of the I, whatever that may be, I may say too, that these eleven properties are almost, in that sense, *attributes* of the I, as far as we can see it or experience it directly.

6 / HIERARCHY OF COLORS
(LEVELS OF SCALE)

Hierarchy of colors: Inca textile made from red, yellow, and blue feathers

Japanese kimono

If we are working at a painting, or the color of a building or an object, as we slowly move it towards inner light, we shall find out almost before anything else that in the vast majority of cases, to make inner light occur, we are led to use *unequal amounts* of different colors. In all those things which succeed in having inner light, we will find that we have followed a broad general rule: the different colors must come in different *quantities*.

This is just as simple as it sounds. The amounts of different colors are numerically different — and usually follow a series of graded steps. So, we find out that as we create light in a thing, and move a thing towards a state of having light, the colors in the composition will move gradually toward a nicely ordered sequence of quantities, as measured by their relative areas. If I want to formulate this as a rule, I can say that inner light is caused first and most strongly by a rule of proportion among colors which creates a clear hierarchy of relative size among the areas of different colors in a picture.

This rule is visible in its most basic form in the Inca feather textile shown on the facing page. There are only three colors: red, yellow, and blue. Red is most, yellow is next, and blue is least. But more than that, there is a stricter hierarchy. The red, yellow and blue are in geometric proportion: 70 percent red, 25 percent yellow, 5 percent blue; all in all, roughly 15:5:1.

We see something similar in this Japanese kimono. The thing has three colors: red, off-white and black. Again the three are in geometric proportion: 4:2:1. In this case, the proportions are more extended. The kimono is really red, but the red is brought to life by the much smaller amount of off-white. The blossoms are off-white, but the off-white is brought to life by the much smaller amount of black. All in all the distribution is as follows: 75 percent red; 19 percent off-white; 4 percent black rings in small amount; 1 percent trace amounts of yellow and pink.

Matisse's beautiful green Moroccan scene has the same quality. If we measure the areas we find the picture mainly green, then white, small amounts of flesh ocher, and very small areas of black. Thus a perfect hierarchy: 66 percent green, 23 percent white, 9 percent ocher, and 2 percent black.

The Persian miniature, opposite, has a similar distribution of areas — light ocher yellows, browns, gray, blue, black, bright yellow, and pale red — but once again follows a careful hierarchy ordering the amounts in sequence. It is mainly very pale brown and ocher yellow, with large areas of red; then a middle amount of gray-green on the horse, shining in between the reds, with one isolated, startling patch of blue. On top of those colors there are small amounts, of dark violet, dark red, and green. Thus: 50 percent light yellow-brown, 20 percent red, 10 percent grey-green, 7 percent bright blue, 5 percent dark reds, 4 percent violet black, 3 percent yellow orange, 1 percent green.

And on the next page, the glorious, subtle, glowing illumination from the 8th century has the same hierarchy, too. It is mainly red, large areas of red; then a middle amount of violet, shining in between the reds; and small amounts — very small amounts — of a pale, glowing, golden yellow tinged with green. Thus: 75 percent red, 20 percent pale violet, 5 percent pale golden yellow.

A successful composition in which there are *equal* areas of several different colors is extremely rare. Instead, what we find in almost all cases where real unity of color feeling is achieved is a well ordered hierarchy of sizes (amounts, quantities, or areas) for the different colors. This means that there is one color which has the largest total area. In the middle there are sometimes two or three colors. Then there are again, other colors, which have still smaller areas. And, usually, near the bottom of the hierarchy, there are colors in

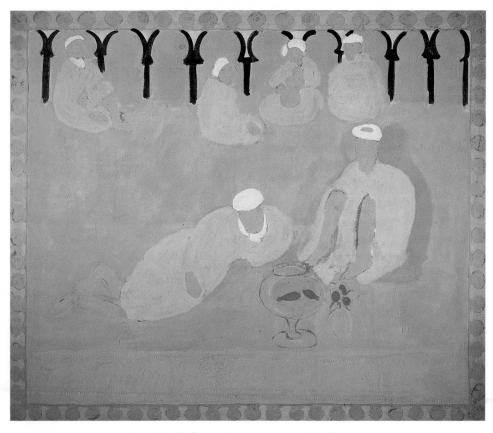

Hierarchy of colors in Henri Matisse, Arab Coffee House

Triumphal Entry of Timur into Samarkand, Persian miniature, Shiraz, 1434

very small amounts which play a major role in the way the wholeness works.

A failure of the painter to follow this rule of hierarchy is the single most common mistake which can be made in a painting. The rule is so basic, and so simple-minded, that it appears trivial. But there are almost no examples of inner light where it is not followed.

This rule can be traced directly to the way the wholeness works. If we think about the field of centers, we know that there must be different centers, of different scales. What is surprising is that the subtle glow of color which is produced in a thing, will only be there when the colors themselves follow the same rule. Thus we see how the field of centers begins to create the glow of light — the glimpse of pure unity.

I want to make it clear that there is no need to follow this rule blindly, as if it were a prescription. But if you work and work at a thing, and keep on trying to push it toward inner light, then you will find out, after the fact, that nine times out of ten, you have been forced (or led) to create a hierarchy of colors in the thing. I do not consider this an arbitrary or externally imposed rule. What makes it important is that it is an observable fact, something you can find out for yourself from your own efforts to make inner light appear.

Medieval illumination, St. Gall Psalter

7 / COLORS CREATE LIGHT TOGETHER
(POSITIVE SPACE, ALTERNATING REPETITION)

The second most fundamental of the color properties is the way that one color approaches another and creates light with it. It resembles the way that smaller centers cooperate to form larger centers. When colors create light together, they create a larger "being."

Suppose we have a swatch of color. I look at it, and ask myself what second color will produce light if I bring it towards the first. When I concentrate, I can summon up this second color in my mind's eye, just from looking at the first color. For example, I look at a certain yellowish color. I keep my mind blank, and ask what color will produce light if I bring it towards the first. I see something bluish perhaps. Then I take bits of colored paper, blue, turquoise, dark blue, light blue, and bring them towards the yellow until light is actually created.

This is the fundamental experiment of all color work, and of all painting. Once I learn how to make this happen, then all the rest will follow. And *until* I can get this to happen, by developing my eye to see it, I can get nothing very valuable.

There are four main variables involved: What is the hue of the second color? How much of it is there? How light or dark is it? How grayed is it?

The first is most critical: What is the hue? Usually I can get my mind to see this. It just arrives in my eye, without effort, as a response to the color that is there. I don't need to work. I need to make my mind and my eye blank. Then it comes by itself, in response to the color that is there. For instance, in the case of this yellow, I see a blue of some sort, perhaps a purplish grayish blue.

I can get a blue of what seems like roughly the right kind, put it on a bit of paper, and bring it towards the yellow. Now the *amount* is critical. I have to keep playing with the amount that is visible. A strip one inch wide may be hopeless.

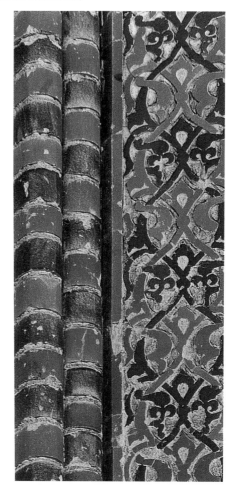

Tilework
from the Sircali Medrese, Konya

Three quarters of an inch wide will be quite different. An eighth of an inch may be just right. I have to keep juggling the amount until the light begins to shine.

Also the lightness and relative greyness may be quite different from what I saw in my mind's eye. I may have seen dark blue initially. But as I do my experiments, I realize finally that what I need is a large area of very pale grayish blue, almost white. The hue is still roughly the one I saw, but the area and degree of saturation are entirely different. To get this part right I have to do experiments.

The main thing to recognize is that the whole process, getting the phenomenon to happen, is an experimental process. If I want to do it, I simply have to try it and try it and try it, until the light begins to shine. As long as that is what I am looking for, I will get it right in the end.

In many cases the light comes from colors which are roughly complementary. Blue is made to shine by yellow and orange, red is made to shine by green, orange by purple. But as we shall see there are also much more sophisticated cases where one color is made to shine by something quite near it: violet by pink and white, black by brown or blue.

In the tilework from the Sircali Medrese (page 179), the effect is mainly yellow and blue, the dark blue and light blue working against each other to create light with the dusky, not very bright yellow. It is almost buff. Yet the light produced is intense.

In Matisse's painting of Madame Matisse, we see intense orange, with blackish yellow-green (this is already not quite complementary).

Henri Matisse, Madame Matisse, 1929

Turquoise and red reverberating: Anatolian keyhole carpet, 17th century

In the Turkish village carpet on page 181, the sea-green turquoise is chosen to vibrate with the reds — the green stares at us, activated by the red. In the shrine of Imam Reza in Meshed, the tilework and the sky work together so that the tiles seem golden, and the sky nearly purple, achieving an effect so strong that the golden mosque actually makes the sky seem purple, while it makes the golden tiles shine.

In the Turkish miniature of a town, magenta and pink, with dark red and turquoise, shine together in an amazing way. When I saw this painting, I thought I had never seen these colors so close together in quality and yet so far from one another in hue, interacting in this way.

In the small photograph of a house wall in a Mayan village (page 184), the brilliant green wall is offset and activated by a small quantity of purple along the base, and by the blood-red shutters with their ocher-orange outlines.

Golden mosaic and purple sky, the shrine of Imam Reza, Meshed

Colors create light in a 15th-century Turkish miniature

geometric properties called POSITIVE SPACE and ALTERNATING REPETITION. The interaction in-tensifies one center (color) by means of another adjacent center (color) lying next to it.

8 / CONTRAST OF DARK AND LIGHT
(CONTRAST)

If the first two properties (HIERARCHY OF COL-ORS and COLORS CREATE LIGHT) are present in the field, but the relative dark and light are not appropriate, then the colors still won't shine. In-ner light is partly *caused* by dark-light contrast.

One of the basic things we have to do while we are making something colored is to squint at it, half close our eyes so that we see only grays, and see if the inner light is still there. If it isn't there — that is to say, if it isn't visible in the dark-and-light pattern of what is in front of me alone — then it will never be there when I open my eyes fully again and the colors come back in. We have to work out the overall pattern of light and dark as if the colors weren't even there in or-der to get them right.

Lion eating bull, Persian, 15th century: the light of black, blue, white, and brown is made to shine by the contrast.

In the floor of the Upham house, the original sketch of yellow, green, red — a little tiny painting — was very helpful (Book 2, Appendix 1). The green was halfway between the yellow and the red in its intensity. The color samples we made were just right, and had the same quality. But when the floor was laid, the mix of the green went wrong, and the green came out a little too dark. This relatively minor accident changed everything. The green had the same darkness as the red, and the pattern didn't make sense any more as one of light and dark. The color feeling of the floor was completely ruined. It was hard to realize the origin of the problem, because with eyes wide open, one was only aware that it looked gloomy and depressing — ugly. But with eyes half-closed, colors disappeared, one saw that the dark-light pattern was fundamentally damaged. We had to work like maniacs to bleach the green terrazzo. Finally we managed it, and the light came back into the floor.

We may define the necessary dark-light contrast in a colored pattern like this: If we take a black and white picture of the colored pattern, the pattern of the dark and light alone (without the color) will still be beautiful.

Consider the Persian miniature of a lion attacking a bull. The strange intensity of this picture comes, of course, from the interaction of blue and black and brown (the brown being, really, a very dark yellow) and white. But the intense activity of the light created by these three colors is activated, above all, by the dark-light contrast, and the continuous inter-folding of the light and dark throughout the picture.

We see a similar phenomenon in this Navajo blanket. In the pattern, the red and blue are beautiful. But the color they have is animated, given most of its life, by the incessant beat of the dark and light, the black and white that accompanies it.

The painting shown on the next page in monochrome and in color, *Shipment of Grain*, a detail of the *St. Nicholas Predella* by Fra Angelico, illustrates the point again. When we look at the color version, it almost seems as though the col-

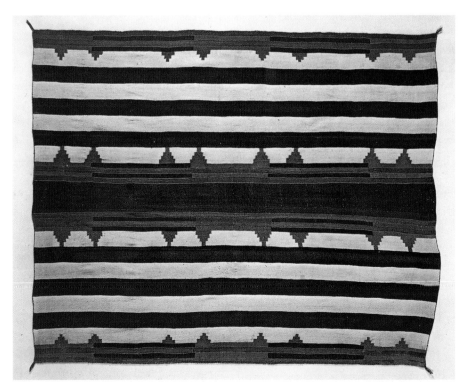

Contrast of dark and light makes the beauty of color in this Navajo blanket, c. 1880.

Contrast of dark and light makes the colors shine in this painting by Fra Angelico, Shipment of Grain

ors have a uniform density. But when we look at the black and white version, we see clearly that even without color, the composition has a beautiful feeling created by the gray tones alone.

The same is nearly always true of paintings when they shine with inner light. To understand the rule, we must first recognize that every color has a tone, and that every painting can be seen as a pattern of black, white, and gray. This way of seeing is hard, since hue sometimes obscures our capacity to see tone. It is useful to remember that we can see the pattern of tones by squinting, half closing our eyes. When we do that, colors go to gray, and we can tell, for any two adjacent colors, which is darker. We can also see the painting as a pure composition of tones. Red, for instance, is nearer to black than one expects; yellow is nearer to white than one expects. Every color has a level of grey.

The simple rule is this: When the pattern of tones — seen purely as blacks, whites, and grays — is a beautiful one, then the colors can shine with inner light. When the pattern of grey tones is not beautiful the colors will always seem muddy and *cannot* shine.

In the Turkish encampment we have a beautiful range of colors, 50 percent soft green, 15 percent strong red, 15 percent pale purple, 10 percent white, 4 percent light blue, 2 percent brown, and various trace amounts of yellow, black, and dark green. But gathering them together, animating the interactions among the hierarchy, is the overall, intense dark-light contrast, a zigzag shape of a river of which like a huge Z slashed through the center of the picture, tying it all together.

In the prayer rug with a yellow border, the yellow shines with reds and blues and purples and greens. When one first looks at the carpet, it is easy to imagine that this wonderful color is coming chiefly from the choice of colors. A careful look shows that, again, the vibrant color is

The color works in this Turkish miniature, The Emperor's Tent, from the 16th century, because the contrast is so good.

caused by the fact of the dark-light contrast woven, in this case, into the colors themselves. If that were not the case the colors would be dull.

Even in Giotto's painting of a river scene formed by muted blues and grays, the subtle beauty of the pattern comes from the fact that, above all, the pattern works as a pattern of dark and light. Take that away, and the subtle soft harmonies just would not amount to anything; the whole way the color works would be undermined.

In the world of black and white, where things are monochrome, the vital importance of contrast is obvious. Without contrast there is no form. But because color is so fascinating, it is easy to become mesmerized by hue and to forget about dark and light. We are so dazzled by the

brilliance of the colors, and by their *color* contrasts, that we assume (often without realizing it) that dark light contrast is no longer essential.

Indeed, almost the most common mistake which students make in their early color studies is to try to produce brilliant color using colors which lie in a too-narrow range of tones. This almost can't be done. There is hardly a single example of great beauty in color, which does not also have considerable dark-light contrast, regardless of the various colors that are used.

In order to make this rule easy to follow, I often find it helpful to consider the painting even more extremely, as if it had only two tones: black and white. We can imagine it like this by making a kind of mental cut at some imaginary threshold of gray: everything above

18th-century Ladik prayer rug: Dark-light contrast makes the colors glow.

*Detail from Piero della Francesca, The Army of Constantine, 14th century: Even in this
very muted picture, dark-light contrast makes the colors shine.*

the cut is considered white, and everything below it black. Using this threshold we can see every painting — or building — as a two-tone composition of dark and light only. The simple rule, then, is this: *The pattern of black and white must be a good one.*

In making a painting (or in placing colors in a building, which is ultimately my main concern), I find it useful to make a thumbnail sketch in black and white — just to see if the basic composition of light and dark has life in it. When it does, it makes sense to go on to color. Until it does, making the painting is almost a waste of paint. And the question, of course, is: What does it mean for the composition of black and white to be beautiful? Here again we go back to the field of centers. When does it come to life? The black and white come to life when they do something similar to the way the yin-yang symbol works. The two establish a polarity in which each defines the other, where each is something solid and established in its own right, and where the two together create a sort of electric tension.

In *shape*, the two things, black and white, must each form positive space, as defined in the geometric properties. In *amount*, the quantities and ratios of dark and light must be enough to electrify each other. This electrifying tension between dark and light does not imply anything so literal as the equal amounts of black and white. The issue is relative. A beautiful painting might be very light, in which even the so-called dark is a rather soft gray — possibly with one or two highlights of black. But the contrast between the two would still cause a polarity. In another case, a painting might be dark all over, with even the so-called light, being a deep dark gray. But again, even in this case, the painting contains, as fundamental to it, a basic pattern in which the polarity of darker and lighter substances creates something and springs to life.

There is one subtle exception to the rule. Sometimes two colors which affect each other very much produce light, because they are of almost similar weight, *without* dark-light contrast. The way that a certain blue flashes on red, or the way that gray sometimes works with pink, are two examples. These cases are rare. But even in these cases the flickering tension between two similar tones, if transformed to be black and white, still has a beautiful pattern.

9 / MUTUAL EMBEDDING
(DEEP INTERLOCK AND AMBIGUITY)

This is a version of the property called DEEP IN-TERLOCK. But, in the sphere of color it is more fundamental, and more necessary, than in the purely geometric cases which DEEP INTERLOCK describes.

In the 17th-century Persian garden carpet shown opposite, each major area, whatever its main color, contains within it small pieces of the other colors that lie in the areas around it. The effect is that each area is tied, subtly, by these internal cross-references, to areas of color which surround it. For instance, the central square medallion contains red and dark blue waves and light blue flowers. The dark blue reflects larger areas of dark blue in the outer squares and outer border. The red reflects elements of red in the outer corners; the light blue reflects the color of the light-blue star-octagons in the four corners of the carpet and of the pale blue ornaments in the main carpet border. The green field contains dark blue motifs in the blue of the medallion, pale yellow motifs reflecting the color of the minor border and the octagon in the middle of the carpet. The brown and pale-blue main border, contains the other colors within it in tiny fragments. The pale blue minor border contains the green and red of the field, the blue of the medallion. It goes on and on.

Let us generalize. Imagine, if you like, that you have a color composition half worked out. You struggle towards making more light in the picture. You seek harmonies which tie things together more. At this stage, you will often find that the thing you have to do to make more light in the picture is, in effect, a process in which you put one color inside another. You have red and blue, say. You want them to shine. You put some blue — small flecks of blue — inside the red.

Persian garden carpet, 17th century

The Book of Kells, 9th century

And you put small dots of red somewhere inside the blue. Slowly, as you do it, the shine of the light increases.

Often, as I get into the later stages of a painting, I find that I have to create additional connections between fields of different colors. For example, I paint a blue bowl of fruit on a black background. The light shines. But everything is a bit too stark, so I have to put spots of purple and blue into the black. Their presence in the black then creates additional connections between the inside and the outside.

In general, if I have two colors next to each other, A and B, then I can create a connection by putting a little bit of A inside B, and a little bit of B inside A. Immediately a connection is formed, and the field becomes more unified.

Suppose we have a green and a red near each other, and they have been chosen to produce a light. Still, there may be some way in which the boundary between the two creates a separation: the overall field is too severely divided into a red field and a green field. To make a better unity in the field, we put little bits of red in the green, and little bits of green in the red. As we do it, the color melts and unifies. Whatever unity can be created by the way that colors create light is then supplemented by a process which unifies and connects the space. Here are some examples of this effect.

In the illustration from The Book of Kells the same process occurs very naively, perhaps with a more spiritual depth: red appears in the blue, flecks of blue appear in the red, flecks of yellow in the blue, flecks of red in the yellow, and so on.

In Bonnard's *Dining Room on the Garden*, it happens with shattering intensity. The blue, the huge and almost horrendous blue, appears in the sky and again, in a touch on the tablecloth. The color of the room wall appears in on the lamp and fruit and table, and in the garden. The green of the outdoors reappears on the floor, and the floor color appears in the blossoms of the bushes outside.

It is possible to generalize this phenomenon beyond color. We may say that each major entity in a living structure must contain references (shapes, structures, colors, motifs, reflections) of the other major elements, so that each element is somehow also *within* the other elements.

Mutual embedding: Pierre Bonnard, Dining Room on the Garden, 1934

10 / SEQUENCE OF LINKED COLOR PAIRS
(GRADIENTS AND THE VOID)

As I have explained under COLORS CREATE LIGHT TOGETHER, the thing which makes any one color glow is its interaction with surrounding colors — both nearby colors and distant colors. If I want to make a red glow, I surround it with a luminescent green. I work at the green. I combine a mid-sea green, with grass green, with white green, patches of yellow that fuse to an intense yellow green — all these, I choose them, because they bring the red to life. We shall go on, now, to examine the spatial arrangement of these interactions.

As I continue trying to create light, the next thing I find most commonly is that the colors essentially work in pairs. They interact spatially to form geometrical sequences of interaction.

In creating light, I find myself having to set up the colors to form centers in a field-like fashion. This works the same way that a sequence of centers can help to form and intensify a center. The gradient formed by the sequence of centers helps to make the larger center strong by focusing attention on the end of the sequence which the gradient points towards. Just so, a gradient of color, or a sequence of colors, or a second color in its impact on the first color, can make the whole thing glow. As I try to make the color glow with light, I have to work at this second color and the third, in their impact on the first.

For example, in the miniature painting of the Persian lady, the eye follows this sequence of linked pairs:

    Gold —> *white*
    White —> *violet gray*
    Violet gray —> *red*
    Red —> *yellow (of collar)*
    Red —> *black shoes*
    Black shoes —> *black writing in*
       yellow gold

We find a definite sequential structure to the hierarchy of colors. When inner light is present, the colors in the hierarchy have a definite spatial sequence, so that the eye moves through the thing from color to color, up and down the hierarchy. In each case, the spatial sequence is built out of linked pairs. We may think of them as arrows. Each color in the field is built as a reaction, or counterpart, to some other particular color that it works with, and forms a pair with. The pairs themselves are linked, and the network of linked pairs or arrows forms the sequence.

The way these spatial pairs are linked and form a kind of sequence is very much like the way that it happens geometrically, in the field of centers. Suppose, for instance, we have a room in which there is a tokonoma, and in the tokonoma there is a vase of flowers. There are three centers. The room center is linked to the tokonoma center and is intensified by it. The tokonoma center is linked to the vase of flowers center and is intensified by it. We experience a sequence of linked pairs.

It is not literally a sequence. There is nothing which says we must see the room first, or the tokonoma second, or the vase of flowers third. Nevertheless, there is this linked structure creating a kind of chain of pairs, and the intensity of the whole is made for us, by this system of linked pairs which keeps pointing and leading from one center to another.

That is how the colors work. Each color talks mainly to one other color above it, and to one other color below it. That makes the chain of linked pairs. It is very helpful, when painting, to concentrate on these pairs, because it allows us, with more intensity, to concentrate on the idea that each color talks to some other one — and by concentrating on it to make sure that it really happens.

Persian miniature, 16th century

Henri Matisse, Nasturtiums and the Dance

In Matisse's *Nasturtiums and the Dance* the orange at the center, small as it is, stands against the red-purple combination; the dark blue stands against the red.

Looking at San Miniato al Monte, in Florence (opposite), again we see this system of linked pairs working:

White —> black
White and black —> blue of sky
White and black —> gold

Sometimes a given color in the sequence talks to, or reacts to, more than one other color that is earlier in sequence. For instance, in the Indian miniature on page 200, the blood red also talks to and reacts with the light turquoise blue. And so does the striking pink which lies in the areas below the red and white. The feeling of moving in the painting, passing from each color to another one which comes forth in answer to it, is very strong. Each color in the sequence is built as a reaction to another particular color in the sequence — and each color then talks to yet another one. It is the network of linked pairs which forms the structure.

Once again, it is easy to see how this series of sequences is connected to the field of centers. In the field of centers each center is propped up or supported by others. As a result there is a sense of orientation caused by the way each center supports another. That is what is happening in the color field, too. Each color helps to support some other color in its life or intensity, and each color is, in its own turn, supported in its life by yet some other color.

A rough rule that is often followed is: the more vivid or more intense colors tend to have small areas, thus be small vivid spots of color further down in the hierarchy. In general, there is an archetypal way of working that exists between two colors. Typically, we see a larger amount of one color, and then we see a second color, present in a lesser amount but more vivid than the first,

and it is the second color which seems to be "what the combination is all about."

Thus the color pairs play a big role in forming the gradient, or arrow, that points to the heart of a given center, and gives it life. We have the golden surround of the Persian lady, and the pale violet grey dress in the center. There is more golden yellow — perhaps three times as much — but the picture is about the violet-grey. Like the hierarchy of colors, the sequence of color pairs helps to create the structure of the field of centers. Each pair which creates movement is a pointer in the field. The pointer is the gradient which actually creates the field. For example, suppose violet and pale yellow are "talking to each other" as they do in the Persian miniature. The haze of gold around the edge talks to the purple dress — it reinforces its centrality. The way the colors talk to each other depends on the fact that the one surrounds, or partially surrounds the other. And vice versa. The violet creates a focus,

San Miniato al Monte, Florence, 11th century.

which induces a greater feeling of centrality in the ring of gold around the outside. Without the violet, the gold would be a weaker center.

In the Indian miniature we see the linked sequence of color pairs most vividly, perhaps, with red and white and blue. The eye moves from the white pavilion to red, blue, gray, white, pink, pale blue, dark blue-green. There is a large area of pale bluish green. The dark blue-green is built up as a definite reaction to this lighter blue. And then the white, which is still smaller in area, is built as a reaction or a counterpoint to this dark blue-green. The brilliant blood red then comes as a foil or as an answer to the white.

In this case, one approximation of the structure we experience might go like this:

White —> blue-green

Mid blue-green —> red of arch

Red of arch —> deep blue-green

Deep blue-green —> small touches of pale blue (of collar)

Pale blue —> original white of arch

We should not forget, finally, that the actual path of the sequence — the way the sequence of color pairs jumps around the page — is also important. When the path has a beautiful feeling, it jumps in an interesting way — in a cascade, or in a circling motion moving inward. A completely

Indian miniature in which the color pairs work very well

simple-minded movement inward is not interesting, and never holds the eye. A dull prison-like walk back and forth across the page is not likely to be interesting. The path which is interesting must be chosen to intensify the centers which exist.

All this follows from the fact that in the field of centers, the way that a given sequence of centers works is most likely to create life when it forms some very large centers at the largest level. This corresponds to the glowing light which comes from the result of these color sequences. The way that a sequence of centers forms a more intense center — the way the sequence of color pairs really works — is reminiscent of the discussion of linked centers creating larger centers in GRADIENTS.

Again, the glowing light itself — which the structure causes — is surprising. Its unity seems to exist beyond the structure of the field which has created it.

11 / BOUNDARIES AND HAIRLINES

(BOUNDARIES)

The intense color of the Persian tilework here, and its great flowers and stems and leaves, is made by its boundaries. Each boundary color strengthens the color which it bounds. The whole pattern is a stunning array of boundaries: the edges, the edges of the edges, the blossoms themselves, and the edges of the blossoms.

This is a general rule in almost all work with color. You will often find that you can intensify colors by making boundaries between them. The simplest boundaries are white and black. If I have a red plum on a blue bowl, and there is a line of white above the plum, it seems like the light on the surface of the plum. But what really happens in the painting is that the whitish line connects the red of the plum and the blue of the bowl, unifies them, and makes a stronger connection. A black line often does the same.

Of course, one doesn't use actual white or actual black — these are usually too stark. A white which has red or green or blue in it will work better — you have to look and see which one does the most. The same is true of black — it will usually be an off-black, with brown or red or blue in it. And boundaries of more subtle color often work to do even more. In my painting of the fruit in the blue bowl, the light first became intense when I put a line of turquoise between the blue of the bowl and the black of the background.

Tilework in which hairlines make the colors shine: Gawhar Shad Mosque, Meshed

As one tries to reach inner light, one is in effect trying to create a deep kind of unity. This unity can be helped, in part, by mutual embedding. But the problem which needs to be solved occurs, in principle, at the boundaries of each color. Each patch of color has the danger of being too isolated. Where two colors meet, there is an imperfect unity just because the two colors, by being different, create a divide. To bridge this divide, it is helpful in the vast majority of cases to have a third color, much smaller in extent and carefully chosen in color, which forms a link across the boundary. That is why hairlines and boundaries originate.

Matisse's *Odalisque in Red Trousers* is almost all boundaries. The couch has boundaries, the ornaments are made of lines and boundaries, the woman's hat has a boundary where it meets her face (the shadow), her breast has a boundary (again the shadow), the stripes on the mattress form boundaries. Each of these boundaries both separates and unites the areas on either side of it, thus simultaneously intensifying them, and uniting them to form larger wholes.

The white field carpet, a 16th-century Ushak, does the same. Here the thin hairlines are explicit as the main structure of the work. The yellow line helps to unify the red and blue on ether side of it. The whole carpet is a structure of boundaries, all working to intensify the simple color and make it something glorious.

In each of these examples the light and unity is intensified by the boundaries between colors. The general phenomenon goes like this: *We have two colors, A and B. Then the unity of A and B together is enhanced by a thin line or zone of a third color C which bears a definite relation to A and B.*

We see this rule employed at two different levels: first, in cases where C is a broad swath, or stripe of color, and second, in cases where C is a thin hairline of color. Occasionally we also see a third case in which these two ideas are combined to give a configuration that has five colors: two major colors, A and B, separated by a broad band of boundary color C, and then A is separated from C by a hairline of color D, and B is separated from C by another hairline of color E.

Henri Matisse, Odalisque in Red Trousers

Brilliance of the color created by the hairlines: Ushak carpet, 16th century

Hairlines painted on traditional Venezuelan houses

for a good hairline as a separator/unifier of these two colors.

There are two laws of a good hairline, defining the choice of the color C. First, a law of contrast. If we define the three color values (darkness), for A, C, B, with C being the hairline, then the three values must always be different. This gives only three possible schemes for the contrasting values:

In general the boundary color must be chosen to do the same as any good geometrical boundary does: that is, to both unite and separate the two colors on either side of it. For any two colors A and B, it is possible to choose a C

A	C	B
FIRST COLOR	HAIRLINE	SECOND COLOR
Dark	Medium	Light
Dark	Light	Medium
Light	Dark	Medium

Second, there is a law of unity. The hues are chosen in such a way that both A to C and B to C

Georges Braque, Olive Trees, La Ciotat, 1907

Hairlines and boundaries as the main motif garden of the Franciscan monastery, Convento de los Leones, Mexico City

have the following properties. C is similar to A in one respect *and* C is different from A in some other respect; C is similar to B in the way that it is different from A. C is different from B in the way that it is similar to A. Thus if C and A are similar in hue, and different in value, then C and B will be more similar in value, and complementary in hue.

In the garden of the Convento de los Leones in Mexico City, we see a Franciscan garden reconstructed in modern times to be as it was originally planted by the Franciscans in the 16th century. Each flower bed is made of green, and the bushes and flowers are arranged in rows to form this boundary effect with the stone and gravel of the paths. It is nice to see a whole garden made like this, of color boundaries.

All these examples show the impact of the boundaries on color: all are similar in the way they work to unite areas, just as geometric BOUNDARIES work. Only the thickness of the boundaries is different.

12 / FAMILIES OF COLOR
(ECHOES)

Another thing we have to do while we are working, if we hope to achieve inner light, is to develop a family quality among the different colors we are using. This unifies the space even further.

The simplest way in which colors become members of one family is similar to the process of mutual embedding. If we want to place a red near a green so as to produce inner light, it is necessary that very small amounts of the red are mixed into the green, and that very small amounts of the green are mixed into the red. This softens the contrast and allows the piece to glow.

Pierre Bonnard, Nature Morte aux Fruits dan le Soleil, 1931

Families of color: Page from the Book of Durrow

Look at Bonnard's painting of fruit on a white tablecloth (page 206). How is it that the colors glow with such intensity? It is because the colors come from a single family. It appears that they have all been mixed in the same gesture, the same proportional feeling. And yet, in the member of this family there are greens, reds, purples, blues, yellows. Somehow they are constructed to be of one family.

Giotto manages the same, in the painting below. In this case the feeling of family resemblance and harmony comes from colors which seem to be quite different; thus, for instance a slate blue, and a creamy white. Even then, harmony comes from the way that the complementary colors (in this case, blue and yellow) are softened by traces of opposite colors — a little gray or green in the yellow: a little yellow or brown in the blue.

Sometimes this family feeling exists simply as a feeling, which is complex and not easy to explain at all. I work on the palette, and I can

Giotto, Flight into Egypt, detail

Church in Tepotzotlan, painted by indigenous Mexican Indians.

tell when I am making colors of the same family: but they are not necessarily related in obvious ways at all.

For instance, I make a yellow which is creamy and white, with a touch of green in it. Then the blue which makes sense with this kind of yellow is a sad blue, grayish. And another blue that makes sense together has a lilac cast. I cannot easily explain this. But I can feel it easily. It probably occurs because these colors make light together, according to the properties mentioned earlier — but now it is happening while actually mixing the colors.

At other times, I mix the family right on the painting. I chop the palette knife into the red, to reveal the yellow beneath it. I chop the knife into the yellow, and traces of red make the yellow glow, become orange in feel, but a deep yellow remains. This happens in a red vase painting I don't have room to illustrate. And the blue which is affected like this, by the chopping palette knife, is an extraordinary blue, eerie, dull

at first sight, but infused with reddish tones than have been cut in. Altogether, then, the color families work together.

A page from the Book of Durrow, covered with red and yellow snakes. All of the colors, and the snakes together, even the browns and whites, seem to be one family. A traditional Mexican church painted by the Indigenas, traditional Mexican people of the region. The gold, red, and blue — glowing colors — are all of one piece. They all come from the same pot. In Giotto's gray-blue mountain, a detail of *The Flight into Egypt*, the "pot" is gray or gray blue. Each color, even the browns, come from this gray-blue harmony. In the Turkish miniature of a town on page 183, this time it is pink and white and turquoise and rose. Although there are green, blues, in this painting, it all seems to be suffused with rose.

Families of color is a color version of the geometric property ECHOES that appears in living structure.

13 / COLOR VARIATION
(ROUGHNESS)

Inner light also requires a certain roughness of individual color, a lively variation within the field of a single color. This is similar to the way that ROUGHNESS works in living structure.

Look at the nearly unbelievable color which is achieved on the wall of Giotto's *History of St. Francis, the Confirmation of the Rule* (opposite). Examine the rippling life in the green of the prehistoric Chinese bronze on page 214. You may call its patina an accident of time, or a skill of the maker. But its effect, and its reality, are undeniable. There seem to be a hundred different greens in the bronze, in its shadows and highlights, and it is this which makes it vibrant. The same has been done in a modern painting, too. Examine the Vuillard painting *Mother and Child* (page 212).

In colors which have light, there are rarely areas of perfectly flat color. Instead, when there are large areas of one color, the inside of these areas vary immensely from point to point so that the overall color is created from the blending or interaction of many slightly different hues. For instance, in one Chinese pillar carpet I used to own, there was an immense golden yellow field, and in this whole field there were almost no two knots of exactly the same yellow.

Another favorite example of mine was a cactus which used to grow in the Berkeley Botanical Garden: a large plant, perhaps forty feet long, on a rock garden, with literally thousands of small flowers, all of the most beautiful and shimmering purple. When you went close to look at the individual purple flower heads you found

Incredible subtlety of color variation. Giotto, History of St. Francis, the Confirmation of the Rule

that they were all different. Their "average" was purple but, individually, they varied all the way from a deep purplish red to a pale reddish blue. What seemed like a homogenous but shimmering purple was actually made up of a thousand hues of purple, deep red-purple, light red-purple, blue-purple, pink-purple, dark blue-purple, violet, and pale blue-purple. That color had life!

It is often variation in color which brings the color to life. To make it happen, the colors which contribute to the effect must be members of the same family, colors which are already close. Then we see the composite effect of the varying shades as if it were a single color which has light in it. Geometry also plays an important role in making it work. The variation works exceptionally well when it is half-regular, so that the regu-

lar and alternating variation of spots of color together create the shimmering unity.

Both in paintings and in buildings, I have
found that this color variation comes about most
easily from a process in which you mix the colors
on the thing itself, not on the palette. Suppose, for
instance, I am painting a surface blue. Suppose
the blue is made of blue and white and a touch of
green. I keep all three colors on the palette, and
mix them on the painting, by taking dabs of one
and dabs of the other as I go, gradually making the
colored surface create the necessary light. Then I
can make sure that the color I put on the plane
itself always does as much as possible to create the
inner light I am looking for. I keep fine-tuning
the color as I go, adjusting it, changing it, bringing
it back to the right perfect one, according to the
overall amount of blue and white and traces of

Variation of color: A cafe table, Greece

Edouard Vuillard, Mother and Child

Color variation in nature: Ripples in a Persian garden pond, Garden of Fin, Iran, 16th century

green I have in that area. Thus like a singer who keeps a perfect tone by vibrato, I use the slight variations from point to point to get a more accurate and perfect color balance in the whole.

Sometimes I do the same thing more geometrically. If we have a particular color, say light red, and we mix black with it, we get brownish dark red; and if we mix white with it we get whitish pink-red. These colors may easily become muddy. But suppose that, instead of mixing the black into the red, we put a fine black (blackish red) tracery of points, dots, lines, and curves over the lighter red. This has the same overall effect on the red — that is, as a whole it moves towards brownish dark red — but it leaves it far more brilliant, with sparkle.

In a similar way, fine pink diamonds dispersed throughout the red may again move it towards lighter red, but again without causing the soupy congealed feeling we sometimes get with pink. Again the red moves towards pink, but the white in it sparkles, and the red retains its brilliance.

We may do the same with more than two hues. If we interlace fine yellow lines or arabesques with red, we can achieve a blazing, light-filled orange, far more delicate than we can get merely by mixing red and yellow in the palette, or by painting a homogenous surface orange on the plane.

Thus we get greater brilliance. This is really how, and why, the variation of roughness works: by creating a mixture out of purer colors, so that we keep the purity of the component colors and their interaction. It is vital to realize that the color variation you use will not do anything if

Chinese Bronze

it is just mechanical. Mechanical variation will be just that—mechanical. To get a variation which is worthwhile, you have to vary the color during your effort to bring the color (and the whole) to life. If you are paying attention to the feeling which the color generates, and mean-while varying the color to make this feeling more intense, then you will find that the variation plays a useful role.

Color variation is a version of the geometric property ROUGHNESS which occurs in all living structure.

14 / INTENSITY AND CLARITY OF INDIVIDUAL COLORS
(STRONG CENTERS, GOOD SHAPE)

Here there is an almost paradoxical ambiguity. Clarity of color is something inherent in the individual color. Yet, its effect is also created by the color interactions and by the impact of other colors on the individual color. Both are true.

Illustrated here are some Shaker boxes. The Shakers were famous for their special colors, the pigments and formulas they used, the clarity and purity of these "Shaker" colors.

And it is true that in the realm of color, we are startled sometimes by the beauty of a particular color — the blue of the sky near Naples, the red of a certain poppy, or the red glaze of certain famous Isnik ceramics from Turkey, so famous that a whole period of Turkish art history is defined by this red color.

I remember once trying to find a particular blue for cabinets in my kitchen. I started with a mid-light blue enamel. I took a piece of board, put a thick coat of this light blue enamel on the board. Then I began rubbing in, with my fingers and hand, colors from tubes of oil paint I had: ultramarine, black, and dark cobalt green. I rubbed some in, mixed it around, moved the color more to gray, intensified the blue with ultramarine, worked in the cobalt green, used more gray, then much more blue, more green again. Finally, I ended with a most glorious color — a deep blue, with traces of green visible, so deeply saturated that the blueness almost could not been seen, and yet it shone. The mixer at the paint store said it was the hardest color he had ever been given to match. But what is im-

Clarity of color that does not depend on interactions: simply on the beauty of individual pigments. Shaker boxes, painted with original Shaker paints.

portant for this discussion is that the color was beautiful *in itself*; it was a pleasure to make it and it is, now, every day, a pleasure to sit and look at it.

When you are in the middle of painting, you can often concentrate only on the color you are mixing, and with great care and concentration, make *that* color by itself carry meaning, and be as beautiful in itself as possible. There is no doubt that you can make this effort, and no doubt that the process of finding a color which is beautiful and clear in itself, which has deep feeling in the color *itself*, is a process which is real.

But what it means — this clarity and beauty of a single color — is paradoxical. Is the color you find which has intense meaning and feeling in itself really a quality of the *individual* color by itself? Or is it a quality of this color in the *interaction* with its surroundings?

It is clear from the history of art that many cultures and artists have treasured particular col-ors — not only because they were hard to make or hard to find — but also because they were so beautiful in themselves. Malachite green, the red from cinnabar (oxide of mercury), the blue of lapis lazuli, Tyrian purple — they were all loved and treasured for the color *itself*. In one famous case, the whole development of a hundred years of Isnik pottery in the 17th century depended on

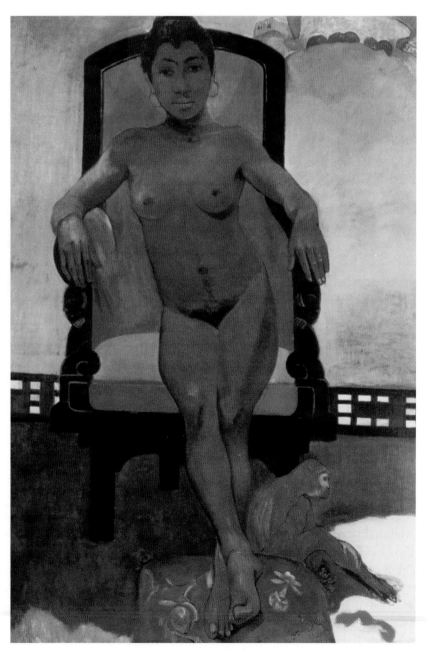

Paul Gauguin, Anna the Javanese, Nude woman in chair with monkey, 1889

the creation (or invention) of a single red glaze. It was the beauty of this one color which made the tradition.

An extreme example of the possible beauty of an individual color occurs in a story recently told by a young American traveller who wrote a book in which he described several years he spent in Turkey and Afghanistan studying with Sufi masters. He spent some months with a master in Turkey. Finally it was time to leave. As he was leaving his master gave him a present, a tiny bottle with a yellow powder in it. He asked what it was. The master told him, "This particular yellow is a perfect reflection of your own soul. If you are sad or tired, look at it, and you will be refreshed. The color will remind you of what you are."

The idea that a *structure* can be a mirror of the soul has been described at length in Book 1. It depends on the idea that the living structure has this property. But the idea that a powder, a single color, could also have this property, is harder to understand. It is interesting, though, because it clearly shows that in Turkey there is a tradition in which it is understood that one color *by itself* may be more profound than another. The point of the precious powder is that *its* yellow is just the right yellow to be a picture of the self: other yellows would not have it. People today, understanding less about color, no longer distinguish profound colors from banal colors. They see only colors. They see only red, blue, yellow, green. They confuse ugly reds made by precise chemical processes with the beauty of the red we see in a poppy.

But the whole subject remains paradoxical. For it also seems doubtful to me that an individual color *can* really be beautiful by itself, and that this even means anything. Most of the rules we have studied in this chapter give examples of this way that light comes from the *interplay* of colors, not from their absolute beauty. We have seen how, to a large extent the beauty of color depends on the *interaction* between colors, on the relative amounts, relative lightness, relative hues. If you take any color — good or bad, no matter what it is — you can choose another color that in hue, lightness, intensity, and amount it makes the first one shine forth intensely. This is precisely the point of COLORS CREATE LIGHT TOGETHER, and it is just this which makes me feel that colors are all relative, work through their interaction, and therefore that there is no such thing as beauty of *individual* color.

This argument would seem to show that it is the *interplay*, the interaction, which produces light, not the absolute beauty of the individual colors themselves. Indeed, this idea does have tremendous force.

However, it turns out that the two ideas are interwoven. As I begin to master the idea of trying to make colors fuse together and glow with inner light, I find out one thing which is rather surprising: to do it, I am really trying to make *each* color shine out as strongly as possible, itself. *Indeed, it turns out that this is the main thing that I need to try to do.*

I work and work to make each color individually beautiful and strong. I get a first sketch of a painting, then step by step I look at each color, and see what I have to do to it to make it shine more beautifully. I do mean this literally, that I want each color to glow in itself. But this is not "individualistic" as it sounds. It sounds at first as if this would inevitably make a babel of color — in which each color is shrieking at the top of its lungs, so the colors will all clash.

The facts are much more subtle. In centers, a strong center is one which stands strong by itself, and yet makes other nearby centers strong. That is part of the definition of a center. Just so, a color which shines strongly is a color which makes other colors nearby shine strongly, too. That is part of the definition of "strong." So, as I try to make the red glow, I have to infuse it with little bits of purple, orange, and pink, work them into the fabric of the red, make places where a tiny spot of blue is showing through. As I accomplish it — as, gradually the red really begins to glow — at the same time the other colors glow also.

This is exactly what I have to do with centers. Nothing can be a center by itself. It becomes a center and gets its life at the same time, and through the same process that brings all the other centers to life. To make a color shine out beautifully and most intensely *actually requires that it is supported by all the other colors in the field*.

Thus, by an odd paradox, by trying to make one color strong and beautiful, I am forced to make the other colors which support it and make it work, harmonious and beautiful both with it, and in themselves. Just so, as I work to make each color beautiful, a center in itself, so I shall, automatically, at the same time also be making beauty in the harmony of the whole.

A perfect example is Gauguin's *Anna the Javanese*. What an intense blue! The force of it is the woman's brown body and this blue together but, in a way the painting is all about the blue! And about the brown! Here it seems that the intensity of color is indeed created by the interaction, not merely by the pigment of the blue itself.

And yet it is also true that the clarity of individual color is a phenomenon which at least appears to exist. Subjectively the phenomenon is real. We certainly sometimes experience one color as having more feeling than another. Sometimes it can take hours of experiment to find the single color which has the most feeling in a given context. The hours of experiment are about

Eastern bluebird. Even here, with brilliant feathers that have their own shining blue pigment, color interaction (the support of the white and of the reddish brown) is used to make the blue shine still more vividly.

something real. The feeling in the color I find for a given situation is absolutely real. That *one* color is clear, beautiful, and full of feeling.

Thus, powerful as interaction is to produce inner light by combination and relative effects, still, also the individual color can be true or false, deep or shallow, clear or muddy. When the color is clear, it shines with inner light *itself* even before it is combined with other colors. In general the colors which occur in nature are beautiful ones. On the other hand, many colors made by mixing pigments are not beautiful. They can be dead, dull, lifeless. Mechanical codification of color, like the Munsell system, with its sphere of colors, leads us mistakenly to believe that all colors are equally valuable, just because each one has a similar looking code name.

So what is clarity of color? Can we define it, or say anything about how to get it? One yellow glows, has an inner light. Another is muddy. The purity of the color is affected, also, by the process through which it is made, and by the actual medium. For example, paint, stain, dye, glaze, deep glaze, wool, and tapestry all have quite different colors. And even within wool, for instance, there is dry wool, lush wool, and dead wool. There is color which is oversaturated, undersaturated. And then, once in a while, there is a brilliant dazzling, shining color, full of light.

One possible explanation of good color (the simplest) is that most paints, pigments, present a mixture of colors. The pigment functions by absorbing light — thus a red pigment gets its red by absorbing blue, yellow, and green wavelength light. However, this absorption is rarely perfect, leaving a muddy effect. On the other hand, pure red light (i.e. laser light or rainbow light) is actually pure, has just one wavelength in it. Perhaps the pigments we consider most beautiful are just the ones which emit a very narrow band of wavelengths, and thus approximate colored light.

However, I believe the correct view is that intensity and clarity of color is mainly an effect of interaction, and that the most important result of color interactions, when they are correct, is not only that the many colors together form a

Intensity and clarity of individual colors: Fra Angelico, The Massacre of the Innocents (detail)

beautiful whole, but that the individual colors also come to life.

This is then exactly like the life of an individual center in the field of centers. The individual color gets its intensity, clarity, beauty, and life from its location among the other colors which together form the context in which we can see and create, the individual color which shines. This is, I think, a version of the properties called STRONG CENTERS and GOOD SHAPE.

15 / SUBDUED BRILLIANCE

(INNER CALM AND NOT-SEPARATENESS)

We come to the most difficult yet most essential aspect of the field effect which produces inner light: subdued brilliance.

Let us imagine that at a certain stage in the development of a colored thing — building, painting, furniture, or cloth — we have gained a wonderful bright feeling where the colors work together, they are brilliant. But they are perhaps too bright, too vulgar, not profound. Let us say that the color is too garish. To make it more profound we have to cut it back. We have to subdue the influence of the whole thing. We quieten it, gently. We quieten it a little more. Then, when we are just to the edge of feeling that we have taken away its brilliance, we put something back — and all of a sudden the color really shines, and the deep meaning shows itself.

That is subdued brilliance.

It can take two different forms. The first form is quiet. Sometimes, to do it, I reduce the intensity of colors by making them more white or more gray. Then the actual pigments are subdued, but I keep the overall brilliance of the field of color — only now somehow it is more profound. That is the first form. The second form is almost opposite. I have pigments which are intense, very bright. But in their interaction they become muted, because they are so carefully chosen, so perfectly chosen, that they melt together and seem quiet even though, individually, as colors, they are bright.

Both these forms work very well. And although they sound different, actually they are the same. In both cases, what I aim to get in the end is subdued brilliance, which shows me I have finally done my work.

8th-century fresco in the Abbey Gateway, Lorsch

Mountains and Streams, Persian miniature, Bihbahan, 1398

The field works, and the unity is created, under those conditions when the colors are both very bright in themselves, and also very much melted together, and indistinguishable from one another. This is the same as the field of centers itself where, in order to succeed, the centers are strong individually in their own life, and also create an overall unity in which the centers are indistinguishably melted in one another to produce a single overall life.

In the case of color, this complex two-sided effect takes a particular form: the colors are bright and intense individually, but very muted, often very light ... and they are, at the same time, pale, muted, and working together, so that there is no overall crass brightness of color.

Persian miniature of yellow mountain and stream (page 221). The colors are very pale, a pale yellow, a pale blue, much white and brown. But the overall effect is unbelievably intense.

Piero della Francesca, *King Solomon receiving the Queen of Sheba*. In this painting the colors

are milky. The main purple robe, is almost white, with the merest trace of purple: the glowing golden color, is again extremely muted. The strong colors are browns, dark and somber. But the intense pale colors shine as if they were the brightest colors they could be.

The subdued brilliance which is central to inner light can be consciously controlled. It happens in two ways, which are usually combined.

The first way involves the use of apparently muted colors, but in a way where each color intensifies the others. For example, suppose we are trying to intensify a red. It will happen, often, through the use of green. But it is often the case that this intensification will be most effective — both most intense, and also most harmonious — if the green is very subdued. Either a white, with a touch of green in it, so that it is almost white — or a green with a very large amount of gray in it, so that it is almost gray. Thus in this case, the brilliance of the combination depends on the use of a fairly intense red, complemented

Piero della Francesca, King Solomon receiving the Queen of Sheba

Subdued brilliance in a mosaic tile panel, Darb-i-Kushk, Isfahan

Smoky rose color, on the exterior of the Hotel Palumbo, Ravello

by a very large amount of very subdued greenish white or greenish gray. So, in this first case, the overall feeling of the color field is muted. It is not gaudy, or garish. It is calm, soft-toned, subdued. This happens because many of the colors have a surprising amount of gray or white in them. They are not pure pigments.

The other way that subdued brilliance helps to produce inner light relies on very intense colors, used in a way which *seems* muted. Gauguin's paintings illustrate this quality well. He might use, for instance, intense purple, orange, green — but somehow makes them muted in their combination. This is a much harder trick than the other. Once again, it happens because the pigments themselves are dampened, muted, by using gray or complementary colors mixed in. Yet at the same time, some of the colors which actually produce this effect, are also, after all intense and brilliant: they are not, themselves, subdued. And this is very surprising — the use of brilliant colors, to produce a muted whole, or an overall unity so profound that nothing stands out, everything melts together, and yet the actual colors that are used are brilliant.

Of course, the reason that this double thing occurs is that the color harmony is so beautifully ordered, so subtle, that the colors seem to melt into one another. When something is made whole, the color *always* has this special subdued brilliance. The subdued brilliance is produced in two different, complementary ways. Bonnard's painting of *Martha in a Red Blouse* has this quality also. Intense color, placed together so that their brilliance is almost muted.

Remember that there are two specific ways in which this phenomenon is helped to happen. First, the bright, or brilliant colors, are often surprisingly light — they have a lot of white in them — like the very pale yellow in the Persian mountain painting. The use of bright colors, in very light versions, which are not whitish (like pink, or cream), but very clear and light: very light red like vermillion, scarlet, washed over white does not look pink, but very light; clear yellow washed over white, does not look cream colored, but clear yellow, again very light.

Second, the other thing which seems to happen is the use of small amounts of deep contrasting colors (for instance the deep blue, almost indigo, in the miniature of a Turkish town, to offset the pale reds; the use of deep purplish black in the Persian mountain painting, to offset the lighter yellow and whites).

So the subdued and bright is often done by a combination of large areas of light, clear colors, contrasted with small quantities of relatively deeper colors, more blackish and more densely saturated.

It is often a feature of this subdued brilliance that the colors are not obvious at all. They are not the simple primaries red, yellow, blue. They tend to be complex and subtle colors . . . a red with gray in it, a blue with slightly greenish hint . . . a yellow with a brownish pink cast . . . or light bluish gray, a yellowish brown, a whitish green. This occurs because it is necessary to make complex and subtle colors, simply in order to meet

Pierre Bonnard, Marthe in a Red Blouse, 1928

Subdued brilliance of a subtle darkening kind. Pierre Bonnard, Garden Gate of the Villa Bosquet, Le Cannet, 1944. A profusion of living centers, in the details and in the whole.

the conditions which have been described in these pages — and thus to bring light to life on the page or in the building. It is always surprising.

In addition, there are often large areas of relatively neutral colors, which contain barely a hint of color. A white which has a touch of blue in it . . . a gray which has a very slight tone of yellow . . . a black, which is not quite black, but has certain reds in it . . . but in all cases, so subdued that one can hardly see them. And yet, these very slightly colored neutral tones play a huge role in the architecture of the color.

Subdued brilliance, when it goes to the extreme, is both gloomy and brilliant, like a smoldering fire, embers glowing, other parts dark or dead, fire waiting to burst forth. Bonnard's

painting *Garden Gate of the Villa Bosquet* is something of this kind, where the greens, grays, pink, dark purple, orange-red, blacks, gray-greens like small flecks of fire, gloom and smolder in the shadows, and a soft light coming from these smoldering embers, like the spirit catching fire, hangs in the picture.

This quality creates the quietness of INNER CALM and NOT SEPARATENESS. Making the colors calm and neutral, we completely prevent the dominance of any one color over the others. It is this which allows the whole to melt, and it is this which then creates the field effect most strongly. The dominance of any one center disappears. All the centers fuse to form a single unbroken whole.

16 / COLOR DEPENDS ON GEOMETRY
(STRONG CENTERS, LOCAL SYMMETRIES)

Throughout this chapter, I have suggested that the light produced by color is a by-product of the geometric field of centers. It is an aspect of wholeness which occurs as color comes to life. This implies, of course, that behind all these color phenomena, it is the field of centers itself which is working to produce the life. The geometric structure of the field is necessary to produce the light within the framework of geometry. Geometric structure is *required* to intensify and unify color.

Look at van Gogh's *The Sower*. This famous painting, tiny and intense, with the green sun, is given its force almost entirely by the force of the dark geometry. The silhouetted tree, the sower's upthrust arm, and the round sun create a force of composition which then intensifies the strange yellowish green and violet colors and encourages them to come to life.

The striking harmony of red, blue and brown in the Yuruk carpet on the next page can be felt in the spikiness of the geometry. If the geometry were different, not so angular, or differently shaped, the particular color harmony we feel in this brown-red-blue would be a different harmony. The light comes directly from the geometric structure of the carpet, acting as the field in which the colors play.

Color and geometry: Vincent Van Gogh, The Sower, 1888

Anatolian Yuruk carpet

The same thing is true in the Turkish plate. The rather extraordinary (and to me previously unknown) interaction of the blue and green, which creates a kind of blue-green-white color mist, is generated by the particular shapes and geometrical interpenetration. If you take the same blue, the same green and the same white, you will not be able to create this particular color feeling with other geometrical forms.

And once again in the Chinese gateway, the powerful, almost regal quality of the red is certainly caused by the strong rectangular shapes, and by the narrow dark boundaries, and small rectangular panels of orange and pink. Again, the very particular and memorable quality of the red is caused by the geometrical interaction, not by the color alone.

Turkish dish, 16th century

Red and gilded arch in the Imperial City, Beijing

The blue tile and brown brick on page 235 shows us the phenomenon again. Again the light comes from the particular geometric interplay of the blue and pale brown. The same colors differently arranged, even if the quantities are the same, will produce an entirely different light.

The hunch that there is an intimate connection between wholeness of color and wholeness of geometry, is borne out empirically. Somehow, apparently then, there is an intimate connection between wholeness of color and wholeness of geometry. Specifically I make this observation: *We can never achieve inner light when the field of centers is not present geometrically.* And the reverse is also true: *We cannot achieve the unity of the field of centers geometrically, unless it is supported by wholeness of color and inner light.*

It is fairly easy to see this in almost all the examples we have looked at. The beauty of color comes not only from the beautiful interplay of colors, but from the geometry as well. We learn the power of this effect fully when we ourselves try to produce inner light. We find then, that it is actually impossible to do unless we also create geometric wholeness as the substrate for the color.

Thus the geometric wholeness is not merely beautiful in itself as an accompaniment to the beautiful color. It is essential, necessary, for the release of light. Color, far from being an incidental attribute of things, is fundamental to the living structure of wholeness. Inner light is not merely a color phenomenon, but the character of wholeness when it "melts."

17 / COLOR AND THE FIELD OF CENTERS

It is obvious that the eleven color properties which I have identified closely resemble the fifteen ways that centers help each other come to life. Like the geometric properties, each describes one way in which colors intensify each other to produce inner light. There is also a literal resemblance between these color properties and the geometric properties, which may be brought out as follows.

HIERARCHY OF COLORS, like LEVELS OF SCALE, establishes the actual areas of color and requires a gradient of areas, by size.

SEQUENCE OF COLOR PAIRS, like CENTERS and GRADIENTS, establishes a direction, an orientation of the colors towards a center which is the target of a given goal.

COLORS CREATE LIGHT, like POSITIVE SPACE, requires the complementarity and cooperative wholeness of adjacent colors, just as positive space is formed by the mutual reinforcement of positive geometric volume and geometric space.

CONTRAST OF DARK AND LIGHT is obviously like CONTRAST: it is virtually the same idea.

MUTUAL EMBEDDING, like DEEP INTERLOCK, requires that when two wholes are near each other, each one partially penetrates the other, to knit the two together.

HAIRLINES AND BOUNDARIES is the same as BOUNDARIES.

FAMILIES OF COLOR is very similar to ECHOES: it requires a hidden similarity among the elements which appear in a given whole.

CLARITY OF INDIVIDUAL COLOR is like STRONG CENTERS and GOOD SHAPE: it requires the individual clarity and beauty of the elements themselves.

COLOR VARIATION, like ROUGHNESS, says that the whole will be more profound, if the individual repetitions (in this case of color in the plane) varies with local circumstance, instead of being homogeneous.

SUBDUED BRILLIANCE is like INNER CALM and NOT SEPARATENESS: it requires the calm humility of the colors, and prevents any one from shouting out too loud by itself.

COLOR DEPENDS ON GEOMETRY, like STRONG CENTERS, like LOCAL SYMMETRIES, places an almost exaggerated emphasis on symmetry and geometry, causing the whole to hold together, and to receive its brilliance.

Evidently the color properties are very similar to the geometric properties we have discussed in the previous chapters. They are not identical, but they deal with the same kinds of issues translated into the world of color. *I wish to emphasize that this is a discovery, not an assumption.* The eleven color properties were derived empirically, without reference to the geometric properties. There was no reason to assume that the properties of color fields would be the same, or even similar, to the properties which create geometric unity. But after identifying them experimentally, it *turned out* that there is a kinship between the two sets of properties.

The parallel between the color properties and the geometric properties underlines the existence of the profound connection between color and geometry. Wholeness of color is evidently very similar both in quality and structure to the geometric wholeness which we have observed. In both cases, we may see this wholeness as a field of centers. It is a structure in which centers intensify one another, to produce increasing unity and in which the field — in the end — melts, as this pure unity is attained more and more.

The following experiment, done in 1982 in my laboratory at the University of California, demonstrates how powerfully color depends on the existence of a harmonious field of centers in the geometry. I asked students to make a number of drawings in which we would study the interaction of color and geometry. Of these drawings, I chose two, one which had a structure that

Landscape: the students coloring is beautiful almost automatically because of the structure of the drawing

Another student's beautiful color

Another student's beautiful color

Another student's beautiful color

would be difficult to color well, and another whose field of centers is so good that it would be hard *not* to color it well.

The "bad" drawing (which we called *Sun Man*) is illustrated on page 232. In a class of ten talented students who tried to color a xerox copy of this drawing, not one student was able to make a beautiful colored version of that drawing. I have shown only two of these examples, because I could not bring myself to put so many ugly pictures in the chapter. The geometry fights against the color. It does not permit creation of inner light, because the field of centers is damaged and not light-producing.

The "good" drawing (which we called *Landscape*) is illustrated on this page. Again, I gave xeroxed copies to all ten students. This time, all the students colored this drawing, beautifully —

even the less gifted students. In *Landscape*, the geometry supports the color, makes it easy for it to come to life, makes it almost automatic.

Let us recapitulate the role of the fifteen properties, now that we have seen how they affect light. In chapters 4, 5 and 6 of Book 1, we have seen that these properties are geometric properties which unify space by providing different ways that centers come to life, and combine to form larger centers. Now, we find that they are also linked, indirectly, to a more pervasive kind of unity — a field-like light — which seems to spread throughout a thing when it is correctly colored.

I conclude that even the inner light which we have observed through color is itself a product of the field of centers: but this product is a *unity*. It is one thing. It is not some other thing, pasted

Sun Man: Horrible in its geometric organization! No matter what you do, the color cannot be beautiful

on top of the field. It is the field itself, shining with light, when it is properly made. But it is one. Thus the color properties are almost exactly parallel to the fifteen geometric properties we have already identified in the realm of geometry.

It also seems that the two sets of properties are *causally* related. Wholeness in geometry somehow helps to create inner light in color. Inner light in color somehow helps to produce wholeness in geometry. Even when all these aspects of the color field are there, it turns out, finally, that you cannot create this inner light, unless the geometric structure of space supports it. In other words, the oneness of space — the properties, the centers, and so forth — is a necessary ground, in which the colors work.

The interaction of color and geometry is unexpected, and difficult to understand. We are aware, of course, that color, brilliance, is affected in some general way by spatial organization. But what we discover from our experiments is much more specific, and much more surprising. Apparently the presence of the fifteen properties in the geometry of a thing, also gives its color life, somehow brings the colors to their maximum potential. Two or three colors in flat areas, side by side, are nice maybe, but nothing special. Yet as we introduce the geometric properties into the space, the colors begin to shine, begin to interact in amazing and deep ways, to produce a sensation of "color" (note the singular) besides

which the original colors (note the "s") are merely flat zones, empty and meaningless vibrations.

Just as the geometry gives life to the colors, so too, the color seems to bring the space to life. It is as though the colors, correctly distributed, affect the space so deeply that the geometric properties themselves are intensified, the oneness of the space is intensified, deepened, altered, by the colors. This is amazing indeed. It is not so surprising that space has the power to affect color. But that color also affects space — that the two are somehow deeply interlocked — that is truly surprising, and poses many unanswered questions. For this implies that the geometrical phenomenon which I have called "oneness" lies in some domain which we can hardly even identify. It is as though the space and the color together create a world of structure, a type of structure, that we cannot define at all — as though the very oneness of space which we seek to define lies in this very inaccessible realm. *It is this fact which makes me suspect that the color phenomenon itself is actually happening in the I.*

Color is thus not an isolated phenomenon. It is not something which is merely "stuck on" to the geometric structure we have been discussing. It is fundamental to the structure of space, and to our understanding of function and geometry, and raises the possibility of seeing living structure more deeply. But its unity, its life, lies in a realm which is not entirely accessible to structural descriptions. The order which we have described by means of the field of centers, touches it, is necessary to it, but it does not catch its essence. That can be understood only in the transcendental realm.

18 / INNER LIGHT AS A GLIMPSE OF THE I WHICH LIES BEHIND THE FIELD OF CENTERS

Let us review the situation. It is clear that what we have understood before as purely geometric order — living structure in buildings, paintings, artifacts — is helped by the additional unity that color brings to it.

This deeper unity depends on a series of qualities in color, like the geometric properties we first learnt to see in the geometric field of centers, but now having to do with unity, not merely structure. In the geometric field, each of these properties is one of the ways in which centers can be built out of centers. In the realm of color, too, these properties somehow generate pure unity, by generating wholeness out of other wholeness. But in the realm of color, we have, for the first time, also been confronted with an additional phenomenon: a purely unitary, non-structural aspect of wholeness. The aspect of wholeness which shines, like light, from the colored thing, and which pervades it, permeates, shines throughout it, as a whole.

This undivided wholeness cannot be seen, or felt, as a *structure*, and should not be *understood* as a structure. It is experienced as an undivided quality which transcends structure, and seems to spring from the very ground of things directly to our consciousness. What we have been looking at is an extension of the idea of order, as I formulated it before, to pure wholeness.

In addition, there are the beginnings of a hint of something beyond purely structural order, a unity more profound, more deeply rooted, than even the word wholeness implies. A hint of something which beckons from, or enters into, a realm beyond. A hint of something which makes connection with a "ground," with the I itself.

There is some fashion in which the unity of color, the perfect, melted unity of inner light, summons up feelings of a deeper sort. We feel, intuitively, that the inner light we have observed is — somehow — unalterably spiritual.

In this sense, we have now begun to look at something in the realm of order, which is new — beyond what we discussed before.

When we say that order is transcendent, we mean to say that somehow, the order makes contact with some other reality, or some other "something," which lies outside of and beyond our normal experience. We need a word for this something. It is hard to find a suitable word, since, by definition, the something is beyond normal experience — and presumably, therefore, outside the range of things which have ordinary names. In accordance with the great religious tradition already quoted in earlier chapters, I use the word "ground" to refer to this something.

The ground is imagined to be a pure reality. It is a state of reality, or substance, which is in the universe, but not accessible to normal perception and normal awareness. It is, however, not assumed to be distant. It is generally assumed to be *here* where we are, and even more real, more authentic, than the reality we normally experience. It is thus supposed to be a state of matter, or state of things, or state of existence, which is more fundamental — and of which one might say that "the universe is really made of *this* stuff." All this is "the ground." It is the ground beneath our feet, the ultimate ground of substance on which all things stand.

Color not only establishes wholeness as a single quality, a oneness beyond structure. It begins to establish a connection with this ground. The inner light we experience in the cases of great color seems to penetrate beyond normal experience, reaching through towards this ground, showing us this ground, making us feel the ground.

19 / THE HINT OF A TRANSCENDENT UNITY

To my knowledge, color theorists themselves have only rarely spoken about the philosophical problems inherent in the transcendent quality of color. However, the strong hint of a transcendent connection with a ground, together with a possible connection to the issue of color, was given in two chapters of the short book MIND AND MATTER by Erwin Schrödinger.[5] Schrödinger, the physicist who discovered the matter-wave equation of quantum mechanics, has a great deal to teach us about color and its real existence. He outlines the following argument. "You and I [he says, in effect], both see yellow. But, according to the prevailing view of science, there is no way of knowing whether the interior experience you have when you see yellow is the same as the interior experience I have when I see yellow. Of course, we know that we shall both say the word yellow when we look at a buttercup, or at light of 5,900 angstroms. But this says nothing about the inner experience we have. You might have the inner experience A (a product of your neurological functioning when your eyes see 5,900 angstroms) and I might have the inner experience B (a product of my neurological functioning when my eyes see 5,900 angstroms). You have learned to call your A by the name yellow, and I have learned to call my B by the name yellow. Thus we both use the word yellow in a consistent fashion to describe wavelengths in the world. But there is nothing to guarantee that your inner experience of yellow, and mine, are the same."

Schrödinger goes on to say that although this point of view is logically consistent, it seems intuitively absurd. Intuitively, it seems to him that the *inner* experience of yellow, *its yellowness*, is something real. He guesses that we all experience it in the same way—in short, that "your" yellowness and "my" yellowness are one and the same thing, not two different things. Most people probably share this intuition. Of course, it remains an intuition, or belief, not a demonstrable fact. Yet, as Schrödinger points out, within contemporary positivistic science, there is not even a way to describe the *content* of this intuition. If it is indeed true—as many people probably believe intuitively—that yellow—*the yellowness itself*—is the same for everyone, then this would imply that there is some domain where this yellowness actually exists. Where is it?

After thinking carefully about this problem, Schrödinger says that he has been able to find no other possible way of explaining this except to say that there is, in the world, only one single mind where the yellow occurs, and that our individual minds are all part of this one mind, and somehow all have access to it. This would explain why we all have the conviction that the yellowness we see is not private, but objectively real and shared. It is the same yellow, because it is all seen by a single mind, of which our individual minds are merely parts.

I have always been deeply impressed by Schrödinger's essay. His AB-experiment (only a thought experiment, of course) is convincing and unexplainable. But I interpret the experiment in a slightly different way. Instead of saying that we all share yellowness because we are all parts of one mind (as he suggests), I draw a slightly weaker conclusion—simply that, at the very least, his thought experiment gives us a realistic hint of the existence of some single realm of mind, which lies beyond normal experience and beyond our present-day mechanical conception

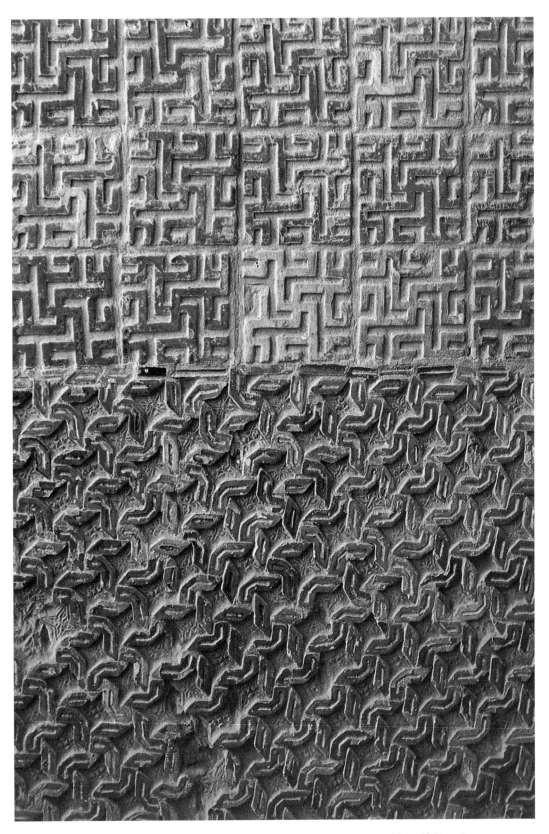

Color and the field of centers: Tile and brick panel on the Sanctuary of Bayazid Bistami

of the world but which we do, occasionally, reach through sense impressions. Most important for my present argument, Schrödinger's thought experiment strongly suggests that color — among all things — might be capable of directly penetrating this realm. This argument implies that the ground is — in principle — accessible to ordinary perception. Furthermore, it suggests that color is especially likely to be helpful in making a direct connection with this ground.

Of course, the inner light I have been discussing is more complex, and more profound, than the simple yellow which Schrödinger discusses. But if it is true in principle that even a single color is capable of making a bridge between our normal experience and some realm of mind beyond matter — a kind of direct pathway, in which we see reality directly — then it is not hard at all to imagine that when the color becomes more intense, more harmonious, more whole — *as it does in the case of inner light* — this bridge might becomes still more effective, and our capacity to see the ground directly, might be intensified.

Schrödinger talks about color sensation in general without reference to good or bad, shallow or profound. He says, in essence, that when we see color, we experience some domain beyond the immediately material one. He locates this domain in the great "self," because it cannot occur merely in individual, private persons, and concludes that in some fashion we are all part of this great self, and that our individual selfness, as we experience it, is there by virtue of our participation in — and belonging to — the greater self.

I extrapolate from Schrödinger's argument, go beyond it, and reach my own conclusion. I suggest that the inner light, which is revealed, seen, when very great color occurs — as it does in nature, as it does in greatest paintings — allows us to experience the great self, in greater degree or in lesser degree, and that our experience of inner light is the experience of the great self directly and openly seen, openly experienced.

In short, the experience of inner light reveals an ultimate world of existence as it really is, perhaps, and shows us a glimpse of a reality which is more profound, more beautiful, than the one we experience every day.

20 / TRANSCENDENT WHOLENESS AS A KIND OF LIGHT

I do not believe that the idea of inner light applies only to color. Rather, I think that this light-like thing which we perceive or feel in the cases of great and harmonious color is also visible in *all* kinds of wholeness — colored or not — and that it is, in fact, the subjective experience of the I which all wholeness ultimately brings us to.

In short, I believe that *all* wholeness, not just harmonious color, may be considered, ultimately as a kind of light, and that all wholeness, not just color, helps us to communicate with the transcendent realm where pure unity exists.

The next three photographs may help to explain what I mean. They are, intentionally, black and white photographs. But the brilliant and shimmering light in these pictures shows the way in which I believe that all wholeness — even without color — has the ability to communicate a kind of light.

Color has helped lead us to a view of order very different from the one examined in Book 1. In this new view, wholeness exists and is perceived directly as an unbroken unity. It is a quality of meltedness in which elementary "parts" and "structures" no longer exist. They give way to something more deeply unified, a single paste.

If we accept this view as a possible general model for order, we are then confronted with the possibility of *all* order as something transcen-

Pure inner light: Marble floor, San Miniato, Florence

dent, in which wholeness is produced — a wholeness connecting us directly with the ground of all things.

What is fascinating about color as a model for this transcendent quality of order is that, like geometric order, it exists first of all as a structure which can be defined. This is suggested, again, by the eleven color properties, which show how deeply all beautiful color is related to the field of centers. Yet it seems that beauty of color *also*

Pure inner light: Leaves in the forest

exists as a transcendent unity which can *not* be described as a structure. Thus in this case, structure is the stepping stone which brings us to the transcendent unity. We may think of the structure as if it were a window that allows us to look through at the transcendent unity.

It — the unity itself — is not a structure. But it can be seen, grasped, felt, perceived, only through the medium of something which is a structure.

Pure inner light: 14th-century Baptistery, Pistoia

21 / CONCLUSION

I believe that our experience of color, if we pay attention to it, strongly suggests that something unusual is going on when we see and experience life. We experience the color in a thing as a feeling as a whole, so that the whole object, the whole plane, is felt, thought and experienced as a single entity — rather like a chord or melody.

With this insight we recognize that the nature of a living thing cannot be understood *merely* as a system of centers. Even though, evidently, it is the centers which do the work —

and largely constitute the whole — still the whole *itself* is an undivided thing, has a *single* feeling.

I regard this feeling of undivided unity, which we experience so strongly in the case of color, as a first direct experience of the I. Or rather, I should say that what we experience in the case of this profound and subtle harmony of color — the deep and mysterious feeling which we see *in* harmonious living color — is the thing called I.

NOTES

1. Color is palpable. Everyone is moved by color. It has a direct appeal. And it is visibly empirical. When people work in the realm of color, the experience is so immediate. The feedback is immediate and clear. You have done it. You haven't done it.

People who take my color class often say that they learn more about architecture in that one class, than in all the others. The extreme sensitivity of the subject is helpful. If in a building, you make a window slightly wrong, too big, too wide, etc., you don't really feel its wrongness as an undeniable fact — you need your sensibilities very acute before you can feel it — so the sensitivity of the space to the subtle changes in proportion and detail, though true is less easy to grasp.

In the realm of color it is immediate and undeniable. You make a line just slightly wrong, in color or position, and it throw the picture off completely. You change the color of the line only slightly, two shades more this way or more that way, and suddenly the whole thing becomes harmonious — the harmony changes drastically and palpably in response to what seems like a very small change in the picture. So the extremely subtle and highly sensitive relation between achieving wholeness and inner light, and the various details, becomes clear empirically. So, the essential task — to create contact with the I — to create inner light — which, in the realm of building may also be called light, or life or spirit — then becomes visible, and practical as a very difficult, but sometimes attainable task.

2. In the case of color — and of things which *have* color — the quality I call wholeness or life elsewhere in these four books is experienced as *light*. Actually this light is an inner light — a light which is mental and emotional as well as physical — a quality which makes us feel the same as we feel in the presence of physical light, but more subtle, something which is in the inner substance of a thing.

This light, or inner light, is a form of wholeness which teaches us profoundly. It teaches me to recognize the feeling of wholeness, as it occurs in me. Once I grasp it as light — experienced in the realm of color — I can then recognize it in other things and then, ultimately, apply it to my own work of building as it evolves. Thus, color and light, show me, by example, what the real feeling-unity is like *as an experience*. It is not until I get this experience, and focus on it clearly as a mental state, that I am able to reproduce it in me, and then use it as a criterion for my work.

By learning to see inner light, we move towards a new understanding of wholeness. As we have seen, the geometric properties play a special role in the creation of inner light. What we have seen, too, is the way that individual geometric properties, geometrically local, have a pervasive effect on the field of vision as a whole. Thus it is the inner light, the connection with the "I," not merely the geometrical structure, which is affected by the presence of the geometric properties.

3. In Book 3, chapter 18, "Color Which Unfolds from the Configuration,", I have given examples of this process, where I describe it happening, in detail, step by step.

4. They are described fully in chapter 5 of Book 1, on the following pages 146–242.

5. Erwin Schrödinger, MIND AND MATTER (Cambridge: Cambridge University Press, 1958). The chapter called "Oneness of Mind" is on pp. 52–68, the chapter on "The Mystery of Sensual Qualities" on pp. 88–104.

CHAPTER EIGHT

THE GOAL OF TEARS

1 / WHY UNITY AND SADNESS ARE CONNECTED

We have seen unity in the case of color. Now I should like to give a few examples of this unity — and what it can look like — in the case of buildings.

Why is unity the same as tears? Why does this chapter have the title "The Goal of Tears"? Unity ties everything together — including joy, happiness and laughter, but also including loss, death, and betrayal. A thing which truly has unity partakes of everything. And through that everything, there must be sadness. The making of this sadness, then, must come through a process where land, details, rooms, form an indivisible whole. Always trying to tie it together, to unify it, to make it disappear.

From the chapter on color, we have the rudiments, now, of a way of understanding the actual unity which appears in buildings. What is remarkable about color — the color phenomenon, inner light — is that we experience it as a *single* unbroken thing, not a system of elements or a system of centers, but we feel the light as a single thing.

Of course, in a great work of building, we see more than living centers: not only large centers tying the whole together, not only many living centers that are I-like. Beyond the living centers, there is an active unity within the work which makes it one thing, and brings it its sadness caused by its impending death. If it is alive, it knows death. If it is truly alive, one can feel its own death within it, even while it lives. It is this, above all, that we mark when we see a living work of art, or the grass on a living hillside.

This unity makes itself felt, to be sure, in some measure, from the higher level properties which appear in the world. For instance, ECHOES and NOT-SEPARATENESS are two of the properties which most strongly tie things together, and create this inner unity in them. In this swan of Matisse's, for example, it is the strokes of the pen, the shapes of the elements, which are all of a piece, and which through their unity, their similarity, create a single whole. We may argue this as if it were created simply by the presence of larger living centers: the wing, the neck and space, and so on. But, beyond all that, we do undoubtedly feel that there is a *single* wholeness here. Partly, this comes about because we feel inner similarity, and inner unity, to the strokes of the pen, to the shapes of the feathers and bars; it is these echoes among the centers which make it all one, tie it all together. In the same fashion, we experience not-separateness between the strokes of the pen, the paper, and beyond. Above all, though, this unity in the swan comes about because of some quality *within*. And it is here that the idea of the pervasive I, in every living center, begins to tell us something.

Living structure in Matisse's Leda: Each bar of the swan's wing, each feather group, the space within the curve of the swan's neck, the half moon of space between the neck and the upper wing — all are living centers, helping one another.

A single material, in variations: Sadness in a beam, ornament, ceiling, columns, and windows.

Martinez house, Christopher Alexander, 1978–83.

243

Fireplace of the kitchen, Martinez House, Christopher Alexander, 1978–83

Mother and Daughter, oil on canvas, Christopher Alexander, 1994

As the brushstrokes in the swan form a unity because of their inner similarity and similarity of intent, in a building this may come from something as simple as a single material used again and again in transformed versions, forming everything. On the left I show an interior from the Martinez House, a building where everything — walls, floors, ceilings, ceiling ribs, columns, beams, column capitals and bases, ornaments — was all formed by shooting concrete. Everything is carved, in this building, from the operation of shooting concrete from a gunite gun.

For if each living center is but a reflection of a single unity, has the same origin in its being, then the whole, the living work, is animated by this same being behind the scenes — and we experience the same living fire in every part of the whole.

It is when this happens that we may — sometimes — feel ourselves to be in the presence of true life, true value. And it is in that situation, so rare in the experience of every maker, that the existence of the I as the source of all being makes itself felt.

Entrance to the West Dean Gardens Visitor's Centre

2 / SADNESS

To set the stage further for understanding unity in a building, I go back to the emotional underpinning of the living structure, its personal character, its rootedness in feeling.

The I, that blazing one, is something which I reach only to the extent that I experience, and make manifest, my feeling. What feeling, exactly? What exactly am I aiming for in a building, in a column, in a room? How do I define it for myself, so that I feel it clearly, so that it stands as a beacon to steer me in what I do every day?

What I aim for is, most concretely, *sadness*. I try to make the volume of the building so that it carries in it all feeling. To reach this feeling, I try to make the building so that it carries my eternal sadness. It comes, as nearly as I can in a building, to the point of tears.

I try to shape the volume so that its volume brings tears to my throat. I can feel, in me, the eternal sadness of all life welling up, to some small degree, in me. This is very highly concrete. I cannot do it in a trivial way. I cannot literally make the building laugh and cry. And it is not gloomy either. This sadness of tears, when I reach it, is also joy. The sky over the Bay Bridge, the lights of the cars, the rain, the existence on this earth. What makes it sad is that it comes closest, in the physical concrete beams and columns and walls, as close as possible, to the fact of my existence on this earth. It reminds me of it, it makes me take part in it. So when it happens, it is also a kind of joy, a happiness.

But to recognize it, I concentrate most on my sadness, and my tears.

3 / GETTING SADNESS IN THE FLESH OF THE BUILDING

Although social pressure — the desire to please others — sometimes makes it hard to reach the I, the difficulty is not mainly a social difficulty. It is mainly an artistic difficulty.

The difficulty arises simply because it is so hard to find that shape, that substance, which actually makes tears well up in me. To many people a roof is just a roof. A column is just a column. It takes a great effort of perception, conscious work, and concentration, to see that the subtle change of the column makes a difference to its sadness, or to its capacity to hold, and reflect sadness.

I look at the shafts of the columns in the Martinez House, while building them. I move them, change them, cut cardboard, modify the shape. At first they seem merely nice. I try to get the flutes that come down the four corners a little better — that means, at first, simply harmonious. Then I notice that the boards need to be a little wider, more substantial.

I try a line across the top. The line seems needed, but perhaps it is a bit too much. I stand back in the room, a few times, to check it, also looking at the base. Simpler seems better.

Gradually, as I achieve a more harmonious shape, even in the plywood forms themselves, I begin to see something which nearly works, in that place. I begin to be aware that this column which I am making can be more austere — and that, as I strip away every bit which is too sweet, that I slowly leave the bare bone of something which can affect me, can make me — almost — choke tears in my throat. Of course, it is just a sensation, not actual tears. It is so slight, I have to watch the growing thing in the room very intensely to notice it at all.

But if I pay very careful attention to the feeling which is welling up in me, I do notice tiny differences, small sensations, and I do notice that threat of tears, that harshness in the back of my throat which moves me towards the shape of the column which will ultimately have a more serious meaning, which will enlarge life in that room, which will then, through its austerity, make more likely the experience of joy.

4 / SADNESS OF COLOR AND GEOMETRY

It is important for me to explain that what I call the quality of "tears," the sadness that necessarily characterizes all living art, is inherent in the *geometry*, it is not only an emotion, but is a character of the geometry itself. I would like to try and explain this in a painting which is, on the surface "nothing but" shapes and color. Yet, I believe the painting does have this quality of tears in some degree.

Please look at the painting on the next page. What I want you to look at is the way the painting is put together. It goes on and on and on. You can't really take it apart, and you go on and on and on going around in it. There's something in it, a living quality I'll just describe as a kind of shimmering. This shimmering exists on a formal level. In reality there is nothing there except paint, and the centers which the paint creates. At the same time one feels the endless connection quality in the thing and in the way it keeps on going.

Getting it took hard work, and the picture went through many versions. In this version that you're looking at there must be a hundred different yellows, and an equal number of different reds.

5 / UNITY AND SADNESS IN A GROUP OF BUILDINGS

Let us go back to the Eishin campus, described in Books 1, 2, and 3, which has several examples of the same kind of unity. Here the unity takes a human form, it is a unity not only in the buildings, but in the buildings, and the people, and their actions. The quality of sadness, underlying this unity, is more visible, because that campus is (in its success) so deeply dependent on the human life that happens there.

I have already shown many photographs, some taken the day the school opened in 1985, some pictures showing what it was like a couple of years later with a very inhabited feeling about it. Here I show only a handful: a spring day in April 1985, and some details, and the lake.[3]

I want to tell you a few short stories about the social circumstances in that school. These are quite important stories, and I am going to try to tie them into the question of the physical unity and sadness — the poignant wholeness — of the place.

First I just want to go back to the beginning of the project to tell you one detail. We were in the days of trying to understand the patterns that were going to govern this campus, and we had, as I have described in Book 2, a special way of asking questions. Part of the process of getting these things out from people was to force teachers, students and others to say what their ideal dreamed-of life was, and how would they like to have life in their campus that was going to come. It was quite difficult to get people to say things, because often they wouldn't take the questions seriously at first. They would say, "What do you expect me to say, we know this is going to be a block in the middle of an asphalt playground." In response, I pushed them and tried to force a more real kind of answer out of them, sometimes begging and cajoling, trying almost anything to help them to say what, deep down, they would really like to have.

Occasionally I would use almost hyperbolic expressions to get them to say things, because they would say "I don't know, what do you expect me to say" and so forth, and I would say things like "Please . . . just imagine that the new campus is like heaven, the most perfect school you could imagine, a school you would like to teach in for the rest of your life — *then* what would it be like?"

Gradually people would start saying deeper things, more connected to their essential feeling, and one of the things I remember several people said in one form or another, "I would like to be able to take a walk along some little stream or some little pool while I am thinking about my next lecture." A number of teachers made, though not exactly the same comment, some comment along these lines. In time, this need for water was incorporated in the pattern language; and then put into the plan, in the lake we built. We made bridges over the lake, we planted lawns coming up to the lake, we planted cherry trees along the lake, and we built a little path along the water.

Now, years later, the campus is built, and has been used for years. The water, dreamed of by those teachers long ago, is actually in the school in the form of that lake.

And now, so many years later, when people are asked what it is about the school that means most to them, many say "the lake." It has become first on many people's list of things they like about the campus. What people originally told us, half ashamed, about their dreams of water and small paths where they could think about their lectures, was something real. Now that the lake is there, this real feeling has room to exist, and has become more real. The connection people expressed as an aspect of their inner selves was not an artificial concept but an inner reality which has been proven in practice.

This lake shows what I mean by "sadness." Of course, superficially, it is mainly happy. The ducks are swimming, the light is beautiful, people walk arm in arm around the lake. But if you

The buildings around the lake at Eishin

Spring blossoms on the Eishin campus

compare it with an asphalt playground, the more usual core of a high school — that asphalt does not allow your sadness to exist. It hardens your heart, you have to stifle your feelings, you can hardly allow yourself to feel anything. But this lake, even though it allows happiness to exist, is much closer to tears. If you have tears, you can feel them at the sight of the lake, or of the wind ruffles on the surface of the water. Its very existence in the school even allows your tears. You become the kind of person who can shed tears — your tears are closer to the surface of your existence.

I want to tell you about other matters on that campus, more human and social matters, which are connected to the living structure of the place. In 1985, Japanese high-school students normally wore stiff, compulsory, almost military-style school uniforms. This was the norm. Yet about a year after moving onto this campus (earlier the school had existed in another part of Tokyo) a decision was taken to abandon the use of school uniforms in this place altogether. This was an extraordinary action, a very unusual action for a Japanese high school at that time. I believe it came about because of the freedom which existed on the campus, the freedom was so sincere, and its joy and sadness so real, that the use of uniforms no longer seemed appropriate.

At about the same time, in the later 1980s, the board of directors took a decision to abandon all school rules on that campus, and to be guided "only by the constitution of Japan." The head of the school became known as the mayor. These things, too, were startling as indicators of a tremendous freedom which was experienced there and which the school's directors felt confident to extend to all their students. Surprising anywhere, this is especially surprising in modern Japan, which is so rigidly bound by rules in its high schools.

Another example of what I mean by tears concerns the profound attachment students felt to the campus after they moved in. In Japan it is common for students to commute to school, often for an hour or more. Many students take fairly long bus rides to get to school in the morning. Before construction of the Eishin campus, the school had been in Musashino-shi, nearer to downtown Tokyo. For going home after school, there were special school buses provided every half hour, starting from 2.00 o'clock, one at 2.30, at 3.00, at 3.30 and so on, throughout the afternoon. The hope of the school had always been to maintain an afternoon program of special and voluntary studies, so the students would stay in school for various afternoon activities. But in Musashino, the fact was that the 2.00 bus and the 2.30 bus were always full, because students did not want to stay there, and the later afternoon buses were mainly empty. After moving to this new Eishin campus, the situation became quite reversed. The early buses were always empty. The last bus of the day was full. It was very difficult to get the students to go home, to get them off campus at all. Even at the very end of the day, it was difficult to round up the students, and get them to get on the buses and go home. All this, because in the new campus, they felt so much at home. They really felt possession of it. They wanted to be there, and they did not want to leave.

More recently, in the late 1990s, a group of students' *parents* pooled money to build themselves a clubhouse on that campus, so that they, too, can be on the campus. Even after their sons and daughters have left the school and are no longer students, the parents still want to be there. They still feel attached to it, and still feel that it is theirs. They want to walk there, hear the students, listen to the voices in the small streets, watch the cherry blossoms blooming in the disorderly back garden of the teacher's building.

In the pictures I show here, of the cherry garden on the Eishin campus, we see something more of what a place which has its sadness may be like. There is roughness, the ordinariness of everyday life. In this garden there are common plastic containers for potting seedlings and cuttings; beyond them are rough bushes and fences. The earth is spilled from some pots. In the distance — about 25 or 30 meters from the camera — the buildings themselves form a backdrop to the scene, and to the rough ordinary life, which makes us feel alive there.

Yet these buildings are rather formal. They provide the necessary formal framework for the informal bushes and spilled earth and clumsy buckets — a framework which brings the whole to life. This is because each thing in this picture is a being — a picture of self — not precious, not sloppy, carefully right — and often geometrically precise and simple in a way that also invites and allows our tears.

On page 256, there is a photograph which shows this quality. For the buildings, the shape of the columns, almost heavily formal, the sharp, well formed, mass of the column at the corner of the building, is just what is needed. If it were looser, less formal, it would not work. The windows too, the eave, the roof — these are all simple, and formal. They have the hard "human-being-like" shape they need to have, in order to make them act as mirrors, or pictures of the self. Below, the pansies near the camera are not formal in the same geometric sense. They are more rounded, apparently rougher, because the appropriate form, for centers, in the flowers, in the leaves, in the space between the leaves, has a different character. Again, each one is just a nearly perfect, but imperfect mirror of the self.

And the spilled sawdust, the earth and the fallen bucket — these too, though they have a rough, nearly dirty quality — again, they are just right, to form a perfect picture of the self. If they were more formal, they would seem less clearly like pictures of my self. If the pansies were more rectilinear, they would be less like pictures of me. But if the buildings were less carefully organized, then they too would seem *less* like pictures of me.

Being like a picture of the self makes each thing take its form and character from what it is. In these photographs there may be some

Living centers as manifolded "beings" in the rough and ordinary cherry garden of the Eishin school

The harmony of everyday life: Pots, seedlings, columns, bushes

glimpse of the modern self, the 20th- and 21st-century character of a many-being landscape, a living structure made — in our fashion — of ten thousand beings. It has the blissful quality which that entails.

All this has its sadness. Mr. Murakoshi, who sat with me one summer afternoon, and told me that I had brought them a new way of life, has been taken forcibly from the school. His deep appreciation of these realities of life, was perhaps not consistent with the demands of an organization, and the board forced him to resign. Now the sequence of great teachers, Mr. Sakaida, Mr. Hosoi, Mr. Murakoshi, are all gone. The spirit that gave birth to that school — at least in its first manifestation — has vanished, like a dying whisper. Its life is too real. And Mr. Murakoshi's appreciation of it, is too real, for a modern organization to tolerate. Yet all this is real, and this sadness, too, connects us to the I.

6 / UNITY AND SADNESS OF LIFE IN A BACK YARD

This deep sadness, when experienced in a living environment, may not always appear outwardly beautiful or harmonious. For example, at one time, my backyard had ducks and fishes. The place where they lived was quite unimposing from a "designer" point of view.

The stones, rocks, concrete were a bit messed up. There were plastic pipes from the water circulating pumps; there was an old red pump propped up on the fence. The duck run, like a coop, was made of unexciting bits of wood and chicken-wire. There was straw on the ground,

Sadness and beauty in a garden and its fence

mud, and so on. Nevertheless, the backyard was the envy of all our neighbors. There is a low wall and an open fence. All our neighbors came to see the fish, even to take their daily walks with an aim of coming to say hello to the ducks and the fish. So it was very open.

I once heard two small boys walking past, in the street, and one said to the other, "I wish I lived in that house." Another day, a young woman was walking by, saw me working in the yard and said, "I love your house so much, it is like a paradise, I wish you would adopt me." Hardly a day went by when it wasn't like that, without someone coming by and telling us how much they enjoyed it. Yet it was the most ordinary thing in the world.

It is gone now. The garden is still there, but that feeling has vanished from it.

7 / THE GROUND

A thing does not get its unity from being "beautiful." The unity comes from the fact that the various centers are harmoniously connected, and that every center helps every other center. That is the great thing and it is this which causes real unity to exist. But above all, it comes from the fact that in the thing, throughout the thing, we see the I in every part, at every scale. We see only one I, the same I, shining out from every part.

In some cases this results in something which we may call beautiful in the ordinary sense of the word. In another case, the result of the helping between centers is beautiful only in the sense that it fills us with life, reminds us of

Roofs of the Eishin campus

ordinary everyday things, reminds us of the messiness and goodness of everyday life — but is not beautiful in the sense that it would make a great picture in an architectural magazine.

The fact that everyday life, in the visceral, raw, down-to-earth sense, is connected to the physical coherence in geometry, which I have described in the red and yellow painting, is unexpected. The unity is not merely a unity in the surface, in the appearance of things — it is a unity of the most fundamental kind, which goes to the raw reality and which has, when it occurs, a highly unexpected, sometimes rambling,

sometimes ferocious, sometimes friendly, even sometimes absurdly crude or comfortable character. This was the message of Bashō, the great Japanese haiku poet who lived from 1644 to 1694. He expressed the unity and sadness of things, visible in the ordinary details of everyday life, perhaps more vividly than any other poet — perhaps more vividly than anyone else has ever expressed it.[4]

> Sadder and much more
> Forlorn even than at Suma
> Is autumn on this shore.[5]

Kitchen at Meadow Lodge, Christopher Alexander, 1995

8 / CONCLUDING SECTION

In these examples, I have perhaps given glimpses of what I mean by making and revealing the sadness in a work. That is real unity. When this is achieved, or touched, to the extent that it is achieved, then, that is what I mean by reaching and touching the I, the blazing one.

Does it prove that the blazing one actually exists? Of course it does not prove it. It is conceivable that what I have described here is only going on within the realm of psychology, that it is a kind of mental trick I play on myself, to reach life in things. The fact that it does work, that it does sometimes reach objective life in structures — even in practical engineering structures like a bridge — might be dismissed as evidence only of the curious way the mind works.

But the so-definite fact of this sadness which enters things, and the fact that through this sadness we — all of us, I, you, and the person I have never known — all experience life in those things — it is hard to believe that it is only a trick or a mental state. The sense of the thing reached — a sadness which connects me to the I in these cases — does appear to me as an actual thing which I reach, which then becomes visible, like a foggy landscape on a brilliant day, becomes visible through the darkening lace of the thin gossamer window curtain.

NOTES

1. For a description of this wide-open eyes state, see Book 1, appendix 3.

2. The original carpet itself, and the diagrams I made while reconstructing it, may be seen in Christopher Alexander, A FORESHADOWING OF TWENTY-FIRST CENTURY ART (New York: Oxford University Press, 1993), 130–37.

3. Photographs of this project are scattered through the four books: Book 1, chapter 10; Book 2, chapters 14, 15, 17; Book 3, chapters 3, 4, 6, 8. 14. 16.

4. His most famous book of poems is the OKU-NO-HOSOMICHI, or THE NARROW ROAD TO THE FAR NORTH, and other books of poems . . . translated many times. For instance, Dorothy Britton, BASHŌ'S NARROW ROAD TO A FAR PROVINCE (Tokyo: Kodansha International, 1980) and Nobuyuki Yuasa, THE NARROW ROAD TO THE DEEP NORTH (London: Penguin, 1970).

5. From THE NARROW ROAD TO THE FAR NORTH.

"We see only one I, the same I,
shining out from every part."

CHAPTER NINE

MAKING WHOLENESS
HEALS THE MAKER

1 / INTRODUCTION

When the I-stuff is created, it nourishes the maker — not only the viewer, but the *maker* too. For some reason, the process of making things which are alive enlarges us, deepens our experience. I feel more alive for having done it. It is like food. From what I have seen, and from the people I have worked with, this is a common experience. Almost every person experiences the making of wholeness, like food. Each person is nourished, made more whole, by making something which has life.

What is the reason for this "food-like" character of the making process? Why should it matter so much, whether a person makes something beautiful or not? Why should it have such a profound effect on the maker?

2 / THE IMPACT OF MAKING BEAUTY ON THE MAKER'S LIFE

It is amazing to fully grasp the impact of making something beautiful. Have you experienced the fact that when you make a beautiful thing, you feel happy for days, sometimes for one or two whole days, the feeling that something wonderful and important has happened in you, lives on in you? And the reverse is true, also. When you make something ugly, you may be depressed for days. A feeling of gloom and dissatisfaction hangs over you. You can't get over it.

This little-discussed effect is, from an empirical standpoint, extraordinary. It is a massive effect, but — within conventional ways of looking at architecture — there is no obvious explanation for it.

Why does the making of life, the making of beauty, have such a profound interaction with our life, with our own happiness? The most joyful and fulfilling love or friendship, after a particularly lovely moment, can make you feel your own well-being for hours — occasionally for days. Or if it goes badly, maybe it has a gloomy effect on you for hours. But making something beautiful — a bench, a windowsill, a song, or making color which is profound — has an effect which lasts, in my experience, for longer. The positive state, nearly like a glow, but more modest, a well-being which exists in us and which is reflected out to others, can last for days. Our well-being is deeply affected by it, in a way that reaches far inside us. For some reason we are very profoundly wrapped up in, affected by, the aftermath of having made a beautiful thing.

Why should such a deep effect exist? Why is beauty so much connected with our well-being, with our happiness? Why does it have such a profound effect on us when we make a living thing?

Whether we have the answer to this question or not, the effect itself is vitally interesting. It underlines our understanding of the whole phenomenon of life in buildings, makes us realize how massively important this life which can occur in the physical world really is. It is not a minor thing, but a major thing, one of the most vital things there is, if indeed it can affect the maker's well-being for so many days at a time.

I believe what happens is something like this. When you make a beautiful thing, the depth of the person within becomes more vivid, lives more intensely for a moment. In each of us, a person is existing, or waiting to exist. This person — the most free version of that person — does exist, occasionally, for brief glimpses. When one of us becomes free, this latent person inside comes to the light of day, exists then for a few moments, more vividly, more intensely.

3 / THE HEALING PROCESS

One of the comments I most often get from students who take part in the unfolding process described in Books 2 and 3 is that they have tremendous fun. It is such a fulfilling thing to do. This is said, of course, in the context of current architectural practice, which is most often not fun at all, or fulfilling, except perhaps to massage the ego. So the unfolding process is understandably enjoyable because it is an alternative to the dreary and repetitive tasks involved in sitting in an office, drafting, far from the sun and wind and concrete on a building site.

During the late 1970s, the University of Oregon used to send its architectural students to work in an office for a few weeks as part of their last year of study. Many came to the San Francisco Bay Area to work for architects. And I was told that of the students who go to work in these offices, 80 to 90 percent come back shocked by the experience, promising, "I will never go to work in an architectural office, that is one way of life I just cannot stand, day after day after day."

But the comment that unfolding is tremendous fun to do has a deeper side. There is a simple and vital fact to contemplate. When I make something which has wholeness or life, I became more alive in the act of making it. When I make something which is dead, or contribute to the making of something which is dead, I become less alive.

For Karl Marx, the problem of the modern world was summarized by the fact that work was no longer refreshing or creative, but alienated and soul-destroying.[1] This of course can be experienced by architects, just as it is by others, in the organization of work as it was in 1990 and as it still is. It is also experienced, more drastically, by construction workers and others who are part of every building process, and who outnumber architects. In California there are 400,000 construction workers and about 30,000 architects. Most of them are doing their work mainly or entirely for the money, with the doubt in their minds of what they are doing, why they are doing it, just grinding away at a boring task.

But when the thing which is made has life, when the process of making the thing come to life plays an important role, *all this changes*. The rewarding and life-enhancing nature of work comes into focus at that moment because the work does actually nourish the world. As it nourishes the world by building centers which have life, the people who are making these living centers themselves then begin to change dramatically.

4 / MAKING WHOLENESS HEALS THE MAKER

The connection between the life of a made thing and the healing effect it has on the maker is, I believe, very succinctly put just as simply as this: *People are deeply nourished by the process of creating wholeness.*

If a person dedicates himself to making the field of centers, to making things whole, the more he or she does it, the more whole he or she becomes within him- or herself. Even one act of making this field of centers, a few minutes, or an afternoon, done honestly and in full pursuit of the real thing, changes a person and brings a level of calmness, quietness, and peacefulness which is quite unusual into that person.

I first noticed this phenomenon in one of the earliest seminars I gave on this topic. This was in 1977. I gave students exercises to make the field of centers in various drawings and paintings.

One of the students in the class, Barbara Winslow, told me after a few weeks that she had reached a peacefulness and health which was almost unknown to her, simply from making these things. During the following months, she wrote her thesis on this topic, simply recording, as in a diary, the way that the activity of making the field of centers coincided, in her experience, with the process of feeling healed.[2]

During the following years I noticed the same thing in myself repeatedly. The more I began to understand the field of centers, and the more I was able to make it in material objects, the more I found a deep satisfaction from the making of these objects, which left me happy, sane, clear headed, and light of heart.

It remains true. When I manage, at some level, to make life (in a big thing or a small thing), I feel more alive. I feel more whole, myself. On the other hand, so long as I am making stuff that does not have life in it, I feel dull, listless, oppressed. And even then, when I am feeling dull and listless like that, because of not making anything alive, the tiniest success, even in a tiny thing — it may be a painting, a detail of a building, a building plan, even just locating a building correctly in relation to a certain tree — all at once I wake up, I feel joyful and happy. The happiness lasts, sometimes for several days. It seems that the smallest success in making life extends and fills my experience for hours or days. The absence of it starves me.

5 / LIFE MADE CREATES LIFE IN THE MAKER

The positive feeling I have described does not come merely from the activity of making. It comes about only when the field of living centers is actually *achieved*.

Indeed, cases of making where living structure is *not* achieved have a tense, unresolved feeling associated with them, that is more like frustration than satisfaction, even when a thing is actually made and finished.

In recent years I have found evidence of the same phenomenon from more and more of my coworkers and associates. I have noticed, over and over again, that when they make things which have life and living centers in them, they experience satisfaction and healing *in themselves*. Apparently, as they make something whole with

their own hands, they also become whole within themselves. When they fail to do it, or are prevented from doing it — whether by the situation, by constraints inside themselves, by outer constraints — they feel dejected, dull, even dead, as if life has been prevented from flowing in them. Yet when they can do it, even for a minute, or an hour, it is joyful, it nourishes for hours beyond the time of the event itself.

It is as if they have taken food, but food for a kind of joy. In that sense, the art of making something living, once a person has experienced it, is sought again and again, avidly. It is like food. It carries its own reward. It seems immensely worth doing — over and above all other things.

6 / THE SOURCE OF THE HEALING EFFECT

Why is life achieved in things, "like food"?

What is the reason for all this? In order to reach an explanation, it will be necessary to

probe, still more deeply, the nature of the "personal." The issue comes down, very simply, to this: *There is a direct connection between the living structure of the world and the achieved person-ness we experience in ourselves.*

This connection is similar to the typical relation between centers in any system of wholeness. The intensity of one center (its degree of life), is directly dependent upon the intensity of other centers within that wholeness.

Now, of course, a person is *also* a living structure, also a field of centers, also a wholeness. This field, like any other, is therefore also linked to the intensity and wholeness of the other centers and other fields immediately round about. Thus, the relation between a person's own wholeness, and the wholeness of things in that person's immediate environment, is a direct consequence of the nature of wholeness itself.

It follows that a person will indeed feel healed, made whole, during any process in which life and living structure are created in the world. And it follows, too, that a person's own feeling of wholeness is the very best criterion for the wholeness of a thing which he is trying to make.

Students and apprentices approach me and tell me that they do not know whether the things they are making are good or not. They get confused. That happens because, somehow, they still experience the quality of what they make as an external thing, one which they are unsure about because, in part, it remains based on external criteria set by others. Many times I have experienced a sequence of events like this: Someone

shows me something and asks me, "Is it any good? What do you think?" I ask her to consider all the different qualities described above. She tells me she has already done that, but that she still feels ambiguous. The thing she has made *seems* to have all these qualities. But she is still unsure if it is really any good.

At such a moment, I simply ask this question: "*Does the thing which you have made, make you feel more whole within yourself?*" The answer to this question is usually immediate, available to inspection. It is much easier to get *this* clear than to find an answer to asking if the thing is good. If she says, "Yes it does make me more whole in myself," and if this statement sounds believable (a true factual description of that person's experience, not merely a breathless positive), then I say, "It may be a good thing. Perhaps you have real living structure there." If she says: "No, it does not make me feel more whole," then I say, "It must not be the real thing. You had better start again. Make sure this time, that you do something which makes you feel more whole within yourself." A thing which has the field of centers *always does make a person near it* feel more whole.

The progress towards the I is happening in you. The structure of wholeness, the more you encounter it, makes you more and more able to feel the reality and existence of the Ground, the existence of the I.

7 / HUMAN GROWTH: THE MOVEMENT OF THE SELF TOWARDS ITS ORIGIN

Here we come to the core connection between the field of centers — the phenomenon of life in the physical world — and the process of human growth, self-knowledge, insight, and human discovery of the true self which resides in every person. They are profoundly linked.

It means that at root, the process by which a person comes in touch with wholeness — as it is

in the world and as it is in the world around them, and as it is inside themselves — the more, then, that person actually discovers the meaning of their own existence, sees himself accurately in relation to phenomena, and the more that person becomes aware of the real structure which exists inside him and which links him to the universe.

Students often ask me to explain the relation between the fifteen properties and the idea that a living work must have its origin in feeling. A typical question is: "If I get the work from my own feeling, then the fifteen properties are just a kind of checklist — they don't really play any active role — isn't that so?"

Another version of this comment refers to the ancient Greek, or Turkish, or Chinese artists. "Obviously these people didn't have the list of the fifteen properties. They did the same thing, but they got it from their feeling directly. So why do I have to bother with the properties? Aren't the properties just an intellectual thing which gets in the way of the feeling?"

There is a muddle here between cause and effect. To explain the muddle, I ask you to consider the example of the ALCOVE pattern in A PATTERN LANGUAGE.[3] In the 1960s, when we wrote A PATTERN LANGUAGE, the architecture of that time had very homogeneous flat spaces, unadorned, most often undifferentiated. We noticed that good space (in good examples of traditional building) often had a configuration of a smaller space opening into a larger one. The smaller one might have a lower ceiling, or be somehow more contained: it helps the larger one, and is in turn helped by it.

Around 1970, it was still the architectural era of modernism — flat ceilings, homogeneous spaces. At that time, it was a daring revelation for me to suggest that a room might contain a small space like an alcove, window seat, or niche.[4] Obvious as it is now, and obvious as it has been in many buildings all over the world, and throughout human history, at that moment it was taboo. The architectural establishment did not permit it. It was, at that time, considered not to be consistent with the clean lines of a proper modern building.

So in 1977 we wrote this pattern down as the ALCOVE pattern.[5] The alcove pattern says that in some kinds of rooms, if people are looking for a more intimate spot away from the crowd, or a place that is more intensely focused even if there is no crowd in the room, they need a smaller space opening off the larger space, looking into

it, only partly separated, connected but protected, and more private. This space needs to be smaller, something more intimate, with a lower ceiling.

Now, what effect did writing it down really have? First, of course, it gave people permission to do something which had been forbidden. It gave legitimacy to something which people had forgotten about. And it gave information, the information that life might increase within a space if there was a smaller space within, looking into it, yet slightly, delicately separate. This was a valuable insight, and an important fact.

But something far more important was also happening. The piece of information unloosed the *possibility* of feelings which people had, but were not aware they had. Many people do not experience what they feel, because they are cut off from it. The deeper and more vulnerable feeling that arises in them as they approach the I, especially, may be unavailable to their experience. They do not necessarily recognize it in themselves when it is happening, sometimes do not experience it at all. But, with an intellectual focus which places attention on the alcove pattern, a person could become aware — in thinking about an alcove, or seeing one, or experiencing one in use — of the subtle feeling of this one kind, which wells up in those who are related to the existence of the alcove, and make them aware, too, of its non-existence, in a room where possibilities of intimacy are missing.

The effect, then, is an awareness of intimacy as a feature of space, and an awareness of the link that exists between this feeling and the physical geometry of the environment. Thus the person becomes conscious of a more rounded and deeper relation between the shape of the physical world, even the existence of the physical world, and the evolution of their own emotions and feelings during daily life.

Of course this one example, by itself, would do little. But there are some 250 comparable patterns, in that one book alone. And the larger sense of awareness, described in these four books, may lead to a similar effect.

It is possible — even probable — that a growing, evolving awareness may hold sway, and a society may come to exist in which the integrated, unified relation to the world, and in which individual feeling, the form of the world, and the feelings of others, are woven together in a less and less broken whole.

Of course, to start with such awareness is likely to be hardly more than a trace. A small trace-like feeling rises, and falls away again. But by being recognized, it is allowed to exist and, like a shoot of a seeding plant, it pushes towards the surface. Next time, that person experiences the same feeling more clearly. The time after that, the possibility of

this sort of feeling grows stronger — it is on the increase.

Gradually, what happens is not only that people feel more deeply, become more aware of the vulnerable feeling in them, but their self-knowledge increases. They become more aware of what is in them. They become aware of the more true nature of their own existence. So, what starts as an almost mechanical thing — the writing down of the alcove pattern, and the writing down of other comparable materials — slowly becomes a deep and true thing: the opening of the person, the budding of a deeper self arriving at the surface. And true feeling, the knowledge of what it is to be a person grows, increases.

8 / TOWARDS FULL KNOWLEDGE OF THE SELF WHICH CAN ARISE IN US

Gradually, as this greater and greater experience of true feeling occurs in a person, as true feeling therefore grows more and more clear within you, you are learning something about *yourself*. The feelings which grow are not manufactured. The ALCOVE pattern does not implant something extraneous and foreign in a human being. What is released is something that is there *already*.

So, what happens is that you, in this state, experience more and more truly the feeling of being free. At first this freedom is a kind of emotional freedom — you experience that you are vulnerable. You experience the vector towards the I. You experience art, grass, leaves, and sky as connected, and yourself as part of it. Your feeling of emotion, happiness, and sadness gradually gives way to a greater and more general feeling — the feeling of connectedness towards the I, that you are a part of the great I along with the grass and the sky.

And here the process comes full circle. Because of course it is this general feeling of connectedness which is needed to recognize life, to evaluate wholeness, to know in what degree the life or wholeness in a thing is working.

But there is also something further. The patterns, the inner knowledge of forms and conditions which create a living world, are not only a useful and important practical necessity for the growth of a healthy person. It is also part of your own inner landscape. Alcoves (of course this example is only one drop in a large ocean) and all the other structures contained in living structure are part of your inner landscape. They are part of *you*. As you become more aware of these things, as the kind of morphological structure of a living world makes itself felt and becomes part of your conscious awareness, then you are in touch with this inner landscape. You become a more rounded, more satisfied, more satisfactory being.

And, of course, being in touch with that landscape, is, in some sense, being in touch with the I. So this inner landscape is a part of you which places you more permanently, more readily, in touch with the "All that is."

The patterns in A PATTERN LANGUAGE, and the fifteen properties in THE PHENOMENON OF LIFE, help to create a mental state in which you are allowed to experience and develop your most vulnerable personal nature.[6] The properties open the door to feelings which you have, but which are suppressed. Thus, although the mechanical application of the fifteen properties is not very desirable, even that mechanical process has some positive role.

The more you use the properties, the more you find out that they create structures which correspond to your feeling. And this gives you permission, more and more, to liberate your feeling, to rely on it.

9 / DRAWING SADNESS FROM YOUR MOST VULNERABLE SELF

Am I creating a thing which generates in me, the sadness of human life? That is the question I must continuously ask myself.[7]

The level of awareness needed to do this is a level which is immensely personal, which is almost like the little child speaking — a level where we let go, entirely, of our adulthood, and the normal regulations of adult society. And, further, this level of awareness is not normally available to us. Indeed, paradoxically, it is only the awareness of order which can allow us to release ourselves enough to even *get* this level of awareness.

To me this seems the root quality which makes the field of centers carry weight. It is the essence, the core of the structure-preserving transformation which makes the building fit, perfectly, into the place where it is to be.

What is fascinating about this root quality, is that it contains an unexpected mixture of the personal and the impersonal. It is *impersonal* in the sense that it is related to the fitness of the thing, to the exactness of the structure-preserving transformation. It is *personal* in the sense that it carries feeling, is full of feeling, originates in a vision which comes from your self.

In order to make this as clear as possible, I shall try to explain more about the way that this emotional substance is indeed personal, and comes from your own most touching core, your own humanity. To do it, I shall go over the following question again: What is the connection between the abstract phenomenon we have learned to identify as the field of centers, and the depth of feeling which appears as the "emotional substance" of a work?

The value of what is done, in any work of art, depends, in the end, on the extent that the artist can reach down into his own humanity, into his own person, and draw the thing he makes from this most ordinary person. This is immensely hard to do. The fact is that it is not easy to reach the genuinely human part of oneself, the childlike part, which is true, and simple.

People sometimes believe that it can be done merely by "expressing" what is in you. But this is almost always shallow, and leads to various forms of "feelies" or so-called art which ought better to have been put on a therapist's couch.

The structure described in these four books might be thought of as the structural part of what you *need* in order to reach this human childlike part of yourself. This happens because this structure, the living field of centers, and its place in the world, really *is* a mirror of the human heart. It is therefore only knowledge of this structure which gives you a key to unlock your own heart.

Thus, paradoxically, it is only when you finally are personal, when you really put your humanness into the things you make, that you genuinely reach the wholeness we are striving for in the external structure we call order. And it is at that moment that we reach the ground. But first you need access to the structure of wholeness in order to *be* human, in order to be personal, and to be able to place your personal feeling out into the world.

Thus, life is a thing which can, finally, only be reached by humanness, by the personal, and by the individual, childish temperament which lets a person be vulnerable to the all the world in the things he makes. But he will only be able to be personal, in this way, to express true feeling, once he has mastered the abstract structure which I call the wholeness. Once you reach the point where you are *able* to be personal, *then*, finally, you are able to make something live.

10 / DO NOT ASK FOR WHOM THE BELL TOLLS

The most direct way in which we may become aware of the ground lies in what happens to us, when we are making things. We become whole, in ourselves, when we make wholeness. That is at the core of the connection between ourselves and the ground.

What is the reason for this nourishing "food-like" character of the making process? Why should it matter so much, whether a person makes something beautiful or not? Why should it have such a profound effect on the maker? Experiments have shown that people do better than normal on intelligence tests, problem solving, and spatial reasoning when Mozart's music is playing.[8] This phenomenon appears to be of a similar order: living structure and the process of creating it, has a positive effect on the process of creation.

People have also reported that the presence of this I-stuff, in works of art, makes people feel closer to God. This has been reported not only by religious people who already believe in God, but also by those who do not.[9] Apparently the phenomenon is of such an order that it induces a religious experience in people whose religious inclinations have been dampened. Does this then mean that God is real, and is discovered through these means? Or is this once again a psychological trick, a psychological phenomenon, in which the *appearance* of God is created in a maker, in an artist, in a builder?

What is undeniable, I think, is that the people who become aware of the extent that making wholeness in the world is like food for them, begin to think that this wholeness is something of vast significance. They become convinced, too, that their connection to it, too, is something of vast significance.

Somehow, a person's own self is mobilized, liberated, made more strong by that person's success in making life in the world. It is as if the life in the world which is created, directly nourishes the person. This is not pride working, or a sense of accomplishment. It is something more literal than that. Somehow, the creation of wholeness in the thing out in the world actually increases, intensifies, the strength of the self in the real world.

If there were indeed a realm of I, as I have suggested, an actual self in the material universe, then we could understand this in these terms: the creation of living centers in the world increases this I in those who have contact with it. Just as the centers in one part of the world nourish the other living centers near them, so the person, who is also a center, is nourished by this appearance of wholeness. It is as if each contribution to the I enlarges each other window to the I (each other person).

Nearly four hundred years ago John Donne wrote of our connection to the I in the most shocking and true terms:

Do not ask for whom the bell tolls
It tolls for Thee.

Each of us participates in the I. Each enlargement of the I enlarges each of us.

NOTES

1. For Marx's theory of alienated labor see Karl Marx, DAS KAPITAL (Berlin: Kiepenhauer, 1932).

2. Barbara Winslow, M.Arch thesis, Department of Architecture, University of California, Berkeley, 1978.

3. Christopher Alexander, Sara Ishikawa, Murray Silverstein, Ingrid King, Shlomo Angel, and Max Jacobson, A PATTERN LANGUAGE (New York: Oxford University Press, 1977), 828–32.

4. This sounds funny now, thirty years later — indeed, almost unbelievable. But I must assure the future reader, for whom the strange character of the mid-20th century lies in the past, that there really was a time when people were so obsessed by clean lines and stark simplicity, that such a thing was virtually unthinkable, was an enormous leap from the pattern of assumptions which architects, universally made, at that time.

5. Alexander et al., 828.

6. Book 1, THE PHENOMENON OF LIFE, throughout.

7. I hope it is intuitively more clear now, how the process of drawing feeling from yourself and the process of relying on your own wholeness allow us to create order. I hope it is also clear that the fundamental questions we have to ask, as we produce order, are the questions: *Does it create feeling in me? Does it make me feel more whole within myself, when I confront it?* — and that we cannot produce order in any other way.

8. This long series of experiments has been conducted by Frances Rauscher and a number of coworkers. A bibliography of papers is given in Frances H. Rauscher and Gordon L. Shaw, "Key Components of the Mozart Effect," PERCEPTUAL AND MOTOR SKILLS, 86 (1998), 835–41.

9. Experiments and observations undertaken by my student Father Tom McGelligot, Berkeley, California, 1994, while preparing for his Ph.D. dissertation, and reported to me by the author.

CHAPTER TEN

PLEASING YOURSELF

"I SAW MY LORD WITH THE EYE OF THE HEART.
I SAID 'WHO ART THOU?' HE ANSWERED, 'THOU.'"

*From a 10th-century poem written by
the Sufi saint and poet Hallaj.*[1]

1 / INTRODUCTION

An implicit assumption I have made repeatedly is that each one of us has, within us, a "best" self, a deep self to which we may appeal, where our sense of harmony and right comes from.

In the language I have used earlier, this best self which lies within us, is also that I or great self of which we are a part, and it is that self to which we appeal when we ask which of two things is more like a picture of the self. It is a constant reservoir, within us, of all that is good.

It is significant, too, that living structure may be identified empirically by the extent to which it is a picture of one's self. Here again, it is this reference which each person can make to a nearly universal entity, existing within all of us, and it is this reference which provides us with the surest guide to what is living structure and what is not.

In this chapter I am embarking on something that is a culminating statement to emerge from these four books — even though it may, at first, sound modest: *In order to create living structure, we must please ourselves.*

This single prescription covers the whole environment, covers everything essential. If you want to create transcendent unity — true living order — in a building, *you need to please yourself.*

And you need *only* please yourself. But you must please yourself *truly.* And to do that you must first discover your own true self, come close enough to it, and to listen to it, so that it can be pleased.

Does this sound absurd? And does it sound too easy? It is not absurd. And it is that kind of "easy" which is so hard that on most days it is almost undoable, because to do it we have to break down every resistant force that remains in us. To reach the ultimate I, the transcendent ground of all existence, you have to reach yourself. To make the great work, you have to do that thing which lies in you like a small child, not hidden, just waiting there, and pushed aside, every day of your life, so that you never realized that it is, after all, this which waits, this which is the ultimate of which we are capable.

If true, and if it can be made practical, this would be amazing. Having grown up in an era of moralistic prescriptions, of laws, rules, theories, regulations, prescriptions — all well-meaning, but all ultimately incapable of creating living structure — it would be astonishing, truly amazing, to find out that if we can only learn how to please ourselves, that prescription by itself will always create living structure.

2 / RECAPITULATION OF BOOKS 1 TO 4 AS "PLEASING YOURSELF"

In Book 1, I have tried to describe a living structure which exists, sometimes, in the world. The core of this living structure, from our point of view, is that it is completely natural to us. The only reason that we no longer understand it well is that we no longer know, instinctively, what pleases us. Learning, again, what pleases us, learning to live in the knowledge, daily and in every moment, what pleases us, is the same, exactly the same, as being able to recognize living structure when it occurs.

But we are so mired in the subjectivity of value that we have lost all connection with the fact — or the idea — that what *truly* pleases us is always living structure, and that living structure might even be defined as "that which pleases us," that which *truly* pleases us. And there, in that one word "truly," lies the whole space of these four books.

In Book 2, I have shown how living structure can only be created by an unfolding process. Once again, when we come to creation of things by people, the form this unfolding takes, always, is step by step to please yourself. We cannot perform the unfolding process without knowing how to please ourselves — *truly*. And if we know how to please ourselves truly, why then the process of unfolding and the fundamental process follow from this pleasing of oneself, as night follows day. All of Book 2 may be understood, really, as the definition of those living processes which occur when people learn to, or know how to, please themselves. The social process of unfolding comes about as society learns how all its men and women may, in the going about of daily life and in the creation of their world, know how to please themselves.

In Book 3, I have shown hundreds of buildings and places in which living structure occurs. Once again, what I have really shown is what kind of world will come about when

people truly please themselves. At least that is what I claim. What I have tried to show is not some personal or arbitrary world created by Christopher Alexander and by others who think as he does. What I have shown may be seen, rather, as an embodiment, at many levels of scale, of the kind of world that will come into being when men and women act to please themselves, when they know what it means to please themselves truly, and have the freedom to carry out this process of truly pleasing.

And, finally, Book 4 is once again the same: yet another way of describing the world, and the world-view that follows, when people truly please themselves. What I have said about "I," what used to be called the religious basis of existence, the contact with that world, and the respect for the ultimate, spiritual nature of matter — all this, too, may be encapsulated through the idea of our pleasing ourselves.

To some traditionalists, this might seem almost like blasphemy or heresy. Yet I believe — indeed, I am nearly certain — that when we learn and practice this pleasing oneself at the very deepest level, that is the same thing, then, and leads to the same thing, that was once created by the most mystical religious art, seeking union with God, creating the greatest and most holy things on Earth. Pleasing oneself, when it is truly done, when we are free enough in ourselves to be able to do it, leads to the most sublime, the most profound, the most truly spiritual art, and is — as I believe — the basis that was ultimately intended by the greatest religious teachers. It is the path they tried to show, the path of a freedom so pure, so perfect, that people might manage to do only what is in their hearts. And in doing it, we might be led to the forms of art, the forms of building, which are most like nature, most nearly in touch with the nature of the universe.

3 / VERONICA'S BLUE CHAIR

During my teaching life I have managed, now and then, to bring from a student something truly remarkable. Almost without fail, the way this thing happened was that the student, bringing in work from an exercise, as my students did every week in response to some request from me, would at first keep something back, not *want* to show it. Sometimes it was intentional; they did not want to show it. Sometimes they forgot about it; it seemed too insignificant. Sometimes it was too vulnerable, too embarrassing to them.

But I could smell this thing happening. And when I did, I would urge, tease it out, say, no, please, that is just the one I want to see, please show it to us.

Then, often shyly, the person would bring this thing out. And that particular thing would turn out to be something remarkable, egoless, beautiful, the stuff I was looking for. I would pin it on the wall, and say, that one, that one after all, is the best of what we have today, that one is really worthwhile, that is the thing I am trying to teach you how to do.

The reason this happened so many times is because of cause and effect. It was just because it was too vulnerable, and the maker knew it, that it was not brought out; or because it might be laughed at; or because it was so far from the beaten track, so utterly without pretension, that it was truly invisible to the person who made it, and he or she really did not know that it was good.

Of course, deep down, they always knew, and they flushed to the roots of their hair when I praised it, and pinned it up, and made everyone look at it, and called forth the shining quality it had, because it was so artless.

I remember one example in particular. It was a very simple painting of a chair, against a deep and rather ochery but bright yellow — the background — and a palest sky blue that was the color of the chair itself.

At first Veronica did not want to show this picture of her chair. She was almost ashamed of it; indeed, there was something nearly laughable about it. After all, you have to remember, it was a class of perhaps twenty students, all top graduate students, vying with one another for who could be sophisticated, who could do something fantastic, who could be the best. In this context it is not surprising that Veronica did not, at first, want to show me the painting of the chair, just a little sketch, in gouache, on a torn scrap of paper.

But it was for the other reason, too, that she did not describe it, or want to bring it forth. It was too close, I think, to the bone, and she did not want to expose it.

And the sketch itself, indeed, it had a nearly heart-stopping quality, something that reminded one of everything, childhood, essence, all wrapped up into one. And yet it was not childish at all.

4 / THE HEART-STOPPING QUALITY

What is that heart-stopping quality? I have told, in Book 1, of a time when I built a house for my friend André Sala.[2] And how he, while we were working, remembered his grandfather's house in the Auvergne, the slope outside the farm kitchen, the sun shining up the slope, inside the great table and the fire — almost nothing else.

That place, too, as André described it, had that same heart-stopping quality. All of childhood was seized up, stopped, in the configuration of that thing, as imagined, as remembered and — I am sure — as it was in actuality as well.

5 / THE THOUGHT POLICE

Pleasing yourself is not so easy. It can even seem frightening.

I remember once I built a house near San Francisco for an investment banker, a very nice man. In his house, we built a kitchen-living-room. I put a lot into that kitchen; in the end the whole inside was hand-painted in gouache, beautiful colors, chartreuse, green, yellow, and red with small dots and dolphins in a turquoise blue. Several pictures of the inside are shown in Book 3.[3] It will give you some idea of the quality that room had if I tell you that my chief carpenter from the project, Chester Cervellino, told me one day as we were finishing that he wished he had been born in that room.

One day while we were building, our client came into the room after coming home from the bank, still wearing his dark suit. We were looking at great sheets of gouache, the color mockups, as I modified and worked through the overall design and colors of the room.[4] He stood there, loving it, and then said to me, musingly, "Is it really OK to have this much fun?"

I did not question him. But ever since, for nearly fifteen years, his remark has reverberated in my mind. I think he meant, "Is it OK to have this much fun when you are making a house?" Or did he mean, at all? Is it OK to have this kind of fun in your *life*? Was he astonished because, for the first time, he saw people making something, and he saw that we were pleasing ourselves and he was part of it?

I want to illustrate how hard it is, and how unusual it is in modern society, to have real fun, to please yourself in this deep sense that he noticed.

6 / NOT PLEASING YOURSELF

It is not so easy to please yourself. Why? Because pleasing yourself is not just having fun or following your whim. Truly pleasing yourself means, in the deepest sense, giving pleasure to yourself, making yourself truly pleased. That is only another way of reaching the I, substantially reaching the eternal self, reaching what Zen calls No mind, reaching what the sufis call drunk in God. That is hard because today, it is not something that society encourages, not something society can easily tolerate.

To have a hope of reaching the I, there is a simple rule that must be followed. You *must* make each thing, shape each thing, so that you really *like* it, so that it really pleases you.

I have suggested that this apparently simple statement lies at the core of the nature of order. All life will come from my activities if, as a maker, I do what I truly *like*. Living structure, the creation of living structure, requires only that the people designing it, planning it, and making it are doing what they like, what truly pleases them. We will never be able to contribute to the world's horrible buildings — too prevalent in recent years — if we make things that we *like*.

On the surface, one might say, surely this statement must not be true. It sounds ridiculous. It must be false! And indeed, this enigmatic statement seems, on the surface, patently false.

After all, isn't it true that the makers of the horrible buildings shown in Book 2 (chapter 4) did do what they liked, all pleased themselves? Yet pleasing themselves did not create life in those cases, did it?

The answer, I think, is no. It did not create life. But also, no, it is not true that they pleased themselves. The makers of these image-ridden, ugly buildings did *not* truly please themselves. Pleasing oneself is harder than what they did.

They made things which *seemed* to please others, and in which they seemed to please themselves. But truthfully, what they did, was more often done out of wilfulness, out of a desire to be somebody, a desire to be important or successful, a desire to be good according to the images and standards of mid-20th-century professional architecture.

All that is very, very different from pleasing oneself. That, in our time, has become very rare.

7 / A GROUP OF ARCHITECTURE STUDENTS WHO WERE NOT PLEASING THEMSELVES

Perhaps ten years ago I was invited, by a fellow professor of architecture at the University of California, to be a critic in the final review of his masters' class.[5] His students were in their last year, and they had spent the year working on a project for an office building.

When I came to the review, the students' drawings were all around the walls. Other jury members began making comments, but, for a long time I kept quiet. I hate juries. It always seems so difficult to say anything useful when one comes in fresh, not knowing the problem. I do not really believe in it as a system of education. So I kept quiet, and sat in my corner.

After half an hour or so, I felt that I couldn't go on keeping quiet, and out of politeness felt I had to say something to the students. I had been studying their buildings as best I could. The designs were for the most part rather conventional five- to ten-story office buildings for a site on Oxford Street in Berkeley, buildings of a typical modern or postmodern flavor.

As I studied the buildings, I began to think—then came to something near a conviction—that there had been very little love or affection for these buildings in the students' hearts while they were working on the project. So, I cleared my throat, and said that I wanted to make an observation. I felt, I said, that the students did not really like their buildings.

There was a minor stunned silence when I said this. One of the students asked me, in an acid voice, what I meant by it. So I went on to say this. "I realize that you have done your best, done work that on some level you like; but it is not *real* liking, you do not really *like* what you have done, in the same ordinary sense that you like a hamburger, or a rose. That is what I mean. I am convinced," I said more emphatically, "that you do not genuinely like your own work, which is hanging on the walls here, in this ordinary sense."

Something like pandemonium broke out. The students were angry with me, they were up in arms, how dare I make such a statement; they had been working on these projects all year, they said, what did I know about it, how could I come in from the outside and suggest that they didn't like what they had been doing.

I explained, then, that I felt the conditions of contemporary architecture were such (at the time around 1990), that it was difficult and almost impossible for anyone, genuinely, in the deep sense I meant, to like what he or she was doing; that the conditions of an architect were such that one was supposed to follow certain norms, show one's proficiency in certain ways, excite the imagination or tease the intellect or show that one was capable of playing the game of professional architecture, able to do it well so as to compete with other architects who had also learned to play this game — but that none of this had anything to do with pleasing oneself, or liking what one did in the true ordinary sense which is familiar to us in so many areas of everyday life.

My discussion with the students lasted about half an hour. Gradually, by the end, I had led them to admit that, in the sense that I meant it, in the ordinary sense, they really did *not* like what they had done, or what they had been doing — that indeed, the conditions of their work had never emphasized this point at all, had made no provision for it, and that it had never even been suggested to them, while students, that they *should* like, or might like, what they were doing. That was just not part of the professional discipline being taught to them.

And yet, I said to them, "How terrible! This means you can expect to live your life making buildings that you do not really like." And, even worse, that the others in society, who live with the buildings, made in this loveless spirit, will spend hours, days, years, living with these products of an unliked and unlikable architecture, done only because it was the thing to do, the way to get jobs, the way to impress one's fellow architects.

I think, by the end of that afternoon, some of the students had begun to wonder very deeply about what they were doing. One or two, perhaps, had resolved that they must find a way of making buildings where they could, afterwards, stand up and say, honestly, "I like what I did. I truly like what I have done. It pleases me."

8 / A MEXICALI STORY ABOUT THE THOUGHT POLICE

Why is it so difficult to please yourself?

The essence of the problem is to make something which is profoundly personal. But to be true — that is, to be truly personal — it must be at the same time personal in an impersonal, eternal sense.

The following short story suggests how hard this is — and especially how hard it was in the intellectual and emotional climate of the late 20th century.

Around 1979, I was asked by my colleagues in the department of architecture, at the University of California, Berkeley, to give a short talk describing my recent work. I showed slides of buildings I had recently built in Mexico — a small group of houses and communal buildings in Mexicali.[6] These houses were — for that time — rather sweet in feeling, innocent architecturally. Though made by technically advanced methods, and using the techniques of earth-concrete construction and thin-shell, lightweight, concrete vaults which my colleagues and I invented in the 1970s, they have a *feeling*

similar to the feeling of buildings that might have been built hundreds of years ago.

During the slide presentation of this project, the faculty — at that time still under the influence of technical modernism — were very cruel, and laughed a good deal at my expense. They told me openly how silly these buildings were, and how unacceptable to the image of architecture and architects that prevailed in those years around 1980. I endured the cruelty quietly, since I thought it was important to show the pictures anyway. But it was not enjoyable. The main point of the ridicule was to say that these buildings had no connection with the image of architecture which an architect, in 1979, was supposed to follow.

Afterwards, as I walked down the passage away from the seminar room, one of the faculty who had been most extreme in his criticism, and who had led the ridicule about the pictures which I showed, came up to me in the passage and said in a half-whisper, "You know, Chris, I have always wanted to design buildings like that

Low-cost housing, Mexicali, Mexico, 1976

myself . . . but I have never dared to." His tone was earnest, almost desperate.

Here was an astonishing acknowledgement of the false state of our art as it was then: this man had feelings and thoughts about the design of buildings, but the thought police in his head censored the possibility, did not allow him to do what he wanted. Indeed, his private thought police were so strong, that in public, perhaps in order to preserve his image as a good architect, and as a good member of the club, he felt it necessary to ridicule my photographs — in opposition to his own feelings.

This contrast between thought and feeling, between the image of architecture as it was supposed to be and the reality of human feelings as they actually are, has been a major theme of these four books. In the theory which I have put forward, the theoretical and factual substance of the world, its structure and its life, are *congruent* with the feelings we all have. They are not congruent with the image of architecture as it is *supposed* to be.

Thus the battle between the theory I put forward, and the then-prevailing myth was not only a battle between the faculty and me, not only a battle between the faculty's view of mainstream architecture and the new view of architecture I was putting forward, but even a battle between their own inner feelings and the mental thought police they had inside their own heads, which repressed these thoughts and feelings and desires.

This middle-aged professor who spoke to me in the passage was, in the secret wishes he described to me, strongly connected to the I. But his social context, his aspiration to be a good member of the profession, had destroyed that connection, distanced him. This was the barrier which, in 1979, anyone in architecture had to overcome.

Do you see why the Mexicali project has this quality, why it pleases? It is rather childish, yes. But what I did was to draw, like a simpleton, only what is charming, what has some feeling in a house that only costs $3,500. Domes, paint, white walls, courtyards. Columns for porches and arcades, wooden windows, each window different according to the inspiration of the place where it occurs. None of these things is arbitrary. Each one is common sense, a natural thing to like. And when you put them together, this is what you get. And, in addition, there are small charming touches. The fountain. The single round block on top of the round dome. The blue paint.

Fountain and community building, Christopher Alexander, Julio Martinez, Howard Davis, and others, Mexicali, 1976

A small arcade inside the community buildings　　　　　*Student sitting in a tiny niche*

9 / PLEASING YOURSELF

What examples can I show where the thing made is what the maker *wants*, what pleases me, what pleases you?

BLUE GLASSES

Here are some glasses I made for the Royal Dutch Glassworks in Holland. While working, I asked myself only what kind of glass would I honestly like. My childish spirit was perhaps running very well at the time, to get these glasses. Of course it took a lot of work to make them, sketching, then turning them in wood to test the shapes, then having someone make them in rough glass, then working with the glassmakers in Leerdam to make them just right with the blue spirals. At the end, even longer, when finally I sat, drawing and painting on them with gold enamel and placing gold leaf on the surface of the glass.

I know these glasses are likeable. Almost everyone likes them. No one says they are ugly.

To make sure you understand the special quality they have, I show one of these blue glasses here, side by side with a well-designed glass from the Royal Dutch Glassworks. The well-designed glass is conventional, elegant. But it is cold and hard, like brittle steel. It was done by one of their best designers from a generation when the kind of thing I am writing about had been forgotten, lost, altogether.

There is a story about these blue glasses. The chief glassblower was a man named Henk Verweg. When I was designing the glasses, Henk and I worked together; each time I had a suggestion, he blew a glass. The hot glass, as it came from his pipe, was put straight onto a conveyor passing through a long annealing oven to cool it down. When it came out the other end we could look at it. Hour after hour, we tried many variants, colors, modifications of shape, thickness, texture, and so on. At the end of the day, as the last glasses were going into the annealing oven, one particular glass caught my eye; but the

An earlier prototype of my finished glasses. Christopher Alexander and Katalin Bende, blown by Dan Reilley

A typical drinking glass, Royal Dutch Glassworks: it is beautifully made, and utterly cold in feeling.

Handblown glasses designed, painted and ornamented by Christopher Alexander, blown by Henk Verweg, 1997

last glasses were too hot to look at until the next day.

Next morning, when I came in, the very nice one, the one that went in last — I couldn't find it. I looked around. Still couldn't find it. I asked the foreman if he had seen it; he had not. He looked around for me, but it was nowhere to be seen. More people started looking. All of a sudden, Henk came up to me and took me aside to a corner where no one could hear us. "Look," he said, "please don't be angry. You know that last glass — it was after the end of our session, and I made that one just like the one before, and I made it for me, for me to take home. It happened to turn out well. After so many years blowing glasses in the factory, that is one of the first glasses I have ever deeply liked. Please don't tell anyone."

And that was that.

To go to such lengths, just to have one of these glasses for himself! You know he really liked it. I was so happy he liked the glass of course I let the matter drop. It will be no surprise

that many of the glassblowers themselves when they were making my blue glasses, came to me, one by one, and told me that they really liked them, they liked making them. I knew, from the way they expressed themselves, that nowadays they rarely blow glasses that they truly like.

So that is the outward manifestation of what I mean when I say that these glasses truly pleased me, while I was making them, truly please others, now that they are made. They please, and appeal, at a lower level, in the belly. To a small degree, they have something of that heart-stopping quality.

These glasses have something of the self in them. Because of that, Henk liked them. And because of that, they are truly likeable.

GREEN TEA-TRAY

I made this tray (on the next page) as part of my experiments in construction, in 1970. It was made in knot-free pine boards. When I was finished I needed to work out a way of making it so that I really, really liked it. I could not imagine paint. Varnish seemed banal. Finally, I began to realize how wonderful it would be if it were a soft glowing green, shining. I made a French polish — shellac and linseed oil — and rubbed the oil with pure oil pigment, the best pigment I could buy. I rubbed it in and rubbed it in, all the time making it more and more likeable, more and more lovely to me.

A WINDOW IN THE GIOJA HOUSE

Randy Schmidt and I made this window in the Gioja house in Texas. We did pay special attention to it, to the formation of a design of small glazing bars which concentrated the mind, which formed the end of the room, and looked out over Lake Travis. Here I can say truthfully

that there is nothing, not one particle in the design, which was foreign to our liking. We were lucky in that. It rarely happens that liking is so pure.

THE GIOJA HOUSE, TEXAS

Here (next page) is a terrace, also on the Gioja house. This house began with a genuinely childish impulse from the Giojas: Geoffrey and Linda wanted somehow to live in a dream they had of a courtyard house — Geoffrey's connection to the Latin and Italian archetype. They designed a house which, ambiguously, had a courtyard that was both outdoors, and also the house's main living room. This ambiguity caused quite a bit of grief — what was inside, what was

Pine tea tray with green French polish, and green oil pigment ad linseed oil, Christopher Alexander, 1972

Dining room window, Gioja house, Austin, Texas, Christopher Alexander, Randy Schmidt and Saul Pichardo, 1996

Terrace overlooking Lake Travis, Gioja House, Austin, Texas, Christopher Alexander,
Randy Schmidt, and Saul Pichardo, 1996

outside, where were security locks, how did one keep a rainstorm out, etc.

But in the end this house did, without question, come from real liking. I made my contribution, too, from real liking, in the shape of the column capitals, the view of the lake, the sultry light, and the open water.

What would it mean to make something one truly likes. How, if someone says, "I like *this*," but what he points to is an artificial thing, not likeable at all. How is this to be seen or understood?

The answer is that the real liking comes from the whole person, it comes from a childish truthfulness, in which one does respect one's own feeling, and does not pay homage to a theory, or to an idea.

THE PINK CLOUD

This pleasing yourself is central to the art of painting, too. I painted a picture not long ago, of a dark pink cloud that I saw by my house while returning home one night. The sky still had a trace of light in it as I parked the car by the garden, and was dominated by a huge cloud, looming, light-filled and dark at the same time.

I wrote later, to a friend, about the experience of trying to paint the cloud:

Sunday afternoon, Nov 23. I did it, I did it. Finally I got back my soul in painting. I have just come from the studio, I had a painting in mind for two days, of a cloud I saw at night, I made a tiny colored sketch of it (in oil) about an hour ago. It

The Pink Cloud, oil on canvas, 35 by 50 cm, Christopher Alexander, 1997

came out fairly good. Then I was supposed to go to the supermarket to get there before they closed. But I thought, if I don't do it now — the actual painting itself — I will lose it, not be able to do it later. So I pulled out a piece of canvas, measured the same shape as the little one, and started, I kept wondering, will I be able to do it, will I be able to do it as well. I worked and worked and worked, purple, red, pink, black, a minute touch of orange, umber, purples, deep blue purple and reddish purple, and in the middle — a dark pink cloud hovering.

When I got . . . no, I have to tell you, I worked and worked so fast. It only took about fifteen minutes to paint it. From the small sketch I knew it would work, it was just a question if I could hold it together at the larger scale.

After I got done, I just stood there sweating, all by myself in the house, I shouted out loud, I did it, I did it, I grunted it out, I felt, for the first time in months I had painted a picture as good as my old pictures. I kept on shouting out in a low voice, I did it. I could not contain myself, it was an ecstasy. Even now, ten minutes after I finished, I am still trembling, I ran in here after finishing in the studio, to get it down on the computer.

I really did it.

I am still trembling, My mouth is dry.

To do this, to do only the simple thing that pleased me, *just to do what pleased me*, I had to do something that was outrageous, obviously wrong in the picture. Of course the sky was not so pink, my inner voices said.

Yet in the end it is this quality — the staring, looming, deep purple pink — which gives the picture any connection to the I that it may have.

10 / THE EFFORT IT TOOK TO GET THE STARK GEOMETRY OF WEST DEAN TO A STATE WHERE IT REALLY PLEASES ME

On this page and the following pages, I show further pictures of the Visitor's Centre at West Dean, with some comments on the issue of what it meant for me to please myself throughout the work of making the building.

I started with a small sketch of the wall; then moved to construction experiments in which I was trying (in that instance with my own hands) to find out how to build a complex structure of poured-in-place concrete pieces, with herringbone bricks laid on edge, in each panel. It took a great deal of work, first to find out how to make the wall structural, while maintaining these heavily disciplined centers. And it also took enormous care, over a period of many months, while the wall was later actually being built, to create the right balance of size, color, and material, so that these centers have a rhythm which maintains the distinctness of the centers, yet also fuses them to form larger centers.

In my view there is no doubt that this is the piece of wall where the deep quality and pleasing yourself are. They are successful because of the severity which I imposed on the arrangement. Each small window has a thistle-like shape above the arch to tie it into the brickwork. This special piece had to be drawn, cut, and shaped in brick material. But its function is to connect centers, on either side of the window arch, to connect these to the line of stone and concrete which runs over the panels, and comes in nearly tangent to the curve of the arch. That was quite a trick. It needed hard-edged, disciplined thinking about geometry to make it happen right. Yet it is just this arrangement of centers which finally allows a person to feel related to it. It is all this which is the embodiment of, "What must I do to it truly pleases me?"

That is the kind of work which must be done, every time, if a thing is truly to please —

first the maker, and then everyone. It has little to do with sweetness. What it does have to do with is stark arrangement — a geometry which is stark and simple, organized so that it creates this pleasure and relatedness in the beholder.

Some people have formed the opinion, during the last few years, that my work is aimed at "something sweet." Nothing could be further from the truth. The north wall of the building, shown in the photograph opposite, provides an excellent example. There is, in this wall, a great sense of pleasure and, I think, a sense of life. But it is caused, in this instance by a great severity and toughness in the centers which have been formed in the north wall.

Consider more carefully what I mean when I say that in the panels of the north wall, I worked and worked to bring them to the state where I could feel them pleasing me — truly pleasing me.

To start with, I think, we must acknowledge how unusual the process, how sensitive the problems are. Suppose I consider a simpler problem — the creation of a concrete frame for a very cheap house. A few columns, connected by beams, are to be filled with bricks or blocks. How shall we make that poured-in-place, cast-concrete frame? I want to make it so that it truly pleases me. But what is to like, or not like, in a concrete frame? It is a subtle business, it is hard work. The column can be five inches or six inches, or perhaps thicker, or more slender. The spacing of the columns can change. The beam can be with profile, or without; there may be a connection at the column's base, or at the place where the column meets the beam; then that connection needs a shape, or a design. And all this must be done so that it is cheap, not fancy, as cheap as the most primitive frame. And above all, I want to find the one which pleases me.

The West Dean Visitor's Centre, West Sussex, Christopher Alexander and John Hewitt, 1996

This is a huge effort. You cannot really tell from a drawing what is good and what is bad. To do it, you need perhaps, a cardboard mock-up, as big as the real members, before you begin to see it. Someone has to hold them for you. It takes two persons, not one. And it is a subtle business. The increase or decrease in feeling is slight; it slips through your fingers. Yet it is this very slight kind of difference you are looking for. Gradually, you see that one is a little better than the other. Gradually, you expose yourself to the fact that even the stubborn, raw geometry

of a concrete frame, in its cheapness and simplicity, can please you more, or please you less. You tune your sensitivity to it; gradually you make enough discriminations so that the column and the beam, their thickness, their spacing, the connections, the base — all please you a little more, rather than a little less.

Now go back to West Dean. In the north wall alone, the one I have illustrated, John Hewitt and I made subtle judgments of this kind — towards the thing which pleased me more, away from the thing which pleased me less, perhaps

287

The Entrance Porch, under construction, West Dean Visitor's Centre, 1995

Dining Room, West Dean Visitor's Centre

five hundred times — just to draw, test, and build that one wall: the thickness of each line of stone, the size of the concrete members, the lay of the bricks, the width of the panels, the rise of the arch above the window, the shape of the keystone at the head of the arch, the relative proportion of brick and flint, the relative amount of concrete, the height of the base, the number of small steps in the plinth, the shape of the cornice, the number of small steps in the cornice, their overhang, the measure not in inches but in quarters of an inch of each bit of the overhang.

And of course the larger centers were even more important: the shape of the horizontal panel below the windows, the shape of the group of fifteen panels, the centers formed by the plinth together with the cornice, holding the panels, in their proportion, just right to increase feeling, so that it pleases me.

Inside the same! Look carefully at the photograph of the interior (page 291). The two people here are somewhat at ease. The shot is not posed. I just photographed them, quietly, while

The north wall: windows, herringbone-brick panels, flint.

View of the West Dean Visitor's Centre from the garden. Christopher Alexander and John Hewitt, 1996

Two people at ease in the dining room, on a rainy day.

they were talking, and I was having lunch at the next table. Their ease was caused by the same kind of work indoors.

To do it, I once again made five hundred separate judgments, each one extracting that version of a thing which pleased me more within

the whole, never — at least trying never — to allow one which pleased me less to stand!

Just the geometry, the lines, the rectangles, their shapes. That is what it takes to make a building which truly pleases you. It is immensely hard work. You need the patience of Job to do it.

11 / EMIL NOLDE'S SUNSET AND PAUL GAUGUIN'S COW

Some painters from the early 20th century did achieve this quality. They made things which they liked.

These two pictures (pages 292–93), each painted near the beginning of the 20th century, show what I mean by pleasing oneself, in the very last and deepest sense. The cow, so ordinary, so beautiful — the golden green around its head, the black and white, the soft curve — a construction in which Gauguin was free to please himself. The sunset — how bold, how wild, how

extraordinary, quite different from the cow. Yet what is the same is that here, too, Nolde pleased himself, was free to paint such an outrageous painting, because he reached a state where he could say I don't care, where the restraints were taken from him, he only allowed his brush to do, autonomously, what blazes of color he really saw when that sunset was shining in on him.

If we look at a sunset, we have all seen one; what more basic, more primitive response is there, than to dip the brush in yellow, scrawl yellow, yellow, yellow, all over the central sun? But who would dare to do it? It would have taken enormous daring to be so absurdly basic. And then to do the hard work after being so basic, to fill in the painting, make the crimson, the blues, the grays, and the white light on the boat in just the right place, by obeying, following that most primitive instinct without inhibition, doing the most obvious thing, most directly.

The cow is more basic still. This one is less knowing than Gauguin's other works. When I saw it at Christie's, the junior auctioneer told me it was a "very nice minor Gauguin," it will go below the estimate. Such a patronizing tone.

If we compare this picture with a great picture by Gauguin — *Parahi te Marae*, for example (*The Sacred Mountain*), illustrated in Book 1 — we find that the cow is more direct. *The Sacred*

Mountain took work, it was a considered construction, carefully done, reaching a profound effect. It is a greater picture, yes. But, to some tiny degree, Gauguin, without a doubt I think, was aware when he made *Parahi te Marae*, aware what he was trying to do, aware of the gallery in Paris where he was sending the painting. *The Sacred Mountain* is a knowing construction, infinitely profound, yes.

But the cow is more innocent, perhaps more truly something that Gauguin liked. There, too, I know he must have worked and worked at it. The cow, so carefully placed, so beautifully drawn. All done just right. But in this picture he was, I think, only trying to please himself. He drew and painted this cow for his own pleasure. It was what he saw, what he wanted, not so knowing — constructed, yes, but far more innocent.

Sunset, Emil Nolde, Sonnenuntergang, 1909

Paul Gauguin, Vache Accroupie, 1900

It is even possible, I think, that Gauguin himself was slightly ashamed of this picture, just as my students were sometimes ashamed of their greatest works, because they were too naive, too direct, too innocent. Just as the auctioneer was slightly ashamed of this picture, called it a minor work, and predicted that it would fetch less than its estimated auction value (it did). But artistically the auctioneer was wrong. In my mind, this cow is a greater work, because it penetrates deeper, it has more grace, it is more that ultimate thing which Gauguin did to please himself.

12 / A SIGNIFICANTLY LARGE STRUCTURE

Pleasing yourself is not only vital in small structures and paintings. It is the core of architecture, the core of all building, and — as an idea — is therefore equally applicable to the very largest structures. In early 1995, I was invited by Scott Hunter of T. Y. Lin International — one of the largest bridge engineering firms in the world — to join him in designing a bridge in Puerto Rico. Two T. Y. Lin teams entered the competition at the same time, one headed by myself and Scott Hunter, the other by another team of T. Y. Lin engineers. In the end, neither of us won.

The bridge that came out of our work was highly innovative structurally. Designed to be made out of light-weight pierced-concrete shells, it had high structural strength, and had unexpectedly low weight and cost.[7] During discussion with the other team, it was, however, viewed as too unusual — almost to the point where they would not take it seriously as a structure. The fact that it did not look like a modern bridge — at that time cable-stay bridges were very fashionable — troubled them so profoundly that they almost could not look at its unexpected engineering attributes. My partner, Scott, tried to persuade me to make it look more acceptable by reshaping the tension chord over the support, and making its curve appear less like the cable of a suspension bridge. Yet the reason I had made the bridge steep and angular at the support was not because I wanted it to look like a suspension bridge, but because we had run extensive finite-element simulations on it, and it was performing very well. In addition, I felt its shape and charac-ter, as well as its structure, came from a deeper level of real liking than the other.

Scott and I had a discussion in our office. I tried to persuade him that what mattered was the fact that this shape of the bridge was based on a profound liking. He and I went back, repeatedly, over the structural features which made its structural performance so good. Indeed, the finite element analysis showed that there were forces flowing near the tower, which were somewhat similar to those in a suspension bridge, and which therefore made this shape highly practical.

He continued to believe that the strange-shaped quality of the bridge we had designed together was somehow uncomfortable. On my side, I remained convinced that a more stream-lined look was not related to structural efficiency, but rather to a stylistic modernism and to a fear of making something truly beautiful that would induce a true liking in people.

Later, Katalin Bende, also working on the project in our office, asked me to explain what I meant by this true liking and about people's fear of it, and why anyone could be afraid of true beauty. "What kind of beauty could go so deep that a person would be afraid of creating it?" she asked.

I told her that, in my view, a difficulty we modern people encounter can sometimes go something like this: When centers are properly distributed in a truly beautiful structure, one cannot avoid seeing the I (what a religious person might also call God). In the 20th century

*Bridge for the Rio Grande de Loiza, Puerto Rico, Christopher Alexander, Scott Hunter,
Randy Schmidt, Katalin Bende and Hana Mori, 1995*

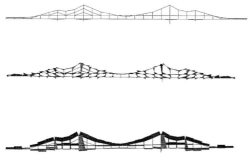

Computer studies for shears, bending moments and axial forces

The Puerto Rico Bridge, prestressed concrete shell design, 500 meter span, by Center for Environmental Structure and T. Y. Lin International, 1995

deep and serious centers in them, for some reason trouble modern architects profoundly. Even when an architect does want to borrow a traditional shape for a building (as postmodernists sometimes do), he often feels he has to make the shape "modern" in order to feel comfortable with it. So, for many decades, architects of the 20th century felt that they had to take a traditional form and distort it, so that they could demonstrate that they have *possessed* it, and so that their colleagues would not laugh at them for being archaic.

Let me put it another way. The history of the 20th century has been one in which people do not *want* to see God nor, therefore, true beauty either. The role of religion has, for many, become uncomfortable. Many people want no part of it. They do not want, even, to get near it. And for that reason, they also do not (cannot) want, in their lives, any kind of true beauty. True beauty is the quality of being in touch with the I. A structure with true beauty — the beauty which brings something in touch with the I — is, in effect, something in which we cannot avoid, in some part, seeing God. For this reason, the underlying design vocabulary of the 20th century, almost throughout the century, asserted that designers should create structures which are "interesting," "pleasing," "fantastic," "exhilarating," "with elan," and so on — anything but *beautiful* — indeed *never* truly *beautiful*. *That* word has unalterable meaning, cannot be contaminated, and during the temporary insanity of the 20th century, struck a nerve which people could not tolerate.

there has been something almost like a taboo, against seeing the I, or true beauty, or God. Hence the discomfort. This discomfort that modern people feel with real beauty — especially that architects and designers feel — is almost legendary. Working with architects, I have experienced it again and again. Many traditional shapes, especially the most profound shapes with

13 / BEING MODERN AND BEING TRUE

Later, when the competition work was almost finished, Scott and I saw drawings of the bridge made by the other T. Y. Lin team. It was graceful, striking, a cable-stay bridge of a type which became important and fashionable towards the

end of the 20th century. It was, in some ways, astonishing because it seemed an engineering marvel, even as a drawing.

Yet, objectively the cable-stay design bridge mainly looks good from the air, or in a model: it is not as satisfying for the driver, when one drives across, or when one experiences such a bridge in reality. That was true, too, of their proposal. It was too big for the landscape, not related to the land, not structure-preserving and thus not really comfortable in that place, not really comfortable to drive across. It was altogether too "technological."

But I cannot truly say that it was altogether bad, and that what we had done was altogether good. In my own heart, I felt something wonderful about the technological marvel of the cable-stay bridge, that could not be denied, and I had to admit too, that our pierced-concrete bridge did not have that something in the same degree. The quality of the bridge which Scott and I designed was troubling — beautiful, yet perhaps not quite right, troubling because it seems not quite of our time!

And yet I know that the more extraordinary, more futuristic-archaic bridge which we designed really *is* a technological marvel. From an engineering point of view, it was more surprising and more innovative than the other. I wonder at the grace of the technical cable-stay bridge, its graceful presentation, its almost flying-airplane gracefulness. And yet I know that this marvel of seeming beauty which I admire is actually alienating, that it does not root me in myself, it takes me, instead, out of myself, and leaves me cold and fearful.

And I know too, that the pierced-concrete bridge is something which will be a pleasure to drive near, a real joy in its feeling, and that you feel more real, more solid in your heart from this bridge.

I do not tell this story because the bridges themselves are important. What is important is the depth, and genuineness, of the real confusion between being *modern*, and being *true*. We are, I believe cut off from ourselves, and cut off from the I, to a very great degree.

Is it even permissible, today, to please yourself? You see from this example of the bridge, how troubling it can be to please yourself, how, in order to please yourself, you may have to make a thing in which God is visible.

Much of the 20th-century difficulty occurred because the vast changes that have occurred in society led ultimately to one conclusion: a person was not allowed to be comfortable with his own self. And it is this which makes wholeness so hard to achieve.

It is hard, so terribly hard, to please yourself. Far from being the easy thing that it sounds like, it is almost the hardest thing in the world, because we are not always comfortable with that true self that lies deep within us. That I is almost frightening in its content. It cannot easily be faced. So we wince when we see it, and are more comfortable with Captain Marvel comics, and Superman, and technology like the cable-stay bridge.

To do that thing which comes only from the heart is so hard not only because it looks futuristic-archaic, not only because others may laugh at us when we do it, but because we may even sneer at ourselves, and wince when we see it, and cannot face the depth and ordinariness which it encompasses. For the sense of that futuristic-archaic feeling, when expressed in its true form, is the I which faces us.

14 / THE CHILDLIKE

The good stuff is always childlike, a pure thing which comes from the heart. It is slightly touchy, in the sense that it is almost too much. One wonders if it is really all right to present such a thing.

I find, even now, after many years of experience, that when I am stuck in making a building, whether it is some large aspect of the thing or a detail, when I am stuck I can always get out of being stuck by asking myself, *which of the options would I really like, if I were doing it for myself . . . only for myself.*

In conventional terms, the idea of pleasing yourself sounds egocentric and completely wrong. It sounds contradictory to say that you get wholeness by pleasing yourself, since we have spent a lot of time discussing the fact that the "it" can only be found by being egoless. How can we become egoless by indulging our personal pleasure?

Yet the process of recognizing that this is true, not false, will get us finally to a full understanding of what living structure, and the deep connection to the ground, does really mean.

I have suggested in Book 2 that it is the process of drawing feeling from yourself which allows us to create order — *and that we cannot produce order in any other way.*[8] This means that the fundamental question we have to ask as we produce order is: *Does it create feeling in me, does it make me feel more whole within myself, when I confront it?*

But what I am emphasizing now is that the level of awareness needed to do this is a level which is immensely personal, which is almost like a little child speaking — a level where we let go, entirely, of our adulthood, even of the normal regulations of professional adult society.

This childish level of awareness is not normally available to us. Indeed, paradoxically, it is only the awareness of order which can allow us to release ourselves enough to even *get* this level of awareness.

What is fascinating about this aspect of the nature of order, is that it contains an unexpected mixture of the personal and the impersonal. It is *impersonal* in the sense that it is related to the fitness of the thing, to the exactness of the

structure-preserving transformation. It is *personal*, in the sense that it carries feeling, is full of feeling, originates in a vision which comes from your self.

The value of what is done, in any work of art, depends, in the end, on the extent that the artist can reach down to his own humanity, into his own person, and draw the thing he makes from this most ordinary person which exists inside. Yet it is not easy to reach the genuinely human part of oneself, the childlike part, which is true and simple. What I have described in these four books is the *structural* part of what you need in order to reach this human childlike part of yourself. It works because living structure — what I call the field of centers — really is a mirror of the human heart. It is only knowledge of this structure, and the practice of making it, which gives you a key to unlock your own heart.

Thus, paradoxically, it is only when you finally are truly personal, when you really put your humanness in to the things you make, that you genuinely reach the *objective* living structure. Living structure is a thing which can, finally, only be reached by humanness — by the personal, and individual childish temperament which lets a person be vulnerable to the all the world, in the things he makes. But a person will only be able to reach the ability to be personal in this way, to express true feeling in this way, once he has mastered the abstract structure which I call the field of centers. It is only after truly being able to experience this field of centers that you reach the point where you are *able* to be personal.

Then, finally, you are able to make something really whole — whenever this personal, light feeling finds its way into the things you do.

15 / THERE IS NOTHING GREATER

There is nothing greater, perhaps, than this "pleasing yourself." Everything follows, comes out right, when we start with real liking, real pleasing of ourselves, of each human being.

At first it may seem funny that I could write four volumes, nearly two thousand pages, and that it would all come down to this: that you must, and each person must please yourself, herself, himself fully. Then the structure of the environment will be a living structure, and everything will be all right.

But you may turn this funny-seeming statement around, and view it backwards. Imagine me saying something like this: The two thousand pages I have written about living structure are — I think — true. But they are to be understood in such a way that every line, every specific structural detail, can be rephrased to say: people will make living structure only when they truly please themselves. If there is any detail about the structure that is not clear, you should understand this fact clearly: *What pleasing yourself truly IS, is the process in which we create living structure.*

Our biggest problem in the world, the absence of living structure, the choked difficulty of finding true freedom, true art, all comes from this: that people do not know — emotionally — how to please themselves. In part, they are prevented by society. And in part, they are prevented by themselves, by their inner thought police.

Creating living structure is to be attained, in the end, by the greatest and most sublime process which can happen: that each person lives, works, exists, in such a fashion that they truly please themselves.

Then we may say, if we wish, that we are close to God.

16 / PURE INNOCENCE AND DEEP ORDER
THE MESSAGE OF ST. FRANCIS

Is not this the ultimate message of St. Francis?[9] The childlike simplicity in which we recognize that God is in us already. The I is inside us and we are made of it.

In trying to achieve a building, or any built thing in the world which means something, we need only touch that part of ourselves, reach to it, pluck it, bring it out. In a world of little children, wholeness — the deepest structure of which the universe is capable — will be satisfied.

It seems to me the message that one must please oneself, perfectly, in order to reach God, was exactly the message of St. Francis. He expressed it differently. He desired, above all things, to please God. He went to extraordinary lengths to do it, is famous for giving up his clothes, dancing barefoot, giving up everything in the material world, in order to praise God and please God.

What I mean here is just that. If you aim to do what will fulfill you and make you happy, what will deeply please you, and succeed in pleasing you, as you really are, to the depth of your soul, then those are the things which will please God.[10]

What is extraordinary is that in our time, this pleasing oneself is almost forgotten. Yet the life of our environment, its deepest reach for living structure, depends on just this: that we learn, again — all of us — to please ourselves. And perhaps, although that is less important, it depends, too, on our awakening: that we learn that in this pleasing ourselves, there lies all that is.

It depends on our learning that this truly pleasing ourselves is not shameful. It is transcendent.

The childish innocence in which we please ourselves is rather like the process when a three-year-old child first starts putting colors on a sheet of paper. She pleases herself, absolutely. She is not confused by any rules, concepts or prohibitions. So she is able to see exactly what is there, and to act accordingly. She is therefore free to place the color exactly *where it has to be*. In intellectual terms, we may say that she sees the structure perfectly, and is therefore free to make the structure-preserving transformation, with perfect accuracy.

This is what we need. That is what we are striving for as we make the field of centers. When we reach the innocence of the child where we only please ourselves, that is the closest we can ever come to the egoless state in which we see the structure perfectly and make the perfect response which preserves the structure perfectly.

This is the crux.

It is worth really contemplating this fact. For when you finally realize that these two things, *(1) pleasing yourself* and *(2) doing what is right*, are one and the same, you will not only feel free to do them, and be able to do them, but you will also have reached a deeper level in your understanding. At that stage, you will finally understand how the oneness of some system in the universe is not only an abstract thing outside your own self but that it is also finally and truly personal, the most personal thing there is. All that I have written in these four books leads, in the end, to the core of what is most vulnerable, most personal in us.

But this is very surprising. This really is a revolution in thought. That that something, the whole thing which I have been writing down, could at one and the same time reach down into the objective truth about the oneness of space and also be intimate, personal, lovely, touching just in our most vulnerable selves — that is almost unimaginable. It implies things about the nature of the universe which are quite beyond any ideas that we have discussed in these chapters.

Now you see how immense this thing is. It tells us that the thing which is most personal and most touching is at the very same time also the most awe-inspiring and objective. You can hardly hold onto this idea without some understanding in you about the way in which ultimate reality combines these two, without some picture of the universe in which something like a great self — the same thing earlier called the I, the source and origin of all our smaller individual selves — is somehow the real stuff that all of it is made of.

But the suggestion which I am making is even more startling. I am not saying only that the objective oneness of space which I have identified as the field of centers is personal. That would be hard enough to understand. But I am also saying that the egoless inner light which sometimes shows itself in a drawing, in a line, in a column, in a color — the I itself — this thing which seems so rarified, so philosophical and which somehow has a religious origin, *is also entirely personal in nature* and that as an artist I shall come closest to it, when I am most direct, most childish, most childlike in the way I make things.

Yes. I am saying that.

NOTES

1. Quoted in Martin Lings, WHAT IS SUFISM (Berkeley: University of California Press, 1975), 49.

2. For more on this process with André Sala, see Book 2, chapter 12.

3. Book 3, chapter 18, "Color Which Unfolds from the Configuration."

4. Ibid.

5. Professor Donlyn Lyndon.

6. The Mexicali project is fully described in Christopher Alexander, Howard Davis, Julio Martinez, Don Corner, THE PRODUCTION OF HOUSES (New York: Oxford University Press, 1981). The loss of connection to the I is not only the repression of one person's ideas, and the repression of a view of the world. It is also repression in the classic psychiatric sense, where a person denies his own feelings, and may even fight frantically to avoid confronting or admitting them.

7. The pierced concrete structure is similar to another pierced concrete structure that is described in detail in Book 3, the chapter called POSITIVE SPACE AND STRUCTURE.

8. Book 2, chapter 13, DEEP FEELING.

9. St. Francis of Assisi, 1182–1226, founder of the Franciscan order, perhaps the best-known and most beloved of all the Christian saints.

10. This very simple formulation was given to me by my daughter Lily, fifteen years old, during a discussion of this chapter.

CHAPTER ELEVEN

THE FACE OF GOD

1 / THIS *IS* GOD

Why does it make me happy when I manage to make something beautiful, and so depressed or sad when I don't manage?

I want to think about the world — what I have been calling the life of centers in the world, the life which appears in wholeness — in one more way.

When the field of centers appears in something, its deep feeling appears and it is literally as though spirit is made manifest. This is a world with lazy bees buzzing, the summer wind, the light on the leaves of the trees, the warm smell of grass. This *is* spirit. This field of centers then makes a window onto some ultimate domain of I — it connects me to myself.

But it is even more concrete to think of this wonderful lazy substance — the quality without a name — as spirit made actual, spirit made manifest. So, when that quiet, happy, sad paste occurs in things, when the subtle harmony occurs, everything is at peace — then spirit is made real, the underlying spirit of the world, its poten-tial, becomes concrete and real. Then, at that moment, we are face to face with that spirit. We are then face-to-face with God.

This quality, when it appears in things, people, in a moment, in an event, *is* god. It is not an indication of God living behind all things, but it is actually God itself. This is spirit made manifest.

It is very hard to take this literally. We are more often in a state of mind where we would like to say one of two things, either, *Everything is God: God is everywhere*, or, *God lies behind things, this is merely the outward material world*.

But in the view which I am explaining here, we must say, more nearly, that it is in this special event, this kind of living breathing situation which appears in us, and in the material world, then this *is* God, it is God appearing, and we do not need to wait for any afterlife, because this wonderful transcendent thing happening before our eyes, is itself God, now.

2 / SPIRIT MADE MANIFEST

As we understand this more, we recognize that a building, or a building detail, or a painting, *is*, to some degree or other, *spirit*. When a thing is well made, it is an actual realization of spirit, a physical appearance and creation, realization, of spirit in this world. As the window to that realm of I, we may see and feel profound things going on, we get a glimpse of something in the made detail.

But it is more than just a glimpse, more than a window, which shows us the real spirit behind the face of matter. The actual substance itself — the building, the painting, the song, made under the circumstances I have described, made to be a center — is itself physically spirit. The process by which a center is made is the process by which spirit becomes manifest, becomes actual. Thus, the tawdry concrete blocks, plaster, and pieces of wood become, in their substance, spirit itself, to some degree or other. A few patches of paint on a panel becomes a painting — and to the extent that this painting has the center, is a window, it becomes spirit. We see spirit in it. But the actual stuff itself becomes spirit. The spirit behind the face of matter is transformed, and the dull mate-rial itself begins to shine, shows us spirit, is spirit. We have contact with actual spirit in that thing.

And this is the ultimate aim of all making: to make a thing which does manifest spirit, which shows us feeling, which makes God visible and shows us the ultimate meaning of existence, in the actual sticks and stones of the made thing.

3 / THE PRACTICAL RESULTS OF THIS KNOWLEDGE

Once I accept that what is happening is actual spirit, it helps me to make a whole thing. Once I understand it, I can seek to do just that. I take everything I know about centers, feeling, and so on, and focus on my inner knowledge of what it means for spirit to appear.

This is a direct humility. Then I am close to making a gift to God.

But my acceptance is more than just humility. Somehow it helps me. If I know that I have to make spirit — I cannot fool around with that. It is a great weight, and a great joy. I keep at it. It is hard work, emotionally. I can do it at any time. But it is so much easier to ignore it, not to do it. Not doing it is easy. Doing it is hard. Concentration, attention, effort — it is all very hard.

But when I actually do it, I pay attention to what I am doing and allow myself to go only in that direction where I can say it is an emerging spirit. That cuts many things out. The inner knowledge that I carry in me, which already knows what is spirit and what is not, will let this instruction, or this knowledge, guide me quite surely towards certain kinds of things.

White slip on black glaze, one of the few times when I felt I had reached something close to the real thing: It is significant, perhaps, that this work is only six inches across. The bigger it gets, the harder it is.

4 / A NECESSARY STATE OF MIND

This brings me, then, to a last aspect of the process which produces life in things, a necessary state of mind. The core of this necessary state of mind is that you make each building in a way which is a gift to God. It belongs to God. It does not belong to you. It is made to serve God, to glorify God. It is not made to glorify you. Perhaps, if anything, it humbles you.

Of course, I do not say this with any intention to suggest that this state of mind is specifically Christian. It is, as far as I can tell, religious in nature, but quite general in its character. And I do believe that it is *necessary*. It is not a pious extra. *I believe it is a necessary state of mind, without which it is not possible to reach the purity of structure needed to create a living thing.*

In Books 2 and 3 about the process of building, I have tried to describe the living processes which are necessary to make a building come to life. I have tried to explain that in these processes we must produce a great deal of structure, most of which must come from the inside of the structure which exists. I have emphasized how, in doing this, and in making a thing whole, we must make centers as intense as possible. I have tried to explain how, as we search to achieve this structure, we must consciously make it like the I or self. In the end I must make every single center in the building a being, and make the whole building a being made of beings.

All these different features of the process must be going on continually while we are making the building. Indeed. But in addition, there is one additional thing — the state of mind which must accompany this process. The essence of this state of mind is that the building must not shout. Emotionally, it must be completely quiet.

It is very hard to allow the wholeness to unfold. To do it, we must pay attention, all the time, only to the wholeness which exists in what we are doing. That is hard, very hard. If we allow ourselves the luxury of paying attention to our own ideas, we shall certainly fail. The things which can and do most easily get in the way, are my own *idea*, my thoughts about what to do, my desires about what the building "ought" to be, or "might" be, my striving to make it great, my concern with my own thoughts about it, or my exaggerated attention to others people's thoughts. All this can only damage the building, because it replaces the wholeness which actually exists at any given stage with some "idea" of what it ought to be.

The reason why I must try and make the building as a gift to God is that this state of mind is the only one which reliably *keeps me concentrated on what is*, and keeps me away from my own vainglorious and foolish thoughts.

Any one of us has a certain natural tendency to want to draw attention to ourselves. Any builder has a natural tendency to hope that people like what he or she has built, a tendency to say, "Look at what I have made," a tendency to want to identify the building which you have made as yours, to have your name on it, to be recognized as its maker, to be recognized as the builder. And in one limited sense this is childish, natural, and all right. But in a more serious sense it interferes profoundly with my ability to make the building right. Instead of paying attention to the structure of the building, allowing it to become just right quietly, paying attention to its wholeness, it will encourage me to change the building, make it more dramatic, make it more identifiable as something which I made, make it so that I can point to it, identify it as a distinct thing in its own right, make it so that other people can point to it.

All this might make me famous as an architect, but it damages the building. It will make me replace care and humble concern for doing just what is required with a frame of mind which wants to shout, just slightly, at each moment, while the design is unfolding. This problem po-

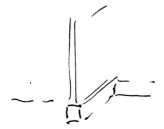

1 inch by 1 inch with 1/8 of an inch offset: Too big, not quiet enough   *3/32 of an inch offset: Still not quiet enough*   *1/16 of an inch offset: Just right, finally quiet enough*

tentially affects every single one of the 100,000 steps which I go through to make the building. So it will infect it very deeply, change its character not in a subtle way, but altogether. The beautiful and living thing which is like water will be replaced by something which shouts out, where I can write my name, which is a little awkward because it tries too hard at every moment.

The effect is tiny, but the impact is enormous.

A few years ago, one of my carpenters was making a kitchen cabinet for me. There are shelves in the cabinet, above the counter. To protect the uprights that come down onto the counter from standing water, I decided to make a sliver of walnut, about three-quarters of an inch by three-quarters of an inch and glued to the walnut of the counter, that would act as a base for the painted pine that came down onto it. If the pine itself were to come all the way down to the counter, the joint would rot out from the water on the counter.

Barton, the carpenter, wanted to make it beautiful. He proposed making this little sliver of walnut slightly bigger, one inch by one inch. He made a mock-up of a piece like that, and we looked at it. It felt too big. I asked him to chamfer the edge. It now stood an eighth of an inch beyond the pine board, with a chamfered edge. It still seemed too much. He reduced it a little, so that it was 3/32 of an inch, again chamfered. It was more delicate, almost OK. But it still seemed just a tiny bit too much. He was disappointed. I could see that at this stage, it still had

a little something, which very quietly said "Look at me." He wanted to keep that in it, because it made him feel good, that he had made a beautiful thing. "Isn't it a beautiful center,?" he said, using the language that would trap me in his own delight. But I looked at it carefully, and finally I said no. It must go down to 1/16th, chamfered again. At 1/16th it will not be noticed. It will still serve to make sure the upper board sits properly on the lower, will make a good joint, and will disappear almost entirely, even though it is still there.

This one was just right. The larger one, I felt I couldn't offer as a gift to God, because it still included someone's pride showing — look at me, look I have made something. But this one, because it is just right, even invisible, I can offer as a gift to God with a clear conscience. And this one is, in the end the most beautiful, the most permanent. It has the most quiet life.

Of course, the desire to make something beautiful is capable of damaging the structure which is actually wanted in the thing itself. It encourages us to let the thing be dominated by an image of "being good," "being beautiful," rather than by being what is actually required. So, in the end, my simple human desire for recognition will interfere with my ability to make a thing which lives. It interferes, concretely, with my ability to get the field of centers right because I am thinking about the wrong thing — my own glory, or my carpenter is thinking about his glory — and neither of us is thinking enough about the actual field of centers in the building which will make it alive. Then it will all come tumbling down. *To get it right, I must think exclusively about the actual field of centers, nothing else.* I cannot think about one tiny particle of myself, or what I want, just what is needed to make the thing come to life.

5 / THE WORLD BEYOND A GIVEN THING

This state of mind is necessary as a practical matter, which will affect the unfolding at every stage. In order to get it right, it means that at each moment, when I carry out an unfolding process, trying to find centers, make the thing more whole, I must be *truly* concerned to make it more whole, I must *truly* abandon my own desire to make a good impression or to make a vivid impression on the other people in the world.

To get it right, I must concentrate very hard on the life of the thing itself, and learn to abandon completely, my own strivings or ideas.

Part of the structure of all life or order, is that it extends beyond itself. To the extent a system has life, it is helping to make some larger whole alive. The field goes out beyond its own immediate confines, and every center draws its strength from other centers, often lying far beyond it. It is, therefore, an essential attribute of all life, that it represents a connection between the space where the order occurs, and the space beyond.

It is certain that life is not something local, a thing which merely happens in a painting or a person or a mountain. It is a relation between the thing

Not-separateness. An inseparable connection between a thing and the world beyond that given thing. —
Lily and Sophie playing in Martinez

where it occurs and the world beyond. It is a phenomenon which depends on the whole universe, and the extent to which the larger order of the universe penetrates and soothes, the order of the part whose order we are looking at. In such a world, the order springs fundamentally, and ultimately, from the connection of each part to its surroundings.

In the preface to Book 1, I showed a yellow tower. The tower embodies everything I have been discussing. It contains, in an imperceptibly simple form, *all* the structure which I have been defining. It has wholeness to an intense degree. It contains each of the fifteen properties which connect space. It gleams with inner light. It has beautiful levels of scale, positive space, a wonderful, simple hierarchy of centers, it has an extraordinary shape, and the space next to it also has such beauty of shape so that we see the tower inseparable from the space around it. It embodies the color properties to an extraordinary degree, and yet is so simple.

And the tower is a mirror of the self to the highest degree, as a whole, and in its parts. Compare all the different buildings I have illustrated in the four books with this tower, and ask which would you take as a mirror of your own self. I believe that there are relatively few things

in these books, or anywhere in the world, which you will choose ahead of it.

And there is one thing more. The yellow tower has the quality of not-separateness to an extent which is very rare. The tower creates the feeling, in a person who sees it, of perfect calmness. It suggests that everything in the world is alright. More extremely, we may say that it creates the sensation that everything — *everything* — is connected. Because it is so deeply connected — its parts to one another, itself to its surroundings — it creates the sensation that nothing is separate, that everything is in harmony.

If we push our perception a little further, and examine our reaction more deeply, we may become aware that the tower even suggests that everything is part of everything else. This happens, of course, because the tower achieves this very thing in itself. It is so deeply made, its field of centers is so perfect, that its wholeness really does extend far beyond its own boundaries. There is no feeling of limitation at its edge. The unity, the stillness which it creates, extends on beyond its walls. It melts perfectly with the paths, gardens, and outbuildings beyond. There is no discontinuity. The world around this thing is almost perfectly at one.

6 / NOT-SEPARATENESS

This state of not-separateness in the yellow tower is not different from what we have discussed before. It is the same thing . . . just wholeness, or life. What is new now is only that I keep attention on the fact that wholeness is *the* state in which each thing is continuous and part of the larger whole. It is a state in which the world is melted. In this view, we finally see wholeness in the most helpful way of all, because here it is quite unpretentious and ordinary. The more any portion of space is unified, the more inseparable it becomes from all the rest. So, in the end, the intricacy and richness of a beautiful thing does not arise from

the desire to make something rich or intricate, it only arises from the particular desire to make it perfectly one in itself, and with the world.

It is perhaps surprising, but necessary to recognize, that *I cannot make a thing which has this not-separateness, unless I honestly want it.* That means I must give up my wish to draw attention to myself. I must honestly want the thing which I am making to become part of the greater world, inseparable from it. In order to see, or feel, or listen for the glimmers of the I, it is necessary to be in a very definite state of mind. I have to want to be not-separate.

As I have described earlier, deep down in my heart there are usually subtle instincts which make me want to stand out, to be identified — instincts, in short, which make me want to be separate. But to feel the quality in the ground, to be able to be sensitive to what it is, I have to have my eye, my ear, my feeling, very finely tuned to listening to the possible conditions in which the feeling of real oneness could occur, what it would be like if it did occur, and so on. For this, I must lose my preoccupation with myself and keep it only with the thing. I must be open to this very vulnerable and subtle substance.

What I have found out is that I cannot be sensitive to this subtle substance unless I have a genuine desire for all things to be one — I myself, the thing I am making, and everything else as well. The desire does not need to be active. But there must be no desire at all for separateness. Any trace of a desire for separateness will destroy completely my ability to hear the one, whispering through, as I go through my trials and efforts in the making process.

Thus, to make a thing which is one, I struggle — myself, the maker — to become one with the world. This sounds nice. It sounds like religious stuff again. But I am doing it only to become better, only because I do want, in the end to make a perfect thing. It is terribly hard, because to become one with the world, I must genuinely *want* to become one with it. I have to catch each flash of "wouldn't this little detail be great" and kill it. Instead I must keep on the hard work of paying attention, trying to understand what I need to make the deep feeling come forth.

This means that I must genuinely give up all the remnants of my desire to be separate. I must genuinely seek, and want, and open my arms to being *not* separate. Most of the time I fail. I fail because, to do it, I must honestly give up every last trace of wanting to be distinct, famous, separate, identifiable. That is one reason why I have to do so many experiments — trying, testing, failing, failing, failing — then once in a blue moon, one time in twenty, occasionally succeeding. I fail those nineteen times because I am trying to think *something*, I think I have a good idea. Then the twentieth time, somehow, when I am lucky, something perfect sneaks in, without my knowing it. But I have to be fast enough to catch it when it comes.

And that I can do best when I am looking all the time to make a gift for God. Because when that twentieth one comes along, even though I did not produce it, I am smart enough, and fast enough, to see it, to know that suddenly, this one is humble, this one moves towards not separateness — this one has a tiny chance of being a gift for God.

Green waves in a tile-panelled bench back, tiles by Christopher Alexander, 1984

This is why, from a practical point of view, there is a connection between building and religion. The connection is not historical. It is empirical, because the religious disciplines are just those which have taught people *how*, practically speaking, to lose themselves. Not only how to become not-separate but — far harder — how to become *willing* to become not-separate.

Because a great work cannot be made except by a person who has become willing to be not separate, it follows that the great works of history are associated with religion. It has been that way simply because the great religions all taught an essential prerequisite for making works of oneness. Few other disciplines have done so.

Let me repeat the argument in slightly different terms. Not-separateness, like everything else we have discussed, is a physical attribute of order. It is something which is visible within any building that has life. But when we concentrate on the problem of creating it, it arises only from a certain state of mind. Thus not-separateness simply means that a thing which is whole will be made, in the end, only by the genuine desire, *on the part of the maker*, not to be separate from the world. In other words, it is the state of mind of the maker, in the end, which produces the deepest forms of order — and these deepest forms cannot be produced *except* by this state of mind. It requires the definite intention to become one with the world.

This idea cannot be realized in a building without a change, a quietness, in the maker. It requires absolute removal of the individual ego, because what is created can no longer stand out and be separated from everything else, and therefore loses its personal identity. And yet, paradoxically, in the moment where this absolute identity and not-separateness is attained in a thing, and it truly becomes one with the things which surround it, it stands out shining with an extraordinary power which could never be reached under any other circumstances.

This is, perhaps, the central mystery of the universe: that as things becomes more unified, less separate, so also they become most individual, and most precious.

7 / MAKING A GIFT FOR GOD

It is in my struggle to want this simple, unobstructed purity that I am helped, most of all, if I try to make each thing a gift to God.

A few years ago I made a coffee table for our office. I made a kind of stand which was to be bolted to the wall, and which was going to be a place to put the coffee machine, cups, and so on. This thing was exactly one of those kinds of things which *fails* to have the quality which I am describing now. It was quite practical. It had a nice shape. It had some good centers, and so on. If I had to use it in a textbook for centers, I could show how it has centers in it in all the right places. But its spirit was very bad. The thing was made to look at. While I was making it, I was half consciously making it to be admired — by my students, by my colleagues, by people who might come into the office.

And how did this "bad" spirit show itself in the thing? It showed itself in the fact that this thing stood out too much. It was not part of the wall. It was not part of the office. It drew too much attention to itself. As a center, it shouted slightly too loud. It was not really arising out of the structure which was there, and gently embellishing it. It was so humble in the way it was made, slightly rounded corners and all, that it was screaming for attention.

This attention it was trying to get was fairly modest. After all, the thing was made of simple pine boards, varnished. But it was clear, *in its spirit*, that it was made to impress. It did not leave things alone. It was too formal, not practical enough. As a result it is trivial. But it would have been impossible to correct its defects, one by one. The only way to correct such a thing is to make it in an entirely different frame of mind.

Thus although what is wrong with it lies in something physical that we can see, it cannot be put right at any concrete practical level in the physical details of the thing. It can only be put right by a change in attitude, and above all, by an entirely different intention, by a different motivation.

In the small picture shown below — an unimportant sketch in gouache — the motivation, at least, was of that kind. It was not made for others to see or admire. Only, for itself, to sit in a certain place in my house, quietly.

Sometimes, when I make something, my mind is so concentrated on it that it becomes different. It becomes a pure thing. I am not concerned with showing off, but only with making the thing itself. How can I set my mind in this egoless direction? At every step in the 10,000 steps during the making of a building, I am always, at each step, asking which of the things that I can do next is the one which will be the best gift to God.

This state of mind, this question, is then in my mind, all the time: when I place the building, when I figure out its volume, when I work out the outdoor space next to it, when I work out its shape, when I decide its height, when I work out the feeling of the interior and its main structural section, when I work out the position of the major rooms, when I work out the width of passages, when I work out the doors that frame the passage, when I work out the surface on the floor — each time, and in each case, I ask myself which of the various things that I can do, which one is the best gift for God?

Not-separateness: A small painting,
Gouache on wooden panel, Christopher Alexander, 1980

In particular, I ask myself if this gift is humble enough to be such a gift. When I ask that, all
the small stupidities of my work come out into
the open. In that state of mind, and with that
question, I always see the egocentric part
clearly — the part which is there to glorify *me*.
Then I have a chance of getting rid of all that
part, because, with the help of this question, I see
more clearly what it is.

At every moment in the process of making,
I am faced with choices of what to do next.
Everything comes down, in the end, to what I do
as I face these choices, how I move forward. So,
if I am choosing among three ways of doing
something, a typical thing that might happen
goes like this: I am at a step where there are three
possibilities in front of me: A, B and C. I ask myself which one is best. When I ask *that* question,
which one is best, I think A is best. But then I
ask in my prayer which one of the three comes
closest to being a suitable gift for God. In answer
to *this* question, I find out that A has some petty
vanity in it, and realize that if this thing is to be
a gift to God, then I must choose C, not A.

Both buildings have this quality in some degree

On this page: Two sketches of classroom buildings for the Waldorf School in Altadena, California

And in fact, this simple question, this arrow in my work trying to make a gift for God, does always lead to C, where the arrow which asks which one is "best" always leads to A. So this question, small and embarrassing as it is, always leads to a different direction from trying to make something "good." That is the fascinating thing.

You may say, well, if it always leads in a different direction, and you already know it, why then not always choose C, keep on asking this question, and keep on going towards C. The trouble is, it is immensely hard work asking this question. It is a bore. It is troublesome. It is pedantic. It is too pious. I can't be bothered with it. It is absurd to keep on asking myself this question. Besides, this question finds me out, and keeps on showing me — what I don't want to know — that my natural inclinations are no good, that my work is too puffed up with pride, that my judgment is imperfect.

So, even just *asking* the question, 10,000 times, is almost impossible.

What I hope to do is to get an instinct which tries to go toward C without my having to ask the question. But it doesn't work. I get the illusion I am doing it, but I really start drifting back to A — Which one is best? — and all the image, pompousness, which that implies.

To get real purity I have to keep on asking the question, which one would I do if it were a gift for God. Then I get my answer. C. Choose C.

It is easy to see how powerful this question is, if it can make a difference like that. I have already explained, many times, that everything we do in making something, hinges on the choices I make, step by step, as the thing evolves. I have seen how different ways of judging what to do next will gradually get me closer and closer to making a thing with life. The mirror of the self, the field of centers, the structure-preserving transformations, feeling, being, simplicity — all of them help me to get better and better at making this judgment.

But even after learning all of them, this question about the gift to God, is necessary to bring me even closer to making something which has true life in it. It is not a different question from the others. It is simply a sharper and more pure form of the question, which, when it is added to the others, and combined with them, gives even better answers than they do.

In effect, what this question does, is it forces me to be humble. I cannot pretend that the small self-glorifications and self-aggrandizements which exist in the thing I am making are not there. So this question gives me the ability to get rid of them, to see beyond them, and to see which path in the making of the thing, is most free of them.

The same state of mind, in which I ask myself if what I am making might be a suitable gift for God, leads to another state of mind. Often, as I work on a thing, I am consciously aware of the ground, the second domain, the "realm beyond." While I work, I am consciously looking for a glimpse of this ground to reveal itself. I wait to catch it. I can see that what I have so far doesn't yet have that thing, and I wait for it, hoping that a little bit of it will shine through.

This is conscious and explicit. I can feel dimly what the ground is like, I have a continual awareness of what it is . . . even though I don't know it in the particular case before me . . . and I wait to try and move what I am doing in that direction.

I try to sense it. I allow my dim feeling of this ground, this heaven, to unfold in my mind's eye. I try to imagine what I would be looking at if I were looking into heaven, and then ask myself what that thing would be in this particular case.

I try to imagine the pale gleam of heaven in the room I am making. I move the window sill, the shape, the height, the glazing bars, until as close as I can get it, this heaven, beyond me, reveals itself, even in a small weak glimpse.

Once again, this question makes up for a great deal of mental laziness. Under normal circumstances, I might choose A or B at a given stage in the process of making. I feel that I am on the right track, and I am comfortable with what I am doing. Then I ask myself if I can feel

The building, as it is affected by the motive: to make a gift for God.
A detail of the cafeteria on the Eishin Campus, Tokyo.

the realm beyond unfolding, looking through at me. Or I ask what it would be like if the realm beyond *were* looking through at me. And then I realize that neither A nor B has the slightest chance of doing this — but that there is a C which does. So I get a glimpse of this C, a kind of hint of it, and start moving towards C instead of A or B. Once again, this deeper question has a big effect.

If I maintain my concentration and stay conscious of this question all the time, then I can — sometimes — keep going towards C instead of A or B — and the end result becomes entirely different.

8 / THE FACE OF GOD

This quality, whether it occurs in a great work or a small work, always has the same essential purpose: to make a connection to the I, to reach, in material substance, the face of God.

For some of us, in our time, this statement is uncomfortable. Part of the positivistic and mechanistic view of the universe which has dominated the scientific thought of the last three centuries was, until recently, a growing effort to "prove" that there is no such thing as God. For me therefore to infer any reliance on God, or to show any aspect of a work which even smacks of this kind of thing, is sentimental, non-factual, perhaps even fanatic.

If it were suggested that we could only give a building life by standing in the mainstream of some extant religion, like Christianity, Islam, or Buddhism, this might indeed be troublesome. That, however, is not what I suggest at all. The intensity of life in the world does not depend on the secular or social body of doctrine and cultural habit which we commonly call "a" religion, or on any one of the recognized religious doctrines. Indeed I suspect that the organized churches and religions are unfortunately rather far from any connection with the ground, or with the facts about the universe which cause an inner connection between the realm of matter and the realm of God or I.

It *is* true that there is a connection between religion and the art of building, and that this connection is functional and inescapable. I have described it partially in chapter 2. But when we examine this connection carefully, we find out that it is a connection with the invariant structure common to all religion, to the psychic center of religion as it exists innately in a person, and to the material nature of the universe.

It is that essence which concerns itself with the connection between our own substance, and the substance of the universe, which is at stake. The depth, the life we have identified, comes into being in the building only when this intimate connection between our own selves, and the great self of the world is made active so that it is entirely within our grasp, because it depends only on the extent to which we can let go of our own small selves, and surrender to the greater self.

Let us go back to the picture of the ground I painted in chapter 6. There are two possible versions of the vision in chapter 6, shown in two diagrams below, A and B.

If I wanted to give a more mechanistic account of the picture, trying to do without the ground, I could say that a building which has life in some way mirrors the structure of our mind, our body, or our self. This is based on the exis-

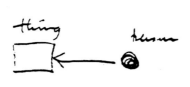

Diagram A. Person and thing: a structural correspondence between maker's mind and building

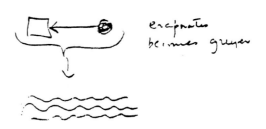

Diagram B. Maker and building together evaporate, together become more transparent in the face of the ground

tence of a connection, a similarity, between our minds and the structure of a building which has life. It could be shown in a diagram like A.

The account I have been giving says, on the contrary, that when we experience this one, either in the act of building, or in the act of enjoying what someone else has built, we somehow ourselves come more closely into relation with the underlying ground-stuff of the universe, with the domain of pure unity or I. This is structurally quite different from the mechanist account. It says somehow, as we enter into this relation with a thing which is one, then we and the thing melt somehow, become more transparent, less form-conscious, more melted into the void of which the universe is made. This is a three-way relation, which might be shown in a diagram like B.

In this second version, as we make or experience this one, we come closer to reality, closer to the stuff, to the void, to the underlying ground of which the universe is made. It is almost as though, as the relation between ourselves and

the thing occurs, we catch on fire, we become more thin, more vaporous, as if the act of relating the two makes both of them transparent, as if, almost, the graphite on the page, which makes the diagram, began to evaporate. All this comes closer to the blinding light, the great void, of which the universe is made.

I cannot make clear common sense of this explanation. I cannot give an operational account of what it might mean. I do not know how to devise an experiment which could establish that it is happening. And yet I am certain that this explanation is the correct one, and that the search for that ground is not merely some psychological exercise in which we look for things which remind us of our inner selves, but an experience in which we approach, as closely as a person ever can, to the underlying non-material stuff of which the world is made, and in which we come as close as possible to a direct experience of what is real, an experience in which we are enveloped, melted, evaporated, lost, and where we touch, for an instant, the inner stuff,

The castle of Eilean Donan, Kyle of Lochalsh, near Skye, Scotland.

behind the stuff, of which we and our world are made.

If we are willing to recognize this ground, whether we call it God or something else, and recognize that this light is behind all things which are at one with themselves, then we may say, simply, that a thing is beautiful to the extent that it reveals this one.

A massive building or a small one, a seat, an ornament, a simple beam, a room, has life, is deep, affects us, moves us to tears, to awe, exactly to that extent that it is a picture of that God behind all things. If you see the watery pale yellow sunlight shining behind dark gray clouds, with the pale blue of heaven shining in between some wintery morning, and you see, in that light, the original light of the universe — then, you may say, in still different terms, that sometimes, very occasionally, an artist who weaves a carpet, or who shapes a building, or who paints a tile, manages to make something which has this same light in it, where this same Self is shining out . . . he has made something as close to a picture of God or Self as it can be, and it affects us, like the light of morning does, because it seems to show us directly to the heart of this self, and connects us with it, almost to the point of pain.

A MODIFIED
PICTURE OF THE UNIVERSE

1 / INTRODUCTION

Throughout these four books there lies, again and again, repeatedly, the single question — a drumbeat, muffled, but insistent — which will not go away, and which must be answered in some fashion, if we are to conceive, and have, a living architecture. That question is: *What is, truly, the ultimate nature of matter?* [1]

I have expressed my conviction that architecture cannot be good so long as we try to do it within a mechanical conception of matter. Because of the recursive nature of life, living centers cannot be well-represented in a mechanical picture; nor can the essential connection between a living building and the "interior" of the human being. Many chapters of this Book 4, and vital parts of Books 1 to 3, deal directly with the architectural problems that emanate from this difficulty. I have argued, in many different ways, that we must have a vision of the world in which life, as the foundation of all architecture, is understood as something objective and inspiring. That idea is beautiful, worthwhile, profound enough to provide a satisfactory underpinning

for our work as architects, artists, ecologists, and builders of the world. But it cannot be understood, or used, successfully, I think, without making changes in our concept of the matter from which the world is made.

The fact that such a modified world-picture might arise in part from *architecture*, not only from physics, is significant. Our present picture of the universe, which does come mainly from physics, is hamstrung by the unavoidable narrowness of physical investigations. The character of wholeness, one of the major unsolved problems in 20th-century physics, is more easily revealed by consideration of architectural problems than by consideration of problems of physics.

Thus architecture, previously the *recipient* of cosmological conceptions that originated in physics, might perhaps itself now become a contributor to cosmology. Cosmology may gain insight from the special problems of architecture, because these special architectural problems crystallize — and can inject new understanding into — profound problems that exist in physics.

2 / THE NATURE OF SPACE AND MATTER

Let us go back to the question, *What is everything made of?* In past eras people have had wildly different ideas about this question. At one time it was thought that the world was ultimately made of earth, air, fire and water; it has been said that it is ultimately made of God-stuff, that it is made of animal spirits, even that it is all a dream in the mind of God.

In the modern era this question, "What is everything made of?" has been given a single, widely accepted answer. We now believe that the world is made of an extended material which we call the matter-space continuum. In the present

view it is generally accepted that this matter-space is extended and approximately continuous. The particles we know as quarks and electrons, the atoms, molecules, crystals, and organisms, all appear as whirlpools or ripples or disturbances in the matter-space continuum. Everything we currently know about the universe can be represented as some (geometric, algebraic, dynamic) consequence of the properties of this matter-space. [2]

The detailed structure of the matter-space is under daily investigation, and is not certainly or completely known. Some physicists use models in which this stuff is mathematically continuous; others use models in which it is discrete — hence string-like or granular — at a very tiny level of scale (10⁻³³ cm). Even the dimensionality and topology of the matter-space are under constant debate.[3] However, one thing is quite clearly agreed upon: *the basic material that everything in the world is made of is the matter-space.*[4] The nature of the world arises from the detailed properties of the matter-space.[5]

In contemporary cosmological theory, the matter-space is assumed to be inert. That was the core assumption made by scientists for the last three hundred years — since Bacon, Descartes, and Newton — and it continues to this day.[6] The fact that space-matter has been considered as inert, does not mean that it is uninteresting. It is very interesting indeed, with fascinating properties and fascinating results. Maxwell's equations, the electromagnetic theory of light, Einstein's relativity theory, quantum theory, most recently the non-local connections predicted by Bell's theorem, have all made it clear that its behavior is not only *very* interesting, but very fascinating *indeed.*[7] *Nevertheless, regardless how fascinating it is, the matter-space is always considered to be inert.* It is above all *dead.*

Even the matter-space of quantum mechanics — which assumes that most events are influenced by the whole, perhaps even by the act of observation, and where events can interact without strictly Newtonian causal interactions — even this quantum matter-space *is still conceived as mechanical in character.* By this I mean simply

that once again it is a lifeless, mathematical structure without spirit — and that any life which appears in it is held to be created only by assemblages and configurations of the inert material. Scientifically speaking, the inertness of the matter-space is the most essential part of its nature, and of its definition in the current physical scheme. Being *inert* is an essential feature of the Cartesian and mechanistic picture, and it must be inert — because the basic idea of our Cartesian model of science is that you *pretend* that it is inert *in order to understand how it works.* It is in this sense that, no matter how complex, the matter-space picture of late 20th-century physics was always still a picture of a mechanism.

Might we be able to create some less mechanical, more comprehensive, picture which provides a substrate for the facts of physics as we know them *together* with the more difficult facts about life in architecture and art that have been held to lie necessarily outside physics? Can we create a picture of matter which will one day become adequate to give us a world not only profound in its mechanical successes, but which also explains our nature, our agony, our relationship to matter, and the existence of the soul?

Before I draw together the strands of Book 4, to explain such a proposal, I summarize two contemporary lines of thought (consistent with the ideas expressed in these four books), which have begun, tentatively, to appear in the physics of the last decades. One of these two lines of thought has to do with wholeness as a structure. The other has to do with mind.

3 / WHOLENESS AS A PHYSICAL STRUCTURE IN THE UNIVERSE

An idea that has recently begun to appear in physics is the idea that wholeness itself is a real structure, something geometrically concrete, not merely a general appreciation for the unity and connectedness which exists in things. It is,

rather, nearly a *substance*, a definite structure, which appears all around us.

We have all had the experience of remembering a human face. We may have experienced, sometimes, the fact that we can remember the *feeling* of this person's face, its gestalt, its effect on us, its kindness or its ferocity, without being able to summon up, in memory, the detailed features that generate this gestalt. Even in such a memory lapse, it is plain that we do remember the most essential thing, the overall *feeling quality* of the face, which allows us later to say, unhesitatingly, "There he is," or "He's the one," if shown a picture.

In this kind of experience, the "something" which is clearly seen, and felt, and understood — the underlying structure which can be carried in memory — *that* is the wholeness.

Although it seems difficult to define, this wholeness is a *structure*. It is not "mere intuition." It is not nebulous. It is a structure lying at such a deep level that we cannot easily describe it in feet and inches, or centimeters and millimeters. In short, the point by point description will not capture it. Efforts have been made to capture this gestalt, but they have not yet succeeded.

In buildings, too, it is the wholeness which governs. What matters about a place, what gives it life, lies in the realm of this kind of global structure, too. It lies in the wholeness. Yet, without a language for talking explicitly about this structure in the past, it is no wonder we have not always done justice to the life, or lack of it, which occurs in different buildings.

In physics, and especially in quantum mechanics, this gestalt, the global configuration of the apparatus, enters into the behavior and experiment in a decisive way. Possibly the most important discovery of the 20th century was that in physics, too, the behavior of matter depends *on the wholeness*, not merely on point by point phenomena.[8] The wholeness influences, guides, and determines, what happens, where things go. Even in the most basic phenomena studied by physics, such as the flight of an electron through a slit onto a wall beyond, it is the wholeness of the electron and the experimental apparatus together, working through the gestalt of the whole, that determines what happens next, where the electron goes, on which part of the wall it lands. That was the essence of quantum mechanics.

And it was thus in *physics* that the vital role of the gestalt of things, the existence of the gestalt as an influential structure, and its influence on events, was first recognized. Since the behavior of electrons, photons, and so forth was for the first time understood to be dependent on the wholeness of the apparatus where the experiment is taking place, for this reason it was necessary to attempt mathematical descriptions of this wholeness. And indeed, in the case of quantum mechanics, the gestalt or wholeness was successfully described by a variety of mathematical formalisms: formalisms so powerful that they predict accurately to many decimal places, the detailed behavior of quantum mechanical systems.[9]

However, although the mathematics of quantum mechanics *works*, it is, even to this day, almost impossible to *understand*. Even now, it is still not entirely clear just *how* it works or what it *means*. For seventy or eighty years, a struggle has gone on to find a way of looking at these phenomena and their mathematical representations which makes them understandable. But the mathematics has outstripped our cognitive grasp of what is happening. Although we know how to predict, with extraordinary accuracy, the flight of the electron, the photon, and other particles, so far, the mathematics itself, although it works, is undecipherable to common sense. *Indirectly* the wholeness has been described by mathematics. But what this gestalt really *is* is still not grasped. We still do not have a clear picture of what the wholeness *is*, nor even how we should think about it or understand it.

I believe this difficulty in quantum mechanics is a special case of the more general difficulty I have been describing throughout these four books. Quantum mechanics has appeared undecipherable because, *altogether*, people alive in the 20th century had the greatest difficulty coming to terms with the idea that it is indeed the *wholeness* — just the very same structural gestalt-aspect of the experimental apparatus which in another case determines the kindliness or ferocity of a human face — that determines where the electron is going to go.

This hurdle to comprehension has occurred because we have not had an adequate way of depicting, in our minds, *what — in general — wholeness is like*, and how it might be depicted. The struggle to reach such an understanding has been very great. In the early years of quantum mechanics, the mathematical models provided by Bohr, Heisenberg, Dirac, Schrödinger, and Feynman were forms of calculation so peculiar in their inner meaning that people struggled for decades to explain to one another what they meant. Above all Schrödinger's wave equation, which essentially gives a map of the wholeness, was very, very difficult to interpret and led to confused discussion of its possible interpretation as waves of probability, the collapse of these wave functions, and so on. The actual meaning of these mathematical descriptions seemed (and I emphasize "seemed") to lead to paradoxes so great that it became common to speak of cats that were both dead and yet not dead, of multiple universes spawned from each event and going forward indefinitely into the future in parallel, and so forth.[10] These strange interpretations, seeming to defy reality, came about in my view because it was too difficult to create workable pictures of just the wholeness itself. In cases of art or buildings, we can feel the wholeness sometimes, intuit it sometimes, grasp it with an artistic eye, but up until now we have had no concrete language for it in the world of everyday phenomena.

Recently, a few adventurous physicists began to see that the "meaningless" mathematical interpretations of quantum physics could be given up and replaced by a more realistic picture of the wholeness which makes sense in a more ordinary meaning. This came about because they gave the wholeness itself a different role and started with the assumption that the mysterious phenomena of quantum mechanics come about because of interactions between things which are extended wholes in the world of space and matter. Einstein argued, for many years, that such an interpretation must be possible. He was followed by Louis de Broglie and David Bohm and John Bell, and

their work has recently culminated in the work of Bohm and Basil Hiley which they describe as "an ontological view" — that is to say, a view of how things *are*, not merely how they are observed, or known, or how they seem to be.[11]

In this ontological view, phenomena of dependence on a larger whole are taken to be real in the ordinary sense. They are real because they are understood against a backdrop of the *structure* of wholeness together with the assumption that one could understand the thing realistically only by formulating an explicit picture of the structure of the wholeness. All this hinges on the idea that space contains a global configurational structure which is not acting mechanically, but is nevertheless guiding and shaping events.

What has been said in these four books goes somewhat further. The key idea is that what grows and unfolds, grows and unfolds as a natural consequence of what is, because it literally grows out of the wholeness — a structure in space — not a vague quasi-religious term, but (at least in my opinion, and according to the definitions given in Book 1) *a structure of symmetries that exist in the way that a given portion of space is differentiated.* Of course, if this hidden structure of symmetries, latent in space, guides and shapes events in a foreseeable way, then it will be quite natural to say that the unfolding of the system is guided by wholeness, because this will be a mathematical consequence of the system of structures.

A growing number of scientists share the vision that the so-called conundrums of quantum mechanics occur because a particle is seen as if it were a tiny bullet . . . and can be solved if we learn to see the particle as a larger portion of space containing a wholeness that then acts in apparently bizarre ways because of its natural interaction with the wholeness of the surrounding configurations. In Bohm's work, and in the work of Bohm and Hiley, the larger wholeness takes the form of the quantum potential, a field which interacts with events. I am not so sure this is exactly the right way to talk about it. As stated earlier, I believe the concepts of

Book 1 may make a better starting point. However, among physicists, even today, the idea that these phenomena of wholeness are real has so far been accepted only hesitatingly, and very reluctantly. All this has arisen because it is so difficult — so very, very difficult — to form an adequate picture of what the wholeness may be like.

For an artist or an architect the task is a little easier. For us, it is more everyday, more commonsense to experience wholeness, easier to see it, and perfectly clear that the phenomenon of wholeness is real. My demonstration with Matisse's self-portraits in Book 1 provides a simple example.[12] Also, for art and building, much of what I have said concerning the fifteen properties that govern the life of buildings is recognizably real. It stems from the structure of the whole. It is undeniable in its impact. In such cases the intuition that wholeness is a deep structure, present in large-scale configurations of the world around us, is unmistakeable and somewhat clear. In this context, talk of disappearing cats, multiple worlds existing in parallel, and collapsing wave functions, though typical of the physics of recent decades, makes no useful sense, and makes no contribution to the solution of real architectural problems. Its absurd character is obvious. Yet the central role of wholeness is the same in both.

The difficulty of achieving a comprehensive picture of wholeness as a structure is considerable. But it can be attempted. For this reason I have tried to make explicit structural accounts of the wholeness, partly in Book 1 (especially chapters 3–6 and the appendices), partly elsewhere. As reported in Book 1, appendix 6, in architecture, even the first approximate calculations made with this structure give remarkably accurate experimental results.[13] Preliminary results of a comparable nature have been obtained for a biological example and are reported in Book 2, appendix 2.[14] I believe it is likely that extensions of the calculations I have made with symmetries and centers can one day be extended to provide an exact geometric picture of the two-slit experiment to show how electrons move under the influence of the wholeness.

4 / CONSCIOUSNESS AS A PHYSICAL FEATURE OF THE UNIVERSE

A second line of thought that has begun to emerge in the physics of recent decades is even more tentative in its acceptance. Towards the end of the 20th century, once a new picture of matter began to come under consideration in which all matter was somehow to be understood as arising from a single unbroken wholeness, for the first time clues began to form that somehow the matter, the space-time continuum, might after all be made of animate material, not just inert stuff, but a mysterious substance, consistent in profundity and grandeur with the universe of the Upanishads.

A hint of this kind is present in the words of George Wald, one of the 20th century's great biologists, Professor of Biology at Harvard for many years, and winner of the Nobel prize for his lifelong work on the evolution and functioning of the mammalian eye, wrote in 1984:[15] *"It takes no great imagination to conceive of other possible universes, each stable and workable in itself, yet lifeless. How is it that, with so many other apparent options, we are in a universe that possesses just that peculiar nexus of properties that breeds life. It has occurred to me lately — I must confess with some shock at first to my scientific sensibilities — that both questions might be brought into some degree of congruence. This is with the assumption that mind, rather than emerging as a late outgrowth in the evolution of life, has existed always as the matrix, the source and condition of physical reality — that the stuff of which physical reality is composed is mind-stuff."*

A number of the major physicists of our era have reached similar conclusions. For example, in 1955 the physicist Wolfgang Pauli wrote: *"It would be most satisfactory of all if matter and mind could be seen as complementary aspects of the same reality."*[16] In 1959, Erwin Schrödinger gave a brief argument which I have referred to, demonstrating what he considered as rather conclusive proof that there must, somewhere in our universe, be a single *"One mind"*[17] in which we are all participants.

The identity hypothesis formulated in 1980 by C.F. von Weizsäcker says: *"Consciousness and matter are different aspects of the same reality."*[18]

David Bohm himself was perhaps foremost among great modern physicists who explicitly came to believe about 1980 that the universe is close to being made of a non-material ground, which he called a plenum, and that both matter and consciousness arise from that ground.[19, 20]

Others, too. In 1985, Brian Josephson, the discoverer of quantum tunneling, speaking of new physics, said *". . . we might hope that appropriate mathematical tools will be developed, so that in not too many years from now we'll have a new paradigm in which God and religion will be right in the middle of the picture . . ."*[21]

John Bell, the originator of Bell's theorem, wrote in 1986: *"As regards mind, I am fully convinced that it has a central place in the ultimate nature of reality."*[22]

And in 1994 Roger Penrose published a book arguing (for nearly the first time in the literature of physics) the necessity (his word) of accepting that consciousness is materially different from the other entities of physics — and cannot be viewed as emergent from them.[23]

All in all, there is a slowly growing consensus among some leading physicists that mind must be an essential part of the material universe. But in spite of this growing consensus, nevertheless a huge problem remains. We do not yet know how to *make sense* of this idea. Just having this idea, by itself does not really solve any problem. This is not because physicists differ greatly on the likelihood that mind and matter must be united. The question is, rather, how this idea can be made to *work*. How can a relationship of mind and matter make a useful, and testable contribution to physics itself? How can such a picture enlarge our understanding practically and change, for the better, our view of how matter *works*?

Here I may have made a small but useful contribution. I have shown how the existence of centers in matter-space (the living centers from which life and all good building form arise) has a recursive character, and I have shown how this recursive character allows a field of centers to exist in space — if we recognize that wholeness is a structure everywhere in space. The intensity of centers and wholes arises within the wholeness, purely as a result of the mathematics of the space itself, as new centers proliferate and concentrate themselves. I have suggested that the intensity of these centers and wholes which are created can be recognized empirically when the observer appeals to feelings of wholeness within himself.[24] And the degree of organization can also be calculated by systematic measurement of the symmetries and subsymmetries appearing in the space.[25] At least in simple cases, these calculations, to a first approximation, do give the same results as introspective examination of the observer's relative wholeness.

The conclusion that there is some *actual* relatedness between the observer's self and the centers which arise in the field is reasonable. After all, this near-identity seems to occur more and more deeply, according to the extent of the living structure which is achieved. When the bootstrap aspect of the field becomes intense — or in the other language we have used, when profound life is created — then the observer experiences the most intense identity between his own self and the bootstrapped portion of the field which he observes.

But to make fullest sense of such arguments we need to know the ultimate substratum, the ultimate material out of which the space-matter is made — the ocean where the bootstrapping of centers occurs. It is in this context that I feel obliged to imagine that matter-space might be either made of, or attached to, or an aspect of, some deeper-lying "self-stuff." Of course this self-stuff would be that ground of I which has been described throughout Book 4. It would be the source of the power we experience in works of art, and would be the same thing which has at different times in history variously been called the great self, or the ultimate source of being, or the void. But it would enter the picture now, as a graspable component, with a clear function, and a clear way of helping the generation of life.

5 / A MODIFIED PHYSICS

Let us try to put together the themes which have appeared in these four books and show that a new physics, of the kind suggested above, might be built on this foundation.

First, a word of caution. In physics, the effort has always been to take the geometry of a material system and to derive from it, predictions about the dynamic behavior, forces, and causal interactions — impacts, effects, consequences, of a mechanical kind — which follow from a particular configuration. That is the nature of physics.

In art and building, we have a different set of problems. Again we have geometry, but here we seek especially to derive from it, or predict from it, the harmony, gracefulness, and quality of life, which different geometries may have. That raises a different set of questions from those raised in physics.

Further, still, in the study of living systems — ecosystems and organisms — we have yet a third set of problems. Here we have geometric structures, and we seek to derive from their geometry both the behavior of the systems (in that regard it is like physics) and the health or degree of life and coherence of the systems (in that regard it is like art and architecture).

In what follows, now, I am taking the view that all three cases are to be included in a single view of matter — and that all these questions, all three kinds of questions, are to be raised. We seek an embracing picture of space and matter in which all these issues can be understood together. Thus, a view of matter-space which gives

us understanding of causal effects; of degree of harmony and degree of life; and of the two together, where degree of life and harmony work together with causal effects to form the underpinning of an organism or of a living ecosystem. We seek a view of space and matter which can lead us, successfully, to all these effects together.

Let us return to the picture I have presented in THE NATURE OF ORDER. According to the arguments I have put forward, and according to the profound everyday nature of architecture as I have described it, our picture of the matter-space of the universe must be modified in a way that is consistent with the insights of 20th-century physics. But to fill out the picture as I have suggested, the matter-space must have certain *additional* features, not provided for by contemporary physics, which allow us to see the wholeness as it occurs in space, thus forming an extension of the present picture.

The existence of centers and wholeness

The first new feature which is needed is simply recognition of the *existence* of wholeness — a pervasive multi-level structure created by centers throughout space, together with the idea that different centers have different *degrees* of life and centeredness. The centers are created by local symmetries, boundaries, hierarchies of other centers, positive space . . . all the geometric properties of Book 1, chapter 5. That is, of course, the origin of wholeness as it is defined in Book 1, chapters 3 and 4. It is this which provides the source of degrees of life in material structures.[26]

As a focus of attention, this emphasis on wholeness with variations in centers caused by their differing degrees of life, is new and not, at present, part of the structures taken into account by physicists. It is possible that this structure requires no new features for the matter-space continuum. The existence of wholeness and centers follows, at least to a first approximation, merely from the local symmetry structure of space, and may (in principle) be calculated just from the space alone, and the differences of material which occur in it.[27, 28]

It is also possible that even for such a system (wholeness and centers and symmetries) an entirely new conception of space may be required, one, for instance, that consists of nested platelets of local symmetry — and that this structure is not merely superimposed on the continuum we know today, but itself becomes the model of space, one which replaces the present conception of space altogether.[29]

Whether innovations are needed or not in the system of space itself, in any case there are certainly other features of the theory of centers which do seem to need modification in our conception of the matter-space. Let us take them one by one.

Value and life as part of space itself

The possibility exists that we might be able to derive the degree of centeredness of each region, by calculating some function of the local symmetries. But whether that is realized or not, the conception of matter-space I have described presents us with something unknown in present-day physics: a conception of matter-space in which each spatial region, at every scale, has a relative *value*, and a relative degree of life.

This is a new idea. The conception of space with degrees of value inherent in it (whether we can calculate it or not), is something very different from the value-neutral view that is deeply entrenched in the present-day physicist's view of matter-space.

The 20th-century matter-space is steadfastly value neutral. The neutrality of value of the different regions in space, is fundamental to its machinelike character, and to the way we think about it. If we succeed in getting a new view which gives each region of space, at every scale, a different value, and we thus have a kind of matter-space which has value attached to every region, and to every point, this then becomes — qualitatively — an entirely new kind of space. It gives us a substratum to our picture of the world which is new, not the same as the present value-neutral view. Whether the value of each region can be calculated from local symmetries, or whether it is observed empirically, still the result — a space in which every region has its own (different) value — is an entirely new kind of thing.

Time asymmetry: Structure-preserving transformations as the origin of the laws of physics and biology

One of the most unsatisfactory aspects of Cartesian physics has been the so-called symmetry of time: the fact that classical equations do not, for the most part, distinguish between forwards and backwards. Like a clock mechanism, the mechanistic universe can run backwards or forwards equally well. Onsager and Prigogine struggled to create a thermodynamics of becoming, within the classical world picture, and succeeded.[30] However, our world picture would be far more satisfactory if there is an overall and natural sense in which 'forwards' and 'backwards' are essentially different.

The world picture which I have been describing provides such an asymmetry in a natural way. In the physics contemplated for a world-picture based on wholeness and its transformations, all laws will (I believe) fall out as natural consequences of the principle of unfolding wholeness (Book 2, chapter 1). That principle will say, only, that the next step after a given configuration will be the one which does most to preserve and extend the structure (structure being defined by the wholeness), and I conjecture that it will be possible to show that all physical laws turn out to be special cases of this principle.

In crystal growth this will allow us to see how snow crystals form, as they truly form (not merely the fuzzy approximations presently available which form something vaguely the right shape), and will explain why the deeper symmetries, not presently explained, occur.[31] In the unfolding of an embryo, this rule will imply that the whole moves to a next state in which the structure of the previous state is strengthened and extended and enlarged. In the electron and the two-slit experiment, it will imply that the probability distribution of the electron throughout space near the slit is given by a function assigning high value to those zones which have the most structure-preserving effect on the configuration as a whole.[32]

The important thing is that for the first time the possibility occurs of a natural way of understanding time-asymmetric laws as the foundation of all physical processes.

The personal quality of space

Another feature of centers, as they appear in the theory I have presented, extends the 20th-century view of matter-space in a more surprising way. I have suggested that each living center, to the degree that it has life, reflects (for each of us) our individual self.[33] Living centers are, in this sense, highly personal. A personal link with our own self is connected to each region of space, in that degree to which that region of the space has life or is centered. Thus, not only value becomes associated with each region of matter-space, but something personal and self-like — *feeling* — also appears in space. And this, then, of necessity, would be part of *physics*.

The idea that matter-space, matter itself, might be personal or linked to the human self *in any way at all*, is utterly different from anything in the 20th-century physicist's picture of space.

Indeed, it violates the most basic attribute of space as it was conceived in the 20th century — namely, that it is (and it used to be held that it *must* be) inert, impersonal, *not* connected with the self, *remote* from the self, and without any personal quality that *could* link it to the self.

Here, for the first time, we are entering the possibility of a view of matter which, in its extent, character, and quality, is personal and self-like in its nature. This is a new kind of matter-space altogether. Something very new and something which, if it ever becomes widely accepted as true, will revolutionize our picture of the universe.[34]

The Ultimate I

To reconcile the vision of matter with the experience of personal relatedness we feel when in touch with living structure, I have, in addition, introduced the conception that living centers open some kind of window or tunnel to a ground *and to an ultimate I which constitutes this ground*.

Here we have a kind of picture in which all matter-space is linked to a single blinding unity, but with the added assumption that different regions of the matter-space are linked more or less to it, according to their structure; and that as the matter-space becomes organized it becomes *more* and *more* strongly linked to this ultimate ground which lies beneath it, or inside it, or throughout it. With this conception, we arrive at something entirely different from present conceptions, something really weird, unlike any present conception of matter-space at all. For this, it seems to me, we have, up until now, had virtually no model at all. This is a conception which almost baffles our imagination, and here we are, truly, in a mental territory of an entirely new kind, with an entirely new conception of the material universe.

Yet I believe that for this conception, too, there are sound arguments, and that the views I have put forward in this book (in the mid-book appendix and in chapter 6) give us sound, if not ironclad, reasons for thinking that it might be so, and almost must be so.

————

All in all, what seems to be required is a conception of the universe in which the matter-space is understood as roughly the same extended continuum which is conceived in present-day physics (with or without strings and granular small-scale structure), but this matter-space continuum is now modified in its behavior so that:

1. We recognize the relative existence of value in different regions of space,

2. The value is personal and space is conceived as having some connection to our personal lives,

3. Space itself is viewed as having connections, or windows, to some undifferentiated plenum of light, or unity, or mind which lies beyond the space and is possibly even in another dimension, but is nevertheless connected to it at every point in the continuum.

Although this suggestion introduces only a fairly small change — the possibility of seeing, judging, and calculating degree of centeredness for every region of space — this could still be understood as an extension of current physics. It would incorporate most present-day physics as it is. However, it would add essential new features making it capable of allowing our world-picture to include *both* contemporary physics *and* the crucial issues of value, feeling, and mystical experience. It could do this in a way that is consistent and continuous with the mechanical facts which are familiar and well explained by the present view of matter. It is conceivable, too, that this picture might have the capacity to contribute substantial insights to the biologists' long-standing search to find a coherent and deep view of what life really *is* when it arises in organic nature. It would, furthermore, provide a new basis for discussion of the profound question: Why does consciousness occur in some living systems?

6 / SUMMARY OF THE MODIFIED PHYSICS

Let me summarize again. In my view, all material order comes from the wholeness — that system of centers of unequal value which appears autonomously in space, as a result of local symmetries and the other geometric properties described in Book 1. The structure appears in space and is generated there because of structure-preserving transformations in the wholeness, and they in turn lead to a type of structure — living structure — thick with the fifteen properties. The degree of life or intensity of any one center is a result of interactions among the other centers which exist in the field, according to the degree that they support this one center. There is, I believe, a constructable mathematical picture of such a field. But it means that the life of any given part of space, the intensity of the centers that occur there, cannot be measured or understood merely as a product of the system of

centers *internal* to that space. The intensity of a center in any one part of space is a product of the combined intensity of all the other centers, both *in* that part of space and *beyond* it — and yet these centers themselves, being products of their fields, are also affected in their intensity by the first center.[35] To make all this possible, the matter, the ground in which this is happening, the character of space itself — that must be different in its composition.

What I have suggested is that space is some sort of pliable material, *which itself comes to life more and more*, as the field of centers gets more and more developed there. This is the different part. This is where the new idea differs from the old.

According to this new view, space is not something which has a fixed and definite nature like a mechanism. It is something whose quality evolves locally, gets better and better (one might even say becomes more and more transparent to the ground). It actually changes in its nature and *as a substance* as the field of centers gets more and more developed in it.

Thus the matter, controlled by the field of centers, is not a mechanism made up by re-arranging fixed components. It is a structure which allows the evolution of the space itself, a process in which the space changes *qualitatively*, step by step, through the intensification of the centers in it. As the structure develops it changes its own *nature*. It is the recursive nature of the wholeness and its system of centers which causes this effect.

In my view, that is not an invention. It is what happens. It is the way that space actually behaves. Thus the phenomenon of life which seems, at first hearing, something very astonishing, is a direct result of a feature of space which can be given a mathematical representation.

The more life a particular center has, the more open the tunneling between the outward manifestation of this center and the ground. So, among the millions of centers which appear in space (buildings, doorknobs, atoms, mountains and so on, all of them), there are different degrees of connection to the ground. When living structure is created, the ground becomes more visible, more discernible, because the connection is quite strong. Occasionally, the connection becomes *very* strong, as in a living human being, where the connection of the centers to the ground then takes the form of consciousness. The phenomenon of human consciousness may

be one of the stronger kinds of connection between matter and the I-like ground.

Also, among great works of music or, sometimes, in very great works of architecture or painting, the connection to the ground is extremely strong. Mozart's 40th symphony and Beethoven's 14th quartet connect us, in some measure, to this ground. So does the Coventry Carol (the music shown opposite). The mosaics of Ravenna, and the temple of San-ju-san-gen-do in Kyoto connect us, in some measure, to this ground.[36] Reaching the ground, having contact with it through the window of a living work, is the experience we refer to as spiritual awareness. In the physical picture of matter I describe here, it occurs when we are connected to the blinding light of the ground, even in a small degree. In the cases of great works of art, the ground becomes accessible, directly visible or experienced through that work. Sometimes we also experience it as love.[37] This new thing happens physically because running through the whole system of space there is a measure (the degree of life of different entities and events) which gives each place, each system, each part of space, each phrase in music, *value*. Entities at all scales — particles, plants, places, buildings, even regions of the world — have relative value, compared with one another. Events, too, have relatively more or less value. The value, in every case, is a measure of the degree to which living structure appears: and the degree to which the living structure, by appearing, then opens a tunnel to the ground of I. Thus value is a measure of the degree of connectedness a given place, or thing, or event, has with the ground.[38, 39]

7 / A NEW PICTURE OF THE WORLD

If we were to take seriously that idea that ordinary matter-space is somehow communicating with a ground of ultimate "I," then of course our view of the universe would be deeply altered.

In order to move our discussion away from abstract speculation, and towards experience, I would like the reader to consider an experiment. Dwell briefly — and for the sake of experiment

51a. Coventry carol

Words from the *Pageant of the*
Shearmen and Tailors (15th cent.)

from the *Pageant of the*
Shearmen and Tailors
(1591 version)

2. Herod, the king,
   In his raging,
      Chargèd he hath this day
   His men of might,
   In his own sight,
      All young children to slay.

3. That woe is me,
   Poor child for thee!
      And ever morn and day,
   For thy parting
   Neither say nor sing
      By by, lully lullay!

This song is sung by the women of Bethlehem in the play, just before Herod's soldiers come in to slaughter their children.

*The original manuscript has F and D in tenor part here.

The Coventry Carol. An instance of profound structure in the sphere of sound, where the self is mobilized, and where a wide-open connection to the I is made. If you do not know it, I strongly recommend that you get someone to play it for you from this music.

only — on the possibility that you are indeed, part of some greater I. In this frame of mind, try, next time you are playing with a favorite animal, to consider this: I have found that if I look at a cat, a favorite cat, and imagine that this cat is part of the very same I that I am made of, then the cat seems entirely different, and my relationship to it, even its relationship to me, seems entirely different. If I consciously regard the cat and think that it is part of the essence of my own being, then the cat, my understanding of it, my perception of it, switches suddenly. I perceive that cat, suddenly, as part of myself; the sense of wonder I feel in the cat's presence, is enormously multiplied, and I begin to see the cat, its beauty, its familiarity, and its strangeness, almost as not cat at all, but rather as something wondrous to which I have the cherished relationship that endears me to it, and makes it part of me. One can do the same with any beloved creature, dog, horse, wild animal, even with a spider in the bathroom. One can do it, of course, with another person (oddly, this is harder). And one can do it with a plant or a flower. It is most poignant with an animal. Each time, when I dwell on it, and gaze on it, with the thought that it is another part of the same I that I am made of, my relationship to it changes, and becomes more precious.

For what it is worth, consider what this experience means. Even though it is no more than a "what if," the reality of the experience may give some small confidence that the underlying assumption is true, not merely abstract speculation.

The character of the universe, then — the character of the whole world and our relation to it — would be very different from what we have assumed for the last three hundred years.

I shall try to complete my sketch of this difference by writing down some new cosmological assumptions, somewhat analogous to the ten "bad" and tacit assumptions described in chapter 1, but consistent now with the view of matter I have put forward. It presents, if you like, a picture of a universe in which life and wholeness appear as the central features.

NEW ASSUMPTION #1. *Matter-space is an unbroken continuum which includes everything, both matter and the so-called space around it, all at the same time.*

For physicists there is nothing new in this assumption. It is new only insofar as it differs from the layman's conviction that space and objects are distinct.

NEW ASSUMPTION #2. *In varying degrees, any given portion of space may be more whole or less whole, more alive or less alive, more healed or less healed, connected or broken, separated or not-separate.*

This assumption implies that the relative degrees of life of different buildings, neighborhoods, paintings, ornaments — even a windowsill — as well as different woodlands, parts of the ocean's edge, mountains, fields, gardens, streets, chairs, and spoons — is largely fact.

NEW ASSUMPTION #3. *Whenever we undertake an act of construction we have the ability to make the world more alive or less alive, more harmonious or less harmonious.*

This follows from the first two assumptions. No action, and no act of building, no matter how small, is exempt from this fundamental aspect of our existence. It is there when we paint the front door. It is there when we lay out the plates for breakfast. It is there when choose a location for a new freeway, and it is there when we decide to pick a single flower.

NEW ASSUMPTION #4. *Everything matters.*

Stated baldly, this perhaps seems commonplace. Yet in our present cosmology, at least as far as the cosmology *itself* is concerned, *nothing* matters. Our present cosmology has built into it a definite refusal to assert the importance of anything, a refusal to define any value, a refusal to define any human reality. It is value-free.

The picture of the world created when we accept the self-like, living character of space and matter has a different character. Because, in this picture, portions of the world can be less alive or more alive, and because the life of a given center has a transcendent quality in which the I of the universe becomes manifested, the degree to which living self occurs in our actions then becomes a matter of immense importance.

In this world *everything* matters.

NEW ASSUMPTION #5. *Value is a definite and fundamental part of the universe, and of the scheme of things.*

Value appears in actions, because of the structure-preserving nature of certain transformations. Each action is valuable, or not, according to the extent that it preserves, and extends, and enhances the wholeness which exists, or does not do so.

In this view the different values which exist in different human cultures are all manifestations of this one value. They appear different, because each one tries to create wholeness in the context of different conditions (including those created by culture, people and society), and therefore takes a different outward form.[40] At root, though, what is valuable is always the same thing: it is that thing which does most to enhance the structure of what is.

NEW ASSUMPTION #6. *Ornament and function are indistinguishable.*

Once we understand that wholeness is the most essential structural feature of the world, there is no room for a narrow distinction between legitimate and non-legitimate forms of wholeness, and there is no moral or practical distinction between the ornamental and the functional. Both ornament and function are equally important — and indistinguishable — aspects of the field of centers which arise as matter-self reveals itself.

NEW ASSUMPTION #7. *Matter itself is not a mechanism: It is a potentially soul-like materiality which is essentially what we call self.*

This is the assumption which most explicitly concerns the linkage of the matter-space continuum with an endless and eternal I.

Although this may seem to be the most fantastic of these new cosmological assumptions, it is this assumption which, in the long run, has the greatest capacity to stimulate experiment. The idea that matter-space and self are two sides of one thing, if true, is not something inconsequential which could be true in all possible universes. The world is emphatically different if it is true, and if it is not true. Thus the truth or falsity of this assumption will have have practical consequences. Experiments can — and I think will — be devised to test the truth or falsity of this assumption. In the long run we shall know, experimentally, whether this is true or not.[41]

NEW ASSUMPTION #8. *If self or I is woken up whenever living structure appears in matter, what we think of as value may then be described as the protection, preservation, nourishment, of the precious self of the universe.*

This paves the way to an ultimately personal view of the world. Matter is personal. We then treat all creation — of buildings, gardens, roads — as the protection of the personal which resides in matter, and which, through our actions, may see the light of day.

NEW ASSUMPTION #9. *The nature of space-matter, being soul-like, is such that the more whole it becomes, the more transparent, the more it seems to melt, the more it realizes itself, releases its own inner reality, the more transparent it becomes, the more transcendent.*

If it is true that the ground of the universe reveals itself whenever order is produced, even as we make a garden, or make a chair, paint the front door, or build an office building ... then this melting, this revealing of the inner stuff of things when order is produced is the single most important thing that is at stake, whenever anything is being made.

NEW ASSUMPTION #10. *Thus art is not merely pleasant or interesting. It has an importance that goes to the very core of the cosmology.*

That is because in such a universe, the task of building things and shaping things is fundamental to the spiritual condition of the world, and to our own spiritual development. It is our closest approach, almost God-like, to creating life, and to seeing and reaching the essential core of things.

NEW ASSUMPTION #11. *The unfolding of the field of centers, and the unfolding of the self, is the most fundamental awakening of matter.*

I believe it may turn out that the considerations which are recorded here will ultimately seem more important than any other facts about the nature of things.

8 / A PHYSICAL BASIS FOR RELIGIOUS AWE

After a lecture of mine, I once heard an architecture student say, "I still don't really see why all this has to be discussed. Isn't it enough to understand the nature of living structure thoroughly, and to try and make life in our buildings? Why do you insist so strongly on the fact that we also need to change our picture of the universe? I have a picture of the universe which is quite flexible enough to contain the idea of living structure."

I did not find myself in agreement with his comment. In my mind, what is most important about the picture painted in these four books is that indeed, our present picture of the universe can *not* contain the idea of living structure, because it contains no natural way of including the idea of value in the idea of space. What I have constructed, on the other hand, has the idea of value in a natural way—first in the relative intensity of different elementary centers as part of the definition of wholeness, and then with more and more depth, as centers are built from living centers, to give structure of real, deep, significant value by essentially the same idea. In this picture, value resides *in the structure* and is part of the structure. Value is written in the same language as the rest of the structure of space-time, the life of the centers arises from the fabric and structure of space itself.

In this conception, value is not something merely grafted onto space, as a passenger might be who carries no weight and does no work. It is part of the same nearly mechanical picture of space that we have come to believe in, and respect, and trust. Yet, at the same time, in a most subtle way, it is also not-mechanical. After all, what we observe is life emerging from space, as we might say "out of the very foam of space."

It *is* a structure, we *can* (tentatively) calculate with it, and it *fits* our structural understanding of space and matter. Yet it creates a bridge to life, feeling, and to our own experience of what it is to be a person: the self, which all of us contain, and are connected to.

That is the structural meaning of what I have described.

George Wald, in the paper quoted earlier, where he says that all matter is ultimately mind-stuff, balks at making any particular connection between mind and matter. He writes, in one place, "Consciousness is altogether impervious to scientific approach."[42] And later, "Though consciousness is the essential condition for all science, science cannot deal with it."[43] Thus, in spite of Wald's fervent belief in the existence of consciousness (or mind, or self), he insists that it is impenetrable, not connected to the structure of space and time as we observe them as a structure.

Yet what I claim is precisely that it *is* connected to the structure. I claim that the field of centers, or some version of it, is a recursive structure in space, which does precisely serve the function of being the bridge between matter and consciousness, between matter and mind; and that it is, indeed, when these extraordinary living structures arise in space, that mind awakens, that space and matter open a window to the mind, and that the great self behind all things actually comes within our experience and our reach.

I believe that one day it will be possible to demonstrate an experimental connection, where it will be shown exactly *how* the field of centers does open a door between space and self, and how, ultimately then, self and matter are permanently intertwined through the construction of this mechanism.

A traditional scientific view, held by many during the 20th century, has been that mechanical pictures of matter, can be consistent with *any* spiritual view of God or consciousness because the two (matter and consciousness) inhabit non-communicating intellectual domains. Such a dichotomy may have been a source of comfort to positivists. But, scientifically speaking, it allows us to get no mileage from the co-presence of the two.

Indeed, I believe continued insistence on the compatibility of the two ("because they do not interact") is almost tantamount to denying any real or useful interaction, and thus inhibits intellectual progress. Polkinghorne, for example, said at one time that everything is OK as it is, and that it is easy enough to reconcile a materialist conception of matter with a spiritual conception of life.[44] All this really said was that we have no understanding of the connection, and that — from an intellectual point of view — there *is* no interaction. But in view of the mechanist predisposition which is so common in our time, and the fact that all practical understanding is mechanical in nature, this means, too, that we have no picture in which self and matter can be coupled: therefore no real way of believing that they *are* coupled.

Even though Polkinghorne and the student who was speaking to me may *believe* the present world-picture is adequate to contain both, I believe it is not so. This broad-minded, intellectually catholic opinion is mistaken. The two views, in their present form, cannot coexist successfully. Even today, we continue underestimating the degree to which we are prisoners of the present mechanistic cosmology; we have a strong tendency to underestimate the effect that this interior mechanistic view can have on us.

Consider, for example, three elementary facts: (1) in our immediate world, at normal temperature and pressure, nearly everything is made of atoms; (2) atoms are little whirling mechanisms which are spinning constantly, (3) people are largely made of atoms too.

Nearly every schoolchild learns these facts in school. We all learnt them. They are, by now, virtually a part of us. Probably we learned them when we were eight or nine years old. As a result, in the western world at least, there are few people alive who do not believe ("know") that they are mechanisms made up of millions of tiny whirling mechanisms.

In case this seems like an exaggeration, or that people do not really believe these things literally as being the whole picture, consider the first paragraph of a recently published book, THE ASTONISHING HYPOTHESIS, by the eminent molecular biologist Francis Crick, co-discoverer of the helical structure of DNA: "The astonishing hypothesis is that you, your joys and your sorrows, your memories and ambitions, your sense of personal identity and free will, are in fact no more than the behavior of a vast assembly of nerve cells and their associated molecules . . ."[45]

At first one might find it surprising that such an eminent scientist should put forward such a crass-seeming reductionist view without flinching. But it simply underlines my point that all of us are susceptible to this oversimplification, so long as we have nothing to replace it with. It is a mark of Crick's honesty and intellectual rigor that he faces the real meaning of the present cosmological scheme and does not try to duck it with pious phrases. Without having access to another structure, so that the structure of matter itself leads to a different view, it seems to me that anyone honest must reach the same conclusions Crick has reached.

But if you believe Crick's mechanized reduction is accurate, how can you take seriously the kinds of ideas which I have described about the life of buildings, and walls, and rooms, and streets? The answer is, you cannot. You cannot, because if you believe the three elementary-school facts, then mentally, you are still living in a universe in which nothing matters, and in which *you* do not matter. And then the life of the environment is not real either.

Ideas about the personal or spiritual nature of reality, no matter how desirable they seem, cannot affect you deeply, *even if you think they do*, until they can be embodied in some *new* picture which leaves the facts of physics intact, and *also* paves the way to a more spiritual understanding of the world by an extended structure which brings in these larger matters clearly and explicitly.

The whole point of the concept which I have described — of wholeness seen as a calculable, recursive, bootstrap field of centers with the consequences that follow from this view — is that within the framework this concept creates, things really are different, and the differences are visible *as new aspects of the structure of space and matter.* This newly seen structure not only *says* that things are different. It shows, through the properties of the structure, exactly *how* things are different.

Within the new view of the structure of matter-space provided by the field of centers, we can reconcile the fact of being a mechanism of whirling mechanisms, because we know that each atom is itself a field of centers, and that in the emergence of these fields, the self comes into view. We . . . you . . . I . . . are thus instances of the field of centers or — if we like to see it more deeply — instances of the self-stuff of the universe, making its way, cumbersomely, from the trap of matter to the light of day.

Armed with this view, we can unite our personal intuition of religious awe with our sensible scientific understanding of the world. It becomes all one, it all makes sense together. Life and religion fall into place and fit together with physics as necessary consequences of the structure of the world — that is, of the way that matter-space is made.

And in this view, the work of building takes on entirely new meaning. It changes in a fundamental way, because we understand what we are doing differently, and realize that our work as builders can — through the forms described in this book — place us in an entirely new relation to the universe.

In this universe, the human self, yours and mine, are indistinguishable, in their substance, from the space and matter where the play of forms occurs. When we make something, its selfness, its possible soul, is part and parcel of our own self.

There is, then, something very like a religious obligation to allow this self to reveal itself. It is our task, as architects, as artists, as builders, to make this stuff, this matter of the universe, reveal itself most fully. This metaphysical obligation will stem directly from our renewed understanding of the substance of the universe. It does not arise merely from our desire to be comfortable, from our desire to avoid alienation. It arises as a supreme spiritual obligation, which is our obligation to the matter/spirit we ourselves are made of.

This feeling, though modern in its form, is, in its essence, similar to the medieval mason's desire to make each stone as a gift to God.

But it arises, now, not as a religious or superstitious belief, but as a result of a new understanding of the structure of the universe.

9 / ESSENTIAL AWE

A few years ago I went to mass in Salzburg's great cathedral. It was, at that time, one of the only places left where Mozart and Haydn's masses were still sung every Sunday. There was a Haydn mass. The church was filled with people thronging, crowding, pushing, to be there while the great mass was sung.

The high point of this mass was the *Sanctus.* Full choir, slowly increasing rhythm, deep sounds of the organ and the basses, high song of the trebles, the church filled, the air became tense with the presence of this mass . . . poised, in the *Sanctus,* as if on the edge of some awakening, and the enormous cave of the building, allowing the sound to roll and fill our minds.

I stood there with my thoughts. At the most awe-inspiring moment, a young man pushed forward to a telephone mounted on one of the columns of the nave. He picked it up, and listened. The telephone was tied to a tape-recording, giving interesting facts for tourists. He listened to the tape-recording of dates and facts, while the *Sanctus* blazed around him.

This man became a symbol for me of the loss of awe and of our loss of sense. Unable to immerse himself in the thing which filled the air and surrounded us, perhaps even unaware of the beauty which surrounded him, unaware of the size and importance of the sounds that he was hearing, he was more fascinated to listen to a tape-recording reeling off the dates when the cathedral was built. For a while, during the 20th century, this had become our world: a place where the difference between awe and casual interest had been sanded down to nothing.

But I realized on that day, that this young man's behavior could summarize what my efforts as an architect have been about. All the efforts I have made have, at their heart, just this one intention: to bring back our awe . . . and to allow us to begin again to make things in the world which can intensify this awe.

NOTES

1. The over-confident statements of quantum physicists in recent decades — no matter how confidently they assert that we are within a hair's breadth of the answer to everything, and that we have 99% of the picture clear — do *not* answer the questions. For references to these exaggerated statements by Stephen Hawking, and others, see chapter 1, note #17. Comparable statements were made by Stephen Weinberg, THE FIRST THREE MINUTES (New York: Basic Books, 1977), where he says that it is all but solved. Interestingly, a portfolio of first-hand statements expressed by some sixty of the century's most prominent scientists shows a widespread contemporary concern that these puzzles have not been answered. Henry Margenau and Roy Abraham Varghese, eds., COSMOS, BIOS, THEOS: SCIENTISTS REFLECT ON SCIENCE, GOOD, AND THE ORIGINS OF THE UNIVERSE, LIFE, AND HOMO SAPIENS (La Salle, Illinois: Open Court, 1992). A surprising number of these scientists, though not all, hold the view that ultimate answers to these questions will require some kind of synthesis of what we now know separately as science and religion.

2. See nearly any contemporary textbook on physics and cosmology.

3. See, for example, recent discussions of string theory, the Kaluza-Klein theories, and the recent contributions by Michael Green, John Schwarz, Edward Witten and others. One accessible overview is provided in Paul Davies, SUPERFORCE: THE SEARCH FOR A GRAND UNIFIED THEORY OF NATURE (New York: Simon and Schuster, 1984), chapter 10. Another is given in Brian Greene, THE ELEGANT UNIVERSE (London: Jonathan Cape, 1999).

4. An interesting (and extreme) version of this view is contained in a letter by Mendel Sachs, "A Speculation On Einstein's Reply To 'Quantum Teleportation,'" PHYSICS ESSAYS (11, No. 2, 1998), 330–31, where Sachs makes the suggestion that Einstein viewed all matter in terms of a continuous holistic field, making interaction at a distance and photon correlations unnecessary.

5. I sometimes find it useful to call it the matter-space *stuff*. The word *stuff*, not often used this way in modern English, but coming from the German *Stoff* meaning cloth or material, is useful. Saying that the universe is given its ultimate character by the stuff that it is made of, is, then, like saying that it is given its character by the cloth from which it is cut.

6. The present-day assumption of the inertness of space and matter has been emphasized in chapter 1.

7. Many excellent books on physics for the lay person have made these points clear, and made the nature of what has been accomplished in modern physics, tantalizing. See Paul Davies and John Gribbin, THE MATTER MYTH (New York: Simon and Schuster, 1992); Gribbin, THE MATTER MYTH, Nick Herbert, David Peat, EINSTEIN'S MOON, for references.

8. First expressed clearly by Niels Bohr.

9. The foundations of quantum mechanics, and the various mathematical formalisms introduced to describe the way the whole guides particle behavior, were due to Planck, Bohr, Dirac, Schrödinger, Heisenberg, Pauli, Feynman, and a number of others. An excellent overview is given by David Bohm, QUANTUM THEORY (Englewood Cliffs, N.J.: Prentice Hall, 1951). Detailed original expositions include Niels Bohr, ATOMIC THEORY AND THE DESCRIPTION OF NATURE (London: Cambridge University Press, 1934); P. A. M. Dirac, THE PRINCIPLES OF QUANTUM MECHANICS (Oxford: Clarendon Press, 1947); Werner Heisenberg, THE PHYSICAL PRINCIPLES OF THE QUANTUM THEORY (Chicago: University of Chicago Press, 1930).

10. Discussion of these strange paradoxes has been widespread in recent years. See, for instance, Bernard d'Espagnat, IN SEARCH OF REALITY (New York: Springer Verlag, 1983); Nick Herbert, QUANTUM REALITY (London: Rider, 1985); John Gribbin, SCHRÖDINGER'S KITTENS AND THE SEARCH FOR REALITY (London: Weidenfeld and Nicholson, 1996).

11. Louis De Broglie, David Bohm; David Bohm and Basil Hiley, THE UNDIVIDED UNIVERSE (London: Routledge, 1993).

12. Book 1, pages 96–98.

13. Book 1, appendix 6, pages 469–72.

14. Book 2, appendix 2.

15. Professor George Wald, "Life and Mind in the Universe," INTERNATIONAL JOURNAL OF QUANTUM CHEMISTRY: QUANTUM BIOLOGY SYMPOSIUM 11 (1984), 1–15, abstracted in Margenau and Varghese, COSMOS, BIOS, THEOS, p. 219.

16. Wolfgang Pauli, "It would be most satisfactory of all if matter and mind could be seen as complementary aspects of the same reality." in Carl Gustav Jung and Wolfgang Pauli, eds., THE INTERPRETATION OF NATURE AND THE PSYCHE (New York: Bollingen, 1955), pp. 208–10.

17. See this book, chapter 7, pages 236–8. See also, Erwin Schrödinger, MIND AND MATTER (Cambridge: Cambridge University Press, 1959), pp. 52–68 and 88–104.

18. Von Weizsäcker's identity hypothesis: "Consciousness and matter are different aspects of the same reality." C. F. von Weizsäcker, THE UNITY OF NATURE, (New York: Farrar, Strauss, Giroux, 1980), p. 252.

19. See, especially, David Bohm WHOLENESS AND THE IMPLICATE ORDER (London: Routledge & Kegan Paul, 1980) pp. 192–213, and D. Bohm and B. J. Hiley, THE UNDIVIDED UNIVERSE (London, Routledge, 1993), pp. 381–390.

20. Bohm and I met, originally, because he had been told that I had some special ability to see wholeness. Based on that, in 1986, he and I spent two days together at the Krishnamurti Center in Ojai, California, in public discussion. In preparation for that event, Bohm was kind enough to read a very early version of THE NATURE OF ORDER. It wasn't more than a sketch when he read it. But after reading the last chapter of Book 4 (what has now been split in two to become chapter 1 and this conclusion), he then declared that in his view this material was the most interesting. I don't remember whether he said interesting, or valuable, or important — but anyway, somehow he thought the conception of matter contained here was the most significant aspect of these books. It came closest, perhaps, to providing a complement to his own views.

21. Brian Josephson, in THE REACH OF THE MIND, NOBEL PRIZE CONVERSATIONS (Dallas: Saybrook Publishing Company, 1985), p. 178.

22. J. S. Bell, "Six Possible Worlds of Quantum Mechanics," PROCEEDINGS OF THE NOBEL SYMPOSIUM 65: POSSIBLE WORLDS IN ARTS AND SCIENCES (Stockholm: August 11–15, 1986), reprinted in SPEAKABLE AND UNSPEAKABLE IN QUANTUM MECHANICS (Cambridge: Cambridge University Press, 1987), p. 194.

23. Roger Penrose, SHADOWS OF THE MIND (Oxford: Oxford University Press, 1994). His argument will not be accepted by everyone. Yet, to me, the argument appears compelling and shows, nearly for the first time, a willingness of a contemporary physicist to recognize the existence of self as something that must be considered by physics.

24. The observation that regions of space are more or less coherent is fundamental, and has been dealt with in many ways by generations of writers including Whitehead's early papers on coherent sets, Wolfgang Köhler's discussion of wholes, and Arthur Koestler's discussion of holons in JANUS (New York: Random House, 1978). Only the concept of centers, itself, is somewhat new. See discussions in note 12 of Book 1, chapter 3 and in notes 2 and 3 of Book 1, chapter 4.

25. In Book 1, I have suggested that the centeredness of a given region is chiefly caused by the local symmetries which occur there. It has perhaps not been noticed before, that the centeredness of a given region might be calculated merely by calculating with local symmetries. But even so, this needs only the present view of space.

The idea that calculating the hierarchy of local symmetries present in a region of space provides a close approximation to the structure of centers, hence to the wholeness, is fully described with operational details, in Book 1, chapter 5, and in appendix 2. I have written "I think" in the text paragraph before as a matter of caution. Although the fifteen properties seem straightforward, I have found that attempts to formulate them exactly by giving necessary and sufficient conditions for their occurrence in a particular case, are surprisingly elusive. It is possible that this hides a greater difficulty than mere precision of mathematical draftsmanship.

26. In an unpublished paper, I have argued that the wholeness, as a structure, is essentially similar to a topology. It is a measure erected on space according to the coherence and life of the different sets and subsets, thus establishing a structure not unlike a topology, but (unlike topology) dealing with value rather than spatial contortion and connectivity. Christopher Alexander, "An Unexpected Structure Underlying Physical Reality," submitted to PHYSICS ESSAYS.

27. See Book 1, appendix 2.

28. It is likely that a more sophisticated calculation will also be needed to show the bootstrap recursive character of the field of centers, and the way that each center is dependent for its life on the life of other centers. Again this will, in all likelihood, not require new mathematics of the space itself. My guess is that this will turn out to be manageable within the present view of Euclidean space. What will be novel will be the way the mathematical self-bootstrapping nature of the field works, not the conception of space. I should be surprised if it needs anything beyond the normal well-understood Euclidean geometry of three-dimensions as a substratum. It is likely (but am not sure) that the calculations which show how each region in space has a different degree of life can be made to follow from the mathematics of the space itself, and can — in principle — be managed perfectly well within our present view of space. See Book 1, appendix 4.

29. This is similar to a suggestion made by David Finkelstein, about viewing the world not as a continuum but as a simplicial complex. See "All is Flux," in B. J. Hiley and F. David Peat, QUANTUM IMPLICATIONS (London: Routledge and Kegan Paul, 1987), 293. Also, see David Peat's remark, in discussing Penrose's work, that space might be seen, in the future, not as continuous, but as a nested structure of sets having only functional properties. F. David Peat, EINSTEIN'S MOON (Chicago: Contemporary Books, 1990), 133–46.

30. See Ilya Prigogine, FROM BEING TO BECOMING (San Francisco: W. H. Freeman, 1980).

31. See discussions of Book 2, 42–43 and appendix 2.

32. Ibid.

33. In chapters 8 and 9 of Book 1, and throughout Book 4. In Book 1, chapter 8, I suggested that wholes and centers are recognizable because each observer sees himself reflected more and more profoundly in these wholes and centers, the more deeply they get organized.

34. The objection could be raised that this is not new at all, indeed that one of the major revolutions of modern physics was the recognition that object and observer are entangled, and indeed it is true that this has been, since the time of Heisenberg, a major feature of 20th-century physics. The observer effect is dealt with in nearly all accounts of quantum physics. But what that observer entanglement meant was something vastly more restricted than I mean here. Perhaps it gave a hint of a possible personal connection between matter and self. But it came nowhere near asserting the personal character of matter as its essential quality.

35. Such a bootstrap phenomenon is slightly reminiscent of something which was at one time important in particle physics. A few years ago, Geoffrey Chew proposed a view in which there are no elementary particles — each particle is somehow built out of others, and out of the interaction of others. What I have just described is somewhat reminiscent of that effort. Geoffrey Chew, LECTURES ON MODELLING THE BOOTSTRAP (Bombay: Tata Institute of Fundamental Research, 1970).

36. See photographs in Book 2, preface, 7–8.

37. The degree to which the ground has ever been reached by living structure, or could be reached, is still relatively undeveloped. So far, anyway, in the history of humankind's experience, it has been something of a rarity, and experienced only in modest degree, when we encounter living structure in the world. It is possible that at some future time, in other civilizations, that the beings, or collections of people, or works of art, or even parts of cities and societies — might reach even further toward the ground, make it more visible. Thus experiences of a depth hitherto unknown may well lie in store for humankind.

38. The direction suggested by these revisions was anticipated, most substantially perhaps by Spinoza in the THE ETHICS, written in the early seventeenth century, first with his idea of matter, and secondly with his idea of value. On matter the ethics offer an exceptionally clear version of these ideas with the statement "Except God, no substance can be or can be conceived." Benedict de Spinoza, A SPINOZA READER: THE ETHICS AND OTHER WORKS, ed and trans. Edwin Curley (Princeton, New Jersey: Princeton University Press, 1994), 93 (from the ethics, II/56, P14). On value Spinoza said, speaking of both objects and ideas "one is more excellent than another, and contains more reality, just as the object of the one is more excellent than the object of the other and has more reality." Spinoza, ibid., 124 (from the ethics, II/97).

39. Although it sounds extraordinary, and unfamiliar to our 20th-century ears, this modified version of our current world-picture does not have to be very greatly unlike the one we have had during the 20th century. Most of the known mechanical phenomena are left largely unchanged by this picture. They appear and work much as we imagine them working today. However, expressions of love, art, and spiritual awareness also have a place in this picture. They make sense within the picture, as they have not done before.

40. I feel a need to revisit, once more, the issue of cultural relativism. For example, building an apartment house which has life in Tokyo is an objectively different problem from building an apartment house which has life in San Francisco. In the two cases, huge numbers of conditions around the building, and in the people who use the building, are objectively different. Making something which preserves and enhances structure in the one case, and in the other case, lead to two different things. Many aspects of the structure, many details of the centers, which have to be created in the two cases, are different. Thus, the one criterion of making things alive will lead us to make things which are Japanese in Japan, and will lead us to make things which are Californian in San Francisco.

41. If this is true, and useful, there will be some detectable interaction between matter and the ground, which must, at some future time, be detected empirically. I-like phenomena must be detectable by experiment or observation. If there is no interaction, the discussion does not mean much. Ultimately, therefore, experiments which detect some interaction must be found. However, even before such interaction is detected, our interpretation of what is going on in the world is made entirely different.

One would expect, for instance, that mental phenomena could be shown to interact with results of quantum phenomena (there is some very slight evidence, already, that such interactions might exist). The hypothesis is that *there is, in the universe, an actual domain of I, that this is physically real, in some form, and attaches somehow to the "back" or "inside" of matter*. What kinds of experiment might lead towards determination of the truth or falsity of this hypothesis?

(1) One class of experiment could try to show a connection between mental events and physical phenomena. During the last ten years a considerable literature has been aimed at discussion of this possibility, and some experiments have been attempted. Among other disussions there is the testing of the Schmidt effect, so far inconclusive but not wholly negative. See Helmut Schmidt, "Toward a Mathematical Theory of Psi," JOURNAL OF THE ASPR, 69 (1975): 301–319, and Henry P. Stapp, "Theoretical model of a purported empirical violation of the predictions of quantum theory," PHYSICAL REVIEW A 50, 1 (July 1994). Other experiments and attempted formulations of possible experiments may be found in James Beichler, YGGDRASIL: THE JOURNAL OF PARAPHYSICS, Volume I, Issue 4, 1998. An overview of experiments of this kind appears in Nick Herbert, ELEMENTAL MIND: HUMAN CONSCIOUSNESS AND THE NEW PHYSICS (New York: Dutton, 1993).

(2) There are some classes of experimental findings which do, for the first time, establish the appearance of

a physical linkage between mind and matter. In one study engineers undertook longitudinal tests over a decade, and showed that in about 2% more cases than expected by chance, reliable and consistent effects of telekinesis were observed. Robert Jahn and Brenda Dunne, MARGINS OF REALITY: THE ROLE OF CONSCIOUSNESS IN THE PHYSICAL WORLD (New York: Harcourt Brace, 1987). Two physicists, Dean Radin and Roger Nelson, made a statistical survey of other scientist's reports, observations and experiments, and concluded that there is an identifiable interaction, with sufficiently high probability to be worth reporting to physicists. See "Evidence for Consciousness-related Anomalies in Random Physical Systems," FOUNDATIONS OF PHYSICS, 19, 1499 (1989). And in medicine, several cardiologists (including Dr. Mitchell Krucoff of Duke University Medical Center, Dr. William Harris, of the Mid America Heart Institute in Kansas City, Missouri, and Dr. Randolph Byrd at San Francisco General) have reported positive findings of the effect of prayer at long distance on patient recovery from heart traumas. Their findings are summarized in Nancy Waring, HIPPOCRATES: PRACTICAL ADVANCES IN PRIMARY CARE, August 2000, Vol. 14, No. 8.

(3) Another class of experiments may shed some light. These are the experiments which show that when music by Mozart is playing, measurements of IQ show increases of about 10 points in people being tested in the room where the music is playing. Of course, this is slender evidence as it stands, but it does suggest that living structure, as I have defined it in works of art, has an impact on something measurable in an observer, over and above the mirror of the self tests. Gary Kliewer, "The Mozart Effect," NEW SCIENTIST, 6 November 1999; Gordon Shaw, KEEPING MOZART IN MIND (San Diego: Academic Press, 1999).

(4) Protocols of people who say that they have seen God, or been very impressed with the presence of God, and their descriptions of the event. One of my Ph.D. students, Tom McGelligot, after having such an experience himself in the church of Notre Dame in Paris, began trying to identify all the kind of places where this was happening, under what circumstances. If such an event were reliably associated with more living structure, it would once again be the slenderest of threads.

(5) A more realistic though more "far out" class of experiments might be directed at the idea that a living structure is a "window" to the I, hence actually gives glimpses of the I *itself*. In this picture of things, at least as I have proposed it, the I is literally light-filled. If so, we would expect to detect some kind of light associated with living structure. The success of the term inner light, which I have associated with color, and the fact that this term, for many, has a feeling of appropriateness, is very slender evidence that this might be true.[46]

42. Wald, 1984, op. cit., p. 8.

43. Wald, 1984, op. cit., pp. 8–9.

44. Polkinghorne, in THE PARTICLE PLAY, p. 125, writes: "I want to say . . . a brief word about whether I detect any consonance between the world view of Christianity and the world view of science. In fact I do, but I do not suppose that I can prove it for you, any more than someone else could disprove it." This elegant, and mildly worded statement, implies, in the nicest possible way, that he really sees little need for establishing such a connection, even though there is no counter-argument against it either.

45. From Francis Crick, THE ASTONISHING HYPOTHESIS (London, 1992), quoted in SCIENTIFIC AMERICAN, February 1992, pp. 32–33.

46. I wish, at the last, to come back to the intensely important question of the connection between consciousness and matter, and the search for empirical evidence of this connection. In the very large corpus of writing on this subject (a few listed in note 41) the prevailing mood of the intellectual inquiry reads as if matter, on the one hand, and mental events or consciousness on the other, are *almost* two comparable entities, two realms between which a link is sought. Thus there is, in much recent writing on this subject, an almost schoolboy quality of looking for a mechanical connection. I believe this kind of connection is unlikely to be found, and is indeed hardly worth finding, since — if such a connection were to be found — the particular version of consciousness or mentality which was discovered like this would be cheapened and made vulgar by the very fact of focusing on this aspect of the connection.

I am certain that to appreciate the subject fully, we must indeed focus on the I from the *inside* (as I have tried to describe it), and think within this framework, focus on what the I really is. It is personal and it comes from within. We must therefore truly ask how matter, the world around us, may be I-like — that is, how it may be like I in its interior, as we may experience matter as if it were in the interior of our own self. We must formulate experimental questions, I believe, while in this contemplative state, so that we are truly aware of the I, and dedicated to reflecting it, while simultaneously formulating the possible nature of the way that matter can reflect, reveal, this I.

Thus there is a contemplative vision, an activity in which we go deeper and deeper inside ourselves, passing mentally through tunnels of matter, while we become more and more alert to the fact that this matter is indeed like the person we experience within.

This contemplation is supremely difficult. But I believe that if the path indicated in these four books is taken seriously, it will lead to that kind of fusion — a fusion of what we know as our interior I and the matter which lies around us. Grasping that fusion, and that identity, may then bring us to an entirely different kind of consciousness, in which these experimental questions may resolve themselves.

EPILOGUE

EMPIRICAL CERTAINTY AND ENDURING DOUBT

1 / AN EXTENSION OF THE SCIENTIFIC IDEA OF WHAT CAN BE KNOWN

In these books, I have tried to show that there are sharable areas of human experience which lie beyond the areas presently touched by science. I have set myself the task of trying to raise these new matters — the deeper issues which mechanistic science has not so far dealt with — to the level of knowledge we are used to, from having a culture based on science.

The experiments and kinds of observation which I have proposed are of a new kind, not so far contemplated by science. They have to do with our interior world, with what we experience when we are exposed to different phenomena. But, though unfamiliar, they are still *experiments*. They appeal to *experience*. And for this reason, they create a new kind of knowledge that people can share.

This new world of reliable knowledge which is then opened goes well beyond the knowledge available to present-day scientific experiments. It allows us to build, collectively, a new picture of the world in which we apply the very high standard first created by Descartes and his colleagues about the year 1600 A.D., but also now going beyond the purely mechanistic into those matters of wholeness, feeling, and experience, which let us make sense of our life in our built world.

This is valuable because it is based on the same high standard as science, but in a new realm of social existence. We only allow ourselves to claim we really know something if that "something" is sharable — in principle — even if it is in the realm we call feeling or experienced wholeness. That is the breakthrough I may perhaps have made. If I am right, the world of science has been extended. I have simply found a way of taking the scientific standard of shared knowledge based on common observation, and extended this idea so that it covers inner realities, not only outer ones. In that process, we discover that the world which we can *know* — truly know — is a much vaster and more complex one than was understood in the earlier days of purely mechanistic science which lasted from about 1600 A.D. to about 2000 A.D.

2 / A NEW METHOD OF OBSERVATION AT THE CORE OF THE WORLD-PICTURE

It is well known that a cosmology may be linked to a particular method of observation. Indeed, the recently-held mechanistic view of the universe itself arises from a particular method of observation, the famous method described by Descartes. In the DISCOURSE ON METHOD, written three hundred years ago, Descartes set out his charming and innocent idea about the method of observation which we ought to follow in order to find out how the world works. He said, quite simply: We must pay careful attention to what happens in the natural world, and keep checking it in detail, and keep making our own model or picture of it also more detailed, constantly checking backward and forward, until the two come into closer and closer correspondence. This is the essence of his famous method.

It is wonderful, reading Descartes, to see how he predicts that the use of this method, when consistently and patiently applied, will lead to the gradual creation of a world picture which is true and detailed. Three hundred years after he described this method, what he predicted had come true. The constant application of his method made it possible for us to know the mechanics of the universe in extraordinary detail. The whole of modern science, the wonderful picture of the world which we have attained today, has come about simply because of repeated application of this method, day after day after day, by hundreds of thousands of people, for three hundred years.

We see, then, that a method of observation can have enormous power to teach us things. However, as we now know, the world-picture we have inherited from these three hundred years of observation and model-making is too mechanical. That came about as a direct result of the method itself. Indeed, it was the genius of Descartes' method to focus attention only on how things work as machines, and to pay no attention to anything else.

But, of course, we had to pay a price for doing it. The mental trick that was needed to achieve these wonderful results required that we separate ourselves from the process of observation — and this had the consequence that our view of the world became mechanical. That is no surprise, because it is precisely the strength of the method that we *choose* to pretend that everything is a little machine. It is this mental trick that lets us find things out. But, at the same time, it has the consequence that the world which is created in our minds then seems to be value-free, and seems to be impersonal.

Descartes himself would have been surprised by this result. I believe he invented his trick, only because during *his* lifetime few people were paying proper attention to the way things really work, and therefore no one had any real idea how the world is actually made. Perhaps they were too busy thinking about spirits and angels. So, in his time, the method he proposed was an antidote to a more religious method of thinking which was making it difficult to find out what the world was really like.

In our time, the tables have turned. In our time, the *only* method of observation considered

scientifically respectable is the one which treats things like machines. So in our time our problem is the opposite of the one which Descartes faced. Our problem is to find a way of supplementing our observation of the mechanical universe with some type of observation which establishes our personal connection to the world.

What I call living structure is directly connected with this issue. The observations presented throughout these four books are based on a method of observation which is entirely different from the Cartesian method. Unlike the Cartesian method, the method I have used invites the observer to make distinctions, constantly, *on the basis of his/her own inner feelings* — but with a framework that guarantees consistency and objectivity to these inner feelings so that they are not idiosyncratic. For example, to discover the fifteen geometric properties reported in Book 1, or the eleven color properties reported in chapter 6 of Book 4, I did not try to observe things as if I myself did not exist. Instead, I kept asking which of two objects was more wholesome, which one had more feeling, and which one created a more wholesome feeling in me — the observer — which then by extrapolation also creates a more wholesome feeling in *all* observers. And I then tried to find out what structural features were correlated with the quality that I observed.

In the canon of contemporary science (as practiced in the second half of the 20th century), this kind of observation would have been considered inadmissible. Yet, as we have seen, without this kind of observation, the very subject matter which I have presented in these books *does not even come into view*. Even the *identification* of the centers which make up the wholeness in a given part of space, together with the relative rank-order of degree of life these different centers have, depend on relative distinctions between centers *because to define the structure at all, we have to select the centers which have the greatest coherence.* The centers identified in the very simple examples of Book 1, chapter 3 cannot be rank-ordered, or even selected at all, without making judgments of their relative coherence. Thus the mathematical structure which underlies the phenomenon of wholeness itself depends on a phenomenon in space which can only be identified, or observed by a method able to make distinctions of value and coherence among the different regions which occur in space.

Within our Cartesian method of observation, it is doubtful if these center-like regions could even be reliably identified, so the structure of wholeness itself would then appear to lie beyond empirical methods of observation. And yet they *can* be identified. I doubt if the reader had any fundamental difficulty recognizing the structures which I described in Book 1, chapters 3, 4, and 5. The fact that some parts of space are more coherent and more salient than others is confirmed by experience and is, to a very large degree, agreed on by different observers. The basis of the theory I have presented lies in the recognition that different regions in space may have different value. In the conception of matter that I have presented, it is the structure based on the value-differences of different regions which is the most fundamental structure of all.

The observations that I have put before the reader in this book are therefore, by and large, *empirical*. They are as objective, as dependent on experience and shared experience as the scientific experiments and observations that are permitted by present-day Cartesian method. But they extend and supplement the arena of permissible observations *in such a way that the self of the observer is allowed to come into the picture*. And they do so in such a way that the self of the observer comes into the picture in an objective, replicable, way.

If we think carefully we shall see how inevitable it is that the way of understanding physical space described in the conclusion of Book 4, and the new method of observation I propose, are intertwined. The point is this. I have argued that space must be considered as a potentially living material — a kind of stuff which, according to the recursive structures that are built up in it, becomes progressively more and more

alive. But of course, this way of understanding space *could not be understood within the confines of a method of observation that insists that everything is a machine* because it is only the facility of assigning value or coherence that allows the structure to be recognized.

Since the matter-space I have described has precisely the character that it is *not* machine-like, *no* method of observation which has to pretend that everything is machine-like will be able to see it as it is, or acknowledge its properties.

The observations I have used to build a modified picture of space and matter are observations which are available to anyone. They are not, in themselves, very astonishing. Many of them were well known to traditional artisans and artists. But, precisely because the observational method of Descartes forbade us from seeing these observables, they have dropped out of awareness. It might be said (by an adherent of mechanistic thinking) that they must not be true, cannot be true, because if they were, something would be wrong with the machinelike representation of the universe. I, on the other hand, started with a different kind of observation. I knew, intuitively, that observation of the inner feeling in a work of building, and the fact that different works of art have more feeling or less feeling, is a real thing. I based my whole method of analysis on the observations that I got by following this method, and on the observables which this method exposes to view.

And since, within this method, there is no arbitrary prohibition against discovering a nonmechanical nature in the structure of space, I was able to consider and discover such a nature.

Thus the characteristics of the field of centers which make it potentially profound — which make it the basis of great art and building — were available to my inspection, *only because I used a method of observation that allowed me to check the feeling of a work as an objective matter*.

Let us be clear that this method of observation, like the method of Descartes, still refers always to *experience*. It is empirical in nature. It dismisses fantasy. It seeks constantly to avoid speculation. In this sense it is experimental, like the method of Descartes. But where Descartes only allowed observation to focus on the outer reality of mechanisms in the world, my method requires that we focus on the inner reality of the observer's feeling of wholesomeness *as well*.

Thus the results I have reported are based on experience, they report experience, and they describe experience. The results are public. Of course the experience is experience of *inner feeling*, but the feelings still refer to experience which can be shared. I have shown that each one of us is capable of feeling the existence of wholeness, feeling the existence of value, and that we can use this capability, constantly, to keep on making distinctions and learning things. In several chapters in these four books, I have demonstrated that these methods of observation are sharable and public. They do not depend strongly on the person who is doing them. So in spite of its novelty, this method is not subjective but objective.

It is not necessary to choose between the method of Descartes and the method which I have described. In a situation where the relevant facts have to do with things that can be viewed in a machinelike fashion, the method of Descartes is best. Pretend the unknown thing is a machine, and find a model which represents its behavior. But in a situation where the relative wholeness of different systems, is the most important, most relevant thing, the method of Descartes, by itself, will not work. We then need a method which can explicitly recognize the relative degree of wholeness in different systems, and can make this objective. In such a case, the method which I have described must be used as well.

If we follow both methods — the method of Descartes for things that are outside ourselves and can be represented as machines; and the method I have explained whenever we have to judge or study wholeness — we may then arrive at a picture of the world which includes the self, and which clearly recognizes the personal nature of the universe.

Whitehead's problem of the bifurcation of nature is then solved.

3 / ENDURING SKEPTICISM AS A SOURCE OF CERTAINTY

But is it all really true, as I have described it? Throughout my life, I have found out everything that I have found out by a continued skepticism, by asking questions, by not accepting anything without questioning it again and again. This habit of a lifetime has not left me just because I have finally finished these four books.

It is sometimes very hard for me to imagine that what I have written about the nature of the universe in this fourth book of THE NATURE OF ORDER can actually be true. Concretely, I am a child of the 20th century, and have been deeply molded by the belief in the mechanical nature of the world. Concretely, I have in my blood a belief in the mechanical nature of my own body, and in the short term of my own existence. Wonder alone does not dispel this skepticism. The wonderful and heart-rending things that happen in different human lives, the ripple that passes down the cat's fur when she jumps to catch the bird, the soft glow of evening in the winter sunset time, the joy of a child born, and the sadness thinking of that child's inevitable death — for all the happiness and sadness in these things, deep down part of me is still convinced that the world is mechanical, just as I learned when still a child.

And yet, in this fourth book, THE LUMINOUS GROUND, I have described a very different reality. I have described a way of understanding the world in which it appears that life is inherent in space itself, and in which soul, or spirit, is an inevitable part of matter, which shows through, as the curtain rends, in which not only people, but buildings, flowering bushes, even window-sills, have their own life and spirit too, as a real thing, which goes far beyond the mechanical world and is part of the nature of their existence.

Is one true and the other false? Is the idea which I have described in this fourth book nothing but an artist's dream, something that is ultimately — from the point of view of physics — *untrue*? I do not think so.

I have written down the view of matter described in this book because I cannot now see another way. For thirty years I have tried to find a consistent and coherent vision of architecture which is able to explain the facts about beauty, buildings, life, and harmony. Almost all of it is rooted in observation. Even during my occasional lapses towards poetic speech, I have not written anything down that is not based on my conviction of its empirical reality. In almost all cases, I have described facts about buildings, intuitions, experiences, as they are, as people experience them.

The scheme I have invented to encompass these things does seem fantastic. But it must also be accepted that the architectural facts which need to be explained will not go away. Just because I believe in the mechanical nature of my own body does not mean that the experiences and feelings described throughout this book are not true. I have been painstakingly accurate as much as I could be. I have tried not to exaggerate. I have used only what I know to be true, *of my own knowledge*. And I have used facts which are, in my experience, sharable. That is to say, others, too, when invited to consider the facts which they experience in the world of building, do make similar observations.

And now, as I consider the possible logical schemes which are consistent with these observations, I can see no genuine alternative. Far-fetched as it is to propose a schema of space and matter which contains life, and which allows a curtain to be pulled aside as matter grows more coherent, looking through to an ultimate reality of I, *I cannot see any other coherent explanation which makes sense of everything in a useful and intelligible way.*

———

As Sherlock Holmes said, if you have examined every possible alternative, and you have gradually eliminated all the alternatives but one, then that one — no matter how fantastic — must be the truth. That is more or less how I evaluate the finding on the interaction of matter and the I reported in this last of my four books. One part of me — the positivistic and 20th-century part of me that grew while I studied mathematics and the sciences at Cambridge — has the greatest difficulty believing it. But at the same time, intellectually I cannot escape the force of the logic that leads to these conclusions. No matter how hard I have tried, I have not been able to construct another scheme of things which gives a believable account of the nature of beauty and life in buildings. All this seems to me, then, like Sherlock Holmes' last alternative: something which seems fantastic, but which remains, nevertheless, the only alternative consistent with the facts, which therefore must be true.

The trained scientist in me, with the prejudices of an earlier era, cannot quite believe it. But as a hard-bitten scientist who goes where the evidence goes, I believe it must be true. And my instinct — lying deeper perhaps than logic, and nourished by years of skepticism — also says that it is true.

It is something like this that I hang onto. I want to believe it. I cannot believe it. But I believe it must be true.

ACKNOWLEDGEMENTS

It has taken twenty-seven years to write these four books. I began in 1976. During this long period, hundreds of people — friends, colleagues, and students — have helped me, often by reading draft after draft, often by arguing with me, sometimes by writing me letters of encouragement, sometimes helping me to sort out the thoughts which are presented here, sometimes just by standing with me and supporting me.

SOME OF MY INSUFFICIENT THANKS
ARE ON THE FOLLOWING PAGES

THANK YOU

Among the hundreds of people who helped me, I want especially to thank the following friends and family whose help is etched in my memory because they gave such unusual amounts of time, friendship, patience and goodwill.

My great friend Nikos Salingaros, for a decade and a half, helped me more than I can ever thank him for. Starting about 1985, he read the text over and over again, in draft after draft, taking time from his work in physics and mathematics ... and has suffered through the most excruciating arguments which we have enjoyed, also while walking in the Berkeley hills, and around my farm in Sussex. His insight and clarity of mind have helped me strongly bring forward the main points which are the essence of the argument, sometimes forcing me, through his stubbornness and refusal to understand too easily what I wanted, to make me formulate things better, helping them to be more clear and more persuasive. Because of our friendship we could surmount these battles. In the later stages of the work, he helped me again and again with editing problems, taking days of his own precious time to sit through sentence after sentence and help me get it right.

My other editor Bill McClung, who introduced himself to me early in 1993, also quickly became a close personal friend. For several years, Bill spent hundreds of hours per year, especially on Book 1, helping me sort through the arguments, clarifying tone and substance, and in this period of the book's production became a kind of life-line for me. His energy and enthusiasm — and his determination, like Nikos, to make me walk in the Berkeley hills around my house, because he thought I needed it — also lent charm and pleasure to the hard work of bringing this book to a final state: and have brought with them a lasting friendship. During that time Bill did more than any other person to make Book 1 what it has become. I am eternally grateful to him.

My wife Pamela has stood by me through all these years. I thank her from the bottom of my heart for many discussions about the book, for her abiding love, and above all for the endless stream of heavenly song which came from her practicing downstairs while I sat upstairs writing: and most recently her Gaelic songs, sung to the harp. She talked with me for twenty years about these matters, and stimulated me to give more and more clear formulations, and also cooked us all the most delicious meals. I do not know how she found time for it. Most exciting for me, in recent years, the insights of this book have even found their way into music — even into the chords and harmonies she uses while she sings. In the realm of song, she has always, I think, been trying to do what I do in the realm of building. And in the last phase of the work she gave me sharp and helpful editing throughout Book 4 which brought, at the last minute, an added new dimension to our friendship.

Lily and Sophie, our children, born while I was already writing this book, growing up while I was still writing it, and now grown up while it is being finished, have given me the most precious comments. They understand perfectly well what beauty is, indeed understand only too well that there is not much of it existing today in the world of buildings. Knowing that I was trying to work out ways in which things could be made beautiful always meant something to them, first as children in sure and childlike ways, later as adults in their maturity. Together, we had many, many discussions about it over the years. I love them for their simple acceptance of the fact that I have been trying to find a way in which the world can become beautiful again, and their enthusiasm and encouragement for this enormous idea — which, to them, seemed so simple and natural.

My dear father, Ferdinand John Alexander, always encouraged me enormously, and spurred me on to take my part in the generation-long family discussions about God v. science and skepticism v. religion, also spurred on by my uncle Johann (his brother), who firmly took the skeptical viewpoint that finally in the 20th century the idea of God must be debunked once and for all. Possibly the greatest thanks of all to my father touch the matter of my education. It was he, on hearing that I wanted to be an architect, who firmly but kindly encouraged me — insisted — that I should study mathematics at Cambridge, before going into architecture. If it had not been for that advice, and his firm hand, this book would have been impossible.

During the last five years of the project Jenny Quillien became my editor and collaborator. We spent weeks at a time going over arguments, the logic of the book, the simplicity and the communication of ideas, the ultimate meaning of the concepts; and she persistently worked with me to clarify ideas and formulate sharper ways of explaining my thoughts. Especially in Books 2 and 3 she became a gentle tyrant, forcing common sense out of me, and, using experience from her own fields to explore the issues of large scale implementation and change in today's world. I can hardly imagine how the closing years of this project, so enormously long and hard on everyone, with the arduous quality of what I came to think of as the final years of the long march, could have been survivable without her support.

It is sad that, in the end, Oxford University Press was not to be the publisher, but I shall never forget what my friends there did for me and for the four books. Many people at Oxford helped this project, over a long period. Among the friends at OUP who helped me, were the three top executives who stood by me for eight years to make this enormous project begin to seem even possible: the President, Laura Brown; the ex-President, Ed Barry; and the Vice-President and Trade Publisher, Ellen Chodosh. My editor Joyce Berry, senior editor at the Press, also undertook detailed editing on each of the four books as it reached its final form. Joyce's work and encouragement continued for years, and always sustained my effort. They all believed in this project at an extraordinary level, and put more effort into it than they had time for. My thanks remain with them.

And I want to say a special word of thanks to Katalin Bende. She came from Hungary to study with me ten years ago, then became my assistant, and for four years became the keeper of the archive and the designer, and typesetter of these books. The beauty of the layout of the four books is due to her efforts. Again and again, while working on a chapter, she would help me, with her eye for graphic beauty and simplicity and elegance of layout, to arrange the pictures in a way that added to the text. In many cases, the layout of the pictures played a guiding role: and this work we did together, in chapter after chapter, kept on until the very final stages of typesetting. She learned professional typesetting, only to help me; and stayed in the United States, keeping her own career as an architect in abeyance, while she helped to finish the books. I am more grateful than I can say, that she had the patience and dedication to stay with me all these years it took to finish.

———

For thirty years, hundreds of my colleagues and co-workers at the Center for Environmental Structure helped me. Their works appear throughout these pages, especially in Book 3. A few of these colleagues stand out because of their quite unusual levels of help and dedication.

Randy Schmidt, now in charge of the offices of CES and of PatternLanguage.com, and my closest co-worker for the last several years, worked and provided inspiration for many of our most difficult building projects. His own dedication and patience and care, sometimes altogether out of the ordinary in seriousness and in intensity, often in situations of the most dire financial hardship, have sustained me through the last few years. Most recently, in the last years, after the decision was made that the Center for Environmental Structure would publish these four books, Randy provided a renewed source of strength, by taking on the arduous and demanding work of book publisher, distributer, and business manager — all in order, simply, to make sure that these books could see the light of day intact. He has been one of my truest friends.

My dear friend Hajo Neis also helped me in innumerable discussions over the years, and through his own inspired efforts to explain these concepts to students. He played a major and most important role in many of the Center's larger building projects, especially the Eishin campus in Japan. In addition, he helped me as a colleague during the vital years when these four books were taking shape: first as a student in seminars at Berkeley, then as a colleague in CES, and most recently as a professor at the University of California in the intensive program where we taught together in the newly established Building Process Area of Emphasis. Hajo has been a part of this work almost as long as the work was going on.

Howard Davis, also a student long ago, and during the last twenty years a dear and greatly valued friend and colleague, stood by me intellectually in many, many situations, helped me again and again with critical reading of whole volumes and many individual chapters, and during this time also wrote his own book, THE CULTURE OF BUILDING, which provided a profound and matter-of-fact picture of construction process in society, making my thoughts richer by the contribution of his thought.

For years, Artemis Anninou helped me again and again. She played an enormous role in helping to arrange and choose pictures, and made some of the most beautiful early pages with her wonderful eye for layout. All this was made more fun by years of dinners and discussions with my family.

Ingrid King, as she has in so many of my books,

once again read and re-read, commented, and helped to formulate vital, basic ideas, and always supported me in my determination to express these ideas. Her subtly different viewpoint often helped me think my way out of one box or another in which I found myself. For thirty years she has been a dear friend and a tower of strength.

Gary Black contributed to many of our projects in the 1980s, and helped to create the professional circumstances which allowed CES to do its early work — much of which is discussed and reported in Book 3. Although we parted company in 1994, I shall not forget him, and remain grateful for his exceptional contribution to the work CES did in those years.

My warm thanks, too, to Katy Langstaff and her husband Stuart Cowan. Katy was first my student, later my teaching assistant who helped to teach early classes on the nature of order. Stuart, a mathematician and ecologist, gave me invaluable information about new developments in the biological and ecological sciences as the years went along. Both of them are very dear.

Beyond these special individuals at CES, others also stand out in my memory as special friends with special dedication. They include, especially, John Hewitt, Miyoko Tsutsui, Carl Lindberg, Saul Pichardo, Bob Walsh, Barton Coffman, Kleoniki Tsotropoulou, Jonathan Fefferman, Lizabeth Chester (now Oxman), Demetrius Gonzales, Susan Ingham, John Lucchesi, Eleni Coromvli, Halim Abdelhalim, Hiro Nakano, Gernot Mittersteiner, Shawn Bradbury, Seth Wachtel, James Maguire, Stephen Duff, Mike Smith, Kurt Brown, Ed Hazzard, Chris Andrews, David Soffa, Hana Mori, Ilhan Kural, Jeannie Ratcliffe, Fanta Lawrence, Harissos Tsiringas, Thymios Demoulas, Marty Shukert, Leonidas Pakas, Alkmini Paka, Walter Wendler, Don Corner, Jenny Young, Chris Gucci, Chuck Han, Keiko Ono, Ismet Khambatta, Annie der Bedrossian, Nili Portugali, Alfred Bay, Olasheni Agbabiaka, David Week. Thank you from the bottom of my heart, to all of you.

And to the hundreds of others.

———

For much needed money and financial support, I am immensely grateful to Bill Joy and Mike Clary of Sun Microsystems. They were far-sighted enough, and deeply kind, to arrange for Sun to give me a major grant which made publication of this work possible. They also provided us with much-needed typesetting equipment and computers. The Graham Foundation for Advanced Study in the Fine Arts later supplemented this subsidy with an additional grant. To them, too, I am extremely grateful.

I want to thank a few special colleagues at the University of California.

My old friend Ken Simmons who so kindly — sweetly really — told me, after reading the manuscript about 1990, that he wanted to be a "fellow-traveller." He was perhaps the first faculty member among my colleagues at Berkeley not afraid of the religious content and cosmological content reported here.

Sim Van der Ryn often inspired me to try and do justice to the ecological side of what is reported here: these discussions were brought to a head in a weekend seminar at the Esalen Institute which we gave together. This gave me the ability to write the opening paragraphs of Book 1, chapter 1.

Yodan Rofe was my principal teaching assistant in the public lectures I gave on this topic during 1990–92. He spent months helping me disentangle the finer points of detail in the theory and helped me especially in re-working Book 2, after I began to understand for the first time that the key of the whole theory lay in the demonstration that the unfolding process is the necessary precondition for life to occur.

Soli Angel, in the early days of the manuscript, more than twenty years ago, on a long drive in Mexico, helped me to understand that most of all I must communicate the basic point that it is our view of the *world* which has to change, not only our idea of architecture.

And Bo Links, my attorney in San Francisco, spent seven years helping me to solve (through the protection of my first amendment rights) the nearly disastrous political problems which occurred at the University of California. He helped me fight the Department of Architecture during a decade when the faculty did their best to prevent the teaching of this material and to close my mouth — because of their fear of the paradigm shift which is reported here. Because Bo won my case against the University, the Building Process Area of Emphasis was created as one of six sub-departments of the Department. The Building Process was founded with the special purpose of allowing the material of these four books to be taught; it was this which made it possible for me to continue teaching this material to generations of students in an otherwise intellectually hostile environment. Without Bo's efforts to control the University's hostile actions, it is doubtful that these four books could have been written at all.

A few special thanks:

To my great friend Hisae Hosoi, the client of our Eishin campus in Japan, who first gave me the opportunity to build something large, and who encouraged me from very early days, simply because he understood from the beginning that "each thing has its life." He has also shared my passionate struggle in the field of architecture, and together we have lived through many of the most drastic political implications of what is formulated here.

To Dick Gabriel and Jim Coplien and many other computer scientists who gave much weight and encouragement to my earlier writings by embodying these ideas in the work of the computer-science community.

To Greg Bryant, who supported me for years by his enthusiastic belief in the value of these ideas, and who so often made special efforts to make contributions and to find financial support.

To Brian Hanson, at one time secretary to the Prince of Wales, and then Director of Studies of the Prince of Wales's Institute of Architecture. He was fearless, and finally lost his own job as a result of his open support of what I was trying to do and its implications in the field of architecture. Many years earlier, Brian was friend enough to be truly frank with me, intellectually, at a time when I thought the manuscript was almost finished (1989, almost fourteen years before it actually was finished). He made me aware of the lack of clarity it then contained. In several wonderful midnight walks near the Villa Lante in Italy, we had fascinating and intense discussions which helped me very greatly to set myself a harder goal.

To David Bohm, whom I met for two days of intensive discussion in the fall of 1986, and who through his wisdom — and in spite of our disagreements — gave me further courage to describe wholeness explicitly as a structure in its own right.

To Stephen Grabow, who helped me in a similar way when he wrote his book in 1980 about the fact that my formulations represented a new "paradigm." This point, perhaps obvious now because he wrote about it, was not so obvious to me then, and talking this matter through with him in the conversations that are recorded in his book helped greatly to clarify and crystallize my thought in the early days. It gave me courage to continue what seemed an impossibly difficult undertaking, only because it was so different from the prevailing thought in the architecture of the late 1970s. Thank you Steve.

And to my dear Maggie, who arrived in my life at the very end of the project, and helped me and supported me in the arduous, long period while we were proofing the four books and sending them off to be printed. Thank you from the bottom of my heart.

Other kind people who gave technical help beyond the call of duty, should be mentioned. First among them, during the last three years, Chet Grycz, former production manager of the University of California Press, helped me to such an extent that it can be said quite truly that these books would not have appeared without him. I owe him an enormous debt. With his great experience of production, he arranged the needed subcontracts, and made it possible to set and print and bind these books so that we may all be proud of them. And my enormous thanks to the Everbest Printing Company, China, especially to Ken Chung and Ching Lam and their staff, and to Duncan McCallum, their representative in California. To all of them my happiest thanks for their patience, for their always pleasant demeanor, and for the beautiful quality of craft in the printed books. They, truly, have made these books what they are.

Thanks, too, to Wilsted and Taylor in Oakland who gave help, advice, and encouragement in the typesetting tasks. Thanks to Susan Edmiston who briefly edited a version of the manuscript in 1992. Other editors, Marion Osmun and Beth Harrison and Jan Ronish were all extraordinarily helpful in final copy editing. And Raffaella Falchi played a vital role in the last two years, by organizing and supervising the proofing process, especially the proofing of color pages. This was arduous work, because of the thousands of images involved. She did it beautifully. And at the very end of the whole process, Rick Wilson and Mehdi Stevens saved me by coming in to tweak the jackets and the final typesetting, like angels of mercy, always patient, always solving the most difficult tiny problems with what seemed like ease and simplicity.

Over the years, hundreds of people all over the United States have been kind enough to read xerox-copies of early versions of these manuscripts, and have then given me the benefit of their comments. This highly positive and almost dialogue-like process was enjoyable, inspiring, and very helpful since, from the beginning, it gave me a chance to see how people would react to these ideas, how they would see them and understand them, and where they would see special difficulties or special points of strength. This was a great pleasure over the years.

I must express my gratitude, also, for the unrelenting hostility of certain of my colleagues in the Department of Architecture at the University of California, Berkeley. The extraordinary levels of attack, open and covert, unremitting over a twenty-year period, and the difficulties these faculty members made, year after year, for those students and faculty colleagues who wanted to study this material, was testimony to the panic they felt — because, under the surface, they knew, I think, that it was true. It threatened them because so many students who came in touch with this material, after reading it, and after helping to make buildings in the way I have described, no longer felt

comfortable studying architecture in the "old way." If what I wrote and taught had not made sense, and had not been so threatening to the professional sensibility of my colleagues, they would never have taken the trouble to make life so difficult for me. For this unintentional, but fervent acknowledgement, I am enormously grateful. At the times of darkest crisis — and in twenty years there are inevitably many — this never failed to give me strength.

Finally I want to thank thirty-seven years of undergraduate and graduate students in my classes at the University of California who read this and earlier texts in innumerable versions, and who struggled through those versions at periods when the arguments were faulty or unclear. The continuous re-writing I have done for twenty-seven years has been largely stimulated by my effort to give them something more clear, each year, and my wish to make it worth the time which they spent studying it.

"A FATHER IS SOMEONE WHO LOVES YOU. MY DAD
WRITES BOOKS AND IS AN ARCHITECT HE LIKES TO GET ME THINGS.
HE LIKES CATS A LOT HE LIKES TO READ WITH ME
HE LIKES TO GO TO THE BEACH WITH ME
MY DAD LOVES BIRDS AND HE LIKES WHALES."

Lily, first grade, June 8, 1988

"I JUST WANT YOU TO KNOW THAT IN SPIRIT I'M WITH
YOU — NO MATTER WHAT HAPPENS. I KNOW WE'LL MAKE
IT THROUGH AND FIND OUR DIRECTION — HOPEFULLY
THE BEST ONE. ANYWAY, I DON'T EVER STOP LOVING YOU
OR CARING ABOUT YOU EVERY MINUTE OF THE DAY."

Pamela, a letter, August 20, 1997

"WE WERE WAVING GOODBYE
ALL THE WAY UP THE LUGGAGE SCANNER
LEAVING MY FATHER
NOT KNOWING WHEN WE WOULD SEE HIM AGAIN
IN ANY PAIN I HAVE PREVIOUSLY HAD
NONE CAME CLOSE TO THAT OF THIS MOMENT"

Sophie, eighth grade, September 21, 1997

Thanks — again — to my family
I can never repay you

PICTURE CREDITS

In addition, I gratefully acknowledge the use of pictures, photographs, and illustrations owned by the following persons and institutions in Book 4. All illustrations not mentioned belong to or are the work of the author, and are reproduced by permission of The Center for Environmental Structure.

Frontispiece
Andre Martin.

Preface
p. 6 George Micheu and Snehal Shah, eds., Ahmedabad, Marg Publications, 1988; pp. 34-35 Dinesh Mehta.

Chapter 2
p. 30 Martin Hurlimann; p. 32 top left: Andre Martin; p. 32 top right: Hirmer Verlag, Munich; p. 32 bottom left: Carl Nordenfalk, *Celtic and Anglo-Saxon Painting*, George Braziller, 1977, plate 1, p. 33; p. 32 bottom right: F.W. Funke; p. 33 left: Everest Films, Norman Dyrenfurth; p. 33 right: Daitokuji Temple, Kohoan; p. 38 Scala/Art Resource; p. 39 The Metropolitan Museum of Art, Rogers Fund, 1906 (06-1046), photograph © The Metropolitan Museum of Art; p. 41 bottom: Emil Nolde, Calm Sea, © The Nolde Foundation; p. 46 Scala/Art Resource; p. 54 Daitokuji Temple, Kohoan; p. 55 Toni Schneiders, Lindau.

Chapter 4
p. 77 Heini Schneebeli; p. 78 Walter Horn and Errnest Born: *The Plan of St. Gall*, v.II, University of California Press, 1979, Title page; pp. 82-83 Ken Longbottom, *Liverpool and The Mersey*, v. 1, Silver Link Publishing, Ltd., pp. 60 and 31; p. 84 top left: Otto von Simpson, *The Gothic Cathedral*, Pantheon Books, 1965, plate 33; p. 85 Editions Houvet, La Crypte; p. 86 top left: Editions Houvet, La Crypte; p. 86 top right: Otto von Simpson, *The Gothic Cathedral*, Pantheon, 1956, plate 38; p. 86 bottom, Editions Houvet, La Crypte; pp. 87-88 Editions Houvet, La Crypte; pp. 89-90 © Sonia Halliday Photographs; p. 91 top: © Sonia Halliday Photographs; p. 91 bottom left and right: Editions Houvet, La Crypte; p. 92 Editions Houvet, La Crypte; p. 93 top: Editions Houvet, La Crypte; p. 93 bottom: © Sonia Halliday Photographs; p. 96 John Ranelagh, Ireland, *An Illustrated History*, Oxford, 1981, p. 20, Photo George Mott; p. 102 Giraudon/ Art Resource; p. 103 Carnegie Museum of Art, Pittsburgh. Acquired through the generosity of the Sarah Mellon Scaife family, 70.50. Photo Peter Hardoldt, 1994.

Chapter 5
p. 132 Giraudon/ Art Resource

Chapter 7
p. 158 © 1990 Amon Carter Museum, Fort Worth, Texas, of Eliot Porter; p. 159 top: Roger Boulton, *Canada Coast* Oxford, 1982, plate 45. Photo Peter Fowler; p. 161 David Magnus Bartlett, *Tibet*, Vendome, 1981, p. 45; p. t Resource; p. 162 bottom: © Country C. Seherr-Thoss; p. 164 Scala/Art Re- que Nationale, Paris, RcB12227; p. letts, Camerapix, Nairobi; p. 166 bot- p. 168 Basil Gray, *Treasures of Asia: Per- Art Albert Skira*, 1961, p. 91; p. 169 Gi- bottom: Hans Jurgen Hansen, ed., 971; p. 150a. Photo Walter Luden; 172 Amsterdam, Van Gogh Mu- Foundation). Scala/Art Resource; p. Art, New York; p. 175 Seiroka Noma, e Arts, John Weatherill, 1979, fig. 37; p. p. 177 Basil Gray, *Treasures of Asia:*

Persian Painting, Editions d'Art Albert Skira, 1961, plate 45, photo Henry B. Belville; p. 178 Ms Codex 23, fol. 9, Stiftsbibliothek, St. Gallen; p. 179 Hans C. Seherr-Thoss; p. 180 Scala/Art Resource; p. 181 Otto E. Nelson; p. 182 Asad Behroozan; p. 183 Geza Feher, *Turkische Miniaturen*, Corvina, Magyar Helikon, Budapest, 1976, XXVII; p. 184 © Jeffrey Becom; p. 185 Giraudon/Art Resource; p. 186 Basil Gray, *Treasures of Asia: Persian Painting*, Editions d'Art Albert Skira, 1961, p. 84; p. 187 Museum of New Mexico, Santa Fe. Photo John Gebhart; p. 188 Scala/Art Resource; p. 189 Geza Feher, Turkische Miniaturen, Corvina, Magyar Helikon, Budapest, 1976, XXXI; p. 190 Ulrich Schurmann, *Oriental Carpets*, Paul Hamlyn, 1966, p. 19; p. 191 Scala/Art Resource; p. 193 Joseph V. McMullan, *Islamic Patterns*, Near Eastern Art Research Center, Inc., 1965, plate 28; p. 194 The Board of Trinity College, Dublin, Ms 58, fol. 5v; p. 195 Solomon R. Guggenheim Museum, New York. Photo Carmelo Guadagno, © The Solomon R. Guggenheim Foundation (Fn 38.432); pp. 198 and 199 Scala/Art Resource; p. 200 Herman Goetz, *Art of the World: India, Five Thousand Years of Indian Art*, McGraw-Hill, 1959, p. 207; p. 201 Roland Michaud/Rapho; p. 202 Giraudon/Art Resource; p. 203 Joseph V. McMullan, *Islamic Carpets*, Near Eastern Art Research Center, 1965, plate 89. Photo Otto E. Nelson; p. 206 Art Resource/New York; p. 207 The Green Studio Limited, Dublin; p. 208 Scala/Art Resource; p. 209 *Tepotzotlan*, Instituto Nacional de Anthropologia y Historia, Mexico, no. 62/63, Vol. XII, plate 57; p. 211 Scala/Art Resource; p. 212 top: Aris Konstantinidis; p. 212 bottom: © Glasgow Museum: Art Gallery and Museum, Kelvingrove; p. 313 Laleh Bakhtiar, *Sufi: Expressions of the Mystic Quest*, Avon Books, New York, 1976, p. 48. Photo Nader Ardalan; p. 214 Photograph by Seth Joel, Metropolitan Musuem of Art, New York; p. 215 Paul Rocheleau; p. 216 Private collection; p. 218 Isidor Jenkin, Cornell Laboratory of Ornithology, all rights reserved; p. 220 Photo Arts of Mankind; p. 221 Laleh Bakhtiar, *Sufi: Expressions of the Mystic Quest*, Avon Books, 1976, p. 56; p. 222 Scala/Art Resource; p. 223 Hans C. Seherr-Thoss; p. 225 Musee National d'Art Moderne, Paris; p. 226 Muskegon Musuem of Art, Gift of Margaret and L.C. Walker Foundation; p. 227 Amsterdam, Van Gogh Museum (Vincent Van Gogh Foundation); p. 228 top: Ulrich Schurmann, *Oriental Carpets*, Paul Hamlyn, 1966, p. 25; p. 228 bottom: Gonul Oney, *Turkish Tile Art*, Yapive Kredi Bankasi, Bir Kultur Hizmetidir, Istanbul, 1976, p. 174; p. 229 Maggie Keswick: *The Chinese Garden: History, Art, and Architecture*, Rizzoli, 1978, Fig. 56; p. 235 Hans C. Seherr-Thoss; pp. 237, 238, 239 Evelyn Hofer.

Chapter 8
p. 242 Jack P. Flan, *Matisse on Art*, E.P.Dutton, 1978, Frontispiece; p. 243 © Mark Darley/ESTO; P. 260 © James Nachtwey, Magnum Photos, Inc.

Chapter 10
p. 292 Emil Nolde, Sonnenuntergang (Sunset), 1909; p. 293 © Christie's Images, Ltd., 1999.